HUNGER AND WAR

INDIANA UNIVERSITY PRESS

Bloomington & Indianapolis

HUNGER AND WAR

FOOD PROVISIONING
IN THE SOVIET UNION
DURING WORLD WAR II

EDITED BY
WENDY Z. GOLDMAN
AND DONALD FILTZER

This book is a publication of

INDIANA UNIVERSITY PRESS
Office of Scholarly Publishing
Herman B Wells Library 350
1320 East 10th Street
Bloomington, Indiana 47405 USA

iupress.indiana.edu

© 2015 by Indiana University Press

All rights reserved

No part of this book may be reproduced
or utilized in any form or by any means,
electronic or mechanical, including
photocopying and recording, or by any
information storage and retrieval system,
without permission in writing from the
publisher. The Association of American
University Presses' Resolution on
Permissions constitutes the only
exception to this prohibition.

The paper used in this publication
meets the minimum requirements of
the American National Standard
for Information Sciences–Permanence
of Paper for Printed Library Materials,
ANSI Z39.48-1992.

*Manufactured in the
United States of America*

*Library of Congress
Cataloging-in-Publication Data*

Hunger and war : food provisioning in
the Soviet Union during World War II /
edited by Wendy Z. Goldman and Donald
Filtzer.

   pages cm
   Includes bibliographical references and
index.
   ISBN 978-0-253-01708-6 (cloth :
alkaline paper) – ISBN 978-0-253-01712-3
(paperback : alkaline paper) – ISBN
978-0-253-01716-1 (ebook) 1. Food
supply–Soviet Union–History.
2. World War, 1939–1945–Food
supply–Soviet Union. 3. Rationing–
Soviet Union–History. 4. Hunger–Soviet
Union–History. 5. Starvation–Soviet
Union–History. 6. Nutrition policy–
Soviet Union–History. 7. Food supply–
Political aspects–Soviet Union–History.
8. World War, 1939–1945–Social aspects–
Soviet Union. 9. War and society–Soviet
Union–History. 10. Soviet Union–Social
conditions–1917–1945. I. Goldman,
Wendy Z. II. Filtzer, Donald A.
   HD9015.S652H86 2015
   363.80947′09044–dc23

                       2014048990

1 2 3 4 5   20 19 18 17 16 15

CONTENTS

· *Acknowledgments*   vii

· *List of Terms and Abbreviations*   xi

· Introduction: The Politics of Food and War
Donald Filtzer and Wendy Z. Goldman · 1

1   Not by Bread Alone: Food, Workers, and
the State *Wendy Z. Goldman* · 44

2   The State's Pot and the Soldier's Spoon:
Rations (*Paëk*) in the Red Army
Brandon Schechter · 98

3   Queues, Canteens, and the Politics of Location
in Diaries of the Leningrad Blockade, 1941–1942
Alexis Peri · 158

4   Nutritional Dystrophy: The Science and
Semantics of Starvation in World War II
Rebecca Manley · 206

5   Starvation Mortality in Soviet Home-Front
Industrial Regions during World War II
Donald Filtzer · 265

- *Bibliography*   339
- *Contributors*   361
- *Index*   363

ACKNOWLEDGMENTS

THE EDITORS JOINTLY WOULD LIKE TO THANK THE AMERICAN Council of Learned Societies for a Collaborative Research Fellowship for their project on "The Soviet Home Front: Work, Life, and Loyalty during World War II" from January 2011 to December 2012. They would also like to thank the Department of History of Carnegie Mellon University for its support of the workshop on "Food, Hunger, and Starvation: Feeding Front and Rear during World War II in the Soviet Union," held in April 2012, at which the contributors to this volume presented drafts of their chapters and offered critical comments on each other's work. Finally, thanks are due to Dan Healey and the anonymous reviewer who read the manuscript for Indiana University Press and offered detailed, constructive suggestions on how the volume as a whole and its individual chapters could be integrated and improved.

The research for Donald Filtzer's contribution to this volume is part of a larger project, "Health, Disease, and Mortality on the Soviet Home Front During World War II," funded by a Research Leave Fellowship from the Wellcome Trust, grant number WT087202MA, during the academic years September 2009–August 2012. He would like to thank Mark Harrison, Bob Davies, Dan Healey, Dave Leon, and Michael David for their advice and comments on earlier drafts of his chapter. Additional material was collected thanks to a research grant from the National Endowment for the Humanities during February–August 2009 and research leave during July–December 2012, as part of the ACLS Collaborative Research Fellowship, held jointly with Wendy Goldman. He expresses his deepest thanks to the archivists and reading room advisors at the

vii

viii   *Acknowledgments*

State Archive of the Russian Federation (GARF) and the Russian State Archive of the Economy (RGAE), and to the librarians at the Central Scientific Medical Library in Moscow.

Wendy Goldman would like to thank the American Council of Learned Societies for its award of the Collaborative Research Fellowship, which made the research and writing of this book possible, and helped fund additional research, publications, and scholarly activity. She is also grateful to the International Department at Russian State University for the Humanities (RGGU), and the exchange program between RGGU and Carnegie Mellon University (CMU) for facilitating her research in Russia, and the efforts of the staff in GARF, RGAE, and the Russian State Archive of Social and Political History (RGASPI) in suggesting and locating materials.

Rebecca Manley's chapter is a much expanded version of papers presented at a conference, "The Soviet Union in World War II" (Paris, May 2011); at the Association for Slavic, East European, and Eurasian Studies (ASEEES) conference in November 2011; and at a workshop, "Food, Hunger, and Starvation: Feeding Front and Rear during World War II in the Soviet Union" (Carnegie Mellon University, Pittsburgh, April 2012). She would like to acknowledge the helpful comments received at these conferences and particularly at the workshop from which this volume evolved. She is grateful to Paul Manley, who served as a medical consultant, to her research assistant, Dinah Jansen, and to Don Filtzer, Dan Healey, and Alexis Peri, who, in addition to commenting on various drafts of her chapter, generously shared research materials with her. Research for this paper was funded by the Queen's University Office of Research Services and the Social Sciences and Humanities Council of Canada and was facilitated by a sabbatical granted by Queen's University.

Alexis Peri would like to thank Middlebury College for its generous financial support in aiding the completion of this chapter. She is also grateful to Joyce Mao, Benjamin Graves, Yumna Siddiqi, Maggie Clinton, Max Ward, Catherine M. Ashcraft, Jamie McCallum, and the other contributors to this volume for comments and critical feedback on earlier drafts. Finally, her heartfelt thanks to Igor' Liubovskii and Natal'ia Afanas'eva who granted her permission to use diaries from their family

Acknowledgments   *ix*

members, and to Tamara Staleva, Ol'ga Prutt, and Tatiana Voronina for helping broker these permissions.

Brandon Schechter would like to thank Thomas Lacqueur, Victoria Frede, Yuri Slezkine, Dan Healey, Jeffrey Hass, Nikita Lomagin, Bair Irincheev, Oleg Budnitsky, Jochen Hellbeck, the members of the Russian History Kruzhok at the University of California, Berkeley, the anonymous reviewer for Indiana University Press, and Milyausha Zakirova for their comments and guidance in writing this chapter. He would also like to thank Konstantin Sergeievich Drozdov, Sergei Vladimirovich Zhuravlev, and Yuri Aleksandrovich Petrov of the Institute of Russian History, Russian Academy of Sciences (IRI RAN) for allowing him access to their fabulous holdings, and the archivists and reading room advisors at RGASPI, GARF, and the National Archive of the Rebublic of Tatarstan (NART) for their help in finding materials. Research for this chapter was generously supported by a Dean's Dissertation Research Fellowship from UC Berkeley and a Fulbright International Institute of Education Fellowship.

TERMS AND ABBREVIATIONS

alimentarnaia distrofiia	nutritional dystrophy, Soviet medical term for starvation or semi-starvation
ASSR	Autonomous Soviet Socialist Republic (Avtonomnaia Sovetskaia Sotsialis- ticheskaia Respublika), autonomous republics within the RSFSR (see below). For example, TASSR (Tatar ASSR), BASSR (Bashkir ASSR), etc.
blokadnik (plural, *blokadniki*)	resident of Leningrad during the blockade
Commissariat	see People's Commissariat
distrofiia	see *alimentarnaia distrofiia*
DOP	division exchange point (*divizionnyi obmennyi punkt*); in the military, a place where supplies were distributed at division level
doppaek (dopolnitel'nyi paek)	supplemental ration given to commanders
fel'dsher	paramedic, physician's assistant, medical assistant; in the army also a field nurse

xi

frontovik	frontline soldier
FZO	Factory Training School (Shkola Fabrichno-Zavodskogo Obucheniia) under the Chief Administration of Labor Reserves, a three- or six-month training school for "mass" trades
GKO	State Committee for Defense (Gosudarstvennyi komitet oborony)
Glavk (plural, Glavki)	Chief Administration, a subdivision of a People's Commissariat
Gossaninspektsiia	State Sanitary Inspectorate (Gosudarstvennaia sanitarnaia inspektsiia), or GSI
GSI	see Gossaninspektsiia
Gulag	Chief Administration of Camps; more generally used as the name for the system of NKVD labor camps (see NKVD)
IMR	Infant mortality rate, calculated as deaths of infants under one year of age per 1,000 live births
ispolkom	executive committee (*ispolnitel'nyi komitet*)
ITR	engineering and technical personnel/ specialists (*inzhenerno-tekhnicheskie rabotniki*)
kolkhoz	collective farm (*kollektivnoe khoziaistvo*)
kolkhoznik (plural, *kolkhozniki*)	collective farmer or collective farm member

Terms and Abbreviations

Komsomol	Communist Youth League, formally known as the All-Union Leninist Communist Union of Youth
LP	*Leningradskaia Pravda,* local newspaper, Leningrad
Militia	Police (Militsiia); the regular police force, as distinct from the secret police
Narkomzdrav	People's Commissariat of Public Health (Narodnyi komissariat zdravookhraneniia)
NKVD	People's Commissariat of Internal Affairs (Narodnyi komissariat vnutrennikh del), in charge of the system of labor camps (Gulag) and police (Militia)
NZ (*neprikosnovennyi zapas*)	literally, "untouchable reserve," commonly called "Iron Rations" in other armies; an emergency ration carried by soldiers to be eaten if they are cut off from supplies
obkom	provincial or regional committee (*oblastnoi komitet*) of the Communist Party, trade union, or other organization
oblast' (plural, *oblasti*)	province or region, depending on context
ORS (plural, ORSy)	Department of Workers' Provisioning (Otdel rabochego snabzheniia)
paek	Ration
People's Commissariat	ministry (e.g., of Internal Affairs, of the Iron and Steel Industry, etc.); after the

	war the title was officially changed to Ministry
Procuracy	Public Prosecutor's Office
Procurator	Public Prosecutor
prodovol'stvennye normy	ration allowances, or list of items to which different groups were entitled
raikom	district committee (*raionnyi komitet*) of the Communist Party, trade union, or other organization
raion (plural, *raiony*)	district (administrative subdivision of a city, province, or other larger territorial unit)
razbazarivanie	literally, "squandering," a catch-all word used to describe a range of misuses of resources, from inadvertent wastage to illegal sale and usage
RKKA	The Red Army (Raboche-Krest'ianskaia Krasnaia Armiia; literally, Workers' and Peasants' Red Army)
RSFSR	Russian Soviet Federative Socialist Republic (Rossiiskaia Sovetskaia Federativnaia Sotsialisticheskaia Respublika), the largest republic within the USSR.
RU	trade school (Remeslennoe Uchilishche) under the Chief Administration of Labor Reserves, a two-year training school in skilled trades
Sovnarkom	Council of People's Commissars (Sovet Narodnykh Komissarov),

Terms and Abbreviations

	equivalent to the cabinet of the Soviet government
SSSR	Union of Soviet Socialist Republics (Soiuz Sovetskikh Sotsialisticheskikh Respublik)
starshina	highest level noncommissioned officer in the Red Army, responsible for supply of basic units (company, section, etc.)
sukhpaek (sukhoi paek)	field ration
SU RSFSR	Statistical Administration of the RSFSR (Statisticheskoe upravlenie RSFSR)
Trudovaia Armiia	Labor Army, consisting of a varied collection of convicts and compulsory laborers, including Soviet citizens of German ancestry, Jews who survived in the territories freed from German occupation, a substantial group of mobilized Central Asian workers, so-called "special settlers" (*spetspereselentsy*—"kulaks" exiled in the early 1930s, Crimean Tatars and other national minorities exiled over the course of the war as potential collaborators with the Axis powers), and other categories of the population placed under the control of the NKVD during the war for a variety of reasons. Some historians note that the state did not officially use the term "Labor Army," but many state documents found in the archives do use the term, often in quotation marks

xvi   *Terms and Abbreviations*

TsSU	Central Statistical Administration (Tsentral'noe statisticheskoe upravlenie)
USSR	Union of Soviet Socialist Republics (Soiuz Sovetskikh Sotsialisticheskikh Respublik)
VKP(b)	Communist Party of the Soviet Union (literally, All-Union Communist Party (Bolsheviks)—Vsesoiuznaia Komunisticheskaia Partiia [Bol'shevikov])
Voenkomat	draft board (*voennyi komissariat*)
VTsSPS	All-Union Central Council of Trade Unions (Vsesoiuznyi tsentral'nyi sovet professional'nykh soiuzov)
ZAGS	Registry Office (Zapis' aktov grazhdanskogo sostoianiia)
ZhU	trade school (Zheleznodorozhnoe Uchilishche) to train skilled workers for the railways; equivalent to an RU

The footnotes use standard abbreviations for Russian archive references, which consist of five elements:

1. The abbreviation of the archive name (the full names of the archives are given in the bibliography).
2. f. = *fond*, or holding. These generally correspond to a particular institution or major subdivision of an institution, for example, the USSR Ministry (pre-1945, People's Commissariat) of Public Health, an industrial commissariat or ministry, or a specific trade union.
3. op. = *opis'*, or inventory. The *opisi* are the primary subdivisions of a *fond*. Sometimes the *opisi* represent subdivisions or departments within an organization; some *fondy* simply divide the *opisi* chronologically.

Terms and Abbreviations xvii

4. d. = *delo,* or file. These are the actual folders containing the documents.
5. l. = *list,* or sheet. Russian archives give files sheet numbers, rather than page numbers, since a file almost always contains many different documents, each of which had its own separate pagination when it was originally written. Each sheet has a separate number, so where sheet numbers are followed by the letters "ob" (for the Russian, *oborot*), this means that the text in question appears on the reverse side of the sheet.

Some smaller or more specialized archives break *fondy* down into *razdely,* or sections, which are then divided into *opisi.*

Thus a typical reference will be something like this: GARF, f. 9226, op. 1, d. 636, ll. 52, 53. This means that the document is in GARF (State Archive of the Russian Federation), *fond* 9226 (State Sanitary Inspectorate of the USSR Ministry of Public Health), *opis'* 1, *delo* (file) 636, *listy* (sheets) 52, 53.

The State Archive of the Russian Federation (GARF) has two reading rooms. The central reading room, Reading Room 1, holds files from administrative divisions of the former USSR. Reading Room 2, in a different location, holds files for administrative divisions of the former RSFSR Documents from Reading Room 2 always have the letter "A" before the number of the *fond.* Thus: GARF, f. A-482, op. 47, d. 4941, l. 11, where *fond* A-482 is the Ministry of Public Health of the RSFSR.

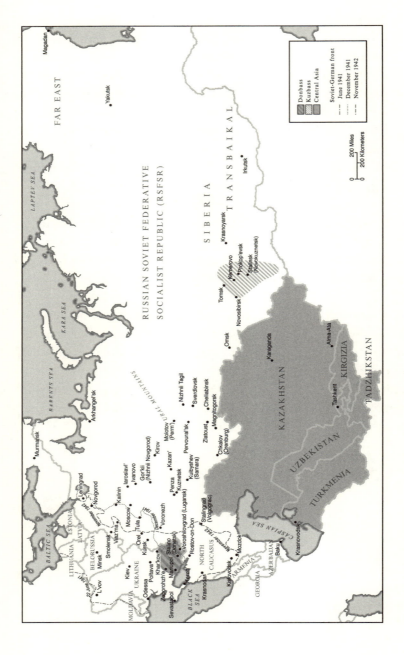

Map of the Soviet Union, 1941–1945: Republics; Major Cities and Industrial Towns; and the Soviet-German Front, 1941–1942. Tanya Buckingham, University of Wisconsin-Madison, Cartography Laboratory.

HUNGER AND WAR

INTRODUCTION:
THE POLITICS OF FOOD AND WAR

Donald Filtzer and Wendy Z. Goldman

EVERY YEAR, VICTORY DAY, OR DEN' POBEDY, THE ANNIVERSARY of Nazi Germany's surrender on May 9, 1945, is celebrated in Russia. In the Soviet period, the day was marked by great festive demonstrations. Elderly men, their medals pinned to worn suit jackets, marched proudly holding the hands of their young grandchildren, and families thronged the streets. The parks were filled with veterans, who met to sing, dance, and remember the war. Today, the ranks of the veterans have thinned, but both state-sponsored events and popular traditions continue. In cities throughout the country, monuments to the war dead are ritual sites of commemoration for wedding parties. In the spring, smiling young girls in bridal dress and their grooms can be seen laying bouquets of flowers at the base of these monuments. The gesture has become a nationwide tradition linking the living and the dead. The wedding party's homage captures a deep, unspoken understanding that future children are in some way consecrated to those young people who did not survive to raise children of their own. Even now, four generations later, the missing are still felt, their memory kept alive, through state-sponsored efforts and family remembrances, from one generation to the next.

The Soviet Union lost more people during World War II, in both absolute numbers and as a percentage of its population, than any other combatant nation: 26.6 million according to the latest figures. More than 8.6 million soldiers died, including almost 3.4 million lost from the ranks or taken prisoner and deliberately starved to death in German camps. Of the civilian population, between 700,000 and 1 million people died in besieged Leningrad. In the occupied territories, 13.6 million perished, including 2.1 million sent to forced labor in Germany; 7.4 million through deliberate extermination, among these, 2 million Jews; and 4.1 million as a result of starvation, lack of medical attention, and other deliberate policies of occupation.[1] Following the German invasion on June 22, 1941, the Soviet state committed the country to "total war": it converted the entire economy to war production, rechanneled consumption into defense, and took control of the food supply. The state shuttered its retail food stores and established an elaborate rationing system to serve soldiers and civilians. Engaged in a process of "total war," the Soviet Union was stretched to the breaking point, hard pressed to meet the needs of the army and the labor force. In 1942, the system was on the verge of collapse. Not a single ounce of additional effort or sacrifice could be wrung from the working population. In fact, many civilians, and not only those in the besieged city of Leningrad, were starving. Research here suggests that Leningrad was an extreme case, but can also be viewed on a nationwide continuum of hunger and shortage. Unlike World War I, however, which ultimately led to revolutions in February and October 1917, the terrible privations on the home front during World War II provoked no mass uprisings against Stalinist rule. Despite devastating losses, the Soviet Union managed to win the war on the eastern front and free the occupied territories.

For many years, the true scale of the damage wrought by the Nazis was unknown. During the Cold War, Soviet leaders concealed the full extent of the human and material losses from both their former Western allies and their own citizens. Following a policy of "We Do Not Divide the Dead," they did not count the dead by nationality (Jewish, Belorussian, Ukrainian, and so on) and were silent about the genocide against

---

1. For total losses, see E. M. Andreev, L. E. Darskii, and T. L. Khar'kova, "Liudskie poteri SSSR vo vtoroi mirovoi voine: metodika otsenki i rezul'taty," on civilian losses, M. V. Filimoshin, "Ob itogakh ischislenniia sredi mirnogo naseleniia na okkupirovannoi territorii SSSR i RSFSR v gody Velikoi Otechestvennoi voiny," and on military losses, G. F. Krivosheev, "Ob itogakh statisticheskikh issledovanii poter' vooruzhennykh sil SSSR v Velikoi Otechestvennoi voine," all in N. A. Aralovets, O. M. Verbitskaia, V. B. Zhiromskaia, Iu. A. Poliakov, and A. I. Repinetskii, eds. *Liudskie poteri SSSR v period vtoroi mirovoi voiny. Sbornik statei* (St. Petersburg: Russko-Baltiiskii Informatsionnyi Tsentr, 1995), pp. 41–42, 127, 75.

Introduction

the Jews in the Nazi occupied territories. The toll the war took on the home front was also tacitly ignored. Everyone from Communist Party leaders to factory workers understood that the country had suffered deeply, but the full extent and specific details of hunger and starvation were not publicly disclosed.

The victory, achieved at such great cost, was eventually enshrouded in heroic myth. Heavily promoted by Soviet leaders, the myth provided the state with legitimacy and gave the people a well-justified pride in the successful struggle against Fascism. It unified people through a memory of common suffering and gave meaning to irrecoverable personal losses. Few families escaped a death: grandparents, parents, children, and siblings were all lost to the war. According to the myth, the Red Army fought valiantly to protect the motherland. The Soviet people united to free their country from the invaders, and the Communist Party played a leading role in organizing the war effort at the front and in the rear. The heroic myth, in many of its lineaments, was true. The battle-hardened *frontoviki* later memorialized were real men and women. They may not have resembled the granite-jawed statues erected to commemorate their service, but real men and women fought fiercely on the outskirts of Moscow, drove horse-drawn carts over the icy wastes of Lake Ladoga to provision Leningrad, and manned tanks with hand-scrawled slogans reading "From Stalingrad to Berlin." The Soviet Union was the first and only occupied country to mount a successful resistance against the Nazi invaders. With the bulk of the Wehrmacht arrayed on the eastern front, the country bore the brunt of Nazi brutality as well as the fighting. Yet the heroic myth also excluded the less savory sides of the war: lack of preparedness, panic at the front, repression in the ranks, collaborationism in the rear, starvation mortality in the non-occupied areas, and the sometimes less than heroic behavior of both officials and ordinary people. Until the collapse of the Soviet Union, the state used the myth to enforce silence on these issues.

Hunger and War focuses on food and provisioning, the very foundation of the military effort and defense production. All the chapters explore topics that were once taboo. Using a wide range of new archival and published primary sources, the book provides a new understanding of state policy, popular responses, and the social costs of victory. In chapter 1,

Wendy Goldman explores the state's food policy, the hierarchy of provisioning, and the new economy that emerged with the collapse of state retail trade. Goldman brings us into the factories, where millions of workers, mobilized from all over the country, worked long shifts on little more than a daily bowl of gruel. In chapter 2, Brandon Schechter focuses on soldiers at the front and their social compact with the state. As Schechter reveals, amid constant death, food took on intense new meanings. In the wake of battle, the surviving soldiers ate the precious bread of fallen comrades. As one soldier noted, "We ate for them." In Leningrad, a city blockaded by the Germans for almost three years, local authorities instituted an iron rationing system but there was not enough food to save everyone. Alexis Peri describes in chapter 3, how people used public spaces like bath houses and bread lines to read new hierarchies of privilege and survival in the starving and fed bodies that surrounded them. In chapter 4, Rebecca Manley focuses on nutritional dystrophy, or starvation disease, and explains how Leningrad's doctors pioneered a new understanding of starvation even as they were perishing from lack of food. Like their dying colleagues in the Warsaw Ghetto, they attempted to chart the stages of dystrophy and find new and targeted treatments for their patients. In chapter 5, Donald Filtzer maps starvation mortality in the rear, demonstrating through statistical analysis that starvation became the largest cause of death in the industrial cities. His research, supported by the other chapters, shows how the food crisis came to envelop not only children, the elderly, and the sick, but the best-fed population sector in the rear: male industrial workers. The five chapters explore the organization, politics, psychology, impact, and multiple meanings of hunger and the rationing system. Taken together, they provide a panoply of experiences at the front and in the rear that have hitherto remained hidden.

THE SOVIET UNION AS NAZI COLONY: THE BACKE HUNGER PLAN AND OPERATION BARBAROSSA

The food crisis in the Soviet Union cannot be understood apart from the Nazi's military, ideological, and political war aims. Operation Barbarossa, launched on June 22, 1941, consisted of a three-pronged attack: north

Introduction

toward Leningrad, center toward Smolensk and Moscow, and south toward Kiev. The three massed army groups constituted the mightiest military force ever concentrated on a single theater of war. Several months earlier, in March 1941, Hitler summoned 250 officers to the Berlin chancellery where he lectured them on the novel nature of war with Russia. The German General Franz Halder summarized the meeting in his diary: "Struggle against Russia: Extermination of Bolshevik Commissars and of the Communist intelligentsia. . . . Commissars and GPU personnel are criminals and must be treated as such. The struggle will differ from that in the west."[2] Heinrich Himmler, as Reichsführer SS, was assigned to take over "special tasks" in the conquered areas with four Einsatzgruppen (task forces) of security police and Security Service (SD) personnel, a force of about three thousand men. At the end of April, staff officers received Field Marshall von Brauchitsch's order setting out the ground rules for relations between army commanders and the SS. According to the Barbarossa orders, Soviet political officers, Jews, and partisans were to be handed over to the SS or Einsatzgruppen. The leaders of these groups were instructed, "to murder all Jews, Asiatic inferiors, Communist officials and gypsies." The political commissars of the Red Army were to be killed if captured. According to further directives, the German armies in the east were to live off the local population, to expropriate whatever they needed, and to send seven million tons of grain back to Germany. Nazi leaders understood the consequences of these orders: Martin Bormann, head of the Nazi Party Chancellery and private secretary to Hitler, later stated, "Many tens of millions will starve to death." He wrote: "The Slavs are to work for us. Insofar as we do not need them, they may die."[3] Members of the armed forces were virtually immune to prosecution for crimes against civilians, including murder, rape, and looting. Officers were given the right to decide on the spot whether any civilian accused of criminal action should be shot. Russian civilians had no right of appeal. Orders also included instructions for collective reprisals

---

2. See Halder's diary notes in Joachim Fest, *Hitler* (Orlando, Fla.: Harcourt, 1974), p. 649. The GPU, or State Political Administration (Gosudarstvennoe politikicheskoe upravlenie) was one of the early acronyms of the Soviet security police. At the time that Halder wrote these words, it was already known as the NKVD.

3. http://www.jewishvirtuallibrary.org/jsource/biography/Bormann.html.

against villages and cities. A guideline of the High Command of the armed forces, issued to 3.6 million soldiers on the eastern front before the beginning of the attack, called for "ruthless and energetic measures against Bolshevik agitators, guerrillas, saboteurs, Jews, and total elimination of all active and passive resistance." A noisy campaign against the "Slavic subhuman" accompanied these orders. As many historians later noted, the orders were not instructions for war, but for mass murder.[4]

By the fall of 1942, the Germans had conquered great sections of the western Soviet Union, including Belorussia, Ukraine, the Crimea, and large portions of Russia. These lands encompassed the vast majority of the Soviet Union's prime farmland, food processing plants, animal herds, and collective farms, as well as coalmines, electrical stations, and industry. The line of occupation in the late autumn of 1942 stretched from the besieged city of Leningrad in the north to the Caucasus in the south. Directly to the north and south of the industrial city of Stalingrad, German forces reached the Volga River, their farthest eastern advance. Soviet General Chuikov's forces were dug in, barely holding several salients on the Volga's western bank, which stretched from the river into the twisted industrial rubble of the ruined city. In a powerful counteroffensive beginning in November, the Red Army launched a massive encirclement of German, Italian, and Rumanian troops. Stalingrad would prove a major turning point in the war: the first mass surrender of Hitler's army. By the end of January 1943, the Red Army began fighting its way back west.[5] Yet liberation would not restore the industrial and agricultural

---

4. On the Barbarossa orders, see Felix Römer, "The Wehrmacht in the War of Ideologies: The Army and Hitler's Criminal Orders on the Eastern Front," in Alex Kay, Jeff Rutherford, and David Stahel, eds., *Nazi Policy on the Eastern Front, 1941: Total War, Genocide, and Radicalization* (Rochester, N.Y.: University of Rochester Press, 2012), pp. 73–100; Christopher R. Browning, *The Origins of the Final Solution: The Evolution of Nazi Jewish Policy, September 1939–March 1942* (Lincoln: University of Nebraska Press, 2004), pp. 222–223.

5. On the battle of Stalingrad and other military campaigns, see Antony Beevor, *Stalingrad: The Fateful Siege, 1942–1943* (New York: Viking Penguin, 1998); John Erickson, *The Road to Stalingrad: Stalin's War with Germany*, vol. 1 (New Haven, Conn.: Yale University Press, 1999); David Glantz, with Jonathan House, *The Stalingrad Trilogy*, 3 volumes (Lawrence: University of Kansas Press, 2009, 2009, 2014); Vasily Grossman, *A Writer at War: A Soviet Journalist with the Red Army, 1941–1945* (New York: Pantheon Books, 2005); Richard Overy, *Russia's War: A History of the Soviet Effort, 1941–1945* (New

Introduction 7

resources that had been lost to occupation. The farms were ruined, cities plundered, mines flooded, and factories demolished. Millions of people lay murdered in pits that pocked the forests and the fields.

The Nazi invasion of the USSR was never a purely military issue. The Germans held special plans for the Soviet lands to the east. Western historians have written extensively about Nazism as a racial ideology, and the genocidal policies against Jews. Yet few have cast German aggression against the Soviet Union as a colonial policy designed to create a vast base of agriculture and raw materials. As historian Adam Tooze notes, "the German invasion of the Soviet Union is far better understood as the last great land grab in a long and bloody history of European colonialism."[6] The USSR had a special place in Hitler's vision of a future Germany. His aim was to destroy Bolshevism, eliminate the Soviet state, and establish German hegemony. The Soviet Union was to serve as a colony for the new Reich, providing food, raw materials, and labor. Its people were to be eliminated or enslaved.

The Nazis saw Bolshevism as both a Great Russian and a Jewish phenomenon. Yet Bolshevism was merely the latest manifestation of a permanent, long-standing conflict between the German and the Slav. Russia was an enemy regardless of her system. In the Nazi view, Slavs were an inferior race, unable to organize a state of their own. Russia was fated to be ruled and dominated by Germany. Its political organizations, from the national to the local level, were to be eliminated. Slavs could not have a state. Most of Hitler's collaborators agreed with these ideas and objectives, although there were some differences over nationality policy. Alfred Rosenberg, the creator of Ostpolitik, hoped to fan and exploit the hostility of specific national groups within the USSR against the Russians. Russia, in his view, should be reduced to a landmass the size of ancient Muscovy and isolated by a cordon sanitaire of Ukraine, Belorussia, the Baltic states, the Caucasus, and Central Asia. Rosenberg argued that these national groups should be permitted to form their own states under

---

York: Penguin Books, 1998); Alexander Werth, *Russia at War, 1941–1945* (New York: Carroll and Graf, 1984).

6. Adam Tooze, *The Wages of Destruction: The Making and Breaking of the Nazi Economy* (New York: Viking Penguin, 2006), p. 462.

German control in order to create anti-Russian allies. Other prominent German leaders, within and outside the Nazi Party, asserted anti-Communist rather than anti-Russian ideas. Emphasizing class rather than nationality, they hoped to turn the Soviet people, especially the peasantry, against Soviet power. Hitler, however, representing the majority within the Nazi hierarchy, contended that Germany had no need of eastern allies; concessions to either national or social groups were not necessary. The entirety of the country should be colonized. Within the first months of the war, Hitler's policy prevailed. The Wehrmacht's rapid military successes and capture of millions of Red Army soldiers confirmed Hitler's belief that the Soviet people were "sub humans" (Untermenschen) to be ruled by violence. All local administration would function under strict German control and all higher administration was to be German. No extension of local authority was envisioned even after the war ended.[7]

The experience of World War I convinced Hitler that Germany could not wage a successful war unless a reliable food source could be provided to the army and the cities. During World War I, the Allied blockade of Germany created great food shortages, leading to mass hunger and food riots during the winters of 1917 and 1918 and, more importantly from Hitler's point of view, to general popular disaffection with the war effort.[8] Historians give conflicting estimates, but somewhere between 425,000 and 760,000 German civilians died of hunger and disease during the war. The food crisis persisted during the winter of 1918–1919, and played no small role in the November 1918 sailors' mutiny that led to the abdication of the Kaiser and the outbreak of the German revolution (including the declaration of a socialist republic in Bavaria) and the creation of workers' councils or soviets throughout the country. Hitler, fearing a repeat of the riots and revolutions of World War I, was obsessed with the need to secure Germany's food supply. The growth and development of capitalism presented Europe with new challenges. Foremost among these, as

7. On planning for the invasion, see Alex J. Kay, *Exploitation, Resettlement, Mass Murder: Political and Economic Planning for German Occupation Policy in the Soviet Union, 1940–1941* (New York: Berghahn Books, 2006).

8. Roger Chickering, *Imperial Germany and the Great War, 1914–1918* (Cambridge: Cambridge University Press, 2003), pp. 141–146.

Introduction 9

historian Lizzie Collingham points out, were the problems that each state faced in feeding a growing urban working class within an emergent, connected global economy. German nationalists saw a route through war, which would allow Germany to dominate Western and Eastern Europe. Yet Hitler faced a conundrum: How could the Nazi state maintain low food prices in the cities, encourage farmers to produce, and support a vast military machine? Unlike the Soviet state, which sought resources from within and required massive sacrifice from the population, Hitler believed the solution lay in eastern colonization, or Lebensraum. He later announced, "What India was for England, the territories of Russia will be for us."[9]

In 1932, R. Walther Darré, who would soon become the Reichsminister of Food and Agriculture, presented a plan at a Nazi leadership conference for large eastern agricultural estates to be run by SS members and worked by enslaved Slavs. The Nazis took power within a year, and Herbert Backe, a fierce proponent of eastern conquest, began to eclipse Darré's limited plan with a more grandiose vision. According to Backe, Germany could become self-sufficient in food only if it conquered the Soviet Union. Backe conceived the agricultural riches of Ukraine and the eastern lands not as spoils of war, but as the very means with which to wage it. Backe thus reversed Darré's view: war was not the path to colonization, but rather, colonization was essential to the conduct of a successful war. In September 1939, the Hitler-Stalin pact neutralized Germany's fear of a two-front war and gave the Soviet Union a much-needed territorial bulwark and breathing space. Poland was divided between the two signatories. Hitler invaded the western half, and Britain declared war on Germany. Hitler then turned west to conquer Denmark, Norway, Holland, Belgium, and France. Yet despite the unbroken string of Nazi victories, Backe remained deeply concerned about Germany's food supply and the British blockade. In May 1940, he noted pessimistically: "If the war lasts more than two years it is lost." Backe urged Hitler to invade the Soviet Union. Occupation would provide Germany with a massive resource base that would support a long war with Great Britain

---

9. Lizzie Collingham, *The Taste of War: World War II and the Battle for Food* (New York: Penguin Press, 2011), pp. 25, 26, 22, 18.

(and the United States) if necessary. To this end, Backe devised his Hunger Plan, which proposed the mass murder of Slavs and Jews and the elimination of "useless eaters."[10]

In January 1941, Backe began aggressively pushing his plan to Hitler, and in February, Hitler and his senior commander, Hermann Goering, approved it. The plan was summarized in the minutes from a May 2 meeting of officials responsible for economic policy. The "Memo on Today's Discussion Regarding Barbarossa" read: "1. The war can only continue to be waged if the entire Wehrmacht is fed from Russia during the third year of the war. 2. As a result, x million people will doubtlessly starve." The Nazi regime would stop the flow of food from Ukraine into central and northern Russia, and divert it to the German army and citizens of the Reich. According to economic guidelines developed shortly thereafter, "x" did in fact represent a number: "many tens of millions" of Soviet citizens were expected to die. Soon leading Nazis such as Himmler and Goering began to quote a figure of "20 to 30 million" Soviets who would starve to death. The cities, in particular, were expected to die out.[11] Those who were to implement the plan were told to stifle any sympathy they might feel for starving Russians. The Wehrmacht, which later attempted to disassociate itself from the mass murder and genocide that followed the invasion, quickly embraced the plan because it solved the problem of feeding the troops via overextended supply lines. The Einsatzgruppen, the mobile task force that followed the Wehrmacht and was responsible for the mass murder of Jews, partisans, and Communists, was also enthusiastic. The head of Einsatzgruppe B, Franz Six, explained: "a 'blazing strip' will emerge in which all life is to be erased. It is intended to decimate around 30 million Russians living in this strip through starvation, by removing all foodstuffs from this enormous territory. All those in-

---

10. Ibid., pp. 32, 25.

11. Alex J. Kay, "Germany's Staatssekretäre, Mass Starvation and the Meeting of 2 May 1941," *Journal of Contemporary History* 41, no. 4 (2006): 685–689. Tooze, *Wages of Destruction*, pp. 479–480. Kay (p. 689) notes, "What one is dealing with here is the blueprint for a programme of mass murder unprecedented in modern history." Tooze (p. 480) quotes official guidelines issued to the Wehrmacht for the implementation of food policy in the occupied territories: "Many tens of millions of people in this area will become surplus to requirements and will die or will be forced to emigrate to Siberia."

Introduction

volved in this operation are to be forbidden on pain of death to give a Russian even a piece of bread. The large cities from Leningrad to Moscow are to be razed to the ground."[12] The Slavic Untermenschen would be eliminated and Germans resettled in their place. Existing towns and villages would be leveled to create a blank canvas. The Slavs would no longer pose an "ecological obstacle to the proper cultivation" of the East. Fourteen million Soviet peasants would be used as slaves, a tiny number would be integrated into German society, and the remaining 70 million would be deported to the Soviet arctic where they would eventually die of overwork. Hitler compared the Slavs to the Native Americans in the United States who were exterminated in the process of Western expansion. Backe's plan fit perfectly with Nazism's racial and political ideology. The idea that the occupation of the Soviet Union was a critical element in Germany's ability to wage war encouraged Hitler to invade in June.[13] The murderous fantasies of the Backe Plan, however, never came to full fruition, as the Wehrmacht found it impossible hermetically to cordon off entire regions. This did not prevent millions of Polish, Jewish, and Soviet citizens from starving to death, including some 800,000 in Leningrad and hundreds of thousands more in the occupied territories and in the rear.[14]

STATE RATIONS AND THE ENERGY FRACTION

The loss of the occupied territories had an immediate effect on the Soviet food supply. Within less than a week of the invasion, the state cut central

---

12. As quoted in Alex J. Kay, "The Purpose of the Russian Campaign Is the Decimation of the Slavic Population by Thirty Million: The Radicalization of German Food Policy in Early 1941," in Kay, Rutherford, and Stahel, eds., *Nazi Policy on the Eastern Front, 1941*, p. 113.

13. Collingham, *The Taste of War*, pp. 33, 36, 37, 38, 39, 41, 42.

14. Kay, "Germany's Staatssekretäre, Mass Starvation and the Meeting of 2 May 1941," p. 699. See also Tooze, *The Wages of Destruction*, pp. 461–551. On the occupied territories, see Christian Gerlach, *Kalkulierte Morde: Die deutsche Wirtschafts und Vernichtungspolitik in Weissrussland 1941 bis 1944* (Hamburg: Hamburger Edition, 1999); Karel Berkhoff, *Harvest of Despair: Life and Death in Ukraine under Nazi Rule* (Cambridge, Mass.: Harvard University Press, 2004); and Alexander Dallin, *German Rule in Russia, 1941–1945: A Study of Occupation Policies* (Boulder, Colo.: Westview Press, 1981).

state stocks available for feeding the civilian population and diverted food to the army. Within a month, it instituted a rationing system that encompassed the urban population and rural waged workers. Retail trade contracted sharply as stores closed or converted to ration distribution centers. Given the loss of territory, agricultural produce, herds, and food processing plants, the Soviet state lacked enough food to provision fully all the groups that needed to be fed: soldiers, mobilized workers, evacuees, refugees, and urban dwellers. The state faced a painful dilemma: how to divide its insufficient stocks among various military and civilian groups.

The state quickly adopted a rationing system structured around basic hierarchies of allocation. Soldiers at the front were fed better than civilians in the rear. Both the military and the civilian spheres, in turn, were divided into their own hierarchies of provisioning, which the chapters that follow describe in detail. The state divided the home front into social categories of provisioning, based roughly on a labor principle of caloric expenditure and importance to defense. Workers in defense production, the energy sector, metallurgy, rubber, and rail and water transport were favored over workers in other branches of industry and municipal services. Workers in all sectors received more food than white-collar employees, adult dependents, and children in a descending order. The state made a special attempt to protect vulnerable population groups, including young children, nursing mothers, workers in hazardous occupations, and teenaged workers, either by boosting the caloric intake of their meals or by giving them privileged access—when supplies were available—to nutritious, deficit foods, such as milk. Leningrad remained a special case because the Germans were successful in blockading the city, especially through the late fall and early winter of 1941–1942. Yet the principles of allocation in Leningrad did not differ appreciably from those in the rest of the country, although the calorie counts were far lower. In both Leningrad and other regions, the state centralized the main sources of food, made strong efforts to provide a daily bread ration, and encouraged decentralized sources, such as collective and individual gardens, to supplement the basic foods allocated by the ration card.

The lack of food made it impossible to protect every social category fully, and provisioning became a zero-sum game that often required various state organizations to take food from one hungry group to supply

Introduction   13

another. Yet the ration hierarchy should not be seen as a direct barometer of nutritional well-being. In order to understand the nutritional status of any particular group, it is necessary to compare the calories it consumed to the calories it expended, a ratio we term the *energy fraction*. If this ratio equaled one, numerator and denominator were in perfect balance: a person would neither gain nor lose weight. If it proved to be less than one, a person would lose weight, and if greater than one, gain weight. The smaller the fraction and the longer this energy deficit persisted, the more likely that malnutrition and eventually starvation would result. A group at the top of the rationing hierarchy that received more food but expended a lot of calories might, therefore, have a lower energy fraction than a group that received fewer calories but expended less energy. Considered over time, this fraction provides the best indication of those groups most at risk of weight loss, nutritional deficiency, and starvation. By placing caloric expenditure as well as consumption into an analysis of the rationing system, the energy fraction allows us to identify the groups most favored by state policy as well as those that bore the greatest impact of food shortage.

The expenditure of energy for all social groups was greatly increased by the difficulty of wartime conditions. Workers experienced intense acceleration of labor and standard working shifts of eleven or twelve hours with few days off and no holidays.[15] Fuel shortages and unremitting cold sharpened people's need for calorie-dense foods and increased their biological requirements. During the long winters, the factories, as

15. Formally, workers in heavy industry were supposed to receive one day off every two weeks, which meant an average work week of six and one-half days. This measure was as often honored in the breach as it was adhered to. For example, at perhaps the extreme end of the scale, in 1943, the *normal* working day for workers at the copper smelting factory in Krasnoural'sk was fourteen to sixteen hours. Only at the end of 1944 were shifts for 62 percent of workers cut to eight hours, but this was made possible only by the arrival at the factory of so-called "special contingents" of prison labor provided by the NKVD. The remaining 38 percent of workers continued to work eleven-hour shifts. Workers had received virtually no days off during all of 1943 and 1944. GARF, f. A-482, op. 47, d. 2030, l. 790b. Factory shifts of ten or twelve hours were common in Britain, too, during the war, but living and working conditions and the diets of British workers were greatly superior to those that prevailed in the Soviet Union. For British workers, malnutrition, not to mention actual starvation, was simply not an issue. Collingham, *The Taste of War,* pp. 363–367, 384–399.

well as the dormitories, barracks, and *zemlianki* (earthen dugouts), were often unheated. Buildings were hastily constructed and offered inadequate protection against freezing temperatures and strong winds.[16] Bathhouses closed for lack of fuel. Hot water for shaving, washing, or even tea was in short supply. Workers lacked warm clothing, footwear, and bedding. Many lived in rickety settlements located many miles from the factory. Public transport shut down for lack of fuel and machine parts, and many workers trudged long distances to and from work. Workers may have used more calories walking to and from work than contained in the single meal the factory canteen provided. Rations alone could not provide the number of calories or the amount of protein people needed to avoid chronic weight loss and depletion of fat and muscle tissue.

Using the energy fraction, how did various groups fare on the ration? Who were the most and the least privileged? Table I.1 and figure I.1 show the number of calories provided by the ration for various groups, their biological requirements, and the percentage of biological need the ration met (the energy fraction). No group, with the exception of leading officials in the armaments industry, received enough food through the ration system to cover their biological needs. (It is important to note that people in all groups received additional food from sources other than the ration.) Older children and adult dependents fared the worst: the ration met only 25 percent of their biological needs (their energy fraction was ¼.) Leading officials in the armaments industry fared the best: they received more calories than they needed. Indeed, unless this small group of officials redistributed their food to family members, friends, colleagues, or neighbors, they may have been the only group in the Soviet Union to gain weight on the ration alone. Only miners working at the coalface

---

16. There is hardly a single report on conditions in factories, dormitories, hospitals, and schools that does not cite this fact. For a typical example, see the discussion of sickness rates in Gor'kii defense factories during 1944, in GARF, f. A-482, op. 47, d. 2202, l. 35. The extreme cold caused other medical and public health problems, besides contributing to morbidity and mortality from starvation. Bathhouses could not operate, laundries could not wash dirty work clothes or bed linen, and doctors and paramedics could not properly dress wounds, all of which contributed to high rates of skin infections, one of the most prominent causes of lost work time due to illness. The risk of typhus was also heightened because of the difficulties of controlling lice infestations.

Introduction

Table I.1. Calorie content of basic rations, different categories of workers, white-collar employees, and dependents, November 1943

Ration category and grams of bread per day each category was allotted	Calories/day	Biological requirement	% biological requirement
Dependents—children (average, ages 4–11)	780	2081	38
Dependents—older children & adults	780	3070	25
White collar—400 grams	1074	3208	34
White collar—450 grams	1176	3208	37
Workers—500 grams	1387	3592	39
Workers—600 grams	1592	3592	44
Workers, special list—500 grams	1503	3592	42
Workers, special list—700 grams	1913	3592	53
Workers, higher norms—600 grams	3181	4112	77
Workers, special higher norms—800 grams	3460	4112	84
Miners, special higher norms + cold breakfast—up to 1,000 grams	4114	4678	88
Miners, special higher norms + cold breakfast + second hot meal	4418	4678	94
Top officials, Group I armaments industry—1,000 grams	4664	3208	145
Workers on heavy jobs in hot shops, armaments—1,000 grams	2661	4678	57
Actual adult consumption, 1943 average	***2751***	***3592***	***77***

Sources: Column 2 (calories per day): rows 3–14, U. G. Cherniavskii, *Voina i prodovol'stvie: snabzhenie gorodskogo naseleniia v Velikuiu Otechestvennuiu voinu, 1941–1945 gg.* (Moscow: Nauka, 1964), p. 77; row 14, calculated from GARF, f. 7678, op. 8, d. 243, l. 6; row 15, calculated from GARF, f. 7678, op. 15, d. 54, l. 114; row 16 from Cherniavskii, p. 179. Biological requirements (column 3) are 1951 figures calculated by the Institute of Nutrition, in GARF, f. 9226, op. 1 d, 1119, ll. 11, 52, 52ob. Column 4 calculated from values in columns 2–3.

Note: In 1951, the USSR Institute of Nutrition determined the biological requirements of children in different age brackets and adults in different occupational categories. Group I included teachers, doctors, office workers, and housewives: 3,208 calories per day. Group II included lathe operators, textile workers, tractor drivers, and other workers doing mechanized labor: 3,592 calories per day. Group III included stokers, blacksmiths, collective farmers, and others performing non-mechanized manual labor: 4,112 calories per day. Group IV included loggers, navvies, miners, and others doing heavy non-mechanized manual labor: 4,678 calories per day. For biological requirements of child dependents, we have taken the average of children aged between 4 and 11. Some children aged 12–13 had already started working, but on the assumption that most were still in school, we have grouped them with adult dependents and for the group as a whole taken the average between teenagers aged 12–15 and adults in Group I. Unless they were disabled, few adult dependents would have led a sedentary existence. They would have helped with essential chores, such as growing food, scouring for food and firewood, or looking after small children. Children aged 14 and over were almost all working, either directly for an employer or as trainees in the Labor Reserve system, and we have treated them as workers. Rows 14 and 15 are from July and May 1943 respectively, that is, before the November reduction in ration entitlements. Row 16 is Cherniavskii's calculation of actual average daily adult calorie intake for all of 1943.

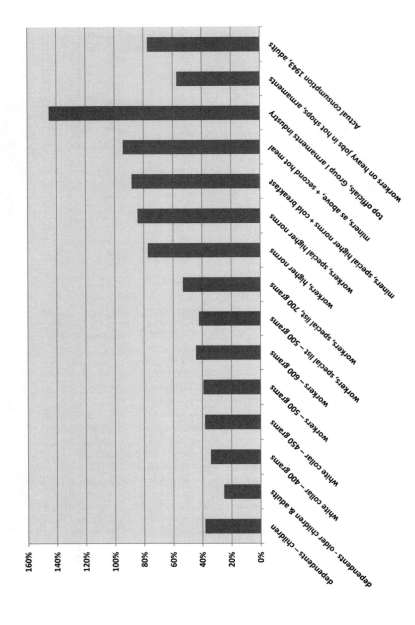

1.1. Ration allowances as a percentage of biological need, calories per day by employment group, November 1943.

Introduction

(face workers) did anywhere near as well: this group received 94 percent of its biological needs through the ration. Given the fact that almost all groups also received supplementary foods from other sources (gardens, collective farm markets, subsidiary agricultural enterprises attached to factories and institutions), miners in all likelihood did not suffer from extended caloric deprivation. Other categories of workers, however, had a greater shortfall to make up: their rations covered from 39 to 88 percent of their needs. White-collar workers fared particularly badly in terms of rations. Despite their lower caloric expenditure, the ration covered only about one-third of their biological needs. In fact, this group fared even worse than young children, who received fewer calories from the ration but required less food (38 percent of their biological needs were covered by the ration).

Two important points emerge from the data in table I.1. First, every group, with the exception of miners and leading armaments officials, could not live on the ration alone. The rations of white-collar workers, industrial workers, children, teenagers, and dependent adults fell considerably short of their biological needs, although the shortfall for most workers was less than that for white-collar employees. By the end of the war, the vast majority of workers had been placed on lists for higher norms, and thus had a caloric shortfall of about 25 percent or less of their biological requirement to make up outside the ration. Yet even with other sources of food added to their daily consumption—mainly potatoes—it is likely that most Soviet citizens still had an energy fraction that fell below one: their caloric expenditure outweighed their consumption. Most of the country went hungry; and in certain periods and places, particularly in poor agricultural areas, some starved. Second, the Soviet ration hierarchy did in fact roughly accord with nutritional status as represented by the energy fraction: ration policy ensured that those who expended more energy, received more food to compensate. Armaments officials were the only group that proved an absolute exception to this rule: they received more food than they required. Relative exceptions to the rule were older children and dependents, who had higher biological requirements than young children, but received the same number of calories in their rations. Their energy fraction (1/4) was lower than that of smaller children (about 2/5). And workers in hot shops in armaments also showed that the labor principle was not applied with complete equality across industries: although they had the same biological requirements as miners, the ration met 57 percent of their needs and 94 percent of those of miners. Yet apart from these exceptions, the energy fraction revealed that the hierarchies of the rationing system, which privileged workers over other groups, were largely synonymous with the hierarchy of nutritional well-being. Those at the top of the rationing hierarchy had a greater percentage of their biological needs met although they expended more calories. The state clearly took caloric expenditure into account in devising its allocation amounts.

SUPPLEMENTARY SOURCES AND THE HUMBLE POTATO

If the Soviet home front had been forced to live on the ration alone, the majority of people would have eventually starved to death. By early 1942, the state was aware of the desperate food situation and moved quickly to supplement the ration with additional sources of food. As Wendy Goldman shows in chapter 1, the state actively promoted subsidiary agriculture, collective and personal gardens, and collective farm markets. These additional sources made a vital contribution to people's diets, especially by providing them with potatoes, vegetables, and, less often, dairy products and meat. The most important of all food products as a supplement to the ration, however, was the humble potato. The potato became "the signature food" of the war.[17] Easy to grow in personal gardens and on farms, a good source of calories, protein, and vitamins, the potato became the main supplementary food available to most of the population.

How much of a supplement did the potato provide to people? Table I.2 shows average consumption by urban residents of potatoes grown on personal garden plots and subsidiary farms attached to factories and institutions in specific provinces in 1943. The subsidiary farms increased potato consumption by roughly one-third over and above the yields of the per-

---

17. Collingham, *The Taste of War*, p. 70. On the potato as more recent supplementary nutrition, see Nancy Ries, "Potato Ontology: Surviving Post Socialism in Russia," *Cultural Anthropology* 24, no. 2 (May 2009): 181–212.

Introduction

Table I.2. Average per capita consumption of potatoes and their daily calorie equivalents for urban residents in selected provinces of the RSFSR, 1943

Location	Annual consumption from garden plots, kilograms	Extrapolated consumption, assuming an additional 33% from factory or institution farms	Grams/day	Kcal/day	Grams of protein/day
USSR average	52	69	189	159	2.84
RSFSR average	65	86	237	199	3.56
Moscow city	24	32	87	73	1.31
Iaroslavl' province	70	93	255	214	3.83
Cheliabinsk province	75	100	273	230	4.10
Omsk province	111	148	404	340	6.06
Novosibirsk province	151	201	550	462	8.25
Kemerovo province	206	274	751	631	11.27

Source: Adapted from Cherniavskii, p. 149. Until 1953, most prewar and wartime calorie and protein calculations used the 1925 nutritional tables produced by the Central Statistical Administration, *Trudy TsSU*, vol. xxii, vypusk 1 (1925): *Normal'nyi sostav i pishchevoe znachenie prodovol'stvennykh produktov.* These assumed that potatoes were new potatoes, consumed soon after harvest, with a value of 63 calories and 1.4 grams of protein per 100 grams of raw product. The VTsSPS (All-Union Central Council of Trade Unions), conducted household budget surveys during 1950–1952, and assumed, more realistically, old potatoes, with a value of 84 calories and 1.5 grams of protein per 100 grams of raw product. We have used this latter standard here. The USSR Ministry of Public Health issued new nutritional tables in 1954, reflecting the improving quality of Soviet food; these listed potatoes as giving 90 calories and 2 grams of protein per 100 grams. *Tablitsy khimicheskogo sostava i pitatel'noi tsennosti pishchevykh produktov* (Moscow: Medgiz, 1954).

Cherniavskii's original table includes more localities than we have listed here: the Central Asian and Caucasian Republics, and from the RSFSR, Arkhangel'sk, Chkalov, Vologda, and Irkutsk provinces, Mordova, Iakutiya, and the Komi Republics, and the Altai, Krasnoiarsk, and Khabarovsk territories. We have chosen only those regions for which we can correlate consumption with starvation mortality data presented by Donald Filtzer in chapter 5. Significantly, Cherniavskii does not give any figures for Sverdlovsk province, where much of the 1943 potato crop was wiped out by potato blight. GARF, f. 5451, op. 43, d. 301, ll. 15, 41, 42, 42ob.

sonal garden plots.[18] Table I.2 converts the average annual consumption in kilograms to calories and grams of protein per day, assuming a caloric value of 84 kilocalories and 1.5 grams of protein per 100 grams of raw product. The caloric and protein supplement provided by the potato were significant. Although in Moscow the contribution of potatoes to the average diet was negligible, elsewhere they proved a valuable, although not always sufficient supplement. Unfortunately, the geographical distribution of potato consumption was uneven. In Iaroslavl' and Cheliabinsk provinces, the potato undoubtedly saved many lives, although as Donald Filtzer shows in chapter 5, its overall contribution was still not enough to prevent large numbers of people in both provinces from dying of starvation. In Western Siberia, however, and especially in the Kuzbass (Kemerovo province), potatoes provided such a large supplement that their consumption may partially explain the lower incidence of starvation mortality there.[19] Moreover, although the state launched the gardening movement in 1942, yields peaked only in 1944. They were considerably lower in 1942 and 1943, and thus provided a smaller buffer against starvation. By 1944, potato consumption from subsidiary farms and garden plots of the average urban resident had nearly doubled from the previous year, from 52 to 101 kilograms (222.2 pounds), or 276 grams (10 ounces) a day, providing each person with an extra 232 calories and 3.5 grams (0.12 ounces) of protein.[20]

If the potato was the war's "signature food," meat, dairy products, and vegetable and animal fats remained in very short supply. As Wendy Goldman notes in chapter 1, some factories set up piggeries, and the state attached some large state farms to the factories. Yet for the vast majority of industrial workers, consumption of fats and animal protein was meager. Fat not only provided a dense source of energy; it was vital to the body's ability to synthesize vitamins and to heal wounds or abrasions.

---

18. U. G. Cherniavskii, , *Voina i prodovol'stvie: snabzhenie gorodskogo naseleniia v Velikuiu Otechestvennuiu voinu, 1941–1945 gg.* (Moscow: Nauka, 1964) does not give potato yields from factory or institutional farms for 1943, but in 1942 the latter added an additional 36 percent to total potato consumption, and in 1944 an additional 28 percent. It would be reasonable to assume that subsidiary farms added an additional one-third in 1943. Any error here is likely to overestimate potato yields, not the reverse.

19. See chapter 5 of this volume.

20. Cherniavskii, p. 145.

Introduction

As Rebecca Manley notes in chapter 4, protein deprivation led to fatigue, muscle wasting, high blood pressure, edema, skin discoloration, and immune system suppression, all symptoms of what Leningrad's doctors soon identified as dystrophy, or starvation disease.[21]

It is very difficult to know the exact number of calories and array of foods that people *actually* consumed. Soviet statisticians did not undertake household budget studies during the war years; thus, the estimates of consumption presented here are based on aggregate figures of food made available through central state stocks and other sources and then divided by the numbers of people in the groups that received them. One reliable estimate suggests that the average urban adult consumed a total of 2,555 calories per day from all sources in 1942; 2,751 in 1943; and 2,810 in 1944.[22] Against what standard do we compare these figures? How many

---

21. Ibid., pp. 179–180, 183. Cherniavskii correctly notes that due to lack of fodder, animals were leaner, and their meat contained far less fat than before the war. The Soviet Union partially compensated for its wartime food deficits through the production of vitamin and protein supplements, in particular pine needle and yeast extracts. Local authorities assumed responsibility for the production of both. One successful case was the city of Stalinsk in the Kuzbass. GARF, f. A-482, op. 47, d. 1416, l. 980b. An example where the policy had less success would be Factory No. 701 in Cheliabinsk, which manufactured mines. GARF, f. A-482, op. 52s, d. 78, l. 60. Pine needle extract was extremely bitter, and factory canteen cooks complained that they needed sugar or saccharine to make it palatable enough to drink. GARF, f. A-482, op. 52s, d. 82, l. 131. A recipe is contained in a Narkomzdrav circular on the local manufacture of vitamins, in GARF, f. 8009, op. 21, d. 43, l. 20b.

22. There are two basic ways to estimate consumption: calculations derived from total food stocks, which is what Cherniavskii attempted in his book, and household budget surveys. Of these methods, the budget surveys are more precise, because they record what people actually consumed, as opposed to what people were allocated on paper according to plan. Before the war, the Central Statistical Administration (TsSU) built up a sophisticated system of household budget surveys, but these were suspended during the war. Cherniavskii, p. 169. Cherniavskii followed commonly accepted international practice and converted average calorie consumption into what are known as "adult equivalent units." These take account of the age and gender composition of the average household, adjust for their differing calorie needs, and express the results in terms of consumption by adult males. Expressing consumption in terms of a standard unit makes it possible to make accurate comparisons between years and localities, even when age and gender compositions differ. To take a simple example, assume we have two families. Family A consists of three people, a man, a woman, and a two-year-old child. Family B also consists of three people, a father, an adult son, and an adult woman. Assume further that each family consumes 6,000

calories did the typical urban adult need, and how well or how poorly did actual consumption meet this need? In the prewar period, nutritionists in all countries, including the USSR, understood that not all adults needed the same number of calories. Those doing heavy physical labor required

---

calories per day between its three members. How do we compare the nutritional well-being of these two families? If we take just a simple average, it appears that consumption in the two families is identical, at 2,000 calories a day per person. However, the nutritional needs of the two families are quite different. Therefore we have to convert their average per capita consumption to a standard unit, an adult male. Before the war, Soviet nutritional statisticians counted an adult woman as 0.8 of an adult male, and a very small child as 0.3 of an adult male, these ratios reflecting their different daily calorie requirements. On this basis, the energy needs of family A are equivalent to those of 2.1 male adults (1.0 + 0.8 + 0.3). These 2.1 male adults (or adult-equivalents) are sharing 6,000 calories between them, giving an average of 2,857 calories each. The energy needs of family B, however, are equivalent to 2.8 male adults (1.0 + 1.0 + 0.8). These 2.8 adult males are also sharing 6,000 calories, or 2,143 calories each. In this way we see that family A is nutritionally much better off than family B. Nutritional scientists and historians of nutrition use this same method to compare the nutritional status of large population groups, including whole societies. If the data are available, they can calculate the daily consumption of the average adult male and use this to compare one group or society with another. Equally, they can use their results to assess the adequacy of nutrition within a single group—in the latter case by comparing actual consumption with the calorie needs of an adult male carrying out levels of activity (work, travel, rest) typical of that society at the time of the surveys. Chernyavskii would have worked out his figure in three steps. First, he would have totaled up all the food stocks available to the urban population in each year and calculated its total caloric value. Second, he would have worked out how many adult equivalents there were consuming this food. Finally, he would have divided the total number of calories available for consumption by the number of adult-equivalent consumers. It is difficult to see how Cherniavskii was able to calculate the number of adult equivalents, since he had no household surveys or population data from which to derive this information. We strongly suspect that he worked out a proxy unit by looking at the size of the different groups receiving rations: workers on extra rations; workers on standard rations; adult dependents; and children. If we apply this method to 1943, the total of 41.8 million people receiving bread rations reduces to 36.6 million adult equivalents. Unfortunately, Cherniavskii does not show his calculations, but he was in all other respects methodologically very careful, so we should take his calculations as valid estimates. Nevertheless, it is probable that his figures overstate actual consumption, since they make no allowance for losses or wastage. Indirect evidence that his estimates are too high comes from the famine of 1946–1947, when the average adult male in workers' families in the main Russian industrial regions consumed either the same number of calories or slightly fewer than Cherniavskii claims for the war years, despite the fact that food deprivation during the war years was more serious. See Donald Filtzer, *The Hazards of Urban Life in Late Stalinist Russia: Health, Hygiene, and Living Standards* (Cambridge: Cambridge University Press, 2010), p. 248.

Introduction

Table I.3. Average daily adult calorie consumption vs. recommended values, 1939 and 1942–1944

	Actual calorie intake	*Recommended*	*Shortfall*	*Actual as % of recommended*
1939	3,370	3,592	222	93.8
1942	2,555	3,592	1037	71.1
1943	2,751	3,592	841	76.6
1944	2,810	3,592	782	78.2

Sources: Calories, Cherniavskii, p. 179; GARF, f. 9226, op. 1, d. 1119, l. 52ob.

Note: For recommended values, we have assumed Group II (mechanized manual labor) as typical of the wartime adult. See Table I.1 for explanation of groups.

more than those doing lighter work, and within any given occupational group, they believed that men needed more calories than women. The Soviet wartime rationing system, however, differentiated only by age and the intensity of labor not by gender. Table I.3 shows what Soviet nutritionists recommended for average daily adult consumption and what average, urban Soviet adults actually consumed. In this instance, the "typical" adult is assumed to be a worker, who performed mechanized or partially mechanized labor, but was not a white-collar employee or a worker doing very heavy manual labor. Table I.3 provides a rough measurement of the adequacy of wartime consumption, showing the number of calories the average adult required and the percentage actually received in each of the three years, 1942, 1943, and 1944.

The data in table I.3 reveal two significant findings. First, they show that 1942 was the nadir of calorie consumption. According to the average of actual consumption, the urban population received only 71.1 percent of its recommended intake. The situation improved slightly in 1943 and 1944, so that the diet met respectively 76.6 percent and 78.2 percent of need. This still left a very large nutritional shortfall. Second, the shortfall between need and actual consumption persisted for several years. Although the food supply improved in 1943 and 1944, the increases did not make up for the nutritional deficit of 1942. On the contrary, the deficit continued, albeit at a decreasing level.[23] Table I.3 and chapters 1 and 5 all

23. It is the cumulative worsening of this nutritional deficit that explains why large-scale starvation mortality among adult working-age males peaked in 1943, rather than in 1942. See chapter 5 of this volume.

show that the food supply reached its lowest level in 1942. Mortality from starvation, however, reached its apex in 1943 and continued into 1944 even after the food supply improved. The year of greatest food shortage was not the year of greatest death. A lag existed between the shortages of 1942 and their subsequent impact. The lag is explained by the fact that food deprivation takes a slow and often irreversible toll on the human organism. There was thus a delayed reaction between the low point for the food supply (1942–1943) and the high point of starvation deaths (1943–1944).

INEQUALITIES

Early twentieth-century nutritionists in the United States, Germany, Japan, the United Kingdom, and the Soviet Union all set dietary standards that differentiated according to age and gender, building upon the observation that the dietary needs of children differed from those of adults, and that the needs of adult men differed from those of adult women. During the 1880s and 1890s, the U.S. chemist W. O. Atwater, one of the founders of nutritional science, worked out the first scale expressing the numerical relationship between the consumption needs of men, women, and children, so that they could be reduced to a common unit, the adult male. Further refinements of the system by Atwater and other scientists also allowed for differences in adult energy expenditure depending on the type of work they performed.[24] During the 1920s and 1930s, Soviet statisticians used a modified version of the Atwater scale, according to which the caloric needs of an active adult male was set at 1.0; an adult woman at 0.8 of an adult male; a baby aged between six and twelve months at 0.1; a child aged between one and six years at 0.3; aged seven to thirteen, 0.55; aged fourteen to eighteen, 0.8; and adults over the age of sixty, 0.8.[25] Wartime rations, however, were not differentiated by gender. Women may have required less food than men, but based on their ration category, they received the same amount.

24. Edith Hawley, "Dietary Scales and Standards for Measuring a Family's Nutritive Needs," United States Department of Agriculture, Technical Bulletin No. 8, 1927.

25. Stephen G. Wheatcroft, "Soviet Statistics of Nutrition and Mortality during Times of Famine, 1917–1922 and 1931–1933," *Cahiers du Monde Russe* 38, no. 4 (October–December 1997): p. 539.

Introduction

On the basis of the Atwater scale alone, the Soviet ration system provided women with a distinct advantage: they needed less food than men in comparable occupational categories, but received the same amount. Yet whether the gender equality of the rationing system proved to be an *actual* nutritional advantage for women remains an open question. Women were frequently responsible for the care of dependents, the elderly, and children, and it is likely that many shared their rations within the family. Thus even if the commonly accepted premise—that women needed only 80 percent of male calorie requirements—is valid, it is still difficult to assess how much of their rations women actually consumed. Indeed, if a woman worker shared part of her ration with an elderly parent or a teenaged son, her choice to redistribute her food within the household may have wiped out whatever small advantage gender equality in rationing provided her. Sharing within the family may have in general provided a leveling effect on the age and occupational hierarchies of the ration system. On the other hand, women may have profited from the combination of lower biological need and gender equality in rations. As Donald Filtzer shows in chapter 5, women had far lower starvation mortality than men. Despite performing heavy labor, caring for children and dependents, and suffering difficult living conditions, very few women starved to death in the rear. One Russian demographer attributes women's higher survival rates to greater biological "hardiness." And if women were hardier than the general population of men, they were considerably hardier than men in the rear, many of whom had been exempted from the army due to physical weakness or defects and were likely to be more vulnerable to diseases such as tuberculosis.[26] Much remains to be learned, however, about gender differences in mortality as well as woman's behavior, and further investigation is needed into the role of work, biology, and psychology in women's wartime experiences.

Just as the male consumption average reveals nothing about sharing of rations among household members, it also obscures inequalities within unofficial social hierarchies and among regions. Wendy Goldman, Brandon Schechter, and Alexis Peri all show a considerable gap between

---

26. N. A. Aralovets, "Smertnost' gorodskogo naseleniia tylovykh raionov Rossii, 1941–1945 gg.," in Aralovets et al., *Liudskie poteri SSSR v period vtoroi mirovoi voiny*, p. 157.

planned and actual consumption based on shortfalls in deliveries, wastage, spoilage, theft, and unequal distribution. Many needy groups, including children, evacuees, and municipal employees, were fed in factory canteens at the expense of stocks allocated for workers. Officials also appropriated workers' stocks for their own managerial circles by creating sharply differentiated canteens serving different groups within the factories. At the Kirov factory in Cheliabinsk (formerly the Cheliabinsk Tractor Factory), one of the largest tank producers, senior technical personnel received per capita each day six times the amount of fats and four times the amount of meat and fish than the factory's workers. Although the state and the unions viewed such informal appropriations as corrupt and even criminal, in Nizhnii Tagil such discrepancies were officially sanctioned and built into the rationing system. Table I.1 shows, for example, that considerable privilege was officially accorded to top managers in the armaments industry. Managers and engineering technical personnel (ITR) also received higher wages, which allowed them to supplement their rations and canteen meals with purchases in local collective farm markets.[27] Regional variation also affected consumption. The cities and towns of the Urals had such high starvation mortality because the agricultural hinterlands were not very fertile and productive. Moreover, garden plots were not always equally distributed. In the Kuzbass, potato production from private plots gave each urban resident on average an extra 631 calories of energy a day. Yet only about half of all Kuzbass town dwellers had garden plots.[28] These plots, which were given to individuals but served entire households, may have covered the urban

27. GARF, f. 5451, op. 43, d. 187, l. 131. There were ample abuses of the system in Nizhnii Tagil, as well. Family and friends of factory management or of the heads of Departments of Workers' Provisioning (ORSy) were fed according to the higher norms reserved for outstanding production workers, and far in excess of the rations to which they were legally entitled. Marina Vasil'evna Gontsova, "Povsednevnaia zhizn' naseleniia industrial'nogo tsentra v gody Velikoi Otechestvennoi voiny (na materialakh goroda Nizhnii Tagil)," Author's abstract of Candidate of Historical Sciences dissertation (Nizhnii Tagil, 2011), p. 28. As noted in chapter 5 of this book, Nizhnii Tagil suffered very high numbers of starvation deaths. Gontsova's dissertation unfortunately does not discuss the city's very high death rates or the contribution made to them by starvation.

28. Cherniavskii, p. 149.

Introduction 27

population adequately, but it is unclear how many residents actually received supplemental garden food and how many did not.

FOOD AND THE SOVIET HOME FRONT IN COMPARATIVE CONTEXT

Of the five principal combatants in the war—the United States, Great Britain, Germany, Japan, and the Soviet Union—only the latter three experienced serious domestic food crises, and of these, only the Soviet Union experienced mass starvation mortality. The United States produced very sizable food surpluses, sufficient not just to sustain its military and its domestic population, but to provide large amounts of food aid to Britain and, to a lesser extent, the Soviet Union as well. The British government instituted rationing of some foods, but restaurants remained open, bread was never rationed, and the country had a glut of potatoes. Indeed, the British did not even bother to ration what provided the mainstay of consumption for the Soviet population: bread and potatoes. The British diet was monotonous, but no one went hungry or experienced malnutrition. On the contrary, the war saw concerted efforts to improve the nutritional health of the population, and the working class ate better during the war than before it.[29] Beginning in mid-1943, the Allies reduced the U boat threat in the Atlantic through the development of radar and successful decoding of enemy communications, and the percentage of imported food lost in torpedoed ships fell to negligible numbers. By the end of 1943, Britain had built up more food reserves than before the war. The food hierarchy among the Allies favored in descending order: the American military, American civilians, the British military, and British civilians.[30] The Red Army benefited considerably from Lend-Lease aid, but only from 1944 on, and Soviet civilians bore the brunt of the shortages created by German occupation.

In Germany, Japan, and the Soviet Union, food supplies for the home front population were badly constrained and led to varying degrees of

---

29. Collingham, *The Taste of War*, pp. 102, 386–399; Juliet Gardiner, *Wartime: Britain, 1939–1945* (London: Headline Book Publishing, 2004), chapter 7.

30. Collingham, *The Taste of War*, pp. 117, 118.

declining nutrition. All three countries introduced rationing systems based on the same basic principle: they favored those in key defense sectors and/or those who expended the most calories. But the degree of deprivation was greater in the USSR than anywhere else—by orders of magnitude greater than in Germany and worse even than in Japan, the country whose food crisis most closely resembled that in the USSR. The Soviet experience of the war was unique, a fact that holds true even if we look at starvation deaths only in the Soviet rear and exclude the victims of the Leningrad blockade.

German and Soviet domestic food consumption was effectively a zero-sum game. In addition to civilians, by December 1943, there were seven million forced laborers in Germany, who also needed to be fed. German agricultural production provided "an adequate civilian ration, a generous ration for the military . . . and a miserly ration for the forced laborers." Germany expected the occupied territories to make up its food deficits.[31] Indeed, German civilian diets remained adequate during the war only because of the food purloined from occupied Europe, over half of which came from Eastern Poland and the occupied parts of the USSR. The Nazis restored the "food balance" in these territories by allowing millions to starve (including around two million Soviet prisoners of war) and by physically eliminating those whom they deemed the most "useless" of "useless eaters" (*unnütze Esser*)—namely, 3.5 million Polish Jews. These were the most immediate victims of Nazi occupation policy.[32]

The Nazi invasion also created a deep and protracted food crisis in the Soviet rear. We see this clearly if we compare civilian consumption in the two countries. Between the German invasion of Poland in 1939 and the end of 1941, consumption (measured in kilocalories per day) of German adults remained very close to the biological standard set by German nutritionists, and the consumption of children and youth (aged 0 to 18) actually exceeded the norms.[33] (See table I.4.) As children in the Warsaw Ghetto began to die of starvation on a ration of less than three

---

31. Ibid., p. 156.

32. Tooze, *The Wages of Destruction*, pp. 481–484, 523–524, 545–549.

33. United States Strategic Bombing Survey, Morale Division, *The Effect of Bombing on Health and Medical Care in Germany* (n.p., 1947), pp. 284, 285, 290A, 365–371.

Table I.4. Estimated consumption (kilocalories per day) of German civilians inside the Reich, 1939–1945

Age or occupational group	German norm	Dec. 1939–Jan. 1940	May 1940	Feb–Mar. 1941	July 1941	Nov.–Dec. 1941	Apr. 1942	Aug.–Oct. 1942	Jan.–Feb. 1943	June 1943	Dec. 1943–Jan. 1944	May 1944	July–Aug. 1944	Oct–Nov. 1944	Jan. 1945
0–3	1,200	1,783	1,795	1,799	2,002	1,921	1,958	2,129	2,181	2,147	2,362	2,141	2,213	2,029	2,026
3–6	1,400	1,689	1,701	1,705	1,940	1,859	1,959	2,130	2,109	2,075	2,290	2,073	2,145	1,945	1,939
6–10	1,750	2,078	2,091	2,099	2,207	2,126	2,178	2,308	2,285	2,254	2,513	2,292	2,370	2,208	2,208
10–14	2,050	2,330	2,342	2,557	2,207	2,126	2,507	2,637	2,615	2,582	2,795	2,577	2,635	2,479	2,474
14–18	2,400	2,343	2,347	2,391	2,728	2,640	2,428	2,506	2,485	2,453	2,666	2,445	2,523	2,388	2,383
Normal consumers	2,400	2,343	2,347	2,298	2,400	2,319	2,052	2,131	2,198	2,165	2,360	2,272	2,347	2,010	2,010
Long/night shift	3,000	2,587	2,610	2,541	2,916	2,835	2,342	2,421	2,493	2,466	2,596	2,500	2,575	2,419	2,418
Heavy labor	3,600	3,422	3,416	3,367	3,357	3,276	2,775	2,854	2,933	2,901	3,096	2,899	2,974	2,742	2,741
Very heavy labor	4,500	4,216	4,168	4,120	4,104	4,023	3,542	3,621	3,704	3,671	3,866	3,674	3,748	3,475	3,477

Source: United States Strategic Bombing Survey, Morale Division, *The Effect of Bombing on Health and Medical Care in Germany* (N.p.: 2nd ed., 1947), pp. 284, 285, 290A, 366, 367, 369, 370, 371.

hundred calories per day, German children were getting plump. Indeed, consumption by children and youth remained well above or almost at the biological standard for the duration of the war. German workers fared less well: their consumption was below the standard in January 1940 and remained below it throughout the war. At the beginning of 1942, the Wehrmacht reduced rations for combat troops, and the Reich Food Ministry followed with a reduction of civilian rations in April.[34] Although these cuts provoked considerable discontent among German consumers, their food intake remained vastly superior to that of Soviet civilians in the rear. A comparison of the consumption figures in tables I.1 and I.4 show that only a small group of Soviet miners doing the heaviest underground work achieved approximate parity with German workers performing very heavy labor. Nutritionists in Germany and the Soviet Union set consumption norms for workers doing heavy labor at 3,600 and 4,678 calories per day, respectively. Yet in the fall of 1943, German workers doing heavy labor consumed about 3,000 calories, while Soviet workers in similar jobs, only 2,661. Soviet workers fell considerably short of both the German and the Soviet standards, and consumed less than their German counterparts.

The starkest difference between the two countries, however, was among children, youth, adult dependents, and white-collar employees. In the Soviet Union, these groups were least protected by the rationing system, whereas in Germany the ration provided the vast bulk of their calories. Their overall consumption either exceeded the nutritional standard (as in the case of children) or fell below it only marginally. Moreover, after April 1942, German calorie intake slowly recovered: it never regained the levels of late 1939, but it did hit a mini-peak in December 1943, at the same time that the Soviet Union was forced to reduce the rations of its own civilians. German food intake remained at safe levels right up until late 1944, even though the German armies were in retreat on both the Western and Eastern fronts and no longer had access to food from their occupied territories. Many German workers were hungry, especially those doing heavy labor, and all Germans had to cope with shortages and poorer quality food. But real hunger and risk

---

34. Tooze, *The Wages of Destruction*, pp. 540–542.

Introduction

of starvation appeared only when the Reich was on the verge of total collapse.

From the point of view of food deprivation, the combatant country that most closely resembled the USSR was Japan. Prewar Japan had never been self-sufficient in food, even in rice, and large parts of the population were either malnourished or on the edge of malnutrition. The population worked very long hours, and calorie expenditure was relatively high. Estimates carried out by various Japanese and international agencies covering the years 1911 to 1939 suggest an average daily intake of between 2,100 and 2,400 calories and between 60 and 70 grams of protein— values very similar to late nineteenth- and early twentieth-century Britain. As in Britain, the laboring population was chronically undernourished, but not to the point where people displayed obvious pathologies or morbidities. The two exceptions in Japan were tuberculosis and beriberi. Japanese death rates from tuberculosis in 1937 were high, roughly comparable to those in Germany and Britain at the turn of the twentieth century, and high rates of beriberi were common due to the shortage of thiamine (B_1) in a diet based almost exclusively on polished rice.[35]

When Japan launched a full-scale Asian war in 1937, domestic consumption came under pressure from two sources: the need to feed its large army, much of which remained stationed and provisioned inside Japan throughout the war, and declining agricultural output. Not only did the home-based army need to be fed, but its rations were appreciably higher than those of civilians. Other factors in the decline included the military draft of men of prime working age; the reduction in agricultural implements, tools, machinery, and fertilizer in the switch to defense

---

35. B. F. Johnston, with Mosaburo Hosoda and Yoshio Kusumi, *Japanese Food Management in World War II* (Stanford, Calif.: Stanford University Press, 1953), pp. 72, 91, 163, 164. On diets in Victorian and early Edwardian Britain, see D. J. Oddy, "A Nutritional Analysis of Historical Evidence: The Working-Class Diet, 1880–1914," in Derek Oddy and Derek Miller, eds., *The Making of the Modern British Diet* (London: Croom Helm, 1973), pp. 214–231. On tuberculosis in Britain and Germany, see Gillian Cronjé, "Tuberculosis and Mortality Decline in England and Wales, 1851–1910," in Robert Woods and John Woodward, eds., *Urban Disease and Mortality in Nineteenth-Century England* (London: Batsford Academic and Educational, 1984), pp. 83–85, and Jörg Vögele, *Urban Mortality Change in England and Germany, 1870–1913* (Liverpool: Liverpool University Press, 1998), pp. 70–73.

Donald Filtzer and Wendy Z. Goldman

production; and military construction of factories on prime land that could have been used to grow food. Unlike Germany, Japan's overseas colonies, including Korea and Formosa, as well as its newly conquered territories in Southeast Asia, did not generate sufficient food surpluses to make up for the decline in homeland agricultural production. Once the Allied blockade began, most imports, other than those from Korea, had no route into the country. The combined total of domestic rice production plus rice imports fell by 43 percent between 1937 and 1945, and by 47 percent compared to the highpoint reached in 1942. Attempts to compensate through the production and import of other grains, such as soya, millet, kaoliang, and corn, proved woefully inadequate.[36]

The core of the Japanese ration was a basic rice allowance (equivalent to bread in the Soviet system) of 330 grams per person per day, containing 1,158 calories. Children received less. After May 1943, workers received more in the form of factory supplements, which varied according to gender, work, and type of factory. For most workers, the supplements offered only a modest increase in calories; for privileged workers the increase was more substantial.[37] However, as overall food supplies contracted, the authorities adulterated the rice ration with other grains and pulses, and even with brown insects. These substitutes and adulterants made up an

---

36. Johnston, et al., *Japanese Food Management*, p. 258. Irene B. Taeuber, *The Population of Japan* (Princeton, N.J.: Princeton University Press, 1965), p. 340. Bernd Martin, "Agriculture and Food Supply in Japan during the Second World War," in Bernd Martin and Alan S. Milward, eds., *Agriculture and Food Supply in the Second World War. Landwirtschaft und Versorgung im Zweiten Weltkrieg* (Ostfildern: Scripta Mercaturae Verlag, 1985), p. 191. Jerome B. Cohen, *Japan's Economy in War and Reconstruction* (Minneapolis: University of Minnesota Press, 1949), pp. 293, 368–370.

37. Johnston et al., *Japanese Food Management*, p. 203; Cohen, *Japan's Economy*, p. 376. In May 1943, the rice ration was set as 1,158 calories a day for "normal" consumers, between 1,369 and 2,562 for male workers below the age of sixty, and 1,229 and 1,966 for female workers in the same age group. Workers older than sixty received considerably less. Collingham (*The Taste of War*, p. 306) mistakenly assumes that this was total food intake, when in fact it covered only rice. How many extra calories workers received from other foods is difficult to assess, although the U.S. Strategic Bombing Survey Medical Division estimated that for the population as a whole, rice provided roughly 60 percent of all calories and 45 percent of all protein during the years 1943–1945. U.S. Strategic Bombing Survey, Medical Division, *The Effects of Bombing on Health and Medical Services in Japan* (n.p., June 1947), p. 52.

Introduction   33

ever-larger percentage of the "rice" ration with each passing year.[38] Late
in the war, foods like potatoes and sweet potatoes, initially available for
purchase, were declared staple foods and available only through the
ration. They no longer provided a supplement to the ration, but rather,
became a substitute for rice. This shift in policy marked a substantial
decline in nutrition.

During 1941–1943, average nutritional intake held reasonably constant, at around 2,000 calories and 63 grams of protein a day. This was
just below 90 percent of official Japanese nutritional requirements for
calories and 25 percent below the requirement for protein. Distribution
of the shortfall between age and occupational groups was, however, highly
uneven. Workers, both male and female, in favored industries remained
fairly well supplied, while those in less privileged sectors continued to
receive roughly what they biologically required. The wellbeing of workers, however, came at the expense of children under the age of ten. Hardest hit were children living outside Japan's six largest cities, and children under the age of six, irrespective of where they lived. In 1943, children
younger than six received no more than 70 percent of the calories they
needed. For Japan's children, cumulative under-nutrition was already
becoming a problem, even if overt signs of malnutrition among adults
were few.[39] It is unlikely, however, that adults failed to share their food
with their children. Once again, important issues of household redistribution remain obscured by the aggregate figures within categories set
by the state. In 1944, the Japanese diet deteriorated markedly, and by 1945
it provided a bare 73 percent of the basic requirement, an average of just
1,680 calories a day.[40] Morbidity from hunger and malnutrition became

---

38. Erich Pauer, "A New Order for Japanese Society: Planned Economy, Neighbourhood Associations and Food Distribution in Japanese Cities in the Second World War,"
in Erich Pauer, ed., *Japan's War Economy* (London: Routledge, 1999), pp. 93–94.

39. None of the sources seems to have attempted to calculate consumption by each
population group. We have estimated this from rice ration data from Johnston et al.,
Japanese Food Management, p. 203, Cohen, *Japan's Economy*, p. 376, and the U.S. Strategic
Bombing Survey, which claim that in 1943, rice provided around 60 percent of total
calories (*The Effects of Bombing on Health and Medical Services in Japan*, pp. 52, 240).

40. U.S. Strategic Bombing Survey, *The Effects of Bombing*, pp. 52, 239–240. As with
Cherniavksii's estimates in the USSR, the Japanese figures were calculated from available
food stocks. Actual consumption would have been considerably lower.

widespread. Adults and children lost weight, became weak, and many suffered the more serious symptoms of starvation, including diarrhoea and edema. New mothers were unable to nurse properly, infant mortality increased, and children showed signs of arrested development.[41]

Yet, in sharp contrast to the Soviet Union, the Japanese food crisis produced little starvation mortality.[42] One protective factor may have been that the fall in protein consumption was not as rapid as the drop in calories.[43] Another was that Japanese workers, in contrast to their Soviet counterparts, were able to curb their energy expenditure due to enforced reduction in work time. Once Allied bombing intensified in March 1945, workers at many factories did not have the materials, parts, or fuel to work a full shift. Workers used their time off either to rest and conserve energy or to forage for food in the countryside, two activities that may have fended off the potentially lethal consequences of the decrease in rations.

"THE GREAT PATRIOTIC WAR" AND ITS MEANING

The war from its inception had a multiplicity of meanings for the Soviet people. Less than three years separated the beginning of war from the end

41. Ibid., pp. 82–85, 90, 181. For personal accounts of hunger, see Collingham, *The Taste of War*, pp. 303–308.

42. Unfortunately there are no data to confirm this. The Japanese system of registering vital statistics collapsed toward the end of the war, and there are no mortality data at all for the years 1944–1946 (Taeuber, *Population of Japan*, p. 287). Extensive interviews with Japanese food officials and their own observations led the United States Strategic Bombing Survey Medical Division to conclude, "Actual famine was not observed in the three southern islands of Japan proper during this survey except among completely homeless migratory persons in bombed areas, e.g., in Tokyo and Osaka, who congregated and camped in public buildings such as railroad stations" (U.S. Strategic Bombing Survey, *The Effects of Bombing*, pp. 90–91). In contrast to the mainland, Japanese soldiers in occupied parts of Asia starved in very large numbers. Collingham, *The Taste of War*, pp. 291–303.

43. The maintenance of adequate protein consumption may in part have been thanks to the substitution of high-protein soya for rice. Toward the end of the war, however, the protein contribution of soya may have been reduced. Soya needs to cook for four or five hours in order for all of its protein to become biologically available. This proved very difficult for Japanese households due to shortages of cooking fuel and the loss of cooking facilities in the wake of Allied bombing. U.S. Strategic Bombing Survey, *The Effects of Bombing on Health and Medical Services*, p. 89.

Introduction

of the mass repressions and purges in the Communist Party, military, and other institutions. A political culture built on arrests, denunciations, and the hunt for internal enemies left people numbed and fearful. The invasion produced a range of responses, including fierce anti-Fascism, Soviet patriotism, multiple nationalisms, individual survival strategies, and collaborationism. Ideology, prewar experience, geographic location, and the pressure of extreme privation all conditioned initial responses and subsequent behavior. To this day, historians debate what motivated the Soviet people to fight.[44] Andrei Dzeniskevich noted that Leningrad's workers eagerly enrolled in the people's militia (*opolchenie*) and spoke of "beating the fascist scum just as we beat them in the Civil War." They fought to defend Soviet power and the revolution they made in 1917. In Ukraine, however, Karel Berkhoff concluded that people greeted the Germans with a "cautious optimism" that only later "turned to hate."[45] Diaries, letters, and memoirs of ordinary people contain a variety of war narratives, some corroborating the heroic myth later promulgated by the state, others bitterly critical of the state's failings and the selfishness of their fellow citizens. Two pieces of writing by survivors of the siege of Leningrad illustrate these differences. Lilia Frankfurt, a librarian in the Saltykov-Shchedrin National Public Library, proudly noted in a memoir written less than a year after the war ended:

> On 26 January 1942, the library lost electricity. The heating and plumbing system had stopped work even before that. Cold and dark reigned in the stacks, the reading rooms, and everywhere else on the premises. Now the patrons had to settle down to work in the only place where life still glimmered—in the

---

44. For a sense of this range, see Robert W. Thurston and Bernd Bonwetsch, eds., *The People's War: Responses to World War II in the Soviet Union* (Urbana: University of Illinois Press, 2000); Ilya Ehrenburg and Vasily Grossman, *The Complete Black Book of Soviet Jewry* (New Brunswick, N. J.: Transaction Publishers, 2001); Vasily Grossman, *Life and Fate,* translated by Robert Chandler (New York: New York Review Books, 2006); Elena Kozhina, *Through the Burning Steppe: A Memoir of Wartime Russia, 1924–1943* (New York: Riverhead, 2001); Anatoly Kuznetsov, *Babi Yar: A Document in the Form of a Novel* (New York: Farrar Straus and Giroux, 1970); Martin Dean, *Collaboration in the Holocaust: Crimes of the Local Police in Belorussia and Ukraine, 1941–1944* (New York: St. Martin's Press, 2000); Berkhoff, *Harvest of Despair.*

45. Andrei Dzeniskevich, "The Social and Political Situation in Leningrad," in Thurston and Bonwetsch, eds., *The People's War,* p. 82; Berkhoff, *Harvest of Despair,* p. 311.

> director's office.... During the winter of 1941–1942, all operations involving patrons were conducted by the light of lanterns, and when the kerosene ran out, we had to search for books on the shelves with a burning piece of wood in our hands. And nevertheless the library never ceased functioning for even a day.

Frankfurt believed that the patrons and librarians were living examples of the city's refusal to submit or surrender. The ballet teacher, Vera Kostrovitskaia, however, skewered the idea that the human spirit survived in the starving city. She wrote with bitter cynicism in her diary:

> Since in April it became necessary to portray the rebirth of the city at the hands of people half-dead, L.S.T [Lidiia S. Tager, the wife of the head of provisions for the Leningrad front] got the vain idea to give the first public concert.

According to Kostrovitskaia, a well-fed Tager threatened the starving dancers with loss of their rations if they did not perform.[46] Where Frankfurt saw the indomitable spirit of resistance in the ongoing cultural life of the city, Kostrovitskaia saw only the vanity and empty display of a well-fed officialdom. Yet regardless of whether war narratives supported or decried the heroic myth that the state promulgated so strongly, all were inescapably shaped by it.

In the immediate aftermath of the war, the state's narrative focused on the unity of the people and the role of Stalin and the Communist Party in leading the country to victory. Stalin's role loomed largest, far greater than that of the party, the military, or any social group. In the words of two historians, "Stalin's position was strengthened to the point of unassailability.... More than anything, the Soviet victory in 1945 was used to validate his role on a popular basis."[47] Stalin himself set the tone. On June 25, 1945, Stalin gave a toast at a Kremlin reception. Raising his glass, he saluted the "little people" who had made the victory possible:

> I would like to drink to the health of those on the lower echelons whose conditions are little envied, to those who are considered as the "screws" of the immense machine of the government but without whom, all of us marshals or commanding officers of the fronts or armies wouldn't be worth, if I may so

---

46. Cynthia Simmons and Nina Perlina, eds., *Writing the Siege of Leningrad: Women's Diaries, Memoirs, and Documentary Prose* (Pittsburgh, Pa.: University of Pittsburgh Press, 2002), pp. 165, 51.

47. John Barber and Mark Harrison, *The Soviet Home Front, 1941–1945. A Social and Economic History of the USSR in World War II* (London: Longman, 1991), p. 208.

Introduction

> express it, a jot. Because it requires only for one screw to disappear and all is finished, I drink to the health of simple folk, ordinary and modest, the "screws" which ensure the functioning of our enormous state machine in all its aspects: science, economy, war. They are numerous and their name is legion because they comprise dozens of millions.[48]

Stalin's view of ordinary people as "screws" offended many, including loyal Communists, who refused to see themselves as mindless cogs in "the enormous state machine." The metaphor attributed victory to the great success of the powerful administrative command system. It certainly permitted no discussion of any possible dysfunctions of the system, the independent creativity and heroism of those within it, or of the individuals and groups who had opposed it.[49]

War literature published between 1945 and Stalin's death in 1953 paid obligatory and repeated tribute to Stalin's role as military commander and organizer. N. A. Voznesensky, the head of the State Planning Commission and deputy of the Council of Ministers, noted, for example, in his book on the Soviet wartime economy written in 1947:

> During the most difficult days of the Patriotic War, Comrade Stalin inspired the peoples of the Soviet Union and their armed forces to all-out effort for victory. Staunchness in the struggle against the German hordes and confidence in the victory of our just cause emanated from the great Stalin and spread to the entire country, uniting the people and the army and making the USSR an impregnable fortress.[50]

In Voznesensky's formula, Stalin rallied a united people in a just cause to create an unconquerable nation. These four elements—Stalin's leadership, united people, just cause, invincible land—formed the basis of the

---

48. Iosif Stalin, *Pravda*, June 27, 1945; also found in *Collected Works*, vol. 16 (London: Red Star Press Ltd., 1986).

49. An excellent discussion of this is in Elena Iu. Zubkova, *Obshchestvo i reformy 1945–1964* (Moscow: Rossiia Molodaia, 1993), pp. 25–32, available in English in Elena Zubkova, *Russia After the War. Hopes, Illusions, and Disappointments, 1945–1957* (Armonk, N. Y.: M. E. Sharpe, 1998), pp. 20–30.

50. N. A. Voznesensky [Voznesenskii], *Soviet Economy during the Second World War* (New York: International Publishers, 1949), p. 11. The book was originally published in 1947 as *Voennaia ekonomika SSSR v period Otechestvennoi voiny* (Moscow, 1947). The date of the American translation coincides with the purge of Voznesenskii in 1949 as part of the Leningrad Affair. He was executed in 1950. Zubkova, *Russia after the War*, pp. 132–133.

state's official and prescribed narrative. The formula guided all speeches, books, and public pronouncements on the war.[51]

Yet as long as Stalin was alive, the cult of the war, which assumed great significance in the 1970s and 1980s, remained relatively undeveloped. In the immediate postwar period, Soviet leaders were less concerned with commemoration, myth, and monuments than the problems of reconstruction. The occupied areas lay in ruins, millions of refugees had to be housed and fed, and the economy had to be rebuilt.[52] An entire generation of men had perished. There was little time for celebration. In the face of a growing Cold War threat, the state established new mass campaigns centered on work discipline and reconstruction. Not much literature about the war was published in the period between 1945 and 1953, and some military leaders were actively discouraged from publishing their memoirs. In 1947, Victory Day itself was changed from a state holiday to a regular working day.[53]

After Stalin's death, Nikita Khrushchev delivered a ringing indictment of Stalin's role in the war in his speech to the Twentieth Congress of the Communist Party in February 1956. An outpouring of literature, memoirs, and history on the war followed the "thaw" Khrushchev initiated in political life. Several Soviet military leaders penned critical memoirs of their battlefront experience, suggesting that the great commander in chief made some serious tactical mistakes. Writers cautiously explored previously taboo topics such as Soviet preparedness for war, military losses, the genocide of the Jews, and collaborationism.[54] This

51. See also the film *Padenie Berlina,* made in 1950 and considered one of the best examples of the cult of personality around Stalin that emerged after the war.

52. On reconstruction, see Donald Filtzer, *Soviet Workers and Late Stalinism: Labour and the Restoration of the Stalinist System after World War II* (Cambridge: Cambridge University Press, 2002); Jeffrey W. Jones, *Everyday Life and the "Reconstruction" of Soviet Russia during and after the Great Patriotic War, 1943–1948* (Bloomington, Ind.: Slavica Publishers, 2008); Karl D. Qualls, *From Ruins to Reconstruction: Urban Identity in Soviet Sevastopol after World War II* (Ithaca, N.Y.: Cornell University Press, 2009).

53. Nina Tumarkin, *The Living and the Dead: The Rise and the Fall of the Cult of World War II in Russia* (New York: Basic Books, 1994), pp. 100–104.

54. See Yevgeny Yevtushenko's poem "Bab'i Yar," at http://remember.org/witness /babiyar.html.

Introduction

period of relative freedom, however, came to an end when Khrushchev was ousted and replaced in 1964 by Leonid Brezhnev.

Under Brezhnev, party and state leaders actively promoted the heroic myth of the war. The war and victory assumed cult status and became central to "the military patriotic upbringing of youth" and the identity of Soviet citizens.[55] Stalin's role was to some degree replaced by a greater emphasis on the organizing efforts of the party. Many issues, tentatively broached during Khrushchev's "thaw," were once again off limits to writers, historians, and filmmakers. In the Brezhnev period, the state's official narrative hardened, clearly delineating what was to be celebrated from what was to be ignored. It prohibited any honest evaluation of the initial defeats of the Red Army, the massive loss in human life, conditions on the home front, or a host of other topics, which became literally unmentionable. In prohibiting discussion of the war's great difficulties, the myth posed a smooth of arc of victory in which the party, army, and state sailed from one valiant success to the next. The narrative, seeking to promote only the heroic, cheapened the victory by obscuring or erasing the very challenges that made it so impressive.

With the collapse of Soviet Union in the early 1990s, historians and others began to challenge the heroic myth. A "stolen victory" narrative emerged that shifted emphasis for the war's success from the state to the broader self-activity of the people. Gennadii Bordiugov forcefully articulated this view in 1995:

> During the war two intertwined but quite different forces were operating: the people and the System, as it was embodied in the Stalinist regime. Each force contributed to the outcome: but whereas the people liberated [the country], the System, following in its wake, immediately seized the liberated [people] in its iron grasp.

Bordiugov advanced the notion, echoed privately by ordinary people both during and after the war, of two separate forces—state and people— each with different roles in the war and hopes for the future. The "people" were responsible for the war's success, but the state had seized their

---

55. On the war myth, see Tumarkin, *The Living and the Dead*; Lisa Kirschenbaum, *The Legacy of the Siege of Leningrad, 1941–1995: Myth, Memories and Monuments* (New York: Cambridge University Press, 2006).

victory for its own ends. In Bordiugov's view, the masses longed to dissolve the collective farms, introduce free trade in consumer goods and land, improve their standard of living, and live in a freer state.[56] Although he provided little evidence for these somewhat contradictory wishes (free trade in consumer goods, for example, would have immediately produced skyrocketing prices and created a far worse standard of living), his article launched a challenge to the reigning dogma. Bordiugov closely linked the policies of the war years with the postwar period, contending that the state's deliberate promotion of Russian nationalism had culminated in the ugly anticosmopolitan campaign. At the same time, he noted that the state relaxed its rigid control of the population and retreated from the hunt for internal enemies. Ordinary people— soldiers, peasants, workers, intelligentsia—fervently hoped for a democratic renewal, but the state discarded the relative freedom of the war years in favor of new political and economic controls once the victory was won.

Bordiugov's article was accompanied by a torrent of publications questioning the previously indisputable dogmas of the war. With the opening of the archives, former Soviet and Western historians began researching previously forbidden topics. New books and articles emerged on the lack of Soviet preparation for war, the military disasters of 1941, genocide of the Jews, collaborationism, Vlasov's army, the postwar fate of Soviet prisoners of war, cannibalism in Leningrad, corruption of party and soviet officials, nationalist hatreds, and many other topics that were previously hidden, forbidden, or ignored for political reasons. This new body of schol-

---

56. Gennadii Bordiugov, "Bol'sheviki i natsional'naia khorugv'," *Rodina*, no. 5 (1995): 72–77; reprinted in English as "The Bolsheviks and the National Banner," *Russian Studies in History* 39, no. 1 (Summer 2000): 79, 80. Bordiugov first developed the theme of the "Stolen Victory" together with Aleksandr Afanas'ev, in a lengthy interview in *Komsomol'skaia Pravda*, May 5, 1990. A more nuanced discussion appeared in the early articles of Elena Zubkova in the journal *Svobodnaia mysl'*, nos. 6 and 9 (1992) and no. 9 (1993), which she reworked as the first part of *Obshchestvo i reformy*, published in English in Zubkova, *Russia after the War*, chapters 1–3. The idea of the "Stolen Victory" was not new, even if the term itself was not used. It forms a central theme of Vasily Grossman's *Life and Fate*, and Vera Dunham articulated a thought-provoking version of it in her 1976 analysis of postwar Soviet literature (reissued in 1990), *In Stalin's Time: Middle-Class Values in Soviet Fiction* (Durham, N.C.: Duke University Press, 1990), pp. 11–15.

Introduction

arship, focused on everything that was previously taboo, undermined the more simplistic formulas of the Brezhnev era.[57]

The new scholarship made significant contributions to knowledge of the war. Yet it was and is still structured around assailing the myth. The topics with the greatest salience were those that were previously taboo. Evidence from the archives of collaborationism, military blunders, and disunity piled up. Yet historians have yet to integrate the new findings into a coherent view of the relationship between state and people. If the older narrative of a united people under the strong organizational leadership of the party could no longer encompass the evidence, how could the victory be explained? Were the people's efforts merely the result of coercion? Roger Markwick perfectly captured the explanatory dilemma: "How could Stalin's draconian state mobilize such large numbers of Soviet citizens who were willing to give up everything in its defense?"[58] Moreover, although Bordiugov's binary concept of "state and people" was an important advance over the earlier overemphasis on the state, it is too simple to account for the enormous diversity of popular responses, which, as the historian, Elena Zubkova notes, were often contradictory, or for the complexity of wartime governance. Much research still needs to be done into the rather grand category of "the people" in terms of experience, social class, nationality, gender, and ideological belief. The wartime state, too, needs to be conceptualized, not only in relationship to "the people" but in terms of its actual organization and operation.

Hunger and War fits within this new wave of scholarship in its focus on a neglected and forbidden topic. Donald Filtzer is the first to tabulate the extent of starvation mortality in the industrial towns of the rear. As Rebecca Manley makes clear, the figure of the *distrofik*, or person dying

---

57. See for example, Richard Bidlack and Nikita Lomagin, *The Leningrad Blockade, 1941–1944: A New Documentary History from the Soviet Archives* (New Haven, Conn.: Yale University Press, 2012); Catherine Merridale, *Ivan's War: Life and Death in the Red Army, 1939–1945* (New York: Picador, 2006); Amir Weiner, *Making Sense of War: The Second World War and the Fate of the Bolshevik Revolution* (Princeton, N.J.: Princeton University Press, 2000).

58. Roger D. Markwick, "Stalinism at War," *Kritika: Explorations in Russian and Eurasian History* 3, no. 3 (Summer 2002): 510.

of starvation, was a powerful symbol of blockaded Leningrad, the German POW camps, and the occupied territories, but it was dangerous for the state to acknowledge that dystrophy was also present in the rear. This book describes for the first time the extent of hunger and the great problems of provisioning throughout the country, not only in Leningrad, but also on the home front and in the army. At the same time, it seeks to advance our understanding by deconstructing the categories of both "people" and "state." Alexis Peri and Brandon Schechter demonstrate that the war upended social hierarchies and comingled national groups. In Leningrad, bread store clerks assumed power over scientists, and workers who did not work fared better than white-collar employees who did. The army brought soldiers from diverse social backgrounds, regions, nationalities, religions, and ethnicities together to break bread and eat from a common pot. Wendy Goldman shows that state and party organizations, representing different constituencies and interests, fought incessantly over the most valuable resource of all: food. *Hunger and War* aims to reconceptualize the state beyond Stalin and his narrow coterie to include the medical establishment, industrial and trade commissariats, unions, the military, and other party and state institutions. In so doing, it engages the wartime paradox of increased centralization coupled with decentralized power and decision-making. The "state" and the "people" as conceived here are far from monolithic.

THE PRICE OF THE VICTORY OVER FASCISM

The suffering of the war has been understood in multiple ways and bent to many ends. The state elevated this suffering into a heroic myth, and at the same time, carefully suppressed its full dimensions. In this sense, the dogma cheapened those very elements of the myth that were great and true. For how can any victory be fully measured and comprehended without a sense of the difficulties that had to be overcome? The greatness of the Soviet victory over Fascism lies in its direct proportion to the losses suffered and obstacles surmounted. Investigation of these painful issues does not lessen the importance of the victory; it only increases it. This is a book about hunger and food. And here, too, we can to some degree measure the victory. The army was fed best, and amid all the grumbling,

Introduction 43

bitterness, and difficulty of everyday life, no civilian ever seemed to have begrudged the soldiers their food. The home front bore the burden of the food shortage. And this burden, too, can be measured. Anecdotal evidence from factory medical reports suggest that even in large defense enterprises, workers consumed considerably less than the 2,750–2,800 actual caloric consumption average of the urban population in 1943 and 1944 (see table I.3). A look back at table I.1 shows that workers in hot shops in the armaments industry were allocated just 2,661 calories a day in May 1943, and their ration fell still farther after the cutbacks of November that year. Yet as table I.3 suggests, even the average estimates for actual consumption point up the fundamental problem of this period: a worker in a Soviet factory in 1942, 1943, or 1944 could not reproduce his or her labor power on the calories they consumed. This was even more true of dependents, those in low-priority white-collar or professional jobs, and non-working adults, whose lower expenditures of energy in no way compensated for their meager access to calories. Indeed, for four years, the Soviet civilian population walked to work, shivered in rags and broken shoes, spent long hours at machines in freezing shops, and turned out the armaments that beat the Fascist armies on the eastern front. By 1944, male defense workers, the country's best-fed civilians, were beginning to die of starvation. The preciousness of the victory over Fascism lies not only in the defeat of the Nazis' murderous colonial fantasies, or in the Red Army's military achievements, but also in the daily actions of millions of hungry, even starving people. The truth does not cheapen the victory; it only makes it all the more remarkable.

ONE

NOT BY BREAD ALONE:
FOOD, WORKERS, AND THE STATE

Wendy Z. Goldman

In the factory canteen, as a rule, there is a system of replacements, in other words, they may tear off the coupon for grain from the workers' ration cards but they give them cabbage or stewed turnips, or very, very rarely potatoes, and then most of those are frozen. The workers are dying from hunger and malnutrition. We have special *zemlianki* (earthen dugouts) *of death* where about five to seven sick people are dying each day. Often, we have seen cases where workers die in the shops and at the gates of the factory.

Handwritten letter of complaint from Ivan Aleksandrovich Bednov, worker in ammunition Factory No. 62, Cheliabinsk, March 16, 1943.[1]

WHEN GERMANY ATTACKED THE SOVIET UNION ON JUNE 22, 1941, the country mobilized for total war. Throughout the summer and fall, as one town after another fell to the Nazi blitzkrieg, the Soviet leadership ordered the evacuation of factories, workers, grain, and raw materials to safer areas in the east. The rail networks were strained to the utmost: boxcars sped west to the front with Red Army soldiers, and then east to the rear with machinery and evacuees. Workers frantically dismantled machinery under a hail of German bombs, loaded it on trains, and reassembled it weeks later in industrial towns hundreds of miles from the front. Often production resumed in bare fields under open skies. Millions of people, mobilized from all over the country, were transported east to work in the defense industry.

---

1. Epigraph source in RGASPI, f. 17, op. 122, d. 47, ll. 6–9, typed version. Italics in original.

44

Not by Bread Alone

The Soviet state faced enormous tasks: not only did it have to wage war against an undefeated and seemingly invincible army; it also had to provide millions of evacuees and newly mobilized workers with food, housing, clothing, and medical care. Moreover, all these tasks had to be accomplished within severe constraints. The newly industrialized economy was beset by shortages and imbalances even before the war began, and the Germans quickly occupied the nation's prime farmlands. As the Germans conquered more territory, Soviet leaders realized that central state stocks could not feed the Red Army and provide the population with all the food it needed to survive.

The Soviet state was not the first to confront this crisis of provisioning. Indeed, history shows that hungry citizens on the home front have overthrown more than one regime struggling to finance a war.[2] In France, years of war created the fiscal crisis that led to revolution in 1789. In Germany, women's food protests merged with the rebellions of workers, sailors, and other groups to bring down the Kaiser in 1918. In Russia, women's bread riots toppled the tsar in February 1917 and helped bring the soviets to power in October. In each of these moments, hungry people lost faith not only in their leaders but in the very systems they represented.[3] Yet despite the terrible food shortages in the Soviet Union, the experiences of the February and October revolutions were not repeated in World War II. The hunger was fiercer and more widespread, yet there were no mass protests, food riots, or rebellions against the Soviet state. On the contrary, state food policy proved remarkably effective in organizing scarce resources and promoting popular support.

---

2. The term "home front" appeared for the first time at the beginning of World War I in German propaganda. It represented the state's recognition that the support of civilians was essential to the war effort. Karen Hagemann and Stephanie Schuler-Springorum, eds., *Home / Front: The Military, War and Gender in Twentieth-Century Germany* (Oxford: Berg, 2002), p. 8.

3. On war and revolution, see Harriet Applewhite and Darline Levy, eds., *Women and Politics in the Age of Democratic Revolution* (Ann Arbor: University of Michigan Press, 1993); Belinda Davis, *Home Fires Burning: Food, Politics, and Everyday Life in World War I Berlin* (Chapel Hill: University of North Carolina Press, 2000); Lars Lih, *Bread and Authority in Russia, 1914–1921* (Berkeley: University of California Press, 1990); Lizzie Collingham, *The Taste of War: World War II and the Battle for Food* (New York: Penguin Press, 2012).

A complex, multi-tiered economy developed in response to the competing demands of the military and the labor force. The economic system that emerged differed from the grain requisitioning of War Communism, the market exchange of the New Economic Policy (NEP), and the developing state retail trade network of the 1930s. A highly centralized rationing system delivered food to the civilian population while a parallel decentralized system of subsidiary farms, local purchasing, gardens, and collective farm markets supplemented the basic ration and produced essential consumer items. Historians, analyzing this multi- tiered structure, differ sharply about the role of the state. Some argue that the state largely abandoned provisioning the home front in order to concentrate resources on the military. William Moskoff, for example, notes that the state's strategy was "to oblige the civilian population to rely upon itself." Other historians assert the opposite. U. G. Cherniavskii, for example, stresses that the state remained the single largest food provider to the urban population as it deliberately developed and incorporated other supplementary sources.[4]

This chapter brings new archival evidence to bear on the role of the state, the hierarchies of rationing, the struggle over food distribution, and conditions in the factories. It seeks to answer several questions. First, what policies did the state adopt to ensure that workers received food? Second, how did these policies function in practice? And finally, how important was the state to the production, allocation, and distribution of food? The chapter argues that the food situation for workers was far worse than either Western or Russian historians have recognized to date.

---

4. William Moskoff, *The Bread of Affliction: The Food Supply in the* USSR *during World War II* (Cambridge: Cambridge University Press, 1990): 111. Moskoff provides the best overview in English of provisioning the civilian population. See also John Barber and Mark Harrison, *The Soviet Home Front, 1941–1945: A Social and Economic History of the* USSR *in World War II* (London and New York: Longman, 1991), pp. 77–93; and A. K. Sokolov, "Sotsial'no-trudovye otnosheniia na sovetskikh predpriiatiiakh v gody voiny," in A. N. Sakharov and A. S. Seniavskii, eds., *Narod i voina, 1941–1945 gg.* (Moscow: Institut Rossiiskoi Istorii RAN, 2010). U. G. Cherniavskii, *Voina i prodovol'stvie: Snabzhenie gorodskogo naseleniia v Velikuiu Otechestvennuiu voinu 1941–1945 gg.* (Moscow: Nauka, 1964) offers a highly sophisticated and detailed account of provisioning. Unfortunately, Moskoff, Barber, and Harrison did not have access to the Russian archives, and Cherniavskii had only limited access.

Not by Bread Alone 47

Starvation, so well documented in the besieged city of Leningrad, could also be found to a lesser degree in other towns.[5] Hunger and starvation-related mortality existed throughout the country. During the war's grimmest years, many workers subsisted on bread and gruel. Central food stocks, distributed through the rationing system, were simply insufficient to provision the Red Army and ensure adequate nutrition on the home front. At the same time, the state actively sought and organized additional sources of food beyond the ration. State, party, and union organizations played an essential role in provisioning. They struggled to provide food to the groups they represented and organized collective initiatives that enabled workers to participate actively in supplementing the ration. Indeed, it was this very combination of state-sponsored collective efforts and individual participation that allowed the country to manage and survive the terrible food shortages of the war years.

PROVISIONING FOOD: A GENERAL OVERVIEW

The Soviet state had considerable experience with economic crisis and mass hunger, and had resorted to rationing several times in its short history. Throughout the Civil War years, it employed requisitioning and rationing to guarantee food to workers and the Red Army. During the upheavals of collectivization and industrialization in the early 1930s, it again rationed basic foodstuffs as it struggled to eliminate private

---

5. Conditions in Leningrad deserve special attention. Over one million people died in the city, which was under siege for nine hundred days. On Leningrad (in English), see Richard Bidlack and Nikita Lomagin, eds., *The Leningrad Blockade, 1941–1944: A New Documentary History from the Soviet Archives* (New Haven, Conn.: Yale University Press, 2007); Richard Bidlack, "The Political Mood in Leningrad during the First Year of the Soviet-German War," *Russian Review* 59 (January 2000): 96–113; Richard Bidlack, "Survival Strategies in Leningrad during the First Year of the Soviet-German War," and Andrei Dzeniskevich, "The Social and Political Situation in Leningrad during the First Months of the German Invasion: The Psychology of the Workers," in Robert Thurston and Bernd Bonwetsch, eds., *The People's War: Responses to World War II in the Soviet Union* (Urbana: University of Illinois Press, 2000), pp. 71–83 and 84–107, respectively; David M. Glantz, *The Siege of Leningrad: 900 Days of Terror* (London: Cassell Military Paperbacks, 2001); Harrison Salisbury, *The 900 Days: The Siege of Leningrad* (Cambridge, Mass.: Da Capo Press, 2003).

middlemen and develop a comprehensive network of state retail stores.[6] The state's decision to use rationing had always been the consequence of extreme shortage and the need to ensure an affordable and stable supply of food to the cities. It never viewed rationing as a permanent or desirable feature of socialism. Rationing created multiple and false prices for the same item, contradicted Marx's labor theory of value, weakened the role of money, and curtailed the assortment, availability, and circulation of goods.[7] As soon as shortages began to disappear, in the aftermath of the Civil War and again in the early 1930s, the state abolished rationing in favor of a monetary system based on wages and retail trade. In January 1935, despite workers' protests, the state eliminated bread rationing and encouraged citizens to use the new, "open-network" retail stores accessible to all consumers.[8] "Closed-network" canteens and special parcels continued to provide meals and supplements to workers, white-collar employees, officials, students, and many other social groups, but town dwellers did a growing share of their food shopping in state retail stores.

The war, however, quickly undermined the relatively new system of retail trade. Large stocks of grain, sugar beets, and agricultural produce as well as poultry and herds were lost to the Germans.[9] Collective farmers in the front-line zones abandoned the fall sowing and harvest. Rural officials poured kerosene over food stocks before fleeing, leaving little for Red Army troops.[10] The Council for Evacuation (Sovet po Evakuatsii), created one day after the invasion, immediately began shipping food stocks and food-processing factories out of the front-line zones, but rescue

6. Lih, *Bread and Authority*; Elena Osokina, *Our Daily Bread: Socialist Distribution and the Art of Survival in Stalin's Russia, 1927–1941* (Armonk, N.Y.: M. E. Sharpe, 2001); Julie Hessler, *A Social History of Soviet Trade: Trade Policy, Retail Practices, and Consumption, 1917–1953* (Princeton, N.J.: Princeton University Press, 2004); Amy Randall, *The Soviet Dream World of Retail Trade and Consumption in the 1930s* (Houndmills, Basingstoke, Hampshire: Palgrave Macmillan, 2008).

7. Cherniavskii, *Voina i prodovol'stvie*, p. 67.

8. Oleg Khlevnyuk and R.W. Davies, "The End of Rationing in the Soviet Union, 1934–1935," *Europe-Asia Studies* 5, no. 4 (1999): 557–609. Meat and fish rationing was eliminated in October 1935, and rationing of manufactured goods in January 1936. See Osokina, *Our Daily Bread*, pp. 140–144.

9. GARF, f. 6822, op. 1, d. 550, l. 19, and d. 92, ll. 1–6, 9, 11–14.

10. RGASPI, f. 17, op. 122, d. 18, l. 6.

Not by Bread Alone 49

efforts were not always successful. In some provinces, the desperate efforts to evacuate livestock failed; the cattle were driven off, and those that were shipped east died en route for lack of food and water.[11]

In areas not immediately overtaken by the Germans, the Council for Evacuation had greater success in rescuing food, machinery, and equipment. In Ukraine's Stalino province, workers, peasants, and provincial party committee officials managed over several days in October 1941 to evacuate 4,210 out of 4,860 tractors, 1,300 out of 1,537 combines, as well as 69,400 head of cattle, 58,700 sheep, 45,600 horses, and 22,200 pigs. Almost 3,000 people, including agronomists, collective farm directors, veterinarians, mechanics, tractor drivers, and brigade leaders, struggled in pouring rain and deep mud to ship machinery and animals out of the province before the Germans marched in. Tons of grain, flour, and vegetables were evacuated, destroyed, or distributed to the peasants and Red Army.[12]

Yet by 1942, despite heroic efforts at evacuation, the overall picture was grim. About 70 percent of the food stocks in the front-line areas were either destroyed or lost to the Germans. The country's total sown area was diminished by more than one-third, falling from 110.4 million acres of grain in 1940 to 67.3 million in 1942. Of the country's 483,000 tractors in 1940, 180,000 were left behind in occupied territory.[13] The quantity of grain consumed in 1942, as a result, was less than 50 percent of the figure for 1940.[14] The loss of food-processing factories also damaged the food supply. Many were successfully evacuated, but their machinery was transferred to the defense industry. The Chimkent oil-extraction factory, for example, was transferred to the Commissariat of Rubber (NKRezinProm). The order was only countermanded after sharp protest from the head of the Commissariat of the Food Industry (NKPishchProm), who fought

---

11. RGASPI, f. 17, op. 122, d. 18, l. 9.

12. RGASPI, f. 17, op. 122, d. 18, ll. 150–9.

13. Moskoff, *The Bread of Affliction*, pp. 71, 72; P. I. Veshchikov, "Rol' tyla v bespereboinom obespechenii deistvuiushchego fronta prodovol'stviem," in V. P. Kozlov, M. V. Larin, N. I. Nikiforov, M. V. Stegantsev, A. O. Chubar'ian, and S. I. Chuvashin, eds., *Edinstvo fronta i tyla v Velikoi Otechestvennoi voine, 1941–1945* (Moscow: Akademiia, 2007), p. 83.

14. N. A. Voznesensky, *Soviet Economy during the Second World War* (New York: International Publishers, 1949), p. 77.

to preserve the last remaining factory that could extract cooking oil from Central Asian cotton seeds. The loss of the food factories, either temporarily to evacuation or more permanently to occupation or reassignment, resulted in a sharp decrease in all processed foods, including jams, oil, butter, margarine, meat and fish products, and canned vegetables, so important to the diets of urban consumers.[15]

Soon after the invasion, Soviet leaders responded to the losses in the occupied territories by slashing central state stocks of food for distribution to the retail trade network. A "mobilizing plan for the national economy" placed the country on wartime footing and replaced the figures for the third quarter (July-September) of 1941 of the third Five-Year Plan.[16] Central state stocks were cut to 70 percent of the 1940 level for flour, 67 percent for grain, and a bare 34 percent for sugar.[17] The planned volume of trade through state retail stores was cut by 12 percent overall to meet the needs of the army.[18] On July 1, the army in the field was given permission to purchase food and fodder at state prices from collective farms in the front line areas.[19]

In contrast to the confusion and panic reigning on the battlefield, Soviet leaders immediately adopted a clear and firm food policy. Using the Commissariat of Trade (NKTorg), the state introduced a rationing system that gradually encompassed all urban inhabitants and rural waged workers. On July 18, the state introduced rationing in Moscow, Leningrad, and specific districts in their provinces (*oblasti*). Foods included in this first, geographically limited decree included bread, baked goods, flour, grain, pasta products, sugar, meat and fish products, candy, and fat. On August 15, ration cards for bread only were introduced in all towns and workers' settlements in the industrial provinces, as well as the provinces of Sverdlovsk, Cheliabinsk, Molotov, Gor'kii, Iaroslavl', Tula, and Ivanovo, and the autonomous republics of Bashkiriia and Tatariia. By the

---

15. GARF, f. 6822, op. 1, d. 64, l. 1; f. 6822, op. 1, d. 438, l. 13; f. 6822, op. 1, d. 469, l. 24.

16. The Third Five-Year Plan was to cover January 1938 to December 1942 but was abandoned as a result of the war.

17. Cherniavskii, *Voina i prodovol'stvie*, p. 67.

18. Voznesensky, *Soviet Economy*, p. 35.

19. Veshchikov, "Rol' tyla v bespereboinom obespechenii deistvuiushchego fronta prodovol'stviem," p. 83.

Not by Bread Alone

end of August, rationing for bread, as well as sugar and candy, was extended to almost all towns. On November 1, the ration card system expanded again to include meat and fish products, fats, grains, and pasta for forty-three towns and workers' settlements. On November 10, the system of bread and sugar rationing was decreed for *all* towns and workers' settlements. Many industrial enterprises, located in areas that were guaranteed only bread and sugar, were provisioned according to the same norms as the forty-three towns entitled to the wider array of foods. The state also provisioned several occupational groups, including teachers and medical personnel, at the higher level regardless of where they lived.[20] Thus by late fall 1941, forty-three industrial towns and workers' settlements as well as many additional enterprises and occupations were guaranteed a basic array of foods, and all urban areas were guaranteed, at minimum, bread and sugar.

The rationing system gradually spread to encompass an assortment of goods, yet bread remained at its heart. The state was committed to providing all towns with an uninterrupted, firm norm of bread. Fresh-baked bread was distributed daily throughout all towns and workers' settlements in relatively egalitarian amounts. Unlike meat, fats, or other foods, bread was not subject to substitutions. The state treated a bakery stoppage as a serious problem meriting immediate investigation. In this way, bread differed from any other foodstuff. Rationing set limits on consumption, but more importantly, it ensured a fixed minimum. People who possessed ration cards for fish, meat, pasta, fats, and grains were better provisioned than those entitled only to bread and sugar.

The Commissariat of Trade and its local organs assumed responsibility for distributing food stocks. The Commissariat's organizational pyramid encompassed central, republic, provincial, and town levels. Originally created to manage retail trade, the Commissariat of Trade was repurposed to handle rationing during the war. Its provincial and town trade departments (*obtorgotdely* and *gortorgotdely*) received food from

---

20. *Direktivy* KPSS *i sovetskogo pravitel'stva po khoziaistvennym voprosam, 1929–1945 gody*, vol. 2 (Moscow: Gosudarstvennoe Izdatel'stvo Politicheskoi Literatury, 1957), pp. 705–706; RGAE, f. 7971, op. 1, d. 895, ll. 39–94. Cherniavskii, *Voina i prodovol'stvie*, pp. 70–72.

central state stocks for distribution to industrial enterprises and stores in their localities. The state also provided regular deliveries of additional foodstuffs from central stocks (*gosudarstvennye rynochnye fondy*) to specific recipients (*fondo-derzhatelei*), including institutions, provincial and district executive committees of the soviets (*ispolkomy*), and industrial enterprises, according to planned allotments and prioritized lists. The Commissariat of Trade planned and accounted for various contingents of the population, worked out norms of provisioning, presided over the transfer of the open-network state retail stores to closed-network distribution centers, and managed public canteens. The Administration of Normed Provisioning (*Upravlenie po Normirovannomu Snabzheniiu*) under the Commissariat of Trade SSSR issued ration cards (*kartochki*) and controlled distribution through special bureaus in the localities.[21] Workers and other urban dwellers received ration cards and coupons (*talony*) entitling them to buy a set amount of bread, foodstuffs, and consumer items. Many also received at least one hot meal daily in their factory canteens. Flour was the only foodstuff exempt from this process of distribution. Placed in a special, highly protected category, flour was not subject to substitutions or scattered dispensation.[22]

In 1942, the Germans conquered more territory, and the demands of the army increased with vast new mobilizations. Central state stocks available for the home front were cut again: flour was reduced to about half the 1940 level, grain to one-third, and sugar to 15 percent.[23] The amount of food available to the civilian population in the non- occupied areas

---

21. Initially the Council of People's Commissars (Sovnarkom) and the executive committees of the soviets were responsible for issuing ration cards through local bureaus. In August 1943, responsibility for ration cards was transferred to the republic Commissariats of Trade and their respective local departments of trade, which set up Bureaus of Ration Cards for Food and Consumer Items (Biuro prodovol'stvennykh i promtovarnykh kartochek) to manufacture the cards. Town and district bureaus distributed cards through enterprises, institutions, schools, and housing administrations. The Administration of Normed Provisioning (Upravelenie po normirovannomu snabzheniiu) provided leadership and control over the process. Cherniavskii, *Voina i prodovol'stvie*, pp. 95–97.

22. Ibid., p. 178.

23. Ibid., p. 67. The population also shrank due to occupation. The cuts were thus not quite as dire as they appear at first glance, but were nonetheless severe.

Not by Bread Alone 53

contracted sharply. By spring 1942, the state recognized that central stocks alone could not cover the food needs of the urban population, and it encouraged local trade organizations and enterprises to develop decentralized sources of food to supplement rations and ease the burden on rail, sea, and river transport. In addition to the ration, the state organized and promoted four additional sources of food: subsidiary farms, decentralized purchasing, gardens, and collective farm markets. Local soviet executive committees granted unused lands to the factories to create subsidiary farms, staffed by factory employees, to benefit their canteens. Factory officials frequently organized piggeries based on swill from the canteens on these lands. The state also attached already existing state and collective farms to particular enterprises and industrial commissariats. The state encouraged industrial enterprises and local trade organizations to purchase food from local food producers, processors, commissariats, and trusts. Factory officials might negotiate a contract with a fishing trust, for example, allowing brigades of workers to fish in their waters and deliver the catch to the canteens. The state launched a nationwide gardening movement to promote collective and personal gardens. Workers received small plots, implements, and seed. The Commissariat of Trade became active in creating collective farm markets. Workers bought food from peasants, who traded produce for money or more preferably, consumer goods. The food in these markets, however, was expensive and dependent on regional crops. Prices were determined by the market, and were often beyond the reach of those who lacked extra cash or consumer items to trade. Factories set up workshops to fashion and repair essential consumer items from cast-off materials to trade with peasants. And union activists bargained in the collective farm markets on behalf of the workers and bought food in bulk for the canteens.

State policy thus promoted five major sources of food for the town population: central state stocks (*gosudarstvennye rynochnye fondy*), subsidiary farms attached to industrial enterprises and other institutions (*podsobnoe khoziaistvo*), decentralized procurement (*detsentralizovannaia zagotovka*), collective and individual gardens (*ogorodnichestvo*), and collective farm markets (*kolkhoznye rynki*).[24] The lines between these sources

24. Ibid., p. 173.

were not firmly delineated, and various initiatives at the local level often blurred. Of all these sources, only the collective farm markets offered food for sale or trade at free market prices.

Table 1.1 shows the five sources of food, and their respective contributions to the calories consumed by the urban population. Central state stocks contributed by far the greatest share of calories throughout the war, from 78.5 percent in 1942 to 68 percent in 1944. They provided the daily bread ration, a mainstay of survival. Subsidiary farms provided only a small percentage of calories consumed (between 3.4 and 4.5) and decentralized procurement even less (between 1 and 0.6 percent.) The percent of food provided by the subsidiary farms increased only very slightly (by 1.1 percentage points) between 1942 and 1944. They made a negligible contribution to the food consumed by the population as a whole, but played a greater role in provisioning workers. Some industrial commissariats and enterprises received large, highly productive state or collective farms, which were successful in providing substantial food to the workers. According to instructions from the Council of People's Commissars (Sovnarkom), whatever was produced on the subsidiary farms served as a supplement to the ration from central stocks and was not to be counted against it.[25] The contribution of state organizations (central stocks, subsidiary farms, and decentralizing procurement) to overall calorie consumption decreased over the course of the war (by 9.8 percentage points) as gardens and collective farm markets increased their combined contribution. By the end of the war, central stocks still provided the main source of food, although gardens and collective farm markets had come to occupy a greater role. Yet the "free" or collective farm markets still played a relatively small part in provisioning, accounting for only 9.1 percent of

---

25. RGAE, f. 7971, op. 1, d. 895, l. 73. In 1944, the state decreed that subsidiary farms had to set aside 50 percent of their fall harvest for delivery to the state (for centralized stocks) and for seed for the next planting. Decree of Council of People's Commissars of the USSR, "O poriadke ispol'zovaniia produktsii podsobnykh khoziaistv predpriiatii i uchrezhdenii," April 3, 1944, no. 337, Order [Rasporiazhenie] of the People's Commissariat of Trade and Gosplan of the USSR, "O poriadke raskhodovaniia i ucheta produktsii podsobnykh khoziaistv predpriiatii i uchrezhdenii'," in *Sbornik ukazov, postanovlenii, reshenii, rasporiazhenii, i prikazov voennogo vremeni—1944* (Leningrad: Lenizdat,1945), pp. 217–218, 218–227.

Not by Bread Alone

Table 1.1. Sources of food for the town population of the USSR (as percentage of calories of all foods consumed)

Food source	All food products			All food products except baked bread and flour		
	1942	1943	1944	1942	1943	1944
State central stocks	78.5	73.0	68.0	46.4	40.3	39.8
Subsidiary farms	3.4	4.2	4.5	9.3	10.4	9.0
Decentralized procurement	1.0	0.8	0.6	2.8	2.2	1.1
Total through state organizations	82.9	78.0	73.1	58.5	52.9	49.9
Individual gardens	8.0	9.4	12.4	22.6	24.0	25.3
Collective farm trade	9.1	12.6	14.5	18.9	23.1	24.8
All consumption	100	100	100	100	100	100

Source: U. G. Cherniavskii, *Voina i prodovol'stvie: Snabzhenie gorodskogo naseleniia v velikuiu otechestvennuiu voinu 1941–1945 gg.* (Moscow: Nauka, 1964), p. 186.

calories consumed in 1942 and 14.5 percent in 1944. The collective farm markets were mainly important for providing foods not offered by the ration or grown in gardens. If bread, for example, was removed from the total calories consumed, the role of collective farm markets in consumption increased to 24.8 percent in 1944. Yet if bread was included in calorie calculations, state organizations provided for almost three-quarters of the calories consumed by urban dwellers in 1944. In other words, the state provided the overwhelming majority of calories consumed. It provided the "staff of life." At the same time, the ration alone was not enough to sustain people. Other forms of provisioning were critical in supplementing the diet. Taken together, these five sources were the key components of a conscious state policy developed in response to extreme scarcity. Food policy did not emerge as a haphazard response to the exigencies of war. On the contrary, it was carefully planned and implemented by a powerful organizational network of party, soviet, and union organizations that drew on broad popular participation. The labor and energy of working people gave life to the organizational network, and the network in turn enabled ordinary people to contribute to the war effort.

HIERARCHIES OF PROVISIONING

The rationing system operated according to a rough labor principle, which aimed to reward those who expended more calories at work with more food. The system thus privileged waged workers over dependents, and blue-collar workers over white-collar employees. Peasants were not provided with rations on the assumption that they had direct access to food and did not need to be provisioned by the state. The system also privileged those workers it considered most valuable to the defense effort. It created geographic disparities by favoring the industrial towns with a better array of foodstuffs than urban areas, which were guaranteed merely bread and sugar, and it favored urban inhabitants over waged workers in rural areas and agricultural enterprises with a slightly larger bread ration. The system also created special sources of food for the most vulnerable sections of the population, including children, nursing mothers, workers in toxic or arduous jobs, and people suffering from malnutrition and starvation. The basic aims of the system were to guarantee a stable minimum of bread to the urban population, to channel extra food to defense workers, and to provide dietary supplements to those at risk of malnutrition.

Ration cards were divided into four basic groups: workers, white-collar employees, dependents, and children under twelve. All able-bodied adults and teenagers who were not caring for small children or invalids were expected to contribute to the war effort either through work, training programs, or school. Workers received the largest rations, followed by white-collar employees, dependents, and children in descending order. Those who worked in industries most important to defense and expended the largest number of calories at work received a higher ration. The labor principle did not, however, entirely define policy, which also provided supplementary feeding to additional categories. Officials and engineering technical personnel received special food supplements (*spetspaiki*); children and nursing mothers had access to milk kitchens, additional rations, and exclusive canteens; and workers suffering the effects of starvation or hazardous chemical exposure also received special supplementary feeding designed to reverse their conditions.[26] In Irkutsk, for

---

26. Cherniavskii, *Voina i prodovol'stvie*, pp. 74–75; RGAE, f. 7971, op. 1, d. 895, l. 62.

Not by Bread Alone

example, local authorities opened a municipal canteen in December 1942 to serve the children of soldiers, evacuees, and needy parents.[27]

Beyond these basic divisions of industrial geography, occupation, and age, however, the system became more complicated. Rationing was also divided by economic branch. The state reserved the highest norms (*povyshennye* or *osobo povyshennye normy*) for those in Category I, which included defense, coal, peat, chemical, rubber, cement, machine-building, and metallurgical industries; electrical stations and electrical industry; rail and sea transport; construction of defense, metallurgical, machine engineering, and railroad sites; and seasonal work in forestry, fishing, and peat. Category II included all other branches of industry, transport, municipal services, and any remaining urban inhabitants not included in Category I. Thus the four basic social groups were also divided according to Category I or II, producing eight possible ration amounts. By the end of 1944, most industrial employment was concentrated in Category I and over 60 percent of workers received these higher norms.[28]

The system was further complicated by the application of varying ranges of differentiation to each food group. Bread, for example, was distributed relatively equally. (See table 1.2.) The highest provisioned group, workers and engineering technical personnel (ITR) in Category I, received only twice as much bread as the lowest, children and dependents in Categories I and II. Moreover, children and dependents in Categories I and II received the same amount of bread (400 grams or .88 lbs.). A child whose mother worked in an ammunition plant received the same amount of bread as one whose mother worked in a laundry.

Sugar and candy products were allocated even more equally: people were still divided by social groups, but the economic branch of workers (Categories I and II) made no difference to the ration size. All workers and ITR received 500 grams of sugar and candy per month (1.1 lbs.); white-collar employees and dependents—300 grams (.66 lbs.); and children—400 grams (.88 lbs.).[29] Children, in this case, received more than either

---

27. RGASPI, f. 17, op. 122, d. 19, l. 1210b.

28. Cherniavskii, *Voina i prodovol'stvie*, pp. 74–75; RGAE, f. 7971, op. 1, d. 895, l. 62.

29. RGAE, f. 7971, op. 1, d. 895, l. 62. Ration amounts as of October 1941.

Table 1.2. Norms of bread per person per day according to ration card, October 1941

Social Group	Category I (Eco. Branch)	Category II (Eco. Branch)
Workers and ITR*	800 grams (1.76 lbs.)	600 grams (1.32 lbs.)
White-collar employees	500 grams (1.1 lbs.)	400 grams (.88 lbs.)
Dependents	400 grams	400 grams
Children under 12	400 grams	400 grams

Source: RGAE, f. 7971, op. 1, d. 895, l. 62.

*Engineering and technical personnel.

white-collar employees or dependents. The difference between the highest and lowest ration was only slightly greater than 50 percent.

Other foods, however, including meat and fish, fats, and grain and pasta were distributed more unequally: the largest share was reserved for only a subset of workers and ITR in Category I, who worked in the "particularly important" industries of aviation, armaments, ammunition, and tank production. (See table 1.3.) Here, differentiation occurred not only by social group, but by a narrow subset of industry that privileged workers in defense. The allocation of meat or fish (protein) showed the largest differentiation, with workers in defense industries receiving more than five times as much as children, who received the lowest amount. Workers and ITR in defense received 20 percent more protein foods that other workers, and almost twice as much as white-collar employees. The distribution of fats was also sharply differentiated: the best-provisioned category (workers in defense) received three times as much as the lowest category (dependents). The state provided a larger ration to children than to dependents, due most probably to its recognition that fats played a critical role in growth. Grains and pasta showed less of a spread between the highest and lowest rations (more than double). Here, too, children received more than dependents and the same as white-collar employees. Thus the official hierarchy of provisioning contained inequalities, but the differentials were not very great. For bread and sugar, the foodstuffs distributed most equally, the highest category received between twice and 50 percent more than the lowest. And for meat and fish, the foodstuff distributed the least equally, the highest category received five times as much as the lowest. Of course, the small amount of food available and

Not by Bread Alone 59

Table 1.3. Norms per person per month by ration card by grams, October 1941

Social Group	Meat or Fish	Fats	Grains and Pasta
Workers and ITR*: aviation, tanks, armaments, ammo	2,200 grams (4.85 lbs.)	600 grams (1.32 lbs.)	1,500 grams (3.3 lbs.)
Workers and ITR: other industry, transport, communications	1,800 grams (3.96 lbs.)	400 grams (.88 lbs.)	1,200 grams (2.64 lbs.)
White-collar employees	1,200 grams (2.64 lbs.)	300 grams (.66 lbs.)	800 grams (1.76 lbs.)
Dependents	500 grams (1.1 lbs.)	200 grams (.44 lbs.)	600 grams (1.32 lbs.)
Children under 12	400 grams (.88 lbs.)	300 grams (.66 lbs.)	800 grams (1.76 lbs.)

Source: RGAE, f. 7971, op. 1, d. 895, l. 76.

*Engineering and technical personnel.

the nutritional deficit suffered by most of the population gave great material significance to even the smallest differentials. For people suffering dystrophy and malnutrition, several hundred grams could make the difference between life and death.

The provisioning of officials added another layer of complexity to the rationing system. In some places, they were provisioned as white-collar employees; in others, well above workers in the most favored industries. Many received special food supplements (*paiki*) in addition to their ration cards. Up to July 1943, when Sovnarkom issued a decree detailing how much food the various ranks of party, union, soviet, and komsomol officials would receive, the norms and categories were not fully regulated by the state. Some directors created a hierarchy of canteens in the factories, diverting central and local food stocks from workers to their own managerial circles and favored groups. Such diversion of food, however, was not condoned by the state. When investigators from the All-Union Central Council of Unions (VTsSPS) uncovered such practices, those responsible were reprimanded or subjected to criminal prosecution. An investigation in Aviation Factory No. 32 in the city of Kirov in May 1942, for example, revealed no less than four canteens, each serving a different group with varying amounts and assortments of food. At the top of the hierarchy, the director's canteen served the director, chief engineer, three deputy directors, the chief bookkeeper, party officials, and two officials from the design office. For breakfast, these favored officials received two eggs, 25 grams (.88 ounces) of butter, cheese, ham, fried donuts, and sweetened tea. Dinner consisted of borscht with meat, ham with potatoes, cheese cakes, and coffee with milk. Supper brought goulash, more cheese cakes, hot donuts, and coffee with milk. The meal was free, and did not require coupons (*talony*) to be torn off the ration card. The second and third canteens, serving the shop and department heads, and ITR and Stakhanovite workers, respectively, offered only one meal, dinner, which required *talony* and consisted of lentil soup, 200 grams (.44 lbs.) of bread for sale, and oatmeal kasha. The fourth canteen, which served the workers, also provided one meal, consisting of pickled cucumbers and flour gruel (*kasha muchnaia*).[30] In this factory, the director had reversed the state's guiding principle and created a system whereby caloric intake was the inverse of caloric expenditure.

At the very bottom of the food provisioning hierarchy were those groups who were poorly protected by the ration system or temporarily excluded from it. These included teenaged workers and apprentices as well as elderly and sick Central Asian peasants, mobilized and shipped to industrial towns, and prisoner laborers. Housed in barracks, poorly clad and fed, these groups did the lowest, most unskilled work and were completely dependent on the canteens for their meals. Many lived on little more than "soup" made from bits of grain and hot water. Prison labor of various types was fed at the expense of stocks allocated through the Commissariat of Internal Affairs (NKVD) and stocks allocated to workers. Prisoners haunted the canteens, desperate and starving. They hovered behind the workers as they ate, staring with wolfish intensity at the food, and waiting to lick the discarded plates.[31] Evacuated workers, temporarily deprived of employment or not yet placed on lists entitling them to allocations from central stocks, also suffered malnutrition and even starvation. Sovnarkom decreed that evacuated workers and their families would receive traveling expenses, support in their areas of

---

30. GARF, f. 5451, op. 43, d. 199, l. 1190b.
31. GARF, f. 5451, op. 43, d. 325a, ll. 115, 114.

Not by Bread Alone

resettlement, and wages once they began work.[32] Yet many refugees, especially those not part of an organized evacuation, struggled for months to find jobs and receive rations. Free market prices were prohibitively high, and without access to a ration of some sort, they soon exhausted the trade value of their limited savings and personal belongings in the peasant markets.[33]

As critical as the hierarchy of provisioning was to the population, it is important to recognize that nutritional status cannot be understood through the categories of apportionment alone. In order to determine how well or poorly a group might have fared, it is necessary to measure the amount of food it received against its caloric expenditure. Workers, for example, received more food than dependents, but they also expended more energy than those who did not work. Similarly, those who did heavy labor, such as miners, generally expended more energy than white-collar employees at desk jobs. As Donald Filtzer shows, by 1943 and 1944, starvation mortality began to make heavy inroads into the industrial towns despite their relatively privileged place in the provisioning system. And as Alexis Peri notes, when the factories shut down in Leningrad for lack of fuel, the groups who received less bread than workers bitterly resented a differential that could no longer be justified by labor. Soviet citizens in all categories of provisioning understood well the basic principle of survival: the calories one consumed had to roughly equal the calories one expended.

PRIVATION AND WANT

State food policy, no matter how well crafted, could not compensate for the loss of prime farmland, labor, agricultural machinery, equipment, herds, and draught animals in the occupied areas. Nor could it fully cover the needs of the vast numbers of mobilized workers and evacuees who flooded the towns and cities. By 1944, the total grain harvest (47.2 million tons) was only 49 percent of the harvest in 1940; wheat, was 42 percent of

32. GARF, f. 5451, op. 43, d. 116, ll. 87–86.

33. See also Rebecca Manley, *To the Tashkent Station. Evacuation and Survival in the Soviet Union at War* (Ithaca, N.Y.: Cornell University Press, 2009) on the plight of the intelligentsia after evacuation, pp. 148–195.

the 1940 yield; and sugar beets were a mere 30 percent. Even the potato harvest, the staple crop of individual gardens, was only 77 percent of the amount produced in 1940. Similar drops occurred in the number of cattle (87 percent of 1940 level), pigs (38 percent), sheep and goats (73 percent), and horses (51 percent). The production of basic foodstuffs reflected these decreases. In 1944, meat (for slaughter) was 55 percent, milk 79 percent, and eggs, 40 percent of their 1940 levels. Even in 1945, after the liberation of the occupied territories, not a single index of agricultural production had reached its prewar level. Agricultural output also dropped in the non-occupied areas of the east. Only one homely item in the east—potatoes—exceeded its prewar level. In the words of historian Iu. A. Gor'kov: "These data show on what paltry rations the workers of the rear existed."[34] Workers were hungry, many were chronically malnourished, and some starved.[35] Personal consumption of food and consumer goods dropped by 40 percent in comparison with the prewar years.[36] The amount, quality, and array of foods contracted sharply. Meat, fish, dairy products, fats, and sugar were all scarce, and many workers suffered from scurvy.

The urban population reached the nadir of calorie consumption in 1942. (See table 1.4). Whereas in 1939, an average adult in the towns consumed 3,370 calories per day, in 1942, the amount was only 2,555 calories, or 76 percent of the 1939 total. There was a rise in consumption in 1943 (to 82 percent of the 1939 level), and some small, continuing improvement in 1944. By 1944, calories consumed had increased 10 percent over the low of 1942 yet were still below the prewar level. These numbers, however, must be taken as the upper limit for actual consumption. In all likelihood, actual calorie consumption was considerably lower than the figures cited in table 1.4 given that the official data on food stocks and population did not account for large gaps between what the Commis-

---

34. Iurii A. Gor'kov, *Gosudarstvennyi komitet postanovliaet, 1941–45. Tsifry i dokumenty* (Moscow: Olma Press, 2002) pp. 172–175. The country only recouped its prewar levels of food production between 1947 (potatoes and vegetables) and 1956 (cows).

35. On starvation, see Donald Filtzer's chapter in this collection.

36. A.V. Mitrofanova, *Rabochii klass SSSR nakanune i v gody Velikoi Otechestvennoi voiny, 1938–1945*, vol. 3 (Moscow: Nauka, 1984), p. 409.

Not by Bread Alone

Table 1.4. Caloric intake of the town population of the USSR (per adult eater per day)

Year	Calories	Percentage of calories	
		1939	1942
1939	3370	100	
1942	2555	76	100
1943	2751	82	108
1944	2810	83	110

Source: U. G. Cherniavskii, *Voina i prodovol'stvie: Snabzhenie gorodskogo naseleniia v Velikuiu Otechestvennuiu voinu 1941–1945 gg.* (Moscow: Nauka, 1964), p. 179.

Note: Table includes data from central state stocks, collective farm markets, and decentralized purchasing.

sariat of Trade planned to supply and what the local trade organizations actually received; nor were bakery stoppages, adulteration, decrease in quality, small-scale pilfering, large-scale embezzlement, wastage, spoilage, and other chronic problems factored in.[37]

37. Calculating *actual* consumption and caloric intake is difficult. There are two basic methods. One uses budget studies of individual or family consumption, which list the foods and their respective amounts that were bought on a weekly or monthly basis. On the basis of these lists, this "bottom-up" method then calculates consumption (including caloric intake) by an individual or a family over time. Unfortunately, the Central Statistical Administration (TsSU) did not collect budgets for the war years. Only scattered budgets of small sampled groups exist. This method is thus impossible to apply. The second method calculates the amount of food available through central state stocks and other sources (subsidiary farms, gardens, etc.) and divides these aggregates by the number of people entitled to these stocks. This is the method used by Cherniavskii, Gor'kov, and Mitrofanova. This method, "top-down," does not tell us anything about hierarchies of distribution, corruption, theft, and so on. It tells us what people should have eaten according to the system of distribution, and it is subject to all the imprecisions inherent in the larger Soviet system of planning. Many sources, however, reveal that factory administrators and other officials sometimes took food for themselves from workers' stocks, and that numerous contingents who were fed from workers' stocks were not entitled to the food according to plan. The statistics cited by the tables contained here can, however, be used as a rough guide in understanding the basic sources of food, state allocations, and rough calorie counts for the provisioned population as a whole. As such, these statistics indicate the upper limits of calorie consumption. It is important to remember that distribution was not precisely according to plan.

By 1942, the array of foods available, which included critical nutrients such as fats, carbohydrates, and protein, contracted sharply. Table 1.5 suggests that 1942 marked the low point of consumption for every food product except bread, which played a fairly steady role between 1940 and 1943, fats, which increased after a sharp drop, and potatoes, which became an ever larger portion of the nation's diet. The loss of fat, a calorie-dense food, was partially responsible for the low calorie intake; protein (mainly from animal and fish sources) and carbohydrate consumption also sharply decreased. People attempted to compensate for the loss of other foods by eating more potatoes, but the loss of protein was irremediable. Dystrophy, or starvation disease, as the Leningrad doctors in Rebecca Manley's chapter discovered, was linked not simply to hunger, but to severe protein deficiency. In 1943 and 1944, the food situation improved: there was an increase in the consumption of all foodstuffs except bread and sugar products. (The consumption of bread, the ration staple, dropped in 1944 due to a poor harvest the previous fall.) By 1944, workers were consuming more grain, beans, and pasta, potatoes, fats, and fish than they did in 1940, but still considerably less bread, vegetables and melons, dairy products, meat, and sugar. One historian suggests that 1943 marked a turning point in consumption. Collective farm market prices went down; garden outputs went up. People consumed more food and a greater variety of essential foods.[38] The supplementary strategy adopted by the state was successful in mitigating the terrible shortages of the early war years.

Given the dearth of food, the state converted its retail stores to ration distribution points. Commercial sale of food in state stores (off the ration card) was increasingly unavailable. In many industrial towns, retail stores closed altogether, and food was distributed according to ration categories through canteens.[39] By early 1942, the state prohibited commercial

38. Cherniavskii, *Voina i prodovol'stvie*, pp. 179–180, 183. Mark Harrison notes that 1943 marked the lowest point in household consumption; see *Accounting for War: Soviet Production, Employment, and the Defense Burden, 1940–1945* (Cambridge: Cambridge University Press, 1996), pp. 104–107.

39. Retail trade dropped sharply, decreasing by 60 percent between 1940 and 1942. It increased again as the occupied territories were liberated in 1943 and 1944, slowly reaching 68 percent of its prewar level throughout the country and 87 percent in the areas that had not been occupied. Cherniavskii, *Voina i prodovol'stvie*, p. 102.

Not by Bread Alone

Table 1.5. Feeding of workers during the war years (including home and canteen feeding, per single family member, as a percent of 1940 level)

Foodstuff	1940	1941	1942	1943	1944
Bread, flour	100	96.9	98.0	98.0	83.5
Grain, beans, pasta	100	95.4	73.0	91.0	114.0
Potatoes	100	128.2	131.6	198.7	234.1
Vegetables, melons	100	66.1	41.4	44.7	40.9
Milk and dairy products (without butter)	100	90.4	58.3	67.3	69.5
Meat and meat products	100	111.3	42.1	55.8	59.5
Fats (animal and vegetable)	100	56.4	65.4	79.9	106.5
Fish, herring	100	87.3	78.4	105.6	111.6
Sugar, candy products	100	50.6	33.8	25.3	22.4

Source: A.V. Mitrofanova, *Rabochii klass SSSR nakanune i v gody Velikoi Otechestvennoi voiny, 1938–1945*, vol. 3 (Moscow: Nauka, 1984), p. 412.

sale of bread in an attempt to consolidate, control, and direct stocks. In the summer and fall of 1941, workers in the textile towns of Ivanovo and Shuia could still buy bread in the factory canteens for commercial prices above the daily 200 grams (.44 lbs.) guaranteed by their ration cards. This practice, however, soon came to an end. By February 1942, all commercial sale of bread in the factories was halted.[40] As retail stores closed, increasing numbers of people ate at work or at school. Shortages of food and fuel, continuous shift work, high overtime, and employment of housewives made home cooking very difficult. Mobilized and evacuated workers, housed in barracks, tents, earthen dugouts, and dormitories, had no access to kitchens, utensils, running water, fuel, or stoves. In the town of Kirov, the factories simply took over the retail stores and transferred them to a closed-network system accessible only to their own workers and employees.[41] Over time, money became increasingly useless, and peasants trading in the collective farm markets demanded consumer goods in exchange for food. Sometimes, even ration cards could not guarantee access: people had coupons for items that were simply unavailable. Substitutions were common, and even bread disappeared for weeks at a time. The link between food and employment became tighter and more direct.

40. GARF, f. 5451, op. 43, d. 199, ll. 41–42.
41. RGASPI, f. 17, op. 122, d. 19, l. 112.

RATION CARDS AND CANTEENS

The ration card and factory canteen were the two most important sources of food for workers. They redeemed their ration cards in the canteens in exchange for hot meals that presumably contained the amounts of food to which they were entitled. In some cases, they received their bread ration outside the factory through retail stores; in others, within the factory with the meal. Over the course of the war, as the population of cities and towns swelled with people mobilized to work, the number of people provisioned with bread increased. (See table 1.6.) The state guaranteed the bread ration above all, promising daily, reliable deliveries of fresh baked bread to the urban and rural population. Workers, evacuees, children, dependents, orphans, invalids in state institutions, and workers in rural enterprises and on state farms received bread. Beginning in 1943, the Red Army began liberating the occupied territories, and the rationing system expanded to include millions of newly freed people. The number of people provisioned by the state with bread grew steadily, increasing from 61,778,000 in 1942 to 80,586,000 in 1945, an increase of 43 percent. The state's role in providing bread, far from diminishing through the war, increased significantly.

The state made every effort to maintain a steady supply of food from its central stocks to the localities, yet even bread could not be fully guaranteed. In 1942, lack of fuel led to stoppages in bakeries, and people in many towns went without bread for days at a time. Throughout the fall of 1942, tens of thousands of people in the industrial town of Gork'ii waited patiently each day for hours, clutching the ration cards that entitled them to 500 grams of bread. Once the stores ran out, however, those still waiting were turned away. The bread factories were short of both fuel and flour. In October and November, fully 30 percent of Gork'ii's bakeries were not working. In October, the bread stores were short one thousand tons of bread, and in November, fifty to sixty thousand people each day failed to receive their rations.[42] In Kirov, a stronghold of defense production, distribution of the bread ration was also disrupted. Sel'mash, the town's agricultural machine plant, was converted

---

42. RGASPI, f. 17, op. 122, d. 49, l. 1. On bread stoppages in Gork'ii, see RGASPI, f. 17, op. 122, d. 18, l. 93.

Not by Bread Alone

Table 1.6. Number of people provisioned with bread by the state (in thousands)

	1942	1943	1944	1945
Total population provisioned with bread	61,778	67,711	73,999	80,586
I. Population provisioned according to urban norms	40,961	43,188	48,373	53,817
A. Population provisioned by ration cards, including:	38,901*	41,830*	47,198	52,818
Workers	18,744	20,333	23,930	26,119
Dependents	9,864	10,370	11,300	12,327
Children	10,293	11,127	11,968	14,372
B. Population provisioned by bread through closed institutions and "kettle" rations, including:	2,060	1,358	1,175	999
Population mobilized for defense construction and reconstruction work	1,296	186	7	130
Population in orphanages, invalid homes, and other closed institutions	764	1,172	1,168	869
II. Population provisioned according to rural norms, including:	20,817	24,523	25,626	26,769
A. According to norms established by rural soviets for district enterprises and institutions, rural intelligentsia, and their families	17,778	15,800	17,021	18,950
B. According to centrally established norms (workers in enterprises in rural areas)	Not available	7,139	7,826	7,549
C. Remaining population (evacuated from western districts)	3,039	1,584	779	270

Sources: Russian State Archive of the Economy (RGAE), f. 1562, op. 41, d. 239, ll. 2, 4, 222–222ob. Also presented in Istoricheskie Materialy. Statisticheskaia Tablitsa TsSU SSSR "Chislennost' naseleniia, sostoiavshego na gosudarstvennom snabzhenii khlebom v 1942–1947 gg.," in http://istmat.info/node/18420, and Iurii A. Gor'kov, *Gosudarstvennyi komitet postanovliaet, 1941–45. Tsifry i dokumenty* (Moscow: Olma Press, 2002) pp. 481–482.

Note: Includes students in Fabrichno-Zavodskoe Obuchenie (FZO) and Remeslennye Uchilishcha (RU) receiving kettle rations (*kotlovoe dovol'stvie*, or communal feeding) in 1942—802,000 and in 1943—54,000; and thereafter, receiving bread by ration card.

68   *Wendy Z. Goldman*

to production of shells, landmines, and aviation bombs in 1939, and the town received numerous machine-building plants evacuated from front-line areas, including the Lepse Factory and Factory No. 32 (Avitek). In January 1942, the bakeries shut down due to lack of electricity, and deliveries of bread, crackers, and flour stopped. Only seven out of the province's forty-three bread stores and stalls were functioning. Problems persisted through the year. The situation improved only in December, when the party town and provincial committees declared that it was "categorically forbidden under any condition to turn off the electricity to the cracker/flour factory, the bakeries, and the water pumping station."[43] Problems with bread provisioning, however, continued to crop up in many places throughout war.[44]

In addition to the daily bread ration, most workers received at least one hot meal in factory canteens. The Commissariat of Trade directly provisioned some factories from central stocks; local trade organizations provisioned others. The local organizations, however, often failed to receive their planned allocations from the Commissariat of Trade's central stocks. The building materials factories in the town of Vol'sk in Saratov province, for example, received food for their canteens from the Vol'sk town trade department. Each diner was allotted about 860 grams (1.9 lbs.) of flour, 500 grams (1.1 lbs.) of grain, 250 grams (.55 lbs.) of fish, 68 grams (.15 lbs.) of meat, and 27 grams (.06 lbs.) of vegetable oil *per month*. The amounts were so small that even those workers doing heavy labor did not receive more than a single dish in any twenty-four hour period. Moreover, there was no retail sale of food anywhere in the town. Desperate families of soldiers and workers petitioned to be allowed to eat at least one meal in a factory canteen, the only steady source of food. The head of the Union of Workers of the Cement Industry responded, "It is not possible to satisfy this request." The canteens, which fed teachers, doctors, evacuees, and the neediest family members of Red Army soldiers as well as their own workers (a total of 6,132 people), simply did not have enough food.[45] Local trade organizations could feed neither the town's cement workers nor its other inhabitants.

43. RGASPI, f. 17, op. 122, d. 19, ll. 109, 110, 112, 2–3.
44. RGASPI, f. 17, op. 122, d. 80, ll. 1–3.
45. GARF, f. 5451, op. 43, d. 199, ll. 114–112, 115.

Not by Bread Alone

Faced with the task of feeding tens of thousands of diners over several shifts, the factory canteens struggled with terrible organizational problems and shortages. New contingents of workers arrived in the eastern towns in desperate need of housing, clothing, bedding, and food. Housed in barracks, tents, or *zemlianki* without kitchens, they were entirely dependent on the factory canteens for cooked food. In Kuibyshev, for example, in May 1942, Factory No. 18 was responsible for feeding almost twenty thousand workers, who had been evacuated or mobilized from other areas.[46] Often contingents arrived unexpectedly, before local officials received orders or stocks to provision them. The Union of Workers in the Ship Building Industry was furious about the treatment of its members after the workers and their factories were evacuated from Leningrad to Kazan'. For months, the workers received a single course (one dish) of low caloric food per day, and their children did not have access to bread, milk, or even semolina.[47]

Plates, bowls, and utensils were in short supply everywhere. Before the war, the Commissariat of Trade managed four factories, which produced kitchen equipment for canteens. Once the war began, they were transferred to defense production. The Commissariat of Trade began creating local workshops in 1942 to repair old equipment and utensils, but production was hampered by lack of fuel and materials.[48] Aviation Factory No. 26 outside of Ufa had fourteen canteens with seats for over 3,300 workers, but only 2,300 plates and bowls. As a result, workers stood in long lines, waiting up to two hours to be served. Shop heads, anxious to meet production quotas, tried to circumvent the lines by allowing their workers to leave thirty minutes early. According to a VTsSPS report, huge crowds would block up the entrance to the canteens, creating "unbearable" conditions for the waiters. Hundreds of workers could not find seats. Kitchens lacked fuel and basic foodstuffs due to shortages in transport. The canteens and kitchens were unsanitary and in need of repair. Dishes and pots were washed in cold water, the food was often spoiled, and food poisoning and stomach illnesses were endemic. Workers had

---

46. GARF, f. 5451, op. 43, d. 199, l. 43.

47. GARF, f. 5451, op. 43, d. 199, l. 49.

48. RGAE, f. 7971, op. 3, d. 258, ll. 38–39. Canteens were also short of utensils in the 1930s. The shift to defense production exacerbated an already existing problem.

no place to wash their hands, which were covered in oil, dirt, and toxic chemicals.[49]

Even in the renowned Kirov tank factory in Cheliabinsk, the canteens were filthy. Crowded with workers as well as people from outside the factory, they were located in the shops. Workers brought their own spoons and wiped them off on their work clothes. Great lines formed before meals, and here, too, people waited hours to eat.[50] Often bread was not delivered due to problems with production or transport, and many workers received only a portion of their daily ration of 800 grams (1.76 lbs.).[51] The canteens in ammunition Factory No. 15 in Chapaevsk were also unsanitary and short of utensils. One canteen, responsible for feeding 1,400 people, had a total inventory of 40 spoons, 40 small plates, 40 bowls, 15 glasses, and 60 metal mugs. Stocks of dishes and utensils were not much better in the others. No less than ninety minutes were required to get food, and workers often returned from their meal break without having eaten. One kitchen had no place to store food, and meat lay wherever it was unloaded. Workers stepped over or around bloody carcasses strewn across the floors. In another kitchen, the damp storehouse was so poorly ventilated that everything, including the food, was covered in mold. Coal gas smoke billowed from a broken stove. Kitchen staffers, regularly overcome by toxic fumes, had to be carried out on stretchers.[52]

Party, union, and factory officials made strong efforts to reorganize the canteens and to establish dinner breaks at staggered times in order to reduce lines. Their efforts to enforce basic hygiene and to provide cooking equipment, dishes, and utensils were successful in improving conditions in many canteens.[53] Yet labor mobilization continued throughout the war, and new contingents of workers kept arriving on site in need of provisions.[54] After the Red Army began liberating the occupied territories in 1943, thousands of workers returned home, and others were dispatched

---

49. GARF, f. 5451, op. 43, d. 199, ll. 12–10, 25, 24.

50. GARF, f. 5451, op. 43, d. 199, l. 142.

51. GARF, f. 5451, op. 43, d. 199, l. 140.

52. GARF, f. 5451, op. 43, d. 199, ll. 79–78.

53. GARF, f. 5451, op. 43, d. 199, ll. 58–580b.

54. On problems with provisioning workers mobilized from Central Asia into the armaments factories, see RGASPI, f. 17, op. 122, d. 50, ll. 5–36.

Not by Bread Alone   71

from distant areas to rebuild the towns and factories. Pubic catering remained a necessity amid the bombed out and smoldering ruins, and the canteens once again faced the challenge of feeding millions of uprooted people under conditions of extreme scarcity.

The harsh fact was that the gap between planned and actual deliveries was considerable, and factories could not meet the needs of their workers with the food allotments they received from central state stocks. Throughout 1942, before subsidiary farms, decentralized procurement, and collective and individual gardens were fully organized, the situation was grim. In the first quarter of 1942, Aviation Factory No. 29 in Omsk received only 42 percent of the fish, 37 percent of the grain and pasta, 29 percent of the animal and vegetable fat, and none of the dairy products, meat, or potatoes allocated from central state stocks. At the same time, the number of meals served by its canteens jumped from 23,200 to 31,100. Meals as a result were very limited: workers received one low-calorie course a day.[55] Factory managers scrambled to find food in the surrounding area. Using factory funds, officials managed to procure 33 tons of meat and fish, 45 tons of milk and dairy products, and several tons of beets and dried fruits from the area's collective and state farms, but even these additional stocks barely covered the workers' needs.[56] In December 1942, the nadir of consumption nationwide, twelve of the closed-network canteens in Kirov received only 16 percent of their planned potato allotment and little else. They served one bowl of potato soup per day per person for ten kopeks. The ingredients were simple: 100 grams (3.5 oz.) of a dirt-encrusted potato, 20 grams (.7 oz.) of flour, and 5 grams (.17 oz.) of salt; no fat or protein. The workers in Kirov's fur and sheepskin factory ate even more poorly. They had a similar soup made from cabbage, vegetables, or flour; they had no potatoes. The town trade department received only a small percentage of its planned allotment of potatoes, meat, fish, butter, and oil, and was unable to provide any food to the retail stores, which were finally closed and transferred to the factories.[57] Workers had few options: their ration cards could not be

55. GARF, f. 5451, op. 43, d. 199, ll. 29–27.
56. GARF, f. 5451, op. 43, d. 199, ll. 101–100.
57. RGASPI, f. 17, op. 122, d. 19, ll. 110, 112.

redeemed in the stores, and the food in the canteens was not enough for subsistence.

Kitchen cooks responded to the lack of state deliveries and burgeoning numbers of diners by cutting portion size, watering down the soup, and adding inedible fillers. In Aviation Factory No. 19 (Zavod im. Stalina) in Molotov, workers received a single bowl of watery soup made from flour or grain with a small bit of fat and salt, and no onions, carrots, or potatoes. The calorie count, about 190 calories per serving, was 50 percent lower than the norm established by the Commissariat of Trade. Meat cutlets, when available, were also reduced in caloric value by half, from 500 to 250 calories. The kitchen simply did not have enough food. The Commissariat of Trade delivered only a portion of the factory's planned allotments of meat, fish, and flour, and there were few farms in the surrounding area to supplement central stocks. While workers on the day shift might receive two meals, workers in the supporting shops and the night shift did heavy labor on a bowl of watery gruel.[58]

At the same time that central stocks were diverted from the civilian population to the army, factory canteens assumed responsibility for feeding many groups not employed in the factory. With factory stocks often being the only steady source of food in town, local authorities used them to feed evacuees, municipal workers, local officials, families of workers, and others. The multiplication of eaters depleted the already meager stores available for workers, forced cooks to dilute meals, and created sharp resentment. Unions protested strenuously, but in many cases, the factories were feeding the children of their own workers. Five daycare centers in Aviation Factory No. 29 cared for 350 children, and the town trade department provided them with less than half of the norms set by the Commissariat of Trade for fat, sugar, meat, fish, milk, and vegetables. Officials estimated that they received far less food than they needed for proper nutrition.[59] Factory-run crèches and daycare centers also provided supplementary food for nursing mothers. Workers in the Stalin sewing factory in Chkalov, for example, fared poorly, but the nursing mothers among them received extra food through the factory's crèche.

58. GARF, f. 5451, op. 43, d. 199, ll. 58–58ob., 75.
59. GARF, f. 5451, op. 43, d. 199, ll. 26, 100.

Not by Bread Alone

Open twenty-four hours a day to accommodate workers on different shifts, the crèche served almost three times as many children as it was designed for, but both mothers and babies were in good condition.[60] The nutritional supplements and childcare offered by the factories enabled women to work, and to feed themselves and their children. The union factory committees (*zavkomy*) also helped the families of workers who were mobilized into the army, providing material aid and wood for fuel.[61] The factories thus became survival centers, feeding municipal employees, officials, evacuees, parents, children, and families of soldiers and workers. And while all these groups were in desperate need of help, they depleted the stocks available for workers.

The lack of food and narrow diet took a toll on the health of workers. Industrial towns in poor agricultural areas in the east and far north were hit especially hard by the reduction in central deliveries. Workers everywhere suffered from edema and other symptoms of dystrophy. In Factory No. 200 in Cheliabinsk, the head of the union's factory committee and factory doctor wrote a panicked letter in February 1943 to Shvernik, the head of the VTsSPS, about high rates of illness and death, especially among workers housed in dormitories and dependent on the canteens:

> We have an increase of cases of protein-deficiency edemas, vitamin deficiency, and dystrophy of the I and II degrees, leading to a high rate of illness and death, especially among single workers living in the dormitories. If measures are not taken quickly to improve the feeding of single workers and those with dystrophy, then we will come to a catastrophic position with the labor force because the factory is already very short of workers.

They pled with Shvernik to find a dependable source of food and vitamin C so that the factory committee might provide two meals a day for the factory's 1,600 workers, and special supplements for those in various stages of starvation.[62]

In 1943, the state launched a major campaign to use a variety of "invented" foods to supplement the diet. Pine needle extract (*nastoi khvoi*), a bitter concoction made from boiled pine needles containing high amounts of vitamin C, was used as a "juice" to counteract scurvy. Scientists searching

60. GARF, f. 5451, op. 43, d. 199, l. 85.
61. GARF, f. 5451, op. 43, d. 199, l. 84.
62. GARF, f. 5451, op. 43, d. 236, l. 19.

for protein additives discovered yeast extract (*belkovye drozhzhi*), and canteen cooks began adding tons of the foul-tasting stuff to soups and foods. Unions organized workers in large groups to gather edible wild greens, including sorrel, nettles, and dandelion leaves, with high nutritional value. The Union of Workers in Pubic Catering (ROP) taught cooks to boil down the starchy water left after cooking potatoes and to create a variety of jelly-like "desserts" by adding sugar to the potato starch (*krakhmal*). In Moscow, ROP members produced eighty-seven tons of potato starch extract, which was then distributed to the factory canteens. Canteen cooks also made jelly (*kisel*) from water used to boil beets and other vegetables. ROP members took state-sponsored cooking courses in the use of these new "foods," which generally tasted badly but provided a much-needed supplement. ROP sent recipes to canteens throughout the country.[63]

SUBSIDIARY FARMS, GARDENING, AND DECENTRALIZED STOCKS

By early 1942, it was clear that central state stocks distributed through the Commissariat of Trade could not cover the food needs of the urban population; even defense workers were suffering from malnutrition. Mobilizing the Commissariat of Trade and the unions, the state launched a campaign to develop local sources of food, including subsidiary farms, gardens, and decentralized purchasing. On January 5, 1942, the VTsSPS issued two decrees. The first established collective factory gardens for canteens; the second made small plots available to individuals.[64] In February, the Commissariat of Trade established Departments of Workers' Provisioning (Otdely Rabochego Snabzheniia, or ORSy) in leading defense, coal, chemical, and ferrous metallurgical enterprises. As food provisioning shifted from retail stores to canteens, ORSy were created as an administrative extension of the Commissariat of Trade in the factories. By linking factories with local trade organizations, it aimed to improve provisioning for workers, to ensure full delivery of allocated

---

63. GARF, f. 5452, op. 22, d. 25, ll. 105, 57, 58, 610b.–65; f. 5452, op. 22, d. 31, ll. 63–630b., 68, 93, 94.

64. GARF, f. 5451, op. 43, d. 199, l. 61a.

Not by Bread Alone 75

stocks, and to procure additional sources of food. The Commissariat of Trade organized approximately 2,000 ORSy in 1942. By the end of 1944, ORSy managed 30,000 subsidiary farms, and by January 1945, 7,000 ORSy served almost half of the population covered by the rationing system.[65] Active in local food procurement, ORSy established fishing brigades, gardens, and piggeries, and contracted with state and collective farms, and local food processors. Their activities varied widely by region.[66] In some industrial centers, ORSy took over the stores once run by town trade departments.[67] In Irkutsk, the ORS cooperated with party, union, and trade officials, and the directors of the town's industrial enterprises to develop a plan for provisioning and to gather 33,000 tons of potatoes and vegetables from the surrounding area. In many factories, ORSy created subsidiary enterprises, including potteries, coopers, and workshops for sewing, furniture, building materials, leather, and baked goods to serve the needs of the workers.[68] ORSy were also charged with reorganizing food procurement in the newly liberated territories where agriculture, industry, and infrastructure lay in ruins.[69]

On April 7, 1942, Sovnarkom and the Central Committee directed local organs to transfer all unused state land around the towns to factories and other institutions for subsidiary farms and personal gardens.[70] The number of subsidiary farms increased rapidly. Many factories received land in time for spring sowing and were able to gather a harvest in the fall. Piggeries, which proved especially easy to maintain, accounted for one-quarter of all subsidiary farms attached to canteens. The subsidiary farms made an important contribution to factory canteens, allowing many enterprises to provision workers with their own potatoes and vegetables without drawing on central state stocks.[71] The state, aiming to

65. Mitrofanova, *Rabochii klass,* p. 413; Cherniavskii, *Voina i prodovol'stvie,* pp. 100–101.

66. GARF, f. 5451, op. 43, d. 199, ll. 61a, 65.

67. RGASPI, f. 17, op. 122, d. 19, l. 112.

68. RGASPI, f. 17, op. 122, d. 19, ll. 123–1230b.

69. GARF, f. 5451, op. 43, d. 199, l. 103.

70. *Direktivy KPSS i sovetskogo pravitel'stva po khoziaistvennym voprosam,* p. 723.

71. The practice of attaching land to factories for farming and animal husbandry was not new. The party promulgated the policy in 1939 at the Eighteenth Party Congress, endorsing the creation of farms and gardens around industrial centers to supplement meat, milk, and vegetables for retail stores and factory canteens. The farms were placed

76   Wendy Z. Goldman

mobilize local initiative and energy, also permitted the industrial commissariats, enterprises, and local food producers and processors not only
to farm and raise livestock, but to trade and conclude contracts. Factory
directors, for example, contracted for fishing rights and food from local
processors. Additional decrees attached hundreds of state and collective
farms to factories and industrial commissariats for the benefit of their
workers.[72]

Union officials also organized the distribution of land to workers for
individual and collective gardens. A Committee for the Creation of Personal and Collective Gardening was created within the VTsSPS to oversee the unions and their factory committees in organizing the gardening
movement. Between 1942 and 1944, the number of collective and individual gardens more than tripled, from 5 million to 16.5 million. In 1942,
about one-third of all urban inhabitants worked in an individual or collective garden, and in 1944, about one-half. Among workers, the share
was even greater: more than 90 percent of workers employed in ferrous
metallurgy, mining, and the railroads participated in the gardening movement.[73] Town soviets gave land and seed to the factories, which in turn
relied on gardening commissions organized by the unions to distribute
plots to the workers. Millions of workers began planting small plots
(about one-tenth of an acre), raising potatoes, cabbage, and other vegetables. The gardening commissions supervised weeding, terracing, and
harvesting, and provided packing materials and winter storage. Factory
No. 29, for example, received about 495 acres (200 hectares) of land located
about 1.5 miles distant, to be divided among its workers. The factory director received over eight thousand requests for land from workers
eager to receive the plots.[74] Some factories borrowed equipment from the

---

under the administration of the local trade organizations. On September 7, 1940,
Sovnarkom and the Central Committee passed a decree ordering various organizations
to establish subsidiary farms on land distributed by the provincial executive committees
of the soviets for use by factory canteens. See Cherniavskii, *Voina i prodovol'stvie*,
pp. 130–132, 134, 145–146.

72. The industrial commissariats alone received 550 state farms. Mitrofanova,
Rabochii klass, p. 413.

73. Cherniavskii, *Voina i prodovol'stvie*, pp. 141–142.

74. GARF, f. 5451, op. 43, d. 199, ll. 6–5.

Not by Bread Alone 77

Machine Tractor Stations, and workers in Magnitogorsk ploughed the large collective plots with captured German tanks they converted to tractors![75]

The State Committee for Defense (GKO) and the VTsSPS, both headquartered in Moscow, attached state and collective farms to industrial enterprises. In an attempt to improve conditions in the Aviation Factory No. 19 in Molotov, for example, a large nearby state farm was attached to the factory and a portion of its produce diverted to the workers and their children.[76] The state encouraged local officials in the ORSy, unions, soviets, and industrial enterprises to exercise initiative in procuring food. Many factory managers set up small workshops alongside the primary industrial shops to produce eating utensils, shoes, and clothing for use in local trade.[77] The Commissariat of Trade's local trade departments also brokered contracts with farms to procure food for industrial enterprises and institutions. Yet the state continued to play a strong role even in these supplementary activities. On October 18, 1942, Sovnarkom and the Central Committee issued instructions to managers of the subsidiary farms, criticizing them for low productivity and failure to gather the harvest in a timely manner. The state set targets for the amount of acreage to be sown, selected the crops, and determined the percentage of the harvest apportioned for livestock. It also provided elaborate directives about storing and sprouting seeds, tools, composting, irrigation, preserving berries, fungicides, and insecticides, and created a system of prizes and bonuses to reward managers who met the agricultural plans.[78] Provincial party and soviet executive committees also supervised the subsidiary farms, drawing up detailed local plans for food production and distribution.

Taken together, the subsidiary farms, decentralized purchasing, and gardens made a substantial contribution to the food available, providing 17.5 percent of all calories consumed in 1944 by the urban population. In most regions, the subsidiary farms specialized in vegetables, and the gardens yielded mainly potatoes, a crop that was easy to grow and required

75. GARF, f. 5451, op. 43, d. 199, l. 94; Mitrofanova, *Rabochii klass*, p. 414.

76. GARF, f. 5451, op. 43, d. 199, l. 570b.

77. GARF, f. 5451, op. 43, d. 199, ll. 86–85, 6–5.

78. *Direktivy KPSS i sovetskogo pravitel'stva po khoziaistvennym voprosam*, vol. 2, pp. 734–743.

little weeding.[79] For the urban population as whole, by far the most important of these three sources were personal gardens, which contributed more than twice as much to consumption (12.4 percent) as the subsidiary farms and decentralized stocks (5.1 percent). (See table 1.1.) Yet for workers within industrial commissariats that controlled large and productive farms, the food supplement could be considerable. Less than 25 percent of all subsidiary farms were controlled by the industrial commissariats, but these produced 60 percent of the potatoes and vegetables, 60 percent of the pigs, more than 50 percent of the cattle, 40 percent of the chickens, and 50 percent of the sheep and goats raised by all subsidiary farms.[80] Decentralized, local sources of provisioning—subsidiary farms, decentralized purchasing, and gardening—provided critical supplements to central state stocks, but they were never independent of central control. Components of a carefully crafted policy, they were organized and run by union, state, and party organizations.

COLLECTIVE FARM MARKETS AND TRADE

The economic arrangements most similar to a "free" market in food were the collective farm markets, known at the time as "free" (vol'nyi), "private" (lichnyi), or "peasant" markets. Here consumer access to food was determined by ability to pay rather than by need, caloric expenditure, or contribution to the war effort. The reduction in central allocations and contraction of the state's retail trade network was a great spur to peasant marketing. Peasants sold the harvest from the collective farms to the state at state-mandated prices, and their share of the proceeds was determined by the number of "labor days" (calculated units of time), they contributed to work on the collective farm. They also sold produce from their private plots and poultry stocks in the collective farm markets. Families split the labor of their members, deploying some in collective farm work and others on the private plot. Household income rested on a combination of payments for the commercial crops appropriated by the state, and produce from the private plot appropriated by the household. Dur-

79. Cherniavskii, *Voina i prodovol'stvie*, pp. 135, 145.
80. Ibid., p. 134.

Not by Bread Alone   79

ing the war, labor day payments were too small to provide subsistence. The state paid too little to the collective farms to support the collective farmers fully. In 1942, for example, the labor day payments amounted to no more than 200 grams (.44 lbs.) of bread and 100 grams (.22 lbs.) of potatoes per person per day.[81] Without the produce from their private plots, the collective farmers would have starved. Peasants traded briskly with workers, and sold produce, milk, and cooked food at train stations and along railroad routes to evacuees and other passengers. They provided a significant and growing share of the food consumed by the urban population: 9.1 percent in 1942, 12.6 percent in 1943, and 14.5 percent in 1944. (See table 1.1.) The collective farm markets were especially important sources of milk and meat, two food products that central state stocks provided only in small quantities.

The collective farm markets, however, were not independent of state food policy. The Commissariat of Trade contained a Department of Collective Farm Trade that actively promoted the markets, tracked their numbers and total sales, and calculated their contribution to the food supply. As of January 1944, for example, the Commissariat of Trade counted two thousand collective farm markets in Russia, six in Iakutiia, and eighty-seven in Bashkiriia. The Commissariat of Trade incorporated the markets into the state's larger food policy, and made every effort to increase their sales.[82] In many instances, local party and soviet officials set up the markets, providing space, sanitary facilities, advertising, and contacts with the urban population.

Prices in the markets, although based on supply and demand, were also strongly influenced by the low subsidized state prices set by the rationing system. Rationing and other sources of provisioning affected the overall demand for food, especially for bread, butter, and oil. Indeed, a close relationship between central state provisioning and collective farm market prices existed throughout the war. When state provisioning of foods increased in 1943, market prices dropped. Likewise, when the state

---

81. Veshchikov, "Rol' tyla v bespereboinom obespechenii deistvuiushchego fronta prodovol'stviem," p. 86. In 1934, peasants were permitted to farm "private" plots in addition to the work they did on the collective farms.

82. RGAE, f. 7971, op. 5, d. 60, l. 1.

cut the bread ration in November 1943, collective farm market prices for flour increased.[83] Other state policies also exercised a restraining influence on prices. Individual and collective gardens reduced demand for food in general, and potatoes and vegetables in particular, and thus helped to lower market prices. Wholesale purchases by buyers from industrial enterprises also provided food to workers at slightly lower prices. Peasants were often willing to reduce price in exchange for the certainty of bulk sales and time saved waiting in stalls or markets, and factory canteens benefited from such purchases. The state also consciously sought to curb price inflation by removing money from circulation through state loans (war bonds), lotteries, taxes, and levies.[84] Finally, local officials made strong efforts to eliminate middlemen and speculators, who bought up large quantities of food for resale at higher prices.

Despite competition from rationing and other sources, the prices in the peasant markets were high and often out of reach of workers. Wages rose during the war, increasing to an average of 575 rubles per month in 1944, and even higher in some branches of heavy industry. Overtime payments and special premiums also added to the wage for workers, engineers, and technical specialists.[85] Yet prices were still high in comparison to the wage. In Ivanovo province, in February 1942, peasants in the collective farm markets were selling a kilogram (2.2 lbs.) of beef for 150 rubles, ham for 200 rubles, potatoes for 18, and milk for 40 rubles per liter (1.05 quarts).[86] Prices in the peasant markets around Kazan' were similar, with meat selling for up to 200 rubles per kilogram; butter, 570; potatoes, 40; onions, 60; milk, 40; and cottage cheese—120. The head of the Union of Shipbuilders noted that such "speculative marauding prices" were "absolutely out of reach" of the shipbuilding workers evacuated

83. The state supplied 82 percent of the butter consumed by the urban population in 1942 and 59 percent in 1944. Cherniavskii, *Voina i prodovol'stvie*, pp. 185, 154–155.

84. State-sponsored lotteries raised money for the war effort and removed it from circulation. Tickets cost approximately 10 percent of the monthly wage. See GARF, f. 5451, op. 43, d. 132, l. 52.

85. Sokolov, "Sotsial'no-trudovye otnosheniia na sovetskikh predpriiatiiakh v gody voiny," p. 95.

86. GARF, f. 5451, op. 43, d. 199, l. 40.

Not by Bread Alone

from Leningrad to Kazan'.[87] The price of a kilogram of meat was more than one-third of a worker's monthly wage. And with few consumer goods available for purchase, peasants were increasingly interested only in barter. In one surveyed market in Ivanovo province, more than half of the collective farmers would trade their food and wood only for manufactured goods such as kerosene, soap, vodka, or tobacco. The workers were so hungry that they regularly set out in large groups from the town of Ivanovo to the village of Palekh, sixty-five kilometers distant, for food and fuel. The secretary of the Palekh district party committee observed "streams of town inhabitants headed toward the countryside." Many collective farmers abandoned the market altogether and let the workers come to them. "We have no need to go to the collective farm market," they said. "They [the workers] bring everything that we need to us."[88] Peasants were not strongly motivated to market their produce. They, too, were caught in the grip of hunger, and could always consume what they did not sell.

The Commissariat of Trade tried to motivate the peasants to increase marketing by providing transport, building covered stalls, organizing special bazaars before holidays, and brokering contracts between peasants and factories and trade organizations.[89] Local party and soviet officials also tried to promote trade by setting up collective farm markets with convenient access for both peasants and workers. After extensive organizing by party officials in Ivanovo province, about 150 collective farms set up over one thousand wagons in a market in Shuia, selling meat, milk, cabbage, potatoes, rye, and rye flour for reasonable prices. Limits were placed on the amount of purchase making it difficult for speculators to buy in bulk and resell at a profit. The markets, however, did not always function as planned, and one official noted that women textile workers were still angry at the long lines and high prices.[90]

The state's endorsement of the markets allowed local officials a new freedom to explore the role of free trade. Officials from party, soviet, and

87. GARF, f. 5451, op. 43, d. 199, l. 48.
88. GARF, f. 5451, op. 43, d. 199, ll. 41, 40.
89. RGAE, f. 7971, op. 5, d. 60, ll. 10b., 20b.
90. GARF, f. 5451, op. 43, d. 199, l. 40.

trade organizations in Ivanovo, Shuia, Palekh, and other towns met to discuss markets in early 1942. Offering a variety of innovative suggestions, local officials aimed to eliminate the middlemen who bought in bulk from the peasants and resold at exorbitant prices to the workers, a practice that hurt the economic interests of both groups. Many workers traded the consumer items they received from the Commissariat of Trade's town stocks (*gorodskoi fond*) for food. Yet middlemen (*perekupshchiki*) disrupted this direct barter by waylaying the collective farmers on their way to market or buying up all the stocks once they arrived. Some officials proposed that the town trade departments limit the amount that might be purchased, but not the price.[91] One suggested a system akin to the ration card whereby officials would issue coupons (*talony*) to workers, entitling them to purchase food from the peasants. Such a system would eliminate the middlemen, and allow local officials to control who gained access to the markets.[92] The secretary of Palekh's district party committee suggested that existing consumer cooperatives and village stores could also displace the middlemen. The village stores (*sel'po*) could use the consumer cooperatives to buy food in bulk from peasants, open their own stalls (*lar'ki*) in the collective farm markets, and sell food to workers at affordable prices. In this way, the struggling village stores would increase the amount of produce brought to market and act as a break on prices. Moreover, if peasants could rely on regular buyers, they could devote less time to marketing and more to fieldwork.[93] Some party officials went even further, suggesting that consumer cooperatives be granted the exclusive right to buy produce from the peasants and resell it to the workers, thus eliminating the market and direct trade between peasants and the urban population altogether.[94]

Local officials, however, faced serious constraints. As one noted pessimistically, "The whole business rests on transport." The collective farms were unlikely to turn their few remaining carts, tractors, and draught animals over to other organizations, and neither the village stores nor the

91. GARF, f. 5451, op. 43, d. 199, ll. 36–35.
92. GARF, f. 5451, op. 43, d. 199, ll. 34–33.
93. GARF, f. 5451, op. 43, d. 199, ll. 38, 37.
94. GARF, f. 5451, op. 43, d. 199, ll. 35–34.

Not by Bread Alone 83

cooperatives had access to transport.[95] Officials also recognized that the peasants had little incentive to cooperate with schemes that reduced the prices they received. Any attempt to overregulate prices ran the risk of antagonizing the peasants and shutting the markets down completely. Local officials could influence trade only to a limited extent.

The collective farm markets were not the only form of "free" trade that developed. As retail trade contracted, street trading and unofficial markets popped up everywhere. Sprawling second-hand markets (*tolkuchki*), where people might buy or trade clothing, shoes, wood, food, and even ration cards, sprang up around the collective farm markets. Here workers traded the consumer items they received from central state stocks, and small traders sold a motley assortment of wares. In Moscow in 1943, huge second-hand markets encircled the collective farm stalls, spilling out over the tramways and stopping traffic. Teeming with criminals, invalids, homeless people, and orphaned teenagers, the markets were so congested and chaotic that the militia could not pass through to pursue the thieves who snatched food from shoppers and peasants' stalls.[96] Legal, semi-legal, and criminal traders all vigorously plied their wares in the second-hand markets. Workers traded underwear for food, clerks sold pilfered goods, and thieves hawked stolen ration cards. Even local trade organizations got involved in shady market dealings. Trade officials in Gork'ii, Kuibyshev, and other towns, who were desperately short of food to distribute to the factories and the urban population, withheld highly valued consumer items from central state stocks earmarked for workers. They traded these items, including matches, soap, and vodka, for food, which they then added to the stocks available to factory canteens and stores.[97] Although this trading was not for personal gain, workers felt the lack of consumer items keenly. Many went for months without washing due to lack of soap, and suffered from lice, rashes, and skin infections. Petty, or hand-to-hand, trade (*torgovlia s ruk*) appeared everywhere. Second-hand markets, attracting hundreds of people each day, even emerged in factory yards and shops. Rations could not fully cover demand,

95. GARF, f. 5451, op. 43, d. 199, ll. 37–36, 33.
96. RGAE, f. 7971, op. 5, d. 60, ll. 20b, 36–37.
97. RGAE, f. 7971, op. 5, d. 60, l. 10b.

and people sold, resold, and bartered anything of value to get the food and consumer items they needed. Party and state authorities took a dim view of this ubiquitous petty trading, but did little to stop it. Given the constant shortages, most efforts to eradicate petty private trade failed, resulting only in a temporary shift of market location. A. V. Liubimov, the Commissar of Trade, noted in a letter in September 1944 to L. P. Beria, head of the NKVD, that private trade had "assumed a mass character" in Moscow: people traded from morning to night on the streets.[98] The large amount of money in circulation, combined with the dearth of consumer goods and food, encouraged a broad range of market activity from state-sponsored collective farm markets to illegal black-market trafficking in stolen goods.

"Free" markets served many purposes and interests. They supplemented an inadequate rationing system by encouraging the peasantry to expand production on their private plots and increase food available to the towns. And they provided a substitute for the contracting network of retail stores, enabling people to barter or buy goods and food they needed. At the same time, however, markets also undermined the rationing system. They were intimately connected to thievery, providing a space in which small-scale thieves and pilferers as well as large-scale scammers and embezzlers could find buyers for purloined products. Clerks who short-weighted bread rations, party officials who appropriated food stocks or consumer items, and cooks who diverted food from factory canteens were all responsible for increasing shortage and hunger. Illegal gain for an individual was a direct loss to those members of the collective who abided by the system. Food theft was ubiquitous. In a vicious circle, shortage bred theft as inevitably and reliably as theft created shortage. In an attempt to stop the thievery of food, the Commissariat of Trade created inspector-controllers in June 1942 to supervise stores and sales.[99] Six months later a system of direct and democratic control was established in the factories through the unions. On January 22, 1943, the GKO decreed

---

98. V. S. Pushkaraev, "Razvitie 'chernogo rynke' v period Velikoi Otechestvennoi voiny i ego vliianie na sostoianie vnutrennego rynka strany," in Kozlov, et al., eds., *Edinstvo fronta i tyla v Velikoi Otechestvennoi voine, 1941–1945,* p. 190.

99. RGAE, f. 7971, op. 5, d. 58, ll. 1–2.

Not by Bread Alone

that the unions would oversee the ORSy. Commissions for Workers' Provisioning (Kommissii po Rabochemu Snabzheniiu) were to be elected directly by the workers to ensure that no food was wasted or stolen. Over 600,000 controllers were elected to check the canteens, stalls, stores, and subsidiary farms associated with their factories.[100] The VTsSPS instructed the chairmen of the unions' central, provincial, and factory committees that they would be held personally responsible for ensuring honest distribution of food. Over the course of the war, both managers and union officials assumed an ever greater role in provisioning. Union officials virtually lived in the factories, eating in the canteens and sleeping in the shops.[101]

THE INTRA-STATE STRUGGLE OVER FOOD

The state was so deeply involved in food provisioning that much of the struggle over food stocks occurred among its own organizations. Officials in central state and party organizations, including Sovnarkom, the Central Committee, the GKO, Gosplan, industrial commissariats, the VTsSPS, unions, and the Commissariat of Trade all participated in allocating, procuring, and disputing food stocks on behalf of their various constituencies.[102] Officials at the highest levels fielded a steady stream of appeals to resolve disputes. Letters of complaint, investigative reports, pleas, orders, and requisitions flew from one organization to another, all demanding the same thing: food for starving people. Despite the state's effort to establish a rationing system with clear geographic, occupational, and social categories, the careful plans provided a deceptive sense of order. In reality, chronic shortages made mockery of the plans and prompted fierce struggles among officials. The introduction of supplementary local stocks, especially subsidiary farms and decentralized purchasing, only intensified the organizational struggle over food. Competition for local

100. Cherniavskii, *Voina i prodovol'stvie*, pp. 111–119.
101. Sokolov, "Sotsial'no-trudovye otnosheniia na sovetskikh predpriiatiiakh v gody voiny," p. 95.
102. In chapter 3, Alexis Peri provides an example of this phenomenon in Leningrad when Elizaveta Sokolova, the head of the Institute of Party History, struggled to have herself and her staff transferred to the highest ration category.

resources provoked fights among central and local organizations, branches of the Commissariat of Trade, and local enterprises.

The Commissariat of Trade (USSR) distributed food from central state stocks to the republic Commissariats of Trade, which sent it to their respective provincial and town trade departments, which in turn provisioned the industrial enterprises and institutions in their areas. The food was distributed according to plans broken down by product, tonnage, and population group. In this sense, food distribution did not differ greatly from that of raw materials, fuel, or other resources needed for production. Local trade organizations also purchased additional decentralized stocks and developed detailed monthly food plans (*gorpishchtorg plany*) based on both centralized and decentralized stocks. These plans, however, were often more aspirational than real. Actual deliveries from both central and local stocks frequently fell short of the plan, and more importantly, of the minimum required to feed the population.

The Commissariat of Trade, the organization at the epicenter of food distribution, was itself beset by shortages at every level of its vast organizational pyramid. In the spring of 1942, the Commissariat of Trade (USSR), sent strict instructions to the Commissariat of Trade (Tatariia) to improve feeding of various social groups within the republic, and specifically, in the city of Kazan'. Yet the republic never received its full allocation of stocks. In March, the Commissariat of Trade (Tatariia) received so little of the meat and fish allocated by plan that none of the canteens in Kazan' received *any* deliveries.[103] In May, republic officials sent 240 tons of grain and flour to the city's trade department, but in June, they sent only 53.5 tons, a mere fraction of what was needed. Moreover, the food was delivered directly to factories, orphanages, and schools, leaving almost no food available to those outside these closed-network institutions. Kazan''s trade department struggled to make up the gap by buying produce from the surrounding collective farms but was hampered by a lack of transport. Trade officials did manage to organize four stores to provision children under the age of three, and to provide milk, semolina and white bread to daycare centers and orphanages. As in many areas, Commissariat of Trade officials were forced to make painful choices about

103. GARF, f. 5451, op. 43, d. 199, l. 102.

Not by Bread Alone

which needy group would receive priority over others. The evacuees, for example, suffered terribly. Tatariia's Commissar of Trade noted, "The canteens of the evacuated shipbuilding plants, scientific institute, and various other industrial enterprises that are provisioned at the expense of republic stocks serve only a single course of extremely low quality." This course consisted of one bowl of noodle soup a day. The Union of Shipbuilding Workers strongly protested conditions to the VTsSPS, which wrote in turn to Liubimov, Commissar of Trade (USSR), who contacted the Commissar of Trade (Tatariia). The chain of complaints ultimately produced an investigation that resulted in the release of additional food from central state stocks.[104] While such protest letters from the localities were common, relief of painful conditions depended, more often than not, on the intercession of powerful officials representing a defined constituency.

Officials sometimes seemed to be in the business of distributing hunger rather than food. The more than one thousand shipbuilders evacuated from Leningrad to Factory No. 402 in Molotovsk, a port city in Arhkangel'sk province, fared even worse than the group evacuated to Kazan'. Leaving Leningrad in a weakened state, their condition steadily worsened. Central stocks of potatoes and vegetables were inadequate, and provincial officials had little supplementary food available in a province specializing in timber, fishing, canning, and shipbuilding rather than agriculture. The factory received land for a subsidiary farm in April 1942, but the soil was poor and the climate harsh; workers planted little, and the harvest was small. Union and industrial leaders interceded repeatedly, pressuring higher officials to authorize the release of food. In October 1942, I. Nosenko, the Commissar of the Shipbuilding Industry, and Shvernik, the head of the VTsSPS, pleaded with A. I. Mikoian, the head of Sovnarkom, to take 2,450 tons of potatoes and vegetables from two adjoining provinces and deliver it to the factory. The losses for the population in these provinces would be a gain for the shipbuilders, but the request was not granted. More than one month later, in November, Sovnarkom finally ordered the Commissariat of Trade to take a small portion of the original request—20 tons of onions and garlic—from an adjoining province and deliver it to Factory No. 402. The amount that was transferred

104. GARF, f. 5451, op. 43, d. 199, ll. 102, 46, 49–48.

was only a fraction of the 2,450 tons of food originally requested, but officials were unable to offer more. In December, a party organizer from the Central Committee wrote to Shvernik again about the failing health of the workers and their families. Apparently, the transfer of onions and garlic had not helped much. Between October and December, scurvy among the workers had increased more than threefold, from 264 to 911 cases, and dystrophy more than tenfold, from 154 to 1,560 cases. The vast majority of workers were now suffering from both. The party organizer begged Shvernik to intercede again and to instruct the Commissariat of Trade to take no less than 1,600 tons of potatoes and vegetables from the other provinces. Local officials continued to squabble over who should feed the workers and their children, but none had any provisions at hand. The secretary of the provincial party committee explained that the province's stocks of cabbage, mushrooms, and berries had already been distributed, and officials had to close the supplemental food programs and the special inpatient units (*statsionary*) set up to nourish starving workers.[105]

Provincial and town trade departments everywhere were short of food, unable to supply even the defense factories with their full allotments. Molotov, a port city on the Kama River in the western Urals, was a center for the production of chemicals, ammunition, and armaments. Many of its factories, 124 in total, had been evacuated from the occupied territories, and were now crammed into buildings and grounds of already-existing factories in the town or the surrounding province.[106] The head of Molotov's trade department explained that the stocks supplied by the Commissariat of Trade covered only 32 percent of the province's demand; the remainder had to come from other sources. Yet other sources failed to materialize, and the canteens could barely feed their workers. Sovnarkom instructed the Commissariat of the Fishing Industry (NKRybProm) to deliver fish to the province, but the deliveries never arrived. Of the plan for decentralized stocks, the town trade department only managed to procure 64 percent for meat, 26 percent for fish, and 3 percent for milk

---

105. GARF, f. 5451, op. 43, d. 236, ll. 9–11.

106. "Velikaia Otechestvennaia voina i promyshlennoe razvitie zapadnogo Urala," *Entsiklopediia Permskoi Oblasti,* http://ru.wikipedia.org/wiki/Пермь

Not by Bread Alone

and dairy products.[107] Officials in the town trade department and factories were desperate: neither central nor local sources were sufficient to feed Molotov's workers and inhabitants.

Constant shortage bred conflict. Local organizations, struggling to help their constituencies, advanced contending claims for local stocks. In Omsk, for example, the provincial trade department brokered contracts with a meat processor, buttery (Rosmaslo), and fishery (Rybtrust) to provide additional food to a large factory. Yet all three food processors failed to meet their planned deliveries. The main obstacle was lack of transport.[108] Bureaucratic confusion reigned. According to orders from the Omsk provincial trade department, the Omsk tobacco trust (Glavtabak) was supposed to supply tobacco to one local factory, but instead shipped its stocks to others in Alma-Ata, Frunze, and Tashkent.[109] Regional and town food enterprises did not know where or to whom to deliver their food, and various organizations squabbled bitterly over every shipment.

Officials responsible for requisitioning food for central stocks fought with local officials responsible for feeding workers. In March 1942, Omsk provincial party and soviet executive committee officials announced that they would set up collective farm markets. Union organizers in Factory No. 20 promptly collected packing materials and one million rubles from the workers. Purchasers from the factory fanned out through the markets to buy meat, butter, cottage cheese, potatoes, grain, flour, and wheat. But when they tried to take the food they had bought, the district branch of the Commissariat of State Purchasing (NKZag), which bought food on behalf of the state, refused to allow them to leave. They claimed that the collective farms had failed to meet their delivery quotas, and therefore, the factory purchasers bought food that rightfully belonged to the state. The factory director and the district officials, arriving at an impasse, each appealed to higher authorities in Moscow. Meanwhile, the object of their furious squabble began to spoil. Officials from the Commissariat of State Purchasing then announced that the factory's purchasing agents could

---

107. GARF, f. 5451, op. 43, d. 199, ll. 560b.–57.

108. GARF, f. 5451, op. 43, d. 199, ll. 22–21, 95. See Moskoff, *The Bread of Affliction*, pp. 72–75, on the shortage of tractors and tractor parts.

109. GARF, f. 5451, op. 43, d. 199, ll. 96–95.

take the ruined produce, but threatened arrest if they removed the grain. After receiving appeals from the factory's director, the union's factory committee, and the provincial party committee, VTsSPS officials in Moscow remanded the problem to the provincial soviet executive committee. In the meantime, the workers discovered they had spent their hardearned wages on spoiled meat and milk.[110]

A similar tussle between central and local organizations occurred when the GKO attempted to supplement decentralized stocks in Saratov by transferring rafts from the Commissariat of the Fishing Industry to the provincial trade organization. Fishing and trade officials were soon locked in a tug of war over the rafts. Trade officials maintained that they needed the rafts to feed workers in the defense factories. The Commissar of the Fishing Industry appealed directly to Mikoian, the head of Sovnarkom, claiming that loss of the rafts would reduce the fish harvest on the Caspian Sea. He asked Mikoian to intercede with the GKO. Central and local officials collided, involving the state at the highest level.[111] Other GKO orders provoked similar fights. When the GKO attached a large state farm piggery to Aviation Factory No. 29 in Omsk, the Commissariat of the Aviation Industry (NKAviaProm) claimed that the piggery had already been attached to Construction Trust No. 2 and Aviation Factory No. 166. An investigator for the VTsSPS contended that the workers in Factory No. 29 had a greater need for the food because they received only one low-calorie meal a day in their canteen. The piggery, in his view, should not be divided among three different organizations.[112] As in most of these disputes, no one group had a greater moral claim on food than any other. Everyone was hungry, and allocation to one group simply meant less for another.

Local officials not only fought for food for their constituencies, they also sought to offload responsibility for feeding dependents, evacuees, orphans, invalids, and disabled workers. Officials often considered these groups a burden because it was unclear which food stocks should be used to provision them. For instance, the director of a clinic (*profilaktoria*) for

110. GARF, f. 5451, op. 43, d. 199, ll. 105–104.
111. RGASPI, f. 17, op. 122, d. 18, l. 2.
112. GARF, f. 5451, op. 43, d. 199, ll. 23–22.

Not by Bread Alone　　　　　　　　　　　　　　　　　　　　　　91

sick and poisoned workers from chemical Factory No. 102 in Chapaevsk fought with the local trade department when it stopped sending food. The latter claimed that the factory's ORS was responsible for the clinic, but the ORS maintained that it never received central state allocations for this purpose. The dispute eventually reached the Union of Workers in the Nitrogen and Special Chemical Industry, which appealed to the VTsSPS, which ended the dispute with an order to the Commissariat of Trade to provide food.[113] Various organizations maintained complex accounting relationships with each other. Continuing disputes over sickened workers in the nitrogen, ammunition, and special chemical factories eventually reached Sovnarkom, which ordered their respective unions to establish *profilaktory* to treat them. The Commissariat of Trade was ordered to provide the food, but the VTsSPS was ordered to pay for it.[114]

The state thus remained involved in food provisioning at every level. Indeed, the entire system was predicated on state-created categories, encompassing constituencies who were represented and defended by state organizations. When officials from one local soviet distributed ration cards to municipal employees, teachers, evacuees, and others entitling them to eat in factory canteens, union officials sought to have the additional diners removed. A VTsSPS investigation revealed that over one thousand people who did not work in Molotov's Aviation Factory No. 19, including employees of the district industrial trust, militia, polyclinic, and shoe workshop, regularly ate in the factory's canteen although the trade department did not allocate extra food for them. The kitchen staff watered down the soup and cut portion size, and the workers received less. The VTsSPS and the unions protested against the use of factory stocks to feed outsiders. One investigator wrote, "We demand an immediate end to handing out dinners to these enterprises and institutions at the expense of the factory's stocks."[115] In Chapaevsk, two groups of party officials, one serving on the union's factory committee and the other on the party city committee, were at loggerheads over the factory's food stocks. A large number of workers in ammunition factory No. 15

113. GARF, f. 5451, op. 43, d. 199, ll. 30–31.
114. GARF, f. 5451, op. 43, d. 132, ll. 96, 99.
115. GARF, f. 5451, op. 43, d. 199, l. 56.

were evicted from their canteen to make room for 450 officials from the Commissariat of the Textile Industry (NKTekhstil) and their families, 150 officials from municipal organizations, and 35 members of an evacuated Moscow operetta ensemble. The union factory committee repeatedly protested the situation, but the party city committee overruled its complaints.[116] The factory committee, responsible for the workers, attempted to protect their interests, and the city committee, responsible for all urban dwellers, sought to feed as many groups as possible at the factory's expense.

Paradoxically, the shift to decentralized purchasing and collective farm markets did not reduce the role of central state institutions but increased it. Every organization had mouths to feed and plans to meet. Shortage was ubiquitous, and officials argued heatedly over access to every potential and actual source of food. Individuals were provisioned according to categories, and problems with provisioning were rectified not by individuals but by state organizations that represented the aggrieved constituency. The VTsSPS launched numerous investigations in the industrial enterprises, and the unions fought aggressively on behalf of their members. Individual workers would have fared far worse without the VTsSPS and unions that intervened on their behalf. Food distribution and the redress of grievances were both determined within, not outside, the state's system of provisioning.

WAGED LABOR AND SUBSISTENCE LABOR

As the state channeled resources from every economic sector to defense, workers increasingly took on the necessary task of producing food and other essential consumer items. Local union, factory, and trade officials organized subsidiary farms, gardens, and decentralized purchasing. Factory managers diverted thousands of mobilized workers from production to the subsidiary economy to work in gardening, fishing, wood chopping, and tending livestock. Workers were used to gather fuel in the face of huge energy shortages created by the occupation of the coalfields and the voracious needs of the defense plants. Schools, hospitals, and workers'

116. GARF, f. 5451, op. 43, d. 199, ll. 79–76.

Not by Bread Alone

dormitories were barely heated. People sent thousands of complaints, pleading for bread, water, light, and heat. In 1942, crippling shortages of electricity resulted in shutdowns of water-pumping stations, bakeries, baths, and laundries in Kirov. The electric power stations in Saratov province were also in crisis, having exhausted their fuel reserves, and some factories were forced to limit production or shut down entirely. The province was desperately short of wood, with only 340,600 cubic meters in place of the 2.365 million required. Workers were organized into groups and sent to the forest.[117] The economy was so strained to meet the needs of the army that sectors producing the most basic elements of subsistence— heat, water, food, light—began to collapse. Workers in the factories increasingly began to produce the items they needed for subsistence.

The line between agricultural, handicraft, and industrial work collapsed as workers began farming, fishing, producing small consumer items, chopping wood, and tending livestock. They received wages for some of these activities; others were voluntary. The blurring of work lines played havoc with nationwide pay scales that were built on differences among the sectors of industry, construction, fuel, timber, and agriculture. Industrial workers, for example, who gathered peat for fuel were paid at 2.03 rubles per cubic meter; state farm workers at 1.10. There were similar differences in the wage for planting potatoes, and other agricultural jobs.[118] Workers in sectors at the lower end of the wage scale complained when they found themselves working alongside others who did the same work but received higher pay. Yet wage discrepancies were only one symptom of a larger change in the economy as industrial workers took on the full panoply of jobs required for subsistence.

The experience of the Kuzbass miners, who mined the coal that powered industrial production, reflected this economic shift. In November 1942, Sovnarkom developed a plan according to which the miners would buy 10,000 calves, 20,000 heifers, and 30,000 suckling pigs for their personal use from state farms in Novosibirsk and Omsk provinces and the Altai region (*krai*). The state farms would divert part of their animal stock from sales to the state to the workers, who would purchase the livestock

---

117. RGASPI, f. 17, op. 122, d. 19, ll. 109, 110, 112, 2–3.
118. GARF, f. 5451, op. 43, d. 199, l. 64.

collectively at the regular state purchase price spread over the course of a year. The Commissariat of Agriculture (NKZem) would also sell the miners for their personal use 150,000 chicks from a local incubator station. The soviet's provincial executive committee would distribute land parcels of 0.15 hectares (about one-half acre) from unused town and collective farm lands for individual gardens. Miners would also build their own houses. In 1943, Sovnarkom ordered the provincial executive committee and the Kuznetsk Coal Trust to supervise miners in constructing 10,000 houses for their personal use. Construction materials would be provided by the state according to set plans. Newly established construction offices would help with design, and subsidiary enterprises would produce the necessary construction materials. The Kuzbass Coal Trust was charged with procuring timber from the Kuzbass Timber Trust (Kuzbasles). Gosplan was to provide 50,000 cubic meters of window glass, 100 tons of nails, and 50 tons of drying oil. Additional glass would be provided by industrial cooperatives (*promkooperatsii*).[119] These central decrees transformed miners into cattle ranchers, chicken farmers, gardeners, and builders, and put the Kuzbass coal trust into the home construction business. The expectation, of course, was that miners' wives would provide the unpaid subsistence labor in all these endeavors. The miners and their families became independent proprietors of a house and small farm, based on stock and materials provided by the state. Part of a larger strategy to supplement provisions and improve conditions, this innovative mix of central directives, state and local allocations, and the unwaged labor of miners' wives and families was central to state policy.

In a larger sense, the wartime economy increasingly embodied a paradox: production became more specialized, but labor became less differentiated. State resources were focused almost entirely on defense production, but workers, in addition to their waged work for defense, assumed a full array of waged and unwaged subsidiary tasks. As the various branches of the consumer economy shut down, basic subsistence required workers to grow their own food, procure fuel, produce shoes, clothing, and utensils, raise poultry and livestock, and even build their own dwellings. The line between agriculture and industry, between consumption and pro-

119. RGASPI, f. 17, op. 122, d. 19, ll. 70–72.

Not by Bread Alone 95

duction, so pronounced in advanced industrial societies, began to dissolve. Barter replaced money in basic exchange between peasant and worker, and the simplest and most primitive economic relationships supported the mighty industrial economy that eventually out produced the German war machine.

CONCLUSION

Many historians of the war suggest that the victory over Fascism belonged to "the people," not to the Soviet state or the Communist Party. According to this view, the war was won by individuals, who united independently and spontaneously to drive out the invader. Inspired by national feelings, they fought neither for socialism nor for Soviet power but for an ancient idea of Mother Russia. Indeed, the people triumphed despite the Soviet state. William Moskoff expressed this view in his summary of provisioning, writing "Civilians were fed not because of the system but in spite of it."[120] The state, however, was not an abstraction, but rather, concretely embodied in the Party, the GKO, the VTsSPS, soviets, unions, the Commissariat of Trade, industrial commissariats, and other organizations. The evidence presented here shows that these organizations were essential to the provisioning of food on the home front. The very system of provisioning, from central to local stocks, cannot be understood apart from the state. Under conditions of terrible shortage and strain, workers could not have survived and produced the armaments necessary for victory without the state's considerable organizational experience. Indeed, the efforts of "the people" cannot be divorced or divided from those of the state. The history of provisioning cannot be read as a struggle of lone individuals to forage, pillage, or secure their own bunkers. Rather, it should be understood as a history of people organized within powerful state institutions that procured, provided, and defended the interests of their respective constituencies. State strategy, built on a combination of central and local provisioning, collective and individual efforts, and rations and free markets allowed workers and peasants to participate fully in the struggle against Fascism. Isolated, atomized

---

120. Moskoff, *The Bread of Affliction*, p. 238.

individuals could never have survived the extreme privations of the war-time economy.

Food policy was, however, limited in its success. The material conditions of warfare and occupation, including the loss of prime farmland, labor, draught animals, and machinery and the addition of millions of uprooted people in need of food, ensured that hunger and starvation were unavoidable. A considerable gap between planned allocations and actual deliveries existed. The state was unable to provision the enterprises and the towns even according to its own established norms. The Soviet economy was stretched to the breaking point. The lines between agriculture and industry, between home and work, collapsed. Increasing numbers of workers ate, washed, mended clothes and shoes, and fashioned basic utensils at work. In the war's darkest days, with no fuel to heat or light the dormitories and houses, workers slept in the shops. For many, evacuation and labor mobilization reduced "home" to a bare barrack or dug-out, and home life in turn colonized the factory. Trade networks, too, became more primitive as workers began growing their own food and making consumer items for trade with peasants. Union, party, and state officials attempted to remedy the most pressing shortages, but they often did little more than redistribute hunger.

During the early years of the war, the crisis of subsistence even threatened to undermine defense production. In December 1942, officials protested the lack of food and cloth for workers in Irkutsk. The factories failed to receive tons of allocated meat, fish, and fats from the Commissariat of Trade's centralized stocks. Yet as Liubimov, Commissar of Trade, pointed out in his response, central stocks were based on deliveries from other enterprises, and the textile and food commissariats had failed to meet their planned deliveries to the Commissariat of Trade.[121] The reason was simple. Textile and food workers, who were also starving, poorly clad, and cold, were unable to meet their own production programs. They were too weak to produce enough to clothe and feed Red Army soldiers *and* workers in Irkutsk. Labor was not infinitely elastic. Workers could not produce for defense, fashion consumer items in workshops, walk to and from the factories, garden, fish, and gather fuel on bread and gruel

121. RGASPI, f. 17, op. 122, d. 19, l. 125.

Not by Bread Alone

alone. In the final analysis, the breaking point of the economy was set by the collective energy of the workers. This energy, determined in part by caloric intake and in part by sheer will, proved sufficient to achieve victory. But the human cost was very great.

Under conditions that might have created mass political unrest and upheaval, the state marshaled its existing resources and fed its people. Relying on its extensive organizational experience, it rapidly converted the Commissariat of Trade's network of retail trade stores to ration distribution centers. It organized the ORSy to link the Commissariat of Trade directly to the factories. It relied on public catering, developed in the 1930s, to feed workers and other groups. Local soviet and union officials, factory directors, and ORS activists established piggeries and gardens, dispensed seed, advised on planting, and organized wood-chopping expeditions, fishing brigades, and workshops. Union activists and party officials exposed poor conditions and mismanagement, and fought for emergency food shipments to starving workers, children, and dependents. Without the participation of workers and peasants, these party and state initiatives would have been little more than paper proclamations, but without the organizational initiative of the state, people would not have been able to contribute so fully to the war effort. In the grimmest years of the war, starvation threatened production. Yet at no time were workers abandoned by the state to a "free" market in which the most aggressive profit seekers triumphed over the most vulnerable. The great victory of the war belonged to "the people," but it was realized through the state's vast array of creative organizational efforts that enabled individuals to convert their energies into collective action.

TWO

THE STATE'S POT AND THE SOLDIER'S SPOON: RATIONS (*PAËK*) IN THE RED ARMY

Brandon Schechter

Without a spoon, just as without a rifle, it is impossible to wage war.

Aleksandr Lesin, diary entry, March 29, 1942[1]

THE SOLDIER WHO WROTE THE LINES ABOVE CAME TO UNDER-stand all too well how important being fed was to being able to fight. Aleksandr Lesin served on the benighted Kalinin Front. In the spring of 1942, he participated in an offensive that bogged down as starving and exhausted soldiers failed to take their objectives.[2] The Kalinin Front eventually became a lightning rod for attracting Moscow's attention to the needs of soldiers' stomachs.

On May 31, 1943, Stalin signed an order underlining the failure of the rear area services of the Kalinin Front to properly feed its troops. Among a list of complaints, ranging from unequal distribution, improper storage, and failures to provide hot food or use qualified cadres to prepare and apportion rations, Stalin described the essence of the "criminally irresponsible, un-Soviet attitude towards soldier's food"[3] found among those responsible for feeding the army:

1. Aleksandr Lesin, *Byla voina: Kniga-dnevnik* (Simferopol': Tavriia, 1990), p. 76.
2. Ibid., p. 146.
3. TsAMO RF, f. 2, op. 795437, d. 11, ll. 546–549, in P. I. Veshchikov et al., ed., *Tyl Krasnoi Armii v Velikoi Otechestvennoi voine 1941–1945 gg.: Dokumenty i materialy. Russkii arkhiv: Velikia Otechestvennaia,* vol. 25 (14), (Moscow: Terra, 1998), pp. 401–405, p. 402. (Note: Here, as further on, citations of printed archival sources are presented as per the printed collection from which they are drawn.)

98

> Apparently our commanders have forgotten the best traditions of the Russian Army, of such eminent commanders as Suvorov and Kutuzov. They taught the commanders of all of Europe and the commanders of the Red Army should learn from them. They demonstrated fatherly care about the everyday life and rations of soldiers and demanded the same from their subordinates. Meanwhile, in the Red Army, as is obvious from the given facts, one can find commanders who do not believe that concern for the everyday life and rations of rank and file soldiers is their sacred duty, demonstrating therefore an un-comradely and unacceptable relationship to fighting men.[4]

Stalin drew on national and revolutionary traditions to shame officers into fulfilling their duties: feeding one's soldiers poorly was not only un-Soviet but also un-Russian.[5] Soldiers took their officers' failure to fulfill "the sacred duty" of demonstrating their "concern for everyday life and rations" to heart. Red Army men had been assured that the state was capable of providing for them and that failures to do so were the fault of those deputized by the regime under conditions of state monopoly. But failure was everywhere.

"The Kalinin Front is not an exception," Stalin noted; "similar conditions occur on other fronts." Stalin's order was distributed to all fronts as a warning, to be read even by battalion commanders.[6] Alongside highlighting failure and prescribing punishments, the document provided extensive corrective prescriptions, reinforcing and setting norms that would remain fundamental until the war's end. This document, as Stalin's word, marked the culmination of a flurry of similar inspections in 1942–1943. It reflected and constructed Soviet norms

---

4. TsAMO RF, f. 2, op. 795437, d. 11, ll. 546–549, Veshchikov et al., *Tyl Krasnoi Armii v Velikoi Otechestvennoi voine 1941–1945 gg.*, p. 403.

5. The shift to Russianness was a significant development of the prewar period that intensified during the war. See David Brandenberger, *National Bolshevism: Stalinist Mass Culture and the Formation of Modern Russian National Identity, 1931–1956* (Cambridge, Mass.: Harvard University Press, 2002).

6. TsAMO RF, f. 2, op. 795437, d. 11, ll. 546–549, Veshchikov et al., *Tyl Krasnoi Armii v Velikoi Otechestvennoi voine 1941–1945 gg.*, p. 405. This order is also mentioned in memoirs by provisioning officers and histories of the war. See F. S. Saushin, *Khleb i sol'* (Iaroslavl': Verkhne-Volzhskoe knizhnoe izdatel'stvo, 1983), p. 56; Anastas Mikoyan, *Tak bylo: Razmyshleniia o minuvshem* (Moscow: Vagrius, 1999), p. 431; S. K. Kurkotkin, *Tyl sovetskikh vooruzhennykh sil v Velikoi Otechestvennoi voine 1941–1945 gg.* (Moscow: Voenizdat, 1977), pp. 202–203.

and expectations of nourishment in the hour of the Soviet Union's greatest challenge—a total war that called on citizens to make great sacrifices.[7]

The ability to provide for the people was an essential claim made by the socialist state, and by 1943, the state was finally in a position to deliver for the army.[8] In the first years of the war, the Soviet Union lost its bread basket, making food all the more central to victory or defeat. Under these conditions, the state's dedication to provide was reaffirmed to *soldiers,* who were promised ample provisions in return for their service to the state.[9] This ideological commitment and the very real consequences of fighting a war on an empty stomach made breakdowns in provisioning deeply disturbing, which in turn forced the state to reaffirm its role as provider.

This chapter will examine the quotidian details of provisioning, which bound Red Army soldiers to the state on the fronts of the Great Patriotic War. It was difficult to imagine such a key resource as food outside of the horizontal bonds between citizens and the vertical relationship to the state. The very term used for rations, *paëk,* implied mutual obligations. Paëk could be seen as the physical embodiment of the socialist adage "to each according to his work," as its etymological root implied an earned share in a common cause.[10] We will see how rations were constructed by the state and later received and used by soldiers at the front—that is,

---

7. TsAMO RF, f.2, op. 795437, d. 9, l. 696, in Veshchikov et al., *Tyl Krasnoi armii v Velikoi Otechestvennoi voine 1941–1945 gg.,* pp. 291–292; TsAMO RF, f.2, op. 795437, d. 11, ll. 66–68, in ibid., pp. 306–308; TsAMO RF, f. 47, op. 1029, d. 83, ll. 53–55, in ibid., pp. 321–325; TsAMO RF, f. 2, op. 795437, d. 11, ll. 293–295; TsAMO RF, f. 47, op. 1029, d. 84, ll. 23–24, in ibid., pp. 380–382.

8. As Donald Filtzer's chapter shows, however, the effect of these resources on civilian health often came too little, too late.

9. This was cemented by published norms in both field manuals and pamphlets and by the soldier's swearing of an oath to the state. See, for example, *Rukhovodstvo dlia boitsa pekhoty* (Moscow: Voenizdat, 1940), pp. 44–45.

10. *1936 Constitution of the USSR,* http://www.departments.bucknell.edu/russian /const/36conso1.html. Chapter 1, Article 12 states: "In the U.S.S.R. work is a duty and a matter of honor for every able-bodied citizen, in accordance with the principle: 'He who does not work, neither shall he eat.' The principle applied in the U.S.S.R. is that of socialism: 'From each according to his ability, to each according to his work.'"

The State's Pot and the Soldier's Spoon

how paëk functioned, was experienced, and occasionally transformed by those in the trenches.[11]

This work is divided into three sections: the first two tell the story of providing, the last focuses on using and consuming. The first section, "The State Provides," describes how the government thought of rationing, where it drew its resources, and what it sought to provide. The second, "An Inviolable Camp," deals with failures in the provisioning system and examines how standards improved as the war continued. The

---

11. A note on historiography: In English language historiography, provisioning often receives treatment in larger works on the Red Army more generally, particularly in the works of military historians interested in combat effectiveness and military science. Colonel David Glantz provides a brief, but very good soldiers' eye view of provisioning. See David M. Glantz, *Colossus Reborn: The Red Army at War, 1941–1945* (Lawrence: University of Kansas Press, 2005), pp. 555–560. William Moskoff's *The Bread of Affliction* is a pioneering overview, but was written before many of the relevant primary sources became available. See William Moskoff, *The Bread of Affliction: The Food Supply in the* USSR *During World War II* (New York: Cambridge University Press, 1990). Nicholas Ganson's contribution to David Stone's *The Soviet Union at War* provides a concise overview of the provisioning situation in the country and makes many astute observations, particularly on ways in which the state often waited until situations became disastrous before getting directly involved in provisioning. See Nicholas Ganson, "Food Supply, Rationing and Living Standards," in David R. Stone, ed., *The Soviet Union at War, 1941–1945* (Barnsley, U.K.: Pen & Sword, 2010), pp. 69–92. Lizzie Collingham's thorough treatment of food during the war provides an excellent global context and fair overview of the situation in the Soviet Union, although her discussion is hampered by the limited availability of non-Russian source material. Her volume is undoubtedly the most broad-based on the subject of food in the Second World War and an indispensable comparative study. See Lizzie Collingham, "Fighting on Empty," in *The Taste of War: World War Two and the Battle for Food* (New York: Penguin, 2012), pp. 317–346. Soviet historiography on the subject tended to be written by participants with an eye for improving provisioning in the future, often taking the form of memoirs. Some of this work is triumphalist, but a great deal of it is quite revealing and surprisingly frank (see Saushin, Antipenko, and others cited below). However, these authors are not consciously concerned with the cultural dimensions of eating in the army and the transformations taking place in society during the war. Both these and later authors are generally more interested in operational art or simple narrative than a cultural history of food. A major exception to this trend is war veteran and food historian Vil'iam Pokhlebkin, who was keenly interested in how the war impacted Soviet culinary culture and whose work has inspired my own. This chapter brings into sharper focus the rhetorical and political meaning of rations and the details of everyday life. What follows is an attempt to write a cultural history of rations in the Red Army rich in ethnographic detail.

third, "Pots and Spoons," describes what soldiers did with their rations and how they responded to failures.

Rations were a key resource in setting the army apart as a separate class of citizens and in creating clear hierarchies within the army; they both brought together and divided those in the ranks. As the best-fed mass institution during the war, the army is key to understanding Soviet provisioning between 1941 and 1945. It was, after all, for the army's sake that civilians were being provided with so little.

THE STATE PROVIDES: WHAT AND HOW

The importance of food to state legitimacy and survival was nothing new. The Bolsheviks, like their French predecessors, came to power during a revolution that started as a bread riot, and struggle for control over food production and the ability to provide were key to the state's claims of legitimacy.[12] Collectivization and the hardships it entailed had been justified by the looming shadow of another world war.[13] After the collectivization-induced famine, the party-state emphasized the creation of a consumer society and established new hierarchies of consumption.[14] This shift in focus from sufficiency to variety was repeated during the Great Patriotic War.

In 1941–1942, the Soviet Union lost vast resources to the rapacious Wehrmacht. Even by 1945, after the war had shifted to enemy territory,

12. The year 1913 was used because it was the last year before the devastation of the Great War and Civil War, and as such served as a "control group" for pre-Bolshevik economics, the measure by which success or failure was calibrated. See, for example, V. P. Zotov, *Pishchevaia promyshlennost'* (Moscow: Pishchevaia promyshlennost', 1967).

13. I. V. Stalin, "O zadachakh khoziaistvennikov," *Socheneniie*, vol. 13 (Moscow: Gosudarstvennoe Izdatel'stvo Politicheskoi Literatury, 1952), pp. 30–31, 38–40. In this February 1931 speech, Stalin asked: "Do you want our socialist homeland to be beaten and lose its independence? If you don't want this, you should liquidate its backwardness in the shortest time and develop a real Bolshevik tempo in the building of its socialist economy" (p. 39). E. A. Osokina, *Za fasadom "stalinskogo izobilia": Raspredelenie i rynok v snabzhenii v gody ndustrializatsii, 1927–1941* (Moscow: ROSSPEN, 1998), pp. 226–227.

14. See, for example, Jukka Gronow, *Caviar with Champagne: Common Luxury and the Ideals of the Good Life in Stalin's Russia* (New York: Berg, 2003); Osokina, *Za fasadom "Stalinskogo izobiliia,"* p. 173.

The State's Pot and the Soldier's Spoon

the gross production of Soviet food industry stood at half of the level of 1940.[15] When Stalin issued his famous "Not One Step Backward" order in the summer of 1942, he pointed out that if the army retreated any farther, it would be dooming itself to starvation:

> The territory of the USSR, which the enemy has seized and strives to seize, is bread and other foodstuffs for the army and rear, metal and fuel for industry, factories and plants, supplying the army with weapons and ammunition, rail roads. After the loss of Ukraine, Belorussia, the Baltics, Donbas and other regions we have a lot less territory, and therefore we have a lot less bread and metal and fewer people, factories, and plants. We have lost over 70 million people, more than 800 million poods of grain a year and more than 10 million tons of metal per year. We are no longer superior to the Germans in manpower or grain reserves. To retreat any further is to ruin yourself and to destroy our Motherland. Every new scrap of land we leave to the enemy will in every way possible strengthen the enemy and in every way possible weaken our defense and our Motherland.[16]

Food was a resource that could mean the difference between victory and defeat, one that would strengthen one side or the other in a zero-sum equation. As a result, both sides would be waging a campaign of scorched earth whenever they were forced to retreat, lessening the resources left not only to their enemies, but also to civilians caught between the two armies.[17] Forced to wage war regardless of a catastrophic loss of material, Soviet leaders strived to establish total control over food distribution

15. Zotov, *Pishchevaia promyshlennost'*, pp. 24–25.

16. RGVA, f. 4, op. 11, d. 72, l. 270, in A.I. Barsukov et al., *Prikazy narodnogo komissara oborony SSSR 1941–1942 g. Russkii arkhiv: Velikaia Otechestvennaia.* vol. 13 (2-2) (Moscow: Terra, 1997), p. 277. Note that 1 *pood* = 16 kilograms, so Stalin is talking about the loss of 12.8 million metric tons of grain.

17. An order that Stalin gave to the Soviet people in his first address of the war (July 3, 1941) was very explicit as to the extent of the scorched earth policy: "In case of forced retreat of Red Army units, all rolling stock must be evacuated, the enemy must not be left a single engine, a single railway car, a single pound of grain or gallon of fuel. The collective farmers must drive off their cattle, and turn over their grain for safe-keeping of state authorities for transport to the rear. All valuable property, including non-ferrous metals, grain, and fuel that cannot be withdrawn must be destroyed without fail." Joseph Stalin, *The Great Patriotic War of the Soviet Union* (New York: International Publishers, 1945), p. 15. Boris Slutskii recalled that the Wehrmacht was even more obsessively destructive in their retreat, destroying almost every single fruit and vegetable in their wake. Boris Slutskii, *O drugikh i o sebe* (Moscow: Vagrius, 2005), pp. 31–32; N. N. Inozemtsev, *Frontovoi dnevnik* (Moscow: Nauka, 2005), p. 46.

under the chaotic conditions of a war it was clearly losing, as well as refining a hierarchy around what was arguably its most precious resource.

Despite these immense losses, in the course of the war the Soviets were able to provide more and more adequately for the military. In 1941, as many resources as possible were moved east, and agricultural production shifted to Central Asia and Siberia. The full-scale development of agriculture in the east, American Lend-Lease aid, as well as the recapture of resources led to palpable improvement in 1943.[18]

Locavores, Pillagers, and Boxed Lunches: Comparative Approaches to Provisioning

Alongside the shift from west to east, another shift took place in the way that civilians and soldiers were eating: provisioning became less central and more local.[19] As the war progressed, responsibility for feeding soldiers became increasingly localized. In the first months, it was typical to appeal to higher ranks and invest them with sole control over both food and transport.[20] In the first two years of the war, the authority and competencies of rear-area officers were expanded and their personal responsibility clarified.[21] While central reserves would provide necessities that

18. Zotov, *Pishchevaia promyshlennost'*, pp. 136–138. For more on Lend-Lease, see Chapter 5 in this volume.

19. Collingham, *The Taste of War*, pp. 390–393. L. P. Grachev, *Doroga ot Volkhova* (Leningrad: Lenizdat, 1983), p. 213, claims that the army provided itself with 65 percent (26 out of 40 million tons) of the foodstuffs it required in the course of the war. Of course, *podsobnoe khoziastvo* is possible only when a front remains relatively stable for a relatively long period of time; it is impossible during a retreat and very difficult to maintain while advancing. For a discussion of how this played out on the home front, see Wendy Goldman's chapter in this volume.

20. See for example Saushin, *Khleb i sol'*, p. 41; N. A. Antipenko, *Na glavnom upravlenii* (Moscow: Nauka, 1967), p. 60.

21. Antipenko, *Na glavnom upravlenii*, pp. 7–8; TsAMO RF, f. 2, op. 795437, d. 5, ll. 545–547, in Veshchiko et al., *Tyl Krasnoi Armii v Velikoi Otechestvennoi voine 1941–1945 gg.*, pp. 90–100; TsAMO RF, f. 208, op. 224922 c, d. 1, ll. 139–140, in ibid., pp. 123–124; TsAMO RF, f. 2, op. 795437, d. 4, l. 378, in ibid., pp. 173–174; TsAMO RF, f. 244, op. 3017, d. 2, ll. 20–23, in ibid., pp. 345–347; TsAMO RF, f. 2, op. 795437, d. 11, l. 370, in ibid., p. 384.

The State's Pot and the Soldier's Spoon

could not be produced locally, subsidiary agriculture (*podsobnoe khoziaistvo*) became an increasingly significant part of people's diets. Agricultural work became a common duty of men in uniform, as military units began to tend their own rear-area farms and soldiers were sent to assist local collective farms (*kolkhozy*) with sowing and harvesting.[22] Unlike their American or British allies, Red Army soldiers often had a hand in producing the rations they were eating and knew who prepared them.

Red Army personnel were, to a great extent, *locavores*, in contrast to their American and British allies and similar to their Wehrmacht foe. The United States had taken pains to develop its famous C and K Rations— prepackaged, ready-to-eat, standardized, and completely self-sufficient meals, containing everything from can opener, wooden spoon, entrée, and dessert to gum, cigarettes, matches, and toilet paper, all prominently displaying brand names.[23] The British were similar to the Americans, being primarily an expeditionary force. The Wehrmacht combined ready-to-eat items with those needing preparation, and were notorious foragers, often living off what they pillaged from Soviet peasants.[24] Indeed the Reich's very strategy called for the extermination by hunger of millions of Soviet citizens.[25] The Red Army relied heavily on whatever

22. See TsAMO RF, f. 2, op. 920266, d. 6, l. 47, in ibid., pp. 313–314; TsAMO RF, f. 2, op. 920266, d. 6, l. 405, 406, in ibid., pp. 388–389; TsAMO RF, f. 236, op. 2719, d. 76, ll. 14–15, in ibid., pp. 659–660; Lesin, *Byla voina*, p. 319; Mikoyan, *Tak bylo*, pp. 469–470; Antipenko, *Na glavnom upravlenii*, p. 117; Grachev, *Doroga ot Volkhova*, pp. 77, 208–213; U. G. Cherniavskii, *Voina i prodovolstviie: Snabzhennia gorodskogo naseleniia v Velikuiu Otechestvennuiu voinu, 1941–1945 gg.* (Moscow: Nauka, 1964), pp. 130–150. For an English-language treatment of subsidiary agriculture, see Moskoff, *The Bread of Affliction*, pp. 94–113. This was, in a sense, a return to "regimental economy," the means by which the Russian Imperial Regime attempted to make the army defray its own expenses. On regimental economy, see Elise Wirtschafter, *From Peasant to Russian Soldier* (Princeton, N.J.: Princeton University Press, 1990).

23. John Samuels, ed., *Ration Development* (Washington, D.C.: Quartermaster Food & Container Institute for the Armed Forces, 1947), pp. 24–48.

24. Collingham, *The Taste of War*, pp. 37–39, 184–187; Douglas Nash, "Tinned Meat in the German Army Iron Ration" and "German 'Iron' Rations (eiserne Portionen)," www.dererstezug.com; Eric Tobey, "The German Army K-Ration," www.dererstezug.com.

25. See Adam Tooze, *The Wages of Destruction: The Making and Breaking of the Nazi Economy* (New York: Penguin, 2006), pp. 467, 469, 476–480, 538–549.

was available locally, drawing from central reserves when local reserves failed.[26] Red Army forces planned on feeding their men whenever possible with hot, fresh food from field kitchens located not far beyond the front line. Mobile bakeries and even herds of livestock were to follow the army, providing for fresh, high quality food. American soldiers, on the other hand, quickly grew tired of quartermaster officers' overreliance on the portable C and K Rations, which became the subject of postwar inquiries, while the Wehrmacht's methods turned locals against them.[27]

The provisioning methods of the Wehrmacht and the Red Army relied on similar logic: a preference for field kitchens, the issuance of a variety of ready-to-eat items in the event that a hot meal was unfeasible, and, most significantly, the extensive use of local resources. There was, of course, a significant difference between their provisioning strategies. The Red Army, while putting the needs of soldiers ahead of civilians, did not have the strategic goal of starving the civilian population of the area from which it drew supplies.[28] The objective of the Red Army was the defense and liberation of these civilians, which meant a return to the Soviet fold for some and integration into Socialist norms for others. The Bolsheviks, for most of the war, were taking from their own citizens in an economy that perceived all resources as "the people's," and thus constituting a horizontal connection between provider and defender. This was in sharp contrast to the Nazi strategy of exploiting racial "others," most of whom were slotted for eventual extermination. Wherever they were provisioning, the Red Army showed concern for the feeding of local civilians. Nonetheless, while the logic, goals, and extent of these two armies' provisioning strategies were very different, the ways that Wehrmacht and Red Army soldiers were fed bore striking similarities.

---

26. From July 1941 on, local resources were under the control of provisioning officers of the Red Army. See TsAMO RF, f. 2, op. 920266, d. 1, l. 480, in Veshchikov et al., *Tyl Krasnoi Armii v Velikoi Otechestvennoi voine 1941–1945 gg.*, pp. 91–92; TsAMO RF, f. 208, op. 3031, d. 2, ll. 501, 502, in ibid., pp. 172–173.

27. The Quartermaster School for the Quartermaster General, "Rations Conference Notes," January 1949, U.S. Army Quartermaster Foundation, Fort Lee, Va., http://www.qmfound.com/history_of_rations.htm.

28. Collingham, *The Taste of War*, pp. 37–39.

The food they ate was often drawn from the same sources, and they could find themselves eating identical dishes. Local provisioning, a key aspect of the Soviet ration system, obscured the borders between military and civilian, as soldiers received similar foodstuffs as civilians, but generally in larger quantities and of better quality. Both combatants and wide swaths of the civilian population received rations during the war. Local provisioning also greatly diversified what soldiers actually ate at the front.

The Rationale of Rationing

The state discussed rations using two terms that effectively meant the same thing and were often used indiscriminately, but which carried with them important semantic differences that are worth parsing. These terms reveal the two major ways of perceiving rations and what was at stake in provisioning. The terms were *paëk* and *prodovol'stvennye normy;* the latter etymologically posited rations as fuel for biological machines and the former as a resource or even form of payment guaranteed to defenders of the state.

Paëk translated simply into "ration," but the etymology of the word revealed a certain moral economy of provisioning.[29] *Paëk* came from the Turkic root *pai,* which meant "share, part in a common cause, coming through mutual agreement to every individual [*paishchik*], in the paying or receiving of a monetary sum or other form of personal property."[30] The root had close associations with an individual's "part, fate, destiny and happiness," and a participant in a common enterprise such as a co-operative was often called a *paishchik.*[31] The root itself presupposed the necessity of a common cause and mutual obligations in the circulation

29. In Russian, the word *ratsion* is also used, but refers to one component of something being doled out (e.g., "your ration of whiskey"), rather than the complex of things being given.

30. P. Ia. Chernykh, *Istoriko-etimologicheskii slovar' sovremennogo russkogo iazyka,* vol. 1, (Moscow: Russkii iazyk, 1993), p. 615.

31. Preobrazhenskii, Aleksandr Grigor'evich, *Etimologicheskii slovar' russkogo iazyka,* vol. 2: P–S (Moscow: Gos. izdat. inostrannykh i natsional'nykh slovarei, 1959), p. 725. Special thanks to Milyausha Zakirova for pointing out the etymological significance of this word as I began this project.

of rations; it was not a form of welfare but part of a bargain based on who earned what.[32] Yet the term also spoke to a certain ambiguity about who owned the paёk—the state or the soldier, and whether this changed at any point in the transaction. The status of paёk remained uncertain even as the army entered Berlin.

Pai-based understandings of state-citizen relations had been key to how both the Tsarist Army in 1914 and the Bolsheviks in 1918 apportioned resources. The *paika,* a special ration issued to soldiers' families in time of war, was instituted by the tsarist government in 1912 and later adopted by the Bolsheviks during the Civil War. As Joshua Sanborn points out, this was a manifestation of the state's understanding that it had a reciprocal relationship with soldiers and owed both them and their families more than other citizens. It was also a powerful tool to control soldiers' actions—cutting off the paika could leave a family to starve.[33] Under the conditions of the Great Patriotic War, the state continued to show concern for soldiers' families, but concentrated much more on feeding soldiers themselves.

A more physiological understanding of rations was conveyed by the term *prodovol'stvennye normy*—"food ration norms." Like paёk, this referred to *anything* regularly provided by the state to soldiers (and civilians) that was intended to be physically ingested or used in relation to the body (soap was included in the soldier's ration). However, prodovol'stvennye normy appealed to physical needs, being akin to a science of sustenance. The hierarchies of the norms were, at least etymologically, based purely on the physical need for calories of people fulfilling different tasks. A new set of basic norms was established in September of 1941, replacing all prewar norms. They totaled fourteen in all, and changes would be made to refine them to meet the needs of various types of cadres and growing possibilities of the state well into the war.[34] As we will see later in this chapter, much like the *blokadniki* discussed by

32. This was in line with earlier provisioning policies. See, for example, Osokina, *Za fasadom "Stalinskogo izobiliia,"* p. 99.

33. Joshua Sanborn, *Drafting the Russian Nation: Military Conscription, Mass Politics and Total War 1905–1925* (DeKalb: Northern Illinois University Press, 2003), pp. 107–110.

34. TsAMO RF, f. 2, op. 920266, d. 1, ll. 718–929, in Veshchikov et al., *Tyl Krasnoi Armii v Velikoi Otechestvennoi voine 1941–1945 gg.,* pp. 147–148.

The State's Pot and the Soldier's Spoon

Alexis Peri in this volume, soldiers seldom perceived their rations in terms of norms.

As in most armies, rations had to keep soldiers functioning while taking up minimal space and weight in their packs or on supply wagons. Colonel Gurov, author of several manuals on marching, declared: "the nutritional value of food does not depend on the quantity, but on its quality. Therefore those products, which contain more calories are assigned for the fighter's food."[35] This logic gave fats and carbohydrates a privileged place in the soldier's ration. Fats took longer to digest and made one feel full longer, while carbohydrates gave both instant and long-term energy. Both provided a high number of calories per volume. Meat (especially salt pork and sausage) and potatoes were looked upon as ideal ingredients, and bread as simply indispensable.[36]

The range of calories guaranteed to men under arms varied depending on position. A manual for *fel'dshers* (a position that was both medical assistant and health inspector) published on the eve of the war stated that a person in a state of total relaxation needed 1,700 calories, a tractor driver 3,000.[37] A soldier received between 3,161 calories (dry rations for soldiers in the field) and 4,063 calories (a special ration for airmen) according to the prewar norms.[38] An official history of the rear-area services claimed that soldiers received between 2,659 calories (for soldiers guarding rear-area objects and institutions—including those soldiers in training) to 3,450 (for soldiers at the front) to 4,712 (for airmen) according to the September 1941 norms, while the official medical history of the war cites the range from 3,088 for soldiers in the rear to 4,692 for airmen in the course of the war.[39] Front-line soldiers were to receive

---

35. S. Gurov, *Boets i otdelenie na pokhode* (Moscow: Voenzidat, 1941), p. 11.

36. F.G. Krotkov, ed., *Gigiena. Opyt sovetskoi meditsiny v Velikoi Otechestvennoi voine 1941–1945 gg.*, vol. 33 (Moscow: MEDGIZ, 1955), pp. 3, 134. A 1940 textbook for food-service workers praised bread for its high calorie content (2,000–2,500 calories per kilogram; i.e., around 1,000 calories per pound) and ease of digestion. I. Ia. Moreinis, *Uchebnik pishchevoi gigieny dlia sanitarno-fel'dsherskikh shkol* (Moscow-Leningrad: MEDGIZ, 1940), p. 126.

37. Moreinis, *Uchebnik pishchevoi gigieny*, pp. 28, 203.

38. Krotkov, *Gigiena*, p. 139.

39. Kurkotkin, *Tyl vooruzhenykh sil*, p. 191; Krotkov, *Gigiena*, p. 139. I have not found a direct discussion of why there were such fluctuations in the numbers. Given that the

3,505 calories.[40] It should be noted that this was what was promised, not necessarily what soldiers received. Control over calories became a common part of front-line inspections, which were also supposed to insure balanced nutrition.[41]

In practice, provisioning officers were often concerned only with calories, ignoring the importance of nutrients. The head surgeon of the 130th (Latvian) Rifle Corps reported immediately after the war that his soldiers had never received the stated norms of complete proteins and vitamins A and C. "We ended up with massive experiments. It turns out that people can get by with far less of these three necessary nutritional elements for much longer than the norms state," he told his interviewer with pride.[42]

The logic of rations posited soldiers as anonymous biological machines that needed fuel and certain vital nutrients to keep functioning; this attitude is normal for any military and in the sciences. Any system of mass catering imagines a generic body that it will be feeding, ignoring differences in age, sex, and mass that might warrant special attention, not to mention culturally constructed differences that could also be of

---

primary ration norms were established in September 1941, when resources were becoming very critical and the Soviet Union was shrinking, I think that it is safe to assume that the wartime reductions in number of calories are a response to shortage.

40. Krotkov, *Gigiena*, p. 139.

41. E.g., TsAMO RF, f. 47, op. 1029, d. 84, ll. 23–24, in Veshchikov et al., *Tyl Krasnoi Armii v Velikoi Otechestvennoi voine 1941–1945 gg.*, p. 381.

42. Nauchnyi arkhiv Instituta Rossiiskoi istorii Akademii nauk Rossiiskoi Federatsii (NA IRI RAN), f. 2, razdel I, op. 223, .d. 10, ll. 2–20b. An earlier interview with a medic in the same unit complained about a major lack of vitamins. See NA IRI RAN, f. 2, razdel I, op. 16, d. 4, ll. 68–680b. Using grains or flour in place of vegetables was a common practice for meeting calorie requirements; it led to various corrective orders, including the May 31, 1943, signal. TsAMO RF, f. 2, op. 795437, d. 11, ll. 546–549, in Veshchikov et al., *Tyl Krasnoi Armii v Velikoi Otechestvennoi voine 1941–1945 gg.*, p. 402. The British Army in World War I acted in much the same manner. See Rachel Duffett, *The Stomach for Fighting: Food and Soldiers of the Great War* (Manchester: Manchester University Press, 2012), pp. 58, 146. This excellent work shows that there were a number of other parallels between the British Expeditionary Force and the Red Army, including something akin to subsidiary agriculture (p. 124), mitigation strategies (p. 187), and rations being a collective rather than a personal good (p. 190).

The State's Pot and the Soldier's Spoon

significance (such as those of Muslim and Jewish soldiers, for example).[43] This was in line with prewar provisioning.[44] Like other armies, the Red Army redefined its soldiers' identities by specialization and rank. Who you were to the army depended not on where you were from, which God you prayed to, or what language you spoke, but rather on your rank, specialization, and location, all of which impacted what kind of food you would receive.

Soviet provisioning negotiated the concepts of prodovol'stvennye normy and paëk. Rations followed several trajectories, up the ranks, from the rear to the front, according to the changing of seasons and climate zones, and finally, soldiers' specializations. Commanders (except the already well-fed airmen), as the *heads* of the military units, received a supplemental ration (*doppaëk*), which included extra meat, cookies, and higher-quality tobacco (amounting to 450 additional calories, or between 3,490 and 4,000 calories total each per day).[45] Those serving in

43. S. Gurov, *Pokhod i otdykh pekhoty* (Moscow: Voenizdat, 1940), pp. 72–73. Gurov acknowledges that age and body-mass are also a factor in calorie use—something that the army's policies did not take into account. In other armies, particularly colonial forces, the maintenance of ethnic and religious custom was critical to organization and discipline. See Tarak Barkawi, "Peoples, Homelands, and Wars? Ethnicity, the Military, and Battle among British Imperial Forces in the War against Japan," *Comparative Studies in Society and History* 46, no. 1 (January 2004): 134–163.

44. See Matthew Payne, "The Forge of the Kazakh Proletariat?" in *A State of Nations* (New York: Oxford University Press, 2001), pp. 234–235, on how provisioning at work sites created tensions between Kazakh and Russian workers during the First Five-Year Plan.

45. TsAMO Rf, f. 2, op. 920266, d. 1, ll. 718–929, in Veshchikov et al., *Tyl Krasnoi Armii v Velikoi Otechestvennoi voine 1941–1945 gg.*, p. 148: "Mid- and higher level command personnel . . . are to be given for free in norms No.1 and No.2 with the addition of per person per 24 hours: butter or pork fat—40 g., cookies—20 g., canned fish—50 g., cigarettes—25 or tobacco—25 g. and matches—10 boxes a month." This weighed in at 450 additional calories according to the official medical history of the war. Krotkov, *Gigiena*, p. 140. The hierarchy of rations had an impact on soldier's language—it became common to refer to strong tea as "general's tea" in the course of the war. F. T. Bulatov, *Budni frontovykh let* (Kazan': Tatknigizdat, 1984), p. 251. As Boris Slutskii recalled, "For almost the entire war our grub [*kormezhka*] was fairly sparse [*izriadno skudnoi*]. . . . The officers' extra paëk provoked real envy among the soldiers." Slutskii, *O drugikh i o sebe*, p. 28.

frigid climates, such as the Karelian Isthmus or Far North, would be offered special rations, such as additional vodka, salt pork, or vitamin C (154 additional calories).[46] In winter (from October until April) soldiers were given one hundred extra grams (3.5 oz.) of bread. Those recovering from wounds had a different set of norms and specific food.[47] The closer to the front a soldier was, the more rations he (or she) was entitled to. Simply put, in risking his (or her) life and thus most directly contributing to the war effort, the soldier earned more resources from the state as citizen, while the extreme physical demands of the front required more energy as a biological machine.[48] This logic translated into civilian rations, where the more directly the civilian's job contributed to the war effort, the more calories he or she was given. Only those with jobs considered vital to the war effort (Category I workers and ITR) received rations comparable to soldiers at the front.[49] Finally, certain specialized troops received particular kinds of rations. Pilots were given a highly portable ration that included condensed milk and chocolate in case of fatigue, a crash, or unexpected landing. Reconnaissance troops received a special ration (including extra meat, sugar, and vodka) for infiltrating enemy territory, while elite formations like Guards units and Shock Army troops, received additional rations, such as much-coveted white bread.[50]

In these situations, we see that it is impossible to separate prodovol's-tvenye normy and paëk. Some privileges seemed based on biological needs, others on status. Soldiers at the front needed more energy because

46. TsAMO RF, f. 2, op. 920266, d. 1, ll. 718–929, in Veshchikov et al., *Tyl Krasnoi Armii v Velikoi Otechestvennoi voine 1941–1945 gg.*, p. 148; Krotkov, *Gigiena*, p. 140.

47. For example, in 1945 one surgeon said that he gave soldiers suffering from gangrene 200–300 grams (6.7–10.1 fl. oz.) of vodka to help their appetite. NA IRI RAN, f. 2, razdel I, op. 123, d. 13, l. 20b. The September 1941 norms also included a special hospital ration.

48. TsAMO Rf, f. 2, op. 920266, d. 1, ll. 718–929, in Veshchikov et al., *Tyl Krasnoi Armii v Velikoi Otechestvennoi voine 1941–1945 gg.*, pp. 149–155. Soldiers received roughly twice the amount of bread at the front as they did in training, and roughly three times the amount of bread given to those in the hospital.

49. See Wendy Goldman's chapter in this volume.

50. TsAMO RF, f. 2, op. 920266, d. 1, ll. 718–929, in Veshchikov et al., *Tyl Krasnoi Armii v Velikoi Otechestvennoi voine 1941–1945 gg.*, p. 148; TsAMO RF, f. 2, op. 795437, d. 10, l. 276, in ibid., p. 414; Mikhail Loginov, *Eto bylo na fronte* (Kazan': Tatknigizdat', 1984), p. 10.

The State's Pot and the Soldier's Spoon

they were engaged in strenuous combat, but they also deserved more because they were risking their lives. It seems inevitable that these two understandings would blur with one another; paëk, after all consisted of prodovol'stvenye normy. Among the items listed under prodovol'stvennye normy were tobacco, rolling paper, matches, and vodka—none of which were necessary for physical survival, but all of which were deficit items that carried important social weight.[51]

The example of special norms for women demonstrates these messy interconnections between a soldier's physical needs and social status. The army, recognizing the female bodies that had entered its ranks, re-examined the norms given to female soldiers. In April of 1943 there was an army-wide order "concerning the increased norm of soap issued to women service personnel," which increased women soldier's soap ration by one hundred grams (3.5 oz.).[52] While this order could have been based on ideas of women as either social or physiological beings, another order concerning tobacco was based more on values than biology. The army also showed more concern for the lungs of its female personnel than the men in its ranks, as there was an official order "concerning the issuance to non-smoking women of chocolate or candy instead of tobacco." Non-smoking female soldiers were to receive two hundred grams (7 oz.) of chocolate or three hundred grams (10.6 oz.) of coffee instead of tobacco.[53] This order was possibly intended to do battle with gray markets in the ranks. Non-smoking soldiers deserved something to replace one of the most coveted parts of a soldier's ration, and leaving them with large amounts of tobacco to exchange could seriously undermine the army's control over soldiers' consumption. Gender provided a window

---

51. TsAMO RF, f. 2, op. 920266, d. 1, ll. 718–929, in Veshchikov et al., *Tyl Krasnoi Armii v Velikoi Otechestvennoi voine 1941–1945 gg.*, pp. 149–156. There was even talk of including postcards as part of a soldier's ration; RGASPI, f. 17, op. 125, d. 200, l. 172.

52. RGVA, f. 4, op. 12, d. 107, l. 677, in Barsukov et al., *Prikazy narodnogo komissara oborony SSSR 1943–1945 gg.*, p. 115.

53. RGVA, f. 4, op. 12, d. 105, l. 169, in Barsukov et al., *Prikazy narodnogo komissara oborony SSSR 22 iiunia 1941 g.–1942 g.*, p. 285. A similar order was later issued concerning nonsmoking males; see RGVA, f. 4, op. 12, d. 106-a. l. 295, in ibid., p. 368. Some accounts point to this order being fulfilled only briefly; see, for instance, V. I. Galaninskaia, *Budni medsanbata* (Saratov: Privolzhskoe knizhnoe izdatel'stvo, 1980), p. 11.

114 *Brandon Schechter*

for exception to what was otherwise a system based entirely on position and the body as an anonymous biological machine.

As a result of multi-vector norms, as well as the variety of sources from which the army drew provisions, a soldier would receive a wide range of rations, even if this variety was unintentional. Periodically, however, food became nauseatingly monotonous.[54] Soldiers in the rear were nearly unanimous in their complaints of hunger while undergoing training, so much so that being assigned to work in the kitchen was a much sought-after assignment.[55] As Grigorii Baklanov, veteran and novelist, recalled: "They fed us there by the rear area norms: you'll live, but even in your sleep you won't have sinful thoughts."[56] Many looked forward to going to the front as a place where they could finally get enough to eat (and sometimes drink).[57]

The Menu

The menu at the front often impressed those who had been wasting away in the rear.[58] Whenever possible, soldiers at the front were to be provided with hot, fresh food by field kitchens twice a day.[59] Hot food was

54. See Slutskii, *O drugikh i o sebe*, pp. 29–31, for a detailed account of how rations changed as his unit moved further west.

55. Lesin, *Byla voina*, p. 53, explained that one could always agree with the cook to get extra food while working in the kitchen.

56. Grigorii Baklanov, *Zhizn', podarennaia dvazhdy* (Moscow: Vagrius, 1999), pp. 47–48.

57. Lesin, *Byla voina*, pp. 64–65, 80.

58. Gabriel Temkin, *My Just War: The Memoir of a Jewish Red Army Soldier in World War II* (Novato, Calif.: Presidio, 1998), p. 115. Anatolii Genatulin, *Vot konchitsia voina* (Moscow: Pravda, 1988), p. 36: Genatulin recalled an early meal at the front: "Such filling food—buckwheat kasha half filled with meat—we wouldn't have dreamt of such a thing in the reserve regiment. There was enough food, you could eat for two or three, for those guys, who didn't make it to this lunch. Some bent over with empty stomachs, others, crippled—they have bigger problems than food now."

59. RGVA, f.4, op.11, d.76, l. 70–75, in Barsukov et al., *Prikazy narodnogo komissara oborony SSSR 1943–1945 gg.*, p. 168; Loginov, *Eto bylo na fronte*, pp. 9–10; TsAMO RF, f. 47, op. 1029, d. 83, ll. 53–55, in Veshchikov et al., *Tyl Krasnoi Armii v Velikoi Otechestvennoi voine 1941–1945 gg.*, p. 324; Krotkov, *Gigiena*, pp. 145–150. As one might expect, *The Experience of Soviet Medicine in the Great Patriotic War* (the official medical history of the war) presents a very rosy picture that emphasizes the situation from 1943 on, treating the

The State's Pot and the Soldier's Spoon

to be brought up just before dawn and just after dark with soldiers receiving bread and meat for a cold lunch in the morning.[60] The soldier's meal was supposed to consist of two dishes—a soup and a porridge—and tea, brought up in twelve-liter thermoses.[61] In practice this could be reduced to one dish, often a kasha-based soup.[62] Cooks were supposed to divide the ration so that every soldier received the same portion of meat in his soup or kasha.[63] Front-line menus varied greatly, but could become monotonous as one type of soup or porridge became constant.[64]

Red Army veteran and food historian Vil'iam Pokhlebkin noted that priorities during the war ignored assortment in favor of sufficiency and practicality in provisioning: "all production of foodstuffs is concentrated on the maximum expansion of so called basic products, without which not one person in the rear or at the front can exist . . . that being first of all bread and salt . . . [then] meat and fish, fats and vegetables. . . . What kind of meat, which kind of fats—this is all unimportant."[65] The state saw categories in terms of meat, bread, grains, vegetables, and so on, without attention to whether the meat was pork or beef or rabbit or fish, or whether it was canned or smoked or fresh or even took the form of

---

latter half of the war as if it were representative of the war as a whole. It does, however, present interesting details as to the percentage of daily calories per meal and the results of a survey of troops as to which concentrates were tasty and which inedible.

60. Polkovnik D. P. Vorontsov, *Prodol'stvennoe snabzheniie strelkovogo batal'ona i polka v deistvuiushchei armii* (Moscow: Voennaia Akademiia tyla i snabzheniia Krasnoi armii imeni Molotova V.M., 1943), p. 12.

61. Kurkotkin, *Tyl sovetskikh vooruzhennykh sil*, pp. 190; see also TsAMO RF, f. 208, op. 14703 c, d. 2, ll. 339–343, in Veshchikov et al., *Tyl Krasnoi Armii v Velikoi Otechestvennoi voine 1941–1945 gg.*, pp. 137–138; TsAMO RF, f. 47, op. 1029, d. 83, ll. 53–55, in ibid., p. 324. Early in the war buckets were often substituted for thermoses, with a predictable loss of food. Additionally, the seals on thermoses had yet to be perfected. Krotkov, *Gigiena*, p. 148. Krotkov's *Gigiena* pointed out that soups and porridges were ideal for the task of feeding troops in the active army, as they were generally tasty and a hot meal in bad weather was of great importance.

62. E.g., TsAMO RF, f. 235, op. 2096, d. 104, l. 9, in Veshchikov et al., *Tyl Krasnoi Armii v Velikoi Otechestvennoi voine 1941–1945 gg.*, pp. 479–480; Khisam Kamalov, *U kazhdoi zhizn'-odna* (Kazan': Tatknigizdat, 1983), pp. 203–205.

63. Vorontsov, *Prodol'stvennoe snabzheniie*, p. 12.

64. RGASPI, f. 88, op. 1, d. 958, l. 7.

65. Vil'iam Pokhlebkin, *Kukhnia veka* (Moscow: Polifakt, 2000), p. 209.

powdered eggs.[66] Meat was meat, fat was fat (and sometimes "meat" too), bread was bread (whether dried into crouton-like *sukhari* or fresh-baked). The Red Army, while the best fed mass institution in the Soviet Union, was not intended to be a space of culinary discovery (although it became one). Provisioning, at least initially and primarily, was concerned with caloric, not culinary, value, although making food tasty had been a goal of prewar Soviet nutrition. Provisioning officers made concessions to taste over pure practicality with the continued use and inclusion of basic spices (bay leaf, salt, pepper, onions, and occasionally garlic) in norms, the only culinary "details" left intact in military provisioning.[67] In part this reduction to bare minimums was forced on the state because of the logistical nightmare that it faced. Everything from pork to pots was in short supply.

Field kitchens were supposed to service no more than 180 soldiers, but were soon forced to service 300 or more, due to a loss of 7,740 of them in the first year of the war. The kitchens consisted of three pots (soup, kasha, and tea) on wheels, with an oven. They were sometimes so close to the front as to endanger the cook's life (in Lesin's regiment, the first man killed was the cook), and sometimes so far away as to guarantee that food would be doled out cold, despite thermoses, at the front.[68] Cooks were supposed to provide nourishment to their comrades a few hundred meters or a few kilometers in front of them, but their ability to do so varied depending on their skills, the resources available to the rear area, and conditions at the front.

In battle, in echelon, and whenever troops found themselves too far from a field kitchen, two types of ration were to provide them with sustenance: the NZ and dry rations (*sukhpaëk*). The *neprikosnovennyi zapas*

66. An official table of exchange existed to ensure that the soldier received the proper number of calories, regardless of their source. See *Pamiatka voiskovomu povaru* (Moscow: Voenizdat, 1943), pp. 14–15. Under this system, 17 grams (0.6 oz.) of powdered eggs were equivalent to 100 grams (3.53 oz.) of fresh meat.

67. Pokhlebkin, *Kukhnia Veka*, p. 210; *Vospominania frontovikov. Sbornik No.1* (Moscow: Voennaia akademiia tyla i snabzhenia Krasnoi armii imena Molotova V.M., 1943), p. 16.

68. Lesin, *Byla voina*, p. 88. Loginov, *Eto bylo na fronte*, pp. 9–10. See also TsAMO RF, f. 208, op. 14703 c, d. 2, ll. 339–343, in Veshchikov et al., *Tyl Krasnoi Armii v Velikoi Otechestvennoi voine 1941–1945 gg.*, p. 138; NA IRI RAN f. 2, razdel I, op. 223, d. 9, l. 10b.

The State's Pot and the Soldier's Spoon

(literally "untouchable reserve"; in the British and German armies referred to as "Iron Rations"), or NZ (sometimes referred to as *nosimyi zapas*—"portable reserve"), was supposed to be carried in a soldier's knapsack at all times, but was to be consumed only upon a commander's order.[69] However, experience showed that soldiers would sometimes eat them without orders, and commanders sometimes kept reserves under their own supervision (in a special dugout), out of the hands of the soldiers.[70] The NZ typically consisted of canned or smoked meat, tea, sugar, salt, and dried bread.[71] The sukhpaëk, often distinguishable only by not being labeled "NZ," was slightly more generous. It consisted partially of things the soldier could prepare himself, such as concentrated soups and grains, and partially of ready-to-eat items, such as dried bread and canned food. Soldiers complained of both the taste and difficulty of preparing the concentrates issued at the beginning of the war. Preparation was a very serious problem, as the army failed to provide enough dry spirits (alcohol that burned without smoke) to allow soldiers to cook these concentrates, while starting a fire could draw enemy fire and prove fatal.[72] As the war progressed, dry rations came to resemble NZ more and more, as concentrates were reserved for field kitchens and soldiers were given foods that they could eat as is.[73]

69. *Rukhovodstvo dlia boitsa pekhoty*, p. 45. Vorontsov, *Prodovol'stvennoe snabzheniie*, p. 16. The increased use of dry rations was a lesson the Red Army took away from the Winter War, where more mobile Finnish units could outmaneuver Soviet formations that were tied to roads. RGASPI, f. 74, op. 2, d. 121, ll. 11, 32.

70. Antipenko, *Na glavnom upravlenii*, p. 92.

71. Vorontsov, *Prodol'stvennoe snabzheniie*, p. 49. According to norms established in September of 1941, the dry rations consisted of 500 grams (17.6 oz.) of dried bread (*sukhari*), 200 grams (7 oz.) of concentrated porridge, 75 grams (2.65 oz.) of concentrated bean soup, 100 grams (3.5 oz.) of sausage (which could be substituted with a variety of things, from dried fish to cheese), 35 grams (1.23 oz.) of sugar, 2 grams (0.07 oz.) of tea, and 10 grams (0.35 oz.) of salt. Dried bread replaced crackers as a primary foodstuff after the Finnish War. See RGASPI, f. 74, op. 2, d. 121, l. 11.

72. TsAMO RF, f. 208, op. 14703 c, d. 2, ll. 339–343, in Veshchikov et al., *Tyl Krasnoi Armii v Velikoi Otechestvennoi voine 1941–1945 gg.*, p. 138. GARF, f. R5446, op. 43a, d. 8627, l.7. Apparently the failure to provide dry spirits was due more than anything else to a lack of vessels in which to transport them.

73. Antipenko, *Na glavnom upravlenii*, p. 92; Kurkotkin, *Tyl sovetskikh vooruzhenikh sil*, p. 206; Krotkov, *Gigiena*, pp. 150–153.

118   *Brandon Schechter*

The contents of NZ and dry rations varied dramatically: they could be freshly killed boiled lamb, salt pork, lard, compressed animal fats,[74] sardines, sausage, or American Spam (ironically referred to as "Second Front"),[75] depending on what was available.[76] Canned goods were often unlabeled.[77] Vil'iam Pokhlebkin remembered different kinds of NZ and sukhpaёk that had been provided to him:

> Usually fats were put into *shchi* [cabbage soup] ([or any] soup) and kasha. So whichever type they were in the army, it would be difficult to recognize them, unless, in connection with different extraordinary situations, it came down to giving out *sukhpaёk* or to open the NZ. In this situation the *starshina* [sergeant major][78] would give out along with dried bread and sugar a can of *tushenka* [stewed meat] or "fats." Their character changed in relation to historical and military conditions. In 1942 I received in my dry rations some sort of hard, dingy, yellowish-gray chunks. This was *kombizhir* ["combined fats"]. I saw it for the first time (and of course, ate it up). At the end of 1943 they gave out in the dry ration a can of a very white, buttery substance. This was American lard, an artificial fat drawn from the processing of pork fat. It was perceived as a luxury. But at the end of 1944 I received in my dry rations a good-sized 500-gram [17.6 oz.] piece of smoked salt pork. To be exact, it was not peasant salt pork, but smoked, with a pretty brown skin, neat and with a [pleasant] smell. I think that this was from captured German stocks, or maybe, more likely Hungarian, captured in the course of the rout of some large enemy grouping.[79]

74. L. Iu. Slezkine, *Do voini i na voine* (Moscow: Parad, 2009), p. 404; Vil'iam Pokhlebkin, *Moya kukhnia i moe meniu* (Moscow: Tsentrpoligraf, 1999), pp. 278–279.

75. Antipenko, *Na glavnom upravlenii*, p. 92. It was common for soldiers to joke that the Second Front had finally been opened when they popped open a can of Lend-Lease meat. Collingham, *The Taste of War*, p. 339.

76. Sukhpaёk could include a roll with ground beef (Saushin, *Khleb i sol'*, p. 140); fresh boiled meat, salt pork, buttered bread (Antipenko, *Na glavnom upravlenii*, p. 148); concentrated grains (Lesin, *Byla voina*, pp. 100–101); sausage (Loginov, *Eto byla na fronte*, p. 9); canned fish (Kamalov, *U kazhdoi zhizn'-odna*, p. 15); and a variety of other animal products. By the middle of the war, salt pork and sausage seemed the most frequent and sanctioned items, and concentrates were officially removed. Krotkov, *Gigiena*, p. 152.

77. Irina Dunaevskaia, *Ot Leningrada do Kёnigsberga: Dnevnik voennoi perevodchitsy, 1942–1945* (Moscow: ROSSPEN, 2010), p. 94; *Instruktsia po ukladke pokhodnykh kukhon* (Moscow: Voenizdat, 1942), pp. 18–19.

78. Sergeant major; in the Red Army lowest level person responsible for organizing provisioning (of food, clothing, weapons, etc.) at the company, battery, etc., level.

79. Pokhlebkin, *Moya kukhnia*, p. 278.

The State's Pot and the Soldier's Spoon   119

The food that soldiers received depended on a variety of factors largely beyond their control, factors that blurred the line between meats and fats, but where calories were king. Even foodstuffs like *kombizhir* would be consumed without question in order to stay alive, though among this random assortment of foods, some memorable delicious meals were to be had.

During the war, food was perhaps *the* deficit resource, something that everyone needed. By creating a hierarchy of distribution, the state directly (and logically) ranked whose contribution was most significant to its continued survival, and made providing for those who were risking their lives for the state their first priority. Soldiers were keenly aware of being better fed than their families and sometimes felt twinges of guilt. Ibraghim Gazi wrote his wife and child in October of 1943, "I am very sorry that I can't help you with anything except money. I wanted to send my ration of chocolate, but they don't take parcels." Later, he lamented, "As soon as we get a chance to eat something good, I say: this is for kids, and our children probably don't have this."[80] While soldiers might be racked with guilt, they certainly felt the pangs of hunger less acutely than their families in the rear or under German occupation.

AN INVIOLABLE CAMP: RHETORIC, REALITIES, AND EXPLAINING FAILURES

Well-traveled soldier Boris Slutskii, writing in 1945, described how the state had managed to feed the army: "The cruel anti-theft laws of war, executions of chauffeurs for two packs of concentrates, were necessitated by the famished convulsions of a country that robbed its own rear to fatten its front."[81] This was *realpolitik* of the stomach. However frightful this concept may be (it left children, dependents and the elderly with the smallest rations, which, in extreme situations, such as the siege of Leningrad, dramatically reduced their chances of survival), it fit perfectly

---

80. *Pis'ma s fronta 1941–1945 gg.: Sbornik dokumentov* (Kazan': Gasyr, 2010), pp. 81–82.

81. Slutskii, *O drugikh i o sebe*, p. 29. Saushin, *Khleb i sol'*, p. 104: When asked how he liked the food they received at the front, one sergeant said: "It depends. . . . sometimes we like it, sometimes not. This is the front you see. At home they don't even have this. Things are very rough with food in the rear. We don't complain."

with the logic of a sovereign power, the continued existence of which was being threatened by total war.[82] The state used rationing in such a way as to openly declare which lives were more valuable, understanding the zero-sum equation forced on it by shortage.

One of the clear messages sent by the Soviet state at the front was that the USSR could provide for its men under arms only so long as they stopped retreating. In his November 6, 1941, address to the Red Army (when German troops could see the spires of Moscow through binoculars), Stalin described how the hardships of the war "converted the family of peoples of the U.S.S.R. into a single and inviolable camp, which is selflessly supporting its Red Army and Red Navy," guaranteeing that "the Soviet rear has never been so strong as it is today."[83] As a result of this rhetoric of an "inviolable camp" making sacrifices for the Red Army, any shortages at the front were not the failure of the Soviet system or the people, but rather of dangerous attitudes and more often of specific, identifiable individuals in whom the state had entrusted the sacred task of feeding:

> The government allocates enough varied and nourishing foodstuffs for the provisioning of the units of the Red Army and only due to a negligent, dishonest, and sometimes criminal attitude on the part of commanders assigned to the leadership of provisioning, the quality of food and norms of provisioning of fighting men have degraded.[84]

This tracking of failure as the result of corrupt individuals was nothing new and would remain a continuous trope of Soviet discussions of provisioning, even as systematic problems became obvious.[85]

From the very beginning of the war, improvement was sought.[86] In the course of the war, the failures of the prewar organization of ration

---

82. See, for example, Nikita Lomagin, *Neizvestnaya blokada. Dokumenty, prilozheniia. Kn. 2* (St. Petersburg: Neva, 2004), p. 185, as well as other chapters in this volume.

83. Stalin, *The Great Patriotic War of the Soviet Union*, pp. 22–23.

84. TsAMO RF, f. 2, op. 795437, d. 11, ll. 546–549, in Veshchikov et al., *Tyl Krasnoi Armii v Velikoi Otechestvennoi voine 1941–1945 gg.*, p. 403.

85. Alexis Peri's contribution to this volume traces the same phenomenon in the civilian world.

86. TsAMO RF, f. 2, op. 795437, d. 5, ll. 545–547, in Veshchikov et al., *Tyl Krasnoi Armii v Velikoi Otechestvennoi voine 1941–1945 gg.*, pp. 90–100; Antipenko, *Na glavnom upravlenii*, pp. 291–300.

The State's Pot and the Soldier's Spoon

distribution became apparent, and were exacerbated by the loss of both agricultural resources and huge numbers of field kitchens as the army retreated. At the same time that the rear was being reformed, fewer troops were assigned there, as the war demanded more and more able-bodied men to fight on the front lines. Many of these rear-area men would be replaced by women. A series of orders emanated from the State Committee of Defense (or GKO, Godarstvennyi komitet oborony) centralizing and perfecting the apparatus of the rear area. The aim was to do more with less, and on the whole, these efforts were quite successful.[87] Despite the constant improvement of organization, including the establishment of rear-area inspections, realizing the type of control over the quality and quantity of food that the GKO demanded was a struggle that would be waged long after the Red Army had moved beyond Soviet borders.

Breakdowns: Their Consequences and Their Culprits

Any breakdown in provisioning had serious consequences. Hunger was devastating to morale. Failures to provide could lead to the impression that the Germans had much better provisioning. One censored letter near Stalingrad stated: "the Germans get chocolate even when they're encircled, and we sit in the open and have only sukhari."[88] Even in the immensely popular and optimistic *Vasily Tërkin* poems, which were widely circulated in print and read on the radio, this suspicion creeps into a duel between Tërkin and a German: "Tërkin knew that in this fight, he was

---

87. Antipenko, *Na glavnom upravlenii*, p. 289; RGVA, f. 4, op. 12, d. 99, ll. 128–143, 146–147, 151–152, in Barsukov, *et al.*, *Prikazy narodnogo komissara oborony SSSR 22 iiunia 1941—g.–1942 g.*, p. 97; RGVA, f. 4, op. 11, d. 67, ll. 164–66, in ibid., pp. 195–196; RGVA, f. 4,op.. 11, d. 65, l. 396–397, in ibid. p. 71; RGVA, f. 4, op. 11, d.70, ll. 149–150, in ibid., p. 213; RGVA, f. 4, op. 11, d. 70, ll. 251–252, in ibid., pp. 213–214. Stalin threatened to stop sending reinforcements to fronts that failed to meet the targets of these orders. RGVA, f. 4, op. 11, d. 65, ll. 396–397, in ibid., pp. 392.

88. TsA FSB RF, f. 14, op. 4, d. 913, ll. 149–150, in Ia. F. Pogonii, ed., *Stalingradskaia epopeia: Materialy NKVD SSSR i voennoi tsenzury iz Tsentral'nogo arkhiva FSB RF* (Moscow: "Zvonitsa-MG," 2000), p. 383.

weaker—the worse fed [of the combatants]!"[89] Many soldiers complained about a lack of salt making their food inedible.[90]

The physical impact of hunger was something commanders could not ignore. Marshal Zhukov is reported to have declared, "A full soldier is worth five hungry ones!"[91] Failures in provisioning were cited by Red Army officers as the direct causes of desertion (even among elite units), illness, and in some cases of the breakdown of combat operations.[92] Soldiers died from various forms of digestive maladies at or on their way to the front, and night blindness (*kurinaia slepota*) due to a lack of vitamin A became a common malady.[93] In a meeting of top political personnel of the army, one officer exclaimed that when soldiers were not fed, "What kind of combat effectiveness can you expect from them?"[94] Wherever breakdowns occurred, culprits needed to be found and punished.

Orders throughout the war would decry the indifference of provisioning officers toward fulfilling the letter of Soviet law. The issue of proper distribution faced two challenges: indifference and greed. Much more disturbing was the practice of *razbazarivanie*,—meaning "squandering," but often used to refer to the treatment of provisions "as personal property."[95] Stalin's 1943 warning from the Kalinin Front declared:

> Many commanders and provisioning officers do not investigate the safety of provisions; they have forgotten, that the state entrusted them with a most important valuable. There are among them such people, who, using their

89. A. T. Tvardovskii, *Vasilii Tërkin: Kniga pro boitsa* (Moscow: Literatura, 1977), p. 72.

90. E.g., N. N. Nikulin, *Vospominaniia o voine* (St. Petersburg.: Izdatel'stvo Gos. Ermitazha, 2008), p. 60.

91. Quoted in Antipenko, *Na glavnom upravlenii*, p. 299.

92. Lesin, *Byla voina*, p. 82; TsA FSB RF, f. 14, op. 4, d. 943, l. 327, in Pogonii, *Stalingradskaia epopeia*, p. 379; Nikolai Chekhovich, *Dnevnik ofitsera* (Moscow: Molodaia gvardiia, 1945), p. 73; NA IRI RAN, f. 2, razdel I, op. 28, d. 30, l. 10.

93. E.g., TsA FSB RF, f. 14, op. 4, d. 777, l. 40–44, in Pogonii, *Stalingradskaia epopeia*, p. 259–260. RGASPI, f. 84, op. 1, d. 84, l. 2.

94. RGASPI, f. 88, op. 1, d. 958, l. 3. See also Lesin, *Byla voina*, p. 146. TsAMO RF, f. 2, op. 795437, d. 9, ll. 394–395, in Veshchikov et al., *Tyl Krasnoi armii v Velikoi Otechestvennoi voine 1941–1945 gg.*, pp. 237–241.

95. See TsAMO RF, f. 47, op. 1029, d. 83, ll. 53–55, in Veshchikov et al., *Tyl Krasnoi Armii v Velikoi Otechestvennoi voine 1941–1945 gg.*, p. 322; TsAMO RF, f. 239, op. 2294, d. 167, ll. 115–120, in ibid., p. 570.

The State's Pot and the Soldier's Spoon   123

authority, dispose of ration stocks as if they were their personal property, illegally expending foodstuffs, and in so doing damaging the Red Army and the security of the fighting men.[96]

Early in the war the draconian laws concerning the theft of socialist property, developed during collectivization, were reiterated, and speculation was to be dealt with by military tribunals.[97] Despite the consequences, officers (both front-line and provisioning), having more or less total control over resources on the ground, would sometimes utilize what during the war had become *the* form of currency for their own profit. As one provisioning officer told his colleagues in January of 1943, "The fighter could be full. But why doesn't he get all of his food? We came to a definite conclusion—starting from the DOP [Divisional Exchange Point]—people steal [*voruiut*] and when food gets to the kitchen—they steal there too."[98]

This ubiquitous theft, while considered to pale in comparison to graft under the old regime, included cases of illegal trade in foodstuffs as well as of officers throwing unsanctioned feasts using the soldiers' (and the state's) rations; the latter problem became worse around holidays.[99] Theft by commanders was considered such a scourge that there was even talk of separating commanders from general provisioning, creating a separate system of provisioning for them alone. However, it was decided that feeding commanders separately from their subordinates would mean "they would just stop looking in on the troops." At the same time, it was

96. TsAMO RF, f. 2, op. 795437, d. 11, ll. 546–549 in ibid., p. 403.

97. RGVA, f. 4, op. 12, d. 98, ll. 210–214, in Barsukov et al., *Prikazy narodnogo komissara oborony SSSR 22 iiunia 1941 g. –1942 g.,* pp. 11–13. It is interesting to note that in the instances I have found, those guilty are not seen as German agents, but merely as self-interested criminals.

98. RGASPI, f. 88, op. 1, d. 958, l. 10. This problem continued throughout the war. See RGASPI, f. 84, op. 1, d. 86, ll. 223–230. David Samoilov recorded in his diary how one commander demonstrated this point graphically when soldiers complained that they didn't receive their sugar ration. "You say that the *starshina* steals sugar? Of course. But you can consider this sin to be simply part of human nature [*pervorodnyi*]." He had the men in a long formation pass a chunk of dirt from one end to the next. When only a tiny portion got the other end he said: "How many hands did it pass though? And you see how much is left. The same thing happens with your sugar." David Samoilov, *Podennye zapisi,* vol. 1 (Moscow: Vremia, 2002), p. 164.

99. See GARF, f. R5446, op. 46a, d. 7395, l. 27–28. RGASPI, f. 88, op. 1, d. 958, l.13.

also understood that commanders often had guests (delegations from the rear, journalists, and so on) whom they needed to feed.[100]

A few cases of theft (or scapegoating) within a unit could have a ripple effect and send men at the top and bottom of the rear area into eminent peril for treating communal property as personal property. At best, a tribunal or punishment battalion meant humiliation; at worst— death. For example, in May of 1944, on the 3rd Belorussian Front, one Private M., a cook, was sent to a punishment battalion for two months for hiding 5.25 kilograms of meat and 4.9 kilograms of flour; a Lt. L. went before a military tribunal for the illegal use (most likely as currency) of a variety of luxury items (including sugar, meat, and fish); the head provisioning officer for their army, a Guards Major General, was removed from his position for allowing these abuses under his command.[101]

Conversely, hoarding resources could be a necessity for periods when provisions could not make their way from the rear to the front. L.P. Grachev, a provisioning officer on the Volkhov Front, recalled that he had set aside resources for a rainy day, which allowed for the successful development of an operation near Novgorod. His commanding officer, who found out about this only after it was clear that the operation would be successful, reminded him, "They shoot people for that!" but never brought it up again.[102] This was not the only time Grachev recalled a superior hinting at the possibility of execution, and such constant pressure undoubtedly impacted the way in which provisioning officers approached their task.[103] It appears that the difference between an illegal misappropriation of foodstuffs and the wily maintenance of resources "off the books" was circumstantial. Clearly, hoarding could be forgiven, or even encouraged by the exigencies of the war. Incompetence or greed, however, could not.

100. RGASPI, f. 88, op. 1, d. 958, ll. 11–13.

101. TsAMO RF, f. 241, op. 2618, d. 12, ll. 131–133, in Veshchikov et al., *Tyl Krasnoi Armii v Velikoi Otechestvennoi voine 1941–1945 gg.*, pp. 591–593.

102. Grachev, *Doroga ot Volkhova*, p. 241. This situation is quite similar to those described by Stephen Kotkin at Magnitostroi, in which cooked books and creative misplacement of resources were common. Stephen Kotkin, *Magnetic Mountain: Stalinism as Civilization* (Berkeley: University of California Press, 1995), pp. 55–61.

103. Grachev, *Doroga ot Volkhova*, pp. 230–231.

The State's Pot and the Soldier's Spoon

Incompetence and greed haunted the issue of both quality and quantity, either leading to the destruction of resources or their unlawful redistribution. Cases of uneven distribution abounded, as did incidents of simply ignoring proper storage and distribution. Food was left to rot or to be consumed by rats, or left unguarded to be stolen by hungry soldiers and civilians. For example, a report from the Transcaucasian Front in January of 1943 noted the "extreme carelessness" and "unsanitary conditions of Division Exchange Points" in which "grain is stored in heaps on a dirty floor" and "400 tons of potatoes were ruined," yet no one was brought to answer.[104] Under the difficult conditions of armies on the move, provisioning officers were forced to find new places to create warehouses during every advance and retreat, often in places utterly ravaged by war.[105] Inspections frequently found both field kitchens and canteens serving military personnel (including Moscow canteens that fed the staff of the People's Commissariat of Defense!) dirty and under-supplied.[106] Sometimes vegetables were boiled without being peeled, ruining them.[107] A fel'dsher was supposed to test all food before it was served to soldiers, and the results of these samplings were to be carefully recorded in a book that traveled with the field kitchen or canteen. Inspectors often complained that these books were nowhere to be seen, while a fel'dsher

---

104. E.g., TsAMO RF, f. 208, op. 2563, d. 47, ll. 212–214, in Veshchikov et al., *Tyl Krasnoi Armii v Velikoi Otechestvennoi voine 1941–1945 gg.*, pp. 258–261; TsAMO RF, f. 2, op. 795437, d. 9, l. 527, in ibid., pp. 261–262; TsAMO RF, f. 2, op. 795437, d. 9. l. 696, in ibid., pp. 291–292. RGASPI f. 88, op. 1, d. 958, l.15.

105. Antipenko, *Na glavnom upravlenii*, p. 125, discusses the difficulty of finding a standing building on liberated territory to set up the rear in 1944, and how this led to significant wastage of grain.

106. E.g., TsAMO RF, f. 208, op. 2563, d. 47, ll. 212–214, in Veshchikov et al., *Tyl Krasnoi Armii v Velikoi Otechestvennoi voine 1941–1945 gg.*, pp. 258–261; TsAMO RF, f. 2, op. 795437, d. 9, l. 696, in ibid., pp. 291–292, TsAMO RF, f. 47, op. 1029, d. 83, ll. 53–55, in ibid., pp. 321–325; RGVA, f. 4, op. 11, d. 73, ll. 299–301, in Barsukov et al., *Prikazy narodnogo komissara oborony SSSR 22 iiunia 1941 g.–1942 g.*, pp. 372–374; RGVA, f. 4, op. 11, d. 75, ll. 38–40, in Barsukov et al., *Prikazy narodnogo komissara oborony SSSR 1943–1945 gg.*, pp. 24–26; RGVA f. 4, op. 11, d. 75, ll. 41–46, in ibid., pp. 26–28; RGVA, f. 4, op. 11, d. 75, ll. 52–54, in ibid., pp. 29–30; RGVA, f. 4, op. 12, d. 107, ll. 307, in ibid., pp. 70–71.

107. RGVA, f. 4, op. 11, d. 75, ll. 38–40, in Barsukov et al., *Prikazy narodnogo komissara oborony SSSR 1943–1945 gg.*, pp. 24–25.

126   *Brandon Schechter*

could be held responsible for an impractically large area.[108] Soldiers could be given raw food with no way to prepare it, or worst of all, simply given nothing.[109]

All of this spoke to a violation of the state's obligation to its soldiers, who were quite conscious of their duties and those of the state. Wherever the state noted that the paëk was not being received, Soviet power was quick to find the culprits and ameliorate the situation. In Stalin's admonition to the Kalinin Front on May 31, 1943, the army was to retroactively make good what it had failed to give fighting men for up to five days of food stuffs and up to fifteen days of luxuries (tobacco, soap, vodka, etc.).[110] These obligations took on a wider scope as the war reached its turning point, as the state promised not only to provide calories, but to emphasize taste.

Improvement

By 1943 the state demanded very high quality rations, and standards sometimes contradicted the logic of provisioning more generally. Vil′iam Pokhlebkin noted that the categories used by the army to apportion foodstuffs were dramatically simplified and made no appeal to variety. As a result of this "came the 'era' of the potato, or pea, and suddenly the 'macaroni period' or continuously only oats or pearl barley"—whatever was on hand was whatever was going to be served.[111] As the war progressed and the Red Army's fortunes changed, these "eras," alongside the tendency to switch one type of product for another (such as egg powder for

---

108. On distances covered by *feld'shers,* see, for example, Vera Vasil′ievna Sokolova (Moskvina), Interview by Ilya Vershinin, Ia pomniu, http://www.iremember.ru/content /view/302/88/1/4/lang,en/ (23 March 2010); Moreinis, *Uchebnik pishchevoi gigieny,* pp. 193, 199–200, 206–208.

109. E.g., RGVA, f. 4, op. 11, d. 71, ll. 472–475, in Barsukov et al., *Prikazy narodnogo komissara oborony SSSR 22 iiunia 1941 g.–1942 g.,* pp. 273–275.

110. TsAMO RF, f. 2, op. 795437, d. 11, ll. 546–549, Veshchikov et al., *Tyl Krasnoi Armii v Velikoi Otechestvennoi voine 1941–1945 gg.,* p. 404.

111. Pokhlebkin, *Kukhnia Veka,* p. 209. See also "Pshennye dni," *Krasnaia zvevda,* June 8, 1943.

The State's Pot and the Soldier's Spoon

meat, potatoes or grains in place of anything else, and so on) became suspect and inexcusable.[112]

By 1943, the army began placing greater emphasis on who was cooking. Alongside the call for better and more varied ingredients, the army sought to improve the skills of cadres doing the cooking in three ways. The first was finding professional chefs who were already serving in the army (many of whom were in combat roles). The second was replacing men with women, as Stalin's order had called for the "preparation of the necessary number of women cooks for the active army by 1 September 1943."[113] This served a dual purpose of freeing men to serve in combat roles by providing what were presumed to be innately more skilled cadres (based on gendered assumptions) to provisioning.[114] Finally, the army showed that it was taking cooking more seriously by celebrating good cooks and shaming bad ones in Red Army publications.[115] Skilled cooks received medals and orders.[116] A special badge was created for "Excellent Cooks" in 1943, furthering their prestige, and intensive training courses were held in 1943 to train new (mainly female) cooks.[117] According to Vil'iam Pokhlebkin, this led to a period of experimentation and untying of the hands of military cooks that would ultimately alter the face of postwar Soviet culinary traditions.[118]

This spirit of innovation was not merely a phenomenon of the front line. Lend-Lease food from America required cooks to come up with new ways to use unfamiliar products, such as Spam, Vienna sausages,

---

112. TsAMO RF, f. 2, op. 795437, d. 11, ll. 546–549, in Veshchikov et al., *Tyl Krasnoi Armii v Velikoi Otechestvennoi voine 1941–1945 gg.,* p. 402.

113. TsAMO RF, f. 2, op. 795437, d. 11, ll. 546–549, in ibid., p. 404.

114. Antipenko, *Na glavnom upravlenii,* p. 322, states that 75 percent of the cadres in provisioning were women.

115. RGVA, f. 4, op. 11, d. 75, ll. 94–96, in Barsukov et al., *Prikazy narodnogo komissara oborony SSSR 1943–1945 gg.,* p. 38. See also "Krasnoarmeiskaia kukhnia," *Krasnaia zvevda,* April 11, 1943.

116. RGVA, f. 4, op. 11, d. 71, l. 472–475, in Barsukov et al., *Prikazy narodnogo komissara oborony SSSR 22 iiunia 1941 g.–1942 g.,* p. 274.

117. Kurkotkin, *Tyl vooruzhenikh sil,* p. 203.

118. Pokhlebkin, *Kukhnia veka,* pp. 212, 227, 230–231; Saushin, *Khleb i sol',* p. 59, agreed that cooks were taking the initiative and demonstrating greater confidence from 1943 on.

and deviled ham. In 1944, a special manual was created on how to read the labels of Lend-Lease products and prepare them.[119] Those further up the chain of command made constant efforts to improve rations and find new ways to stretch the finite resources of food. At the initiative of provisioning officers, soldiers often were assigned to agricultural work in areas to their rear. Beyond this, provisioning officers experimented with "vegetarian days,"[120] specialized foods for those in hospitals,[121] foraging for and utilizing wild herbs,[122] frozen foods (especially potatoes), and various types of foods that could be prepared in the rear and given to troops at the front. In one particularly innovative moment, F. S. Saushin, a provisioning officer on the Kalinin Front (after May of 1943), described how meat dumplings (*pelmeni*) were air dropped frozen to troops caught in encirclement.[123]

Food was an object that could turn rhetoric into a material reality. With rations, failure or success was physically apparent: soldiers could literally *feel* when the state was not holding up its end of the bargain. The state had promised to feed its soldiers and to punish those responsible for any failures in provisioning. This was a promise that the state intended to keep despite tremendous losses in every type of resource imaginable. As battlefield successes began to show the army's worth, as well as to return (often heavily damaged) resources to the state, a new set of expectations emerged, which led to greater demands on the part of the soldiers. Political and provisioning officers encouraged soldiers to speak honestly with them about how they were being fed and whether they had enough.

---

119. *Novye vidy produktov, postupaiushchikh na dovol'stvie Krasnoi Armii* (Moscow: Voenizdat, 1944) also included information on the new concentrates the army had developed.

120. These were days soldiers were given extra potatoes, bread, grains, and sugar instead of meat. Soy flour was used to compensate for the lack of protein. See *Pamiatka voiskovomu povaru*, p. 4. When asked how they liked this type of provisioning, one *starshina* stated: "The troops have come to really love the second vegetarian day . . . and all of them as one say that if on that day they could get a piece of meat, too, there would be nothing more to wish for" (Antipenko, *Na glavnom upravlenii*, pp. 213–214).

121. Antipenko, *Na glavnom upravlenii*, p. 131, describes specially raising rabbits in the rear to feed soldiers in hospitals.

122. TsAMO RF, f. 217, op. 1250, d. 183, l. 188, in Veshchikov et al., *Tyl Krasnoi Armii v Velikoi Otechestvennoi voine 1941–1945 gg.*, p. 417.

123. Saushin, *Khleb i sol'*, pp. 44, 59–61.

The State's Pot and the Soldier's Spoon   129

At a conference for propagandists and agitators in 1943, a new key method of agitation was discussed: "We should have taught agitators to start with *makhorka* [soldier's tobacco]: Is there enough of it? Have you eaten today? Every agitator—the new and old—should start with this."[124] Military psychologists also discovered a strong correlation between morale and provisioning.[125] One commander told war correspondent Vasily Grossman: "The worse the front, the more food reminds you of peacetime."[126] In conversation with the soldiers, agitators and provisioning and political officers learned how important hot food, tea, spices, and a smoke could be to men risking their lives in defense of the state. Indeed, the party-state showed a great deal of attention to the conditions soldiers lived under, undermining the oft-repeated assumption that Stalin and his associates viewed Soviet citizens solely as cannon fodder, a means to an end.[127] Soldiers' food and living conditions (*byt*) more generally were important enough to garner the attention of the most powerful people in the Soviet Union.

POTS AND SPOONS: EATING AND DRINKING IN THE RED ARMY

Conditions and Improvisation

The state had mandated that soldiers should be served a hot meal at least twice a day, with a cold course to be given out between them. While efforts were increasingly made to achieve this, the contingencies of war meant that even if the food was fresh and hot when it was ladled into thermoses, the soldiers did not always receive it warm. As Mikhail

---

124. "Soveshchaniie nachalnikov otdelov agitatsii i propagandy Politupravlenii frontov i okrugov," *Propagandist i agitator Krasnoi Armii*, no. 5–6 (1943): 22. With the introduction of *edinonachaliie* (the end of the dual command system of commissar and commander), political officers were encouraged to make surveillance of the material situation of soldiers, especially food, their top priority. See RGASPI, f.88, op.1, d.958, l.1.

125. Benjamin Zajicek, "Scientific Psychiatry in Stalin's Soviet Union: The Politics of Modern Medicine and the Struggle to Define 'Pavlovian' Psychiatry, 1939–1953." (PhD dissertation, University of Chicago, 2009), pp. 153–154.

126. Vasily [Vasilii] Grossman, *Gody voiny* (Moscow: Pravda, 1989), p. 362.

127. RGASPI f. 88, op. 1, d. 958, ll. 1–17.

Loginov, a platoon commander on the Kalinin Front recalled, after the ten-kilometer round trip to the field kitchen, his soldiers brought back "cold soup, cold kasha and cold tea. There is nothing and nowhere to heat up the food—neither dry spirits, nor firewood, and anyway, to start a fire at the front is forbidden. The enemy would notice and immediately bombard us."[128] Hot food was often an unrealizable goal, with field kitchens servicing three hundred or more men at a meal sometimes too far away to provide troops scattered over a wide front with food that was still hot. Posting kitchens close to the front endangered them with bombardment and capture. In the chaos of the front, some field kitchens ended up delivering themselves to the enemy.[129] The men sent for food could be killed, the thermoses destroyed.[130] During successful offensives, troops could outrun their rear area services, and were sometimes left to live on what they could capture (sometimes so successfully that they had no need to replenish their stocks).[131]

Making do in the absence of resources is part of the experience of military service everywhere, and the Red Army was no exception. Soldiers' rations could not help but reflect the situation the army found itself in at any given time. Sometimes, the issuing of luxuries was a sign of utter disaster: as one soldier remembers, in Sevastopol', days before its surrender to the Germans, he was given champagne because there was simply nothing else to drink.[132] Another soldier recalls that in the Caucasus Mountains, he and his paratrooper comrades subsisted on chocolate.[133] When matches became a rarity, soldiers "lived as in the times of [Hans

128. Loginov, *Eto bylo na fronte*, p. 9. See also NA IRI RAN, f. 2, razdel I, op. 223, d. 9, ll. 1–10b.

129. Loginov, *Eto bylo na fronte*, pp. 33–34.

130. Ibid., pp. 9–10.

131. TsAMO RF, f. 67, op. 12001, d. 5, ll. 202–217, in Veshchikov et al., *Tyl Krasnoi Armii v Velikoi Otechestvennoi voine 1941–1945 gg.*, p. 36; Boris Suris, *Frontovoi dnevnik: Dnevnik, rasskazy* (Moscow: ZAO Izdatel'stvo Tsentpoligraf, 2010), p. 65; and Tvardovskii, *Vasilii Tërkin*, p. 73. Indeed, part of the reason for the increased emphasis on food in 1943 was the fact that the army was going on the offensive, and provisioning would become increasingly difficult as it moved forward. RGASPI f. 88, op. 1, d. 958, l. 2.

132. Grigory Efimovich Zamikhovskii, Interview by Grigory Koifman, Ia pomniu, http://iremember.ru/krasnoflottsi/zamikhovskiy-grigoriy-efimovich/stranitsa-3.html (10 November 2013).

133. Boris Tartakovskii, *Iz dnevnikov voennykh let* (Moscow: AIRO-XX, 2005), p. 50.

The State's Pot and the Soldier's Spoon

Christian] Andersen," improvising "devilish contraptions" of flint, broken file, and wick.[134]

The need to improvise touched even the most everyday act of eating. Making do was a necessity in a world without chairs, tables, napkins, and other trappings of civility. The soldiers took their food in conditions that were quite different from the kitchens and canteens of the civilian world. Tvardovskii's hero *Tërkin* recalls how soldiers' new habits are inexcusable in "heaven"—the civilian world as exemplified by a rear-area hospital:

> In heaven you can't eat off your knee
> Only from the table
> And no one in heaven can
> Run to the kitchen with their mess tin
> And you can't sit in your threads
> And mangle bread with a bayonet.[135]

Eating in the active Red Army was something that was done wherever the food found its consumers—in bunkers, mud-filled trenches, woods, bombed-out cities, and along dusty roads.[136]

The calculations done in the rear concentrated on the body, not the psyche, and many soldiers felt that provisioning officers failed to take into account the extreme conditions under which they were living. Mansur Abdulin, serving near Stalingrad, mused:

> Irregular food, chronic lack of sleep, hunger, constant physical overload.... We drink dirty water, from melted dirty snow from dirty mess pots.... How did we suffer through this? The mind can't conceive of it! I repeat, the conditions of foxhole life in the steppes near Stalingrad were very difficult. This is without mentioning the threat of death hanging over your head every minute.[137]

---

134. Suris, *Frontovoi dnevnik*, p. 37. See also *Vospominaniia frontovikov*, p. 8. Here supply officers discuss tying strikers and flint to soldiers' rain capes.

135. Tvardovskii, *Vasilii Tërkin*, p. 124.

136. M. G. Abdulin, *160 stranits iz soldatskogo dnevnika* (Moscow: Molodaia gvardiia, 1985), p. 40.

137. Abdulin, *160 stranits iz soldatskogo dnevnika*, p. 40; Loginov, *Eto bylo na fronte*, p. 10, recalled that "For civilians this isn't a bad ration, but in the trenches, for *frontoviks*, it's a bit small. The cold, damp, sleepless nights and nervous tension take a lot of energy. Soldiers don't get enough sleep and don't eat enough, and so they want to sleep and eat all the time."

Conditions on the front could be extreme, and even when food was ample, soldiers suffered from nerves and exhaustion. At times, they found it difficult to eat even when there was ample food, as Mikhail Loginov, a platoon commander on the Kalinin Front recalled: "From no man's land a little wind blows, bringing the slightly sweet smell of corpses, filling the trench. We have trouble breathing and a few get nauseous and throw up. Dinner is brought up in thermoses, but I can't look at the meat or kasha. I give my portion to the soldiers, and myself have only bread and cold tea from my canteen."[138] Stress and trauma both created a greater physical need for sustenance and complicated the body's ability to consume. Some soldiers could shrug off the sights and smells of the trenches, but others could not eat under such conditions, thus subverting the science of provisioning.

During the first two years of the war, when the situation with meat in the army was critical, soldiers and resourceful cooks found a solution on the battlefield.[139] Boris Slutskii remembered how: "In the first spring of the war, when supply became unlikely, we came to eat horse meat. We killed healthy horses (illegally); I can still remember the sweet, sweaty smell of soup with horse."[140] Numerous accounts and archival documents recall how horsemeat became a common source of protein at the front as soldiers cut off from supply found themselves eating their four-legged comrades killed in battle.[141] Lesin recalled how in April of 1942, horsemeat was the main source of food for him and his comrades.[142] At first this idea disgusted him: "To him, a Tatar, *makhan* [slang for horsemeat] is the same as pork to a Russian. We all have a taste for horsemeat now . . . . We ate it without salt. It was appetizing all the same. We ate without bread, a second or third pot-full."[143] Military translator Irina Dunaevskaia initially described soldiers mocking Kazakhs who ate horse, but later noted that she and a comrade were "lucky" when a shell

138. Loginov, *Eto bylo na fronte*, p. 10.
139. As to the crisis with meat, see Zotov, *Pishchevaia promyshlennost'*, p. 128; Saushin, *Khleb i sol'*, p. 115–116; and Pokhlebkin, *Kukhnia veka*, p. 209.
140. Slutskii, *O dugikh i o sebe*, p. 29.
141. E.g., RGASPI, f. 88, op. 1, d. 958, l. 2.
142. Lesin, *Byla voina*, pp. 85, 89, 99, 102, 149–150.
143. Ibid., p. 99.

The State's Pot and the Soldier's Spoon

killed a horse, and they ate "makhan (there is no other way than this Tatar word that this is called at the front)."[144] Horse carrion (*propastina*), was of course of questionable quality, but as surgeon Vera Malakhova noted, it was something "we ate all the time."[145]

Given the unequal distribution of rations along the front, units that were worse off than those around them could get a bad reputation for their love of horseflesh. A report filed after an inspection of the 50th Army (on the Kalinin Front, where Saushin, Lesin and Loginov served) noted that Colonel Samsonov admitted his division had eaten 175 of its horses:

> The situation in this division has gotten so bad, that the 116th Division has become known throughout the units of the army. For example, Lt. Bychkov in the 10th Army's 385th Rifle Regiment stated in our interview about the possibility of moving into the area of the 50th Army—be careful, don't leave your horses standing around, because the "Samsons" will eat them right away.[146]

Horses were not part of paëk, and their consumption could be both demoralizing and counterproductive. But in the darkest days of hunger, they soon found their way into the soldier's pot as an expedient way to make up for what the state could not provide.[147]

Troops sometimes resorted to theft (even on the front lines) as a means of insuring survival. This sort of theft could undermine unit morale, as when a group of former convicts stole all of a unit's food. On the other hand, it could bring a unit closer together as they put their

---

144. Dunaevskaia, *Ot Leningrada do Kënigsberga,* pp. 158, 296.

145. Vera Ivanovna Malakhova, "Four Years a Frontline Physician," in Barbara Alpern Engel and Anastasia Posadskaya-Vanderbeck, eds., *A Revolution of Their Own: Voices of Women in Soviet History* (Boulder, Colo.: Westview Press, 1998), pp. 175–218; pp. 209–211; Kharis Yakupov, *Frontovye zarisovki: zapiski khudozhnika* (Kazan': Tatknigizdat, 1981), p. 30, describes "soldiers shish-kebabs" of artillery horses on the cleaning rods of guns, while Abdullin, *160 stranits iz soldatskogo dnevnika,* p. 22, recalls his bread ration being given to horses to keep them alive, while he himself, p. 59, experimented with (and almost died from) eating *kombikorm,* a concentrated horse fodder.

146. TsAMO RF, f. 2, op. 795437, d.9, ll. 394–395, in Veshchikov et al., *Tyl Krasnoi Armii v Velikoi Otechestvennoi voine 1941–1945 gg.,* p. 237.

147. Less depressing examples of making do come from Nikolai Chekovich, *Dnevnik ofitsera,* pp. 47–48, who wrote home about fishing with hand grenades, and Yakupov, *Frontovye zarisovk*i, p. 73, who recalled that on the Dnepr men ate fish that had been stunned by German shelling.

134   *Brandon Schechter*

needs above those of the army at large.[148] The state had taken very harsh measures to discourage theft, but for people enduring prolonged hunger and possible starvation, the risks seemed worth taking.

Yet theft, or the perception of thievery, could destroy bonds within a unit, so a means of fair distribution of rations was key to morale. At the front, exact measurements of food, especially the multiple components of dry rations, proved impractical. Some *starshiny* found their own way out of this, using magazines and discs from weapons as ersatz weights, a practice noted and condemned by *Krasnaia zvezda,* the army's daily newspaper.[149] However, the most common arrangement in order to ensure fairness in the distribution of rations was a system found in many armies throughout history:

> Bread, sugar and meat are divided into portions and spread out on a *plash-palatka* [rain cape]. One of the soldiers turns to the side and the one who divided the rations points to a portion and asks:
> "Whose?"
> The soldier turned to the side names any name.
> With this sort of division no one is offended.[150]

148. See Izo Davidovich Adamskii, Interview by Grigory Koifman, Ia pomniu, http://iremember.ru/minometchiki/adamskiy-izo-davidovich.html (10 November 2013); Meir Faivelevich Toker, Interview by Grigory Koifman, Ia pomniu, http://iremember.ru/svyazisti/toker-meir-fayvelevich.html (10 November 2013). See also TsA FSB RF, f. 14, op. 4, d. 418, ll. 19–20, in Pogonii, *Stalingradskaia epopeia,* pp. 246–248. Theft and begging were often forced on soldiers who for one or another bureaucratic reason found themselves outside of the responsibilities of one or another provisioning officer—i.e., those whose paperwork were not in order or found themselves on the territory of another unit.

149. "Dolg voennykh khoziastvennikov," *Krasnaia zvezda,* July 4, 1943. It is worth noting that the *starshina* was a figure often derided and assumed to be corrupt. See, for example, Viktor Astaf'ev, *Prokliati i ubity* (Moscow: Terra, 1999), p. 109: "although Shpator never drank, smoked and was a totally unselfish person—all the same no one believed this, because *starshini* are all swindlers, boozers and womanizers, so he must be such."

150. The *plash-palatka* was a soldier's piece of equipment that served as both a rain cape and half of a tent. Loginov, *Eto bylo na fronte,* p. 9–10. Anatoly Nikolaevich Muzhikov, Interview by Bair Irincheev, Ia pomniu, http://iremember.ru/minometchiki/muzhikov-anatoliy-nikolaevich.html (November 10, 2013), discusses the occasional envy this caused, while Abdulin, *160 stranits iz soldatskogo dnevnika,* pp. 6–8, recalls that his comrade divided up their rations and was trusted to do so.

The State's Pot and the Soldier's Spoon   135

Such a system ensured that any inequality in rations was an act of god, rather than an act of nepotism or ill will. This maintained a sense of fairness at the lowest level of ration distribution, and kept disputes over what was probably the most valuable commodity to a minimum.

Eating from the Same Pot

Eating in the Red Army was a collective activity that could strengthen bonds between the diverse men and women in the ranks. It was a time of rest, when soldiers took stock of their situation, remembered home, got to know each other, and replenished their physical strength.

While soldiers seemed to always want more to eat, situations where food was ample were not necessarily occasions for celebration. The strict ratios of products to soldiers proved difficult to fulfill as casualties mounted on the front, as the head of provisioning of the 1st Belorussian Front, N. A. Antipenko, recalled:

> In the course of an operation, as we all know, troops take casualties. Their computation is always behind—a more detailed account comes only significantly later. There are fewer people, sometimes one half or one third of the original number, but the higher authorities continue to send food for the entire unit. Therefore, a soldier in the course of an offensive received unlimited food.[151]

This sudden abundance could be less than a joyous occasion, as one soldier recalled:

> There was no one living around. Near the morning the cook crawled up with thermoses of vodka and boiled horse. But there wasn't anyone to drink up or eat. It fell to me to drink a large cup of vodka for everyone.[152]

Moments of rest and feeding actually underlined the losses that a unit had suffered, as those who remained consumed the portions of their absent comrades.[153] A passage from the autobiographical novel *Naveki*

---

151. Antipenko, *Na glavnom upravlenii*, pp. 148–149.

152. Genrikh Zinov'ievich Kats, Interview by Grigorii Koifman, Ia pomniu, http://iremember.ru/razvedchiki/kats-genrikh-zinovevich.html (10 November 2013).

153. Temkin recounts that he had been counted dead, a mistake no one noticed until an "extra mouth" was found in his unit; Temkin, *My Just War*, pp. 117–118.

deviatnadtsatletnii (Forever Nineteen), written by a veteran, captures this moment eloquently:

> Only after he swallowed, did he look at what he was eating. In his mess pot was thick, yellow pea soup. And with this spoon, with his eyes closed, he mentally held a funerary feast for those, who today were no longer with them. They were still here, all the same, they could stumble into the kitchen at any moment, sit in the sun.[154]

Eating was when you realized that you were alive, a visceral moment that separated the living and the dead.[155] As a result, army food could evoke strong emotions and potent memories, and, as we see from this quotation, could create the sense that those who had fallen were near.

A sense of communality was supported by the most quotidian details of provisioning. Soldiers were supposed to receive two dishes yet they were issued only one mess pot, and given that shortage was a general rule, there were often many fewer pots than soldiers.[156] Red Army pots came in two styles. One was a copy of the German mess-tin issued in both world wars, which was a kidney shaped aluminum pot with a bail-like handle and a shallow top that doubled as a cup.[157] The other was a simple round pot of varying depths with a bail handle but no top. The mess pot was not entirely the soldier's and not entirely the state's, much like the food that was consumed in it.[158] The pot was issued by the state,

---

154. Grigorii Baklanov, "Naveki deviatnadtsatletnii," in *Voennye* povesti (Moscow: Sovetskii pisatel', 1981), p. 280.

155. Abdullin, *160 Stranits iz soldatskogo dnevnika*, p. 134, describes a touching moment in his memoirs where the smell of kasha and act of eating is when he realizes that, somehow, he has survived.

156. As late as August of 1944, Khrulev complained that there was a deficit of 2.7 million mess-tins at the front. GARF, f. R5446, op. 46a, d. 7161, l. 2.

157. This model was deemed more useful. TsAMO RF, f. 208, op. 14703 c, d. 2, ll. 339–343, in Veshchikov et al., *Tyl Krasnoi Armii v Velikoi Otechestvennoi voine 1941–1945 gg.*, p. 137.

158. Several documents speak to the attention paid by the state to shortages of pots and spoons, including orders to manufacture them locally. See TsAMO RF, f. 47, op. 1029, d. 83, ll. 53–55, in Veshchikov et al., *Tyl Krasnoi Armii v Velikoi Otechestvennoi voine 1941–1945 gg.*, pp. 321–325; TsAMO RF, f. 233, op. 29302, d. 6, ll. 15–18, in ibid., p. 419. Anatolii Genatulin, *Strakh* (Moscow: Sovetskii voin, 1990), p. 25, describes spoons and mess pots being taken from the dead by their surviving comrades.

The State's Pot and the Soldier's Spoon

but it was one of the few items of a soldier's kit that seemed to belong specifically to him or her (if there were enough to go around). It was not uncommon for soldiers to decorate their pots with their name, a place where they had served, or the name of a friend or random acquaintance. Lev Yur'evich Slezkin carved the names of two Estonian women he met before the war onto the side of the pot he carried through most of his service "in memory of a pleasant, romantic meeting."[159] By carving names, initials, places, and dates into government-issued items, soldiers turned an anonymous piece of metal into a deeply personal item that recorded parts of their biography.

Mess-pots served not only for consuming and occasionally preparing food; they could also be used for individual washing. As one female soldier recalled, "Mess-tins! We had them for food, to wash our clothes in, to wash up ourselves with—everywhere mess-tins!"[160] One soldier informed his correspondent that he was using the bottom of his mess-tin as a desk.[161] Many soldiers lacking vitamin A suffered from night blindness, which created serious problems on long marches under the cover of darkness. In this case, banging a rod on the mess-pot of the man in front enabled the blinded soldier to complete night marches.[162] A soldier's mess-pot was something like a room in a portable home, serving as dining room, and sometimes as kitchen and shower. However, as all activities in the army took place in the company of others, the soldier shared the pot with his or her comrades.

159. Slezkin, *Do voiny i na voine,* p. 347.

160. Golubkova Iudif' Vladimirovna, Interview by Artem Drabkin, Ia pomniu, http://www.iremember.ru/content/view/385/85/1/3/lang,en/ (14 March 2010). See Malakhova, "Four Years a Frontline Physician," pp. 199, 204–205.

161. Gamilzhan Valiev, *Soldat khatlar* (Yar Chally, 2000), p. 57.

162. Genadii Tokarev, *Vesti dnevnik na fronte zapreshchalos'* (Novosibirsk: Svin'in i synov'ia, 2005), p. 137: "We moved only after sun down, so that enemy planes wouldn't spot us. . . . So a company is marching in the dark, and on the side of the road a chain of 'the blind' being led by somebody who can see. Later they didn't form a separate column, as we found a simpler way to ease the march of the 'blind men.' Every 'blind man' was given a cleaning rod and placed behind someone who could see. From time to time the 'blind man' would bang his cleaning rod on the mess pot hanging off the pack of the 'seeing man' in front of him. In the night all you could hear was the quiet ring of cleaning rods against mess pots."

When food was doled out to soldiers, one pot was filled with soup, the other with kasha.[163] Soldiers would eat in pairs, as Gabriel Temkin remembers:

> We ate from one *kotelok* (mess tin), using approximately the same size wooden spoons. We would eat by turns, I a spoonful and then he a spoonful, slowly, as becoming among comrades. Having finished the soup or kasha, we would lick clean our personal spoons and put them back in place, where they were customarily kept—behind the top of the right or left boot. Front-line soldiers would sometimes, in panicky retreats, throw away their heavy rifles, but never their spoons.[164]

Such an arrangement helped to build a sense of comradeship, as soldiers of different ages and ethnicities would often find themselves eating from the same pot.[165] Nonetheless, the soldier still had at least one item that was exclusively his, and in many ways the mark of a front-line soldier— the spoon that he was even less likely to give up than his rifle.

Spoons

Very little of what soldiers carried belonged to them. Their clothes were the property of the state. When they went to a bathhouse to wash up, they were not guaranteed to get their own set of underwear back. Their weapons also belonged to the state, as did the food they ate. However, the spoon was something that the individual soldier owned. Draft notices told inductees to bring a spoon, a cup, towel, and change of underwear.[166] Given that the towel and underwear would soon be worn out, the spoon and cup were among the few items from the civilian world that soldiers would carry throughout their service. Spoons were frequently individualized with initials and artwork, and are often the only way to identify soldiers whose remains are found today. The spoon could be wooden or metal, a traditional Russian triangular spoon or an oval soup-spoon. German and Finnish folding spoons were also popular, as they

---

163. Loginov, *Eto bylo na fronte*, p. 9.
164. Temkin, *My Just War*, p. 104.
165. Loginov, *Eto bylo na fronte*, p. 24.
166. "Mobilizatsionnoe predpisanie (oborot)," Soldat.ru, http://www.soldat.ru/doc /original/original.html?img=mobpredpis&id=2 (Accessed 25 January, 2014).

The State's Pot and the Soldier's Spoon

were easily carried and their handles doubled as forks. Some soldiers made their own spoons out of scraps found on the battlefield, such as downed planes.[167] In one case, an officer found craftsmen from among his soldiers, took them from the front line, and put them to work carving spoons for soldiers in need.[168] Spoons were a frequent item in government supply orders throughout the war: in the third quarter of 1942 alone, 1.9 million wooden spoons were ordered.[169]

The spoon was the only utensil a soldier was expected to have; all of his or her food was designed to be eaten either with a spoon or bare hands. As such, the spoon became a mark of a real soldier. Vera Malakhova, a front-line surgeon, recalled an embarrassing moment near Odessa. While joining a group of soldiers sitting down to a meal, she realized that she lacked something the men around her all possessed: " 'Well, why don't you eat?' 'I don't have a spoon,' I answered. 'What sort of a blankety-blank are you? Just what sort of soldier are you? Why don't you have a spoon?' "[170] Even the sukhpaëk could not be consumed without a spoon, meaning a soldier reduced to a minimum carried a spoon and a rifle. The soldier's spoon helped to separate the military experience from the civilian world. In a letter home in 1939, Lev Slezkin describes eating in a café "like troglodytes, looking with tender emotion at knives and forks (in the barracks we eat only with spoons)."[171] Spoons were the implement of individual consumption and a deeply prized, rare piece of personal property. Yet every aspect of the soldier's paëk could be treated as if it were personal property, and not only by corrupt commanders.

Currencies, Rituals, Substitutes, and Valuables: Tobacco, Tea, Vodka, Water, and Bread

Food became a tradable commodity under conditions of extreme scarcity. People receiving rations throughout the country were often willing to part with durable goods (such as clothing and jewelry) for consumables

---

167. Kats, Interview.
168. *Vospominaniia frontovikov*, p. 7.
169. RGASPI, f. 84, op. 1, d. 83, l. 172.
170. Malakhova, "Four Years a Frontline Physician," p. 201.
171. Slezkin, *Do voini i na voine*, p. 328.

(such as bread, meat, and vodka). As one war correspondent recorded in his diary in January of 1943, "The modern form of payment is vodka and bread."[172] Exchanges, especially of "luxury" items, were very common at the front, as Boris Slutskii recalled: "In the trenches there was a lively exchange business! Tobacco for sugar, a portion of vodka for two portions of sugar. The prosecutor struggled with this barter in vain."[173] Boris Komskii, a mortar man, recorded in his diary that he exchanged a watch (a particularly valuable item that he had taken from a German soldier whom he shot) for food while lying in a field hospital.[174] These types of exchanges both highlighted the rituals of consumption that took place in the army, and allowed those who did not drink or smoke to participate in or profit from them by either exchanging their portions of tobacco and alcohol or giving them away.[175] These coveted items were not only potential commodities, but also consumables that were used collectively.

"Let's smoke one together, comrade!" was the chorus to a popular wartime song.[176] Tobacco was considered to be so important that the provisioning officer of the Kalinin ront was flown to Moscow to procure it in the spring of 1944 and ordered not to return without *makhorka*. He did this despite orders not to send delegations from the front to beg from manufacturers.[177] Tobacco was such an integral part of military culture that

172. Aleksandr Ustinov, " 'Zavtra uedem v armiiu': Iz frontovogo dnevnika fotozhurnalista," *Rodina*, no. 6 (2011): p. 23.

173. Slutskii, *O drugikh i o sebe*, p. 29.

174. Boris Komskii, "Dnevnik 1943–1945 gg.," in *Arkhiv evreiskoi istorii*, vol. 6. (Moscow: ROSSPEN, 2011), p. 30.

175. Rakhimzan Koshkarbaev, *Shturm: Den'1410* (Alma-Ata: Zhalyn, 1983), p. 109. The author tells of an Uzbek soldier in his platoon who would divide his vodka ration among his comrades.

176. A. Lukovnikov, *Druz'ia-olnopolchane: Rasskazy o pesniakh, rozhdennykh voinoi, melodii i teksty* (Moscow: Muzyka, 1985), pp. 32–33.

177. Saushin, *Khleb i sol'*, pp. 87–93; the quality of this tobacco was very poor, and it was referred to by even those sending it to the front as " *feliton*"—given the purplish smoke it created, which was much like the purplish ink used in the Soviet Union. As to the order forbidding delegations in both 1941 and a repeat order in 1943, see RGVA f. 4, op. 12, d. 98, ll. 507–508, in Barsukov et al., *Prikazy narodnogo komissara oborony SSSR 22 iiunia 1941 g.–1942 g.*, p. 48; RGVA, f. 4, op. 11, d. 75, ll. 16–17, in Barsukov et al., *Prikazy narodnogo komissara oborony SSSR 1943–1945gg.*, pp. 18–19. However, it appears that appealing to the center for items in serious deficit was a standard part of how provisioning

The State's Pot and the Soldier's Spoon

the state was dedicated to providing its soldiers with smokes despite a nationwide reduction to 25 percent of prewar production.[178] Smoking, a communal activity that was often experienced as a different form of time, brought soldiers together in moments of rest and was often accompanied by sugary black tea.[179]

Tea, which, according to a nutrition textbook from 1940, was "almost without nutritional value" was to be given to soldiers *hot*, twice a day, and manuals reminded soldiers that it was preferable to water.[180] Some aspects of the soldier's ration were clearly aimed at psychological, rather than nutritional benefits and were invested with important social meaning. Tobacco and tea were useful stimulants; the latter, served warm, could save men dying of frostbite. Tea was a particularly good delivery system for sugar and quick calories, something that has contributed to its global popularity.[181] Both caffeine and nicotine could enliven men psychologically numbed by the lack of sleep that accompanied hard fighting and long marches. They also leant themselves to ritualized, habitual use.[182] Vodka, a depressant, could calm the nerves of men who had seen ghastly sights.

Vodka had only recently returned to the Red Army soldier's ration, the experience of the Finnish War having shown its value in staving off frostbite and death by exposure. Still, its distribution was constantly modified and a cause of concern.[183] In the spring of 1943, Colonel Dulov,

---

worked. A front seemed more or less invisible to the center while its provisioning was in order, and became visible in moments of crisis.

178. Zotov, *Pishchevaia promyshlennost'*, p. 483.

179. On cigarettes and relaxation, see Richard Klein, *Cigarettes Are Sublime* (Durham, N.C.: Duke University Press, 1993), especially chapter 5, "The Soldier's Friend."

180. Moreinis, *Uchebnik pishchevoi gigieny dlia sanitarno-feldsherskikh shkol*, p. 146; S. Gurov, *Boets i otdelenie na pokhode* (Moscow: Voenzidat, 1941), p. 22; TsAMO RF, f. 2, op. 795437, d.9, l. 696, in Veshchikov et al., *Tyl Krasnoi Armii v Velikoi Otechestvennoi voine 1941–1945 gg.*, p. 291; TsAMO RF, f. 47, op. 1029, d. 84, ll. 23–24, in ibid., p. 381; Krotkov, *Gigiena*, p. 39.

181. Sidney W. Mintz, *Sweetness and Power: The Place of Sugar in Modern History* (Penguin: New York, 1986), pp. 108–109, 114, 122.

182. See ibid., pp. 110, 122, on the ritualization of goods.

183. RGVA, f. 4, op. 14, d. 2737, ll.58–70, in N. S. Tarkhov, ed.,"*Zimniaia voina*": *Rabota nad oshibkami (aprel'–mai 1940 g.): Materialy komissiy Glavnogo voennogo soveta*

commanding the 146th Rifle Division from Tatarstan, wrote to his representative in the Presidium of the Supreme Soviet of the Tatar ASSR, Comrade Dinmukhametov, about which gifts from home were useful and which were better left in the Republic:

> I have a request. If you are going to send us packages, do not send vodka, it is issued by the order of the People's Commissar. Extra vodka sent by you is exactly that—extra and is used by many commanders to satisfy excessive personal needs, which creates an unhealthy mood and a number of other consequences coming from this. Instead of vodka, it is better to send other gifts, especially foodstuffs, leather, etc.[184]

More so than any other component of the soldier's ration, vodka presented a potential threat that required careful regulation. A drunken soldier was a danger to himself and others, more likely to steal, harass civilians, be rude to his superiors and subordinates, and die foolishly.[185] In any army alcohol could pose a serious problem, as numerous accounts attest. As a result, vodka rations were constantly being re-regulated and the issuing of extra rations censured.

Beginning with the Finnish campaign, soldiers received a winter ration of one hundred grams (3.4 fl. oz.) of vodka.[186] On August 25, 1941, one hundred grams of 80-proof vodka per day was introduced for all soldiers on the front line, pilots, and technical support troops at aerodromes. Vodka was to be given out only to those persons who earned it by risking their lives. It was also to be guarded and accounted for with vigilance. Dispensation depended on a monthly application with details

---

Krasnoi Armii po obobshcheniu opyta finskoi kompanii (Moscow-St. Petersburg: Letnii sad, 2004), p. 118; Antipenko, *Na glavnom upravelneii*, p. 149; RGVA, f. 4, op. 11, d. 65, ll. 413–414, in Barsukov et al., *Prikazy narodnogo komissara oborony SSSR 22 iiunia 1941 g.–1942 g.* 73; RGVA, f. 4, op. 11, d. 70, ll. 548–549, in ibid.; RGVA, f. 4, op. 11, d. 71, ll. 191–192, in ibid., pp. 252–253; RGVA, f. 4, op. 11, d. 73, ll. 154–155, in ibid., 365–366; RGVA, f. 4, op. 11, d. 75, l. 51, in Barsukov et al., *Prikazy narodnogo komissara oborony SSSR 1943–1945gg.*, p. 28; RGVA, f. 4, op. 11, d. 75, l. 649, in ibid., p. 145.

184. NART, f. R-3610, op. 1, d. 327, l. 40.

185. See Genatulin, *Strakh*, pp. 19–22, on what it felt like to go into combat having drunk a double ration of vodka, and Komskii, "Dnevnik," pp. 27–28, on the results of an assault led by a drunken officer.

186. RGVA, f. 4, op. 14, d. 2737, ll. 58–70, in Tarkhov, *"Zimniaia voina,"* p. 118.

The State's Pot and the Soldier's Spoon   143

as to the number of troops in a unit and the amount consumed.[187] This was not the last word on vodka. By mid-May 1942, vodka became an inducement to fight, as only "units successfully advancing" were to be given vodka—and two hundred grams (6.8 fl. oz.) of it, twice the amount previously given to the army at large. Meanwhile, their comrades received one hundred grams of vodka only on revolutionary holidays.[188] The distribution of vodka on those holidays remained the most consistent aspect of vodka use in the Red Army. Within a month, the May order was replaced by a new rule giving one hundred grams to all troops engaged in offensive operations and on revolutionary holidays. This latest order also noted that it was illegal for officers to use their rank to drink vodka whenever they pleased, and called for greater vigilance in securing vodka at the front.[189] By November 13, 1942, the rules changed yet again: everyone under fire would receive one hundred grams per day; reserves would receive fifty grams (1.7 fl. oz.), and those serving in the Caucasus would receive fortified wine in place of vodka. This order also established limits per front for the period from November 25 till December 31, 1942, amounting to anywhere between 364,000 and 980,000 liters by front and 5,691,000 in the army as a whole, with 99,000 going to the 7th Separate Army and 1.2 million liters of wine being issued to the Transcaucasian Front.[190] Finally, in May of 1943, the army returned to the principal of offensive operations and holidays being the only times a soldier earned his hundred grams.[191]

The state's approach to rationing vodka rested on the notion that it could manage the delicate balance between calming nerves and inducing drunkenness. Soldiers, however, disposed of their rations in various ways.

187. RGVA, f. 4, op. 11, d. 65, ll. 413–414, in Barsukov et al., *Prikazy narodnogo komissara oborony SSSR 22 iiunia 1941 g.–1942 g.,* p. 73.

188. RGVA, f. 4, op. 11, d. 70, ll. 548–549, in Barsukov et al., *Prikazy narodnogo komissara oborony SSSR 22 iiunia 1941 g.–1942 g.,* p. 228.

189. RGVA, f. 4. op. 11, d. 71, ll. 191–192, in Barsukov et al., *Prikazy narodnogo komissara oborony SSSR 22 iiunia 1941 g.–1942 g.,* pp. 252–253.

190. RGVA, f. 4, op. 11, d. 73, ll. 154–155, in Barsukov et al., *Prikazy narodnogo komissara oborony SSSR 22 iiunia 1941 g.–1942 g.,* pp. 365–366.

191. RGVA, f. 4, op. 11, d. 75, l. 649, in Barsukov et al., *Prikazy narodnogo komissara oborony SSSR 1943–1945 gg.,* p. 145.

Some women soldiers reported never having received a vodka ration; others noted that they gave theirs away.[192] Among Muslim soldiers, several accounts mention believers giving their vodka to their comrades.[193] Trade and gift-giving disrupted the state's attempt to manage soldiers' use of vodka

By its nature alcohol was potentially dangerous. Mansur Abdullin recalled the catastrophe that ensued when Red Army soldiers discovered an intact distillery abandoned by the Germans in retreat:

> How could you take a distillery and not get tight? That seemed unnatural. What a cursed self-hypnosis! . . . Many of our guys "tied one on" . . . and thirty fascist tanks with flamethrowers came at us full speed ahead. . . . It is painful to remember. Sober, on stable feet, you can orient yourself and maneuver. Many people who had heroically fought perished in the sticky flames.[194]

Similar accounts abound in the second half of the war. Drink offered one of the few escapes for men under severe stress. While obviously unwise from a self-preservation standpoint, "tying one on" for men who had no ability to make long term plans and who could be killed despite their best efforts to survive may have made sense despite the presence of the enemy. Access to alcohol only increased as the war continued, as Red Army men came to the wine cellars of East Central Europe.[195] Once this happened, it became increasingly difficult to control the consumption habits of Red Army men.[196]

The ambiguities of vodka as doled out by the state had a peculiar effect, according to Pokhlebkin: "by 1945, the use of vodka, which had

192. Nina Ivanovna Kunitsina, Interview by Artem Drabkin, Ia pomniu, http://iremember.ru/letno-tekh-sostav/kunitsina-nina-ivanovna.html (Accessed 10 November 2013), and Klavdiia Andreevna Deriabina (Ryzhkova), Interview by Artem Drabkin, Ia pomniu, http://iremember.ru/letchiki-bombardirov/deryabina-rizhkova-klavdiya-andreevna-letchitsa-po-2.html (Accessed 10 November 2013). See also Slezkine, *Do voini i na voine*, p. 401, concerning his distaste for vodka.

193. E.g., Koshkarbaev, *Shturm*, p. 109.

194. Abdulin, *160 stranits iz soldatskogo dnevnika*, p. 105.

195. See Slutsky, *O drugikh i o sebe*, p. 30, Temkin, *My Just War*, p. 197, and Nikulin, *Vospominaniia o voine*, pp. 144, 169. 187, 199, for further anecdotes concerning alcohol at the front.

196. Some diarists record an increase in drinking in 1945. See, for example Suris, *Frontovoi dnevnik*, p. 204–205, 234, 236; Inozemtsev, *Frontovoi dnevnik*, pp. 199, 208–209, 226.

The State's Pot and the Soldier's Spoon

been low-class and forbidden suddenly became very prestigious among the mid-level leadership . . . and refusing your allotted portion of spirits was already understood as an element of opposition and disloyalty."[197] Who, after all, would refuse part of their paëk?

The state did not plan to provide soldiers with water. A moderately active male needs around three liters of water per day to remain hydrated. Most soldiers would have needed more. Getting fresh water at the front was an immensely difficult task, to which poet Aleksandr Tvardovskii alluded in the opening of his poem *Vasily Tërkin*:

> From a well,
> From a pond,
> From a water pipe,
> From the impression of a horse shoe,
> From a river, anyhow,
> From a brook, from underneath ice—
> There is nothing better than cold water,
> As long as the water is water.[198]

Soldiers were issued half-liter canteens and were supposed to bring their own mugs upon mobilization. The canteen, however, often suffered from several shortcomings. In order to economize on precious aluminum, the material used for both canteens and parts of planes, the army began manufacturing glass canteens. A report concerning equipment in the first three months of the war concluded: "The canteen in and of itself is convenient, but the glass ones are very fragile and the aluminum ones are too few and expensive to make."[199] Glass canteens would continue to be manufactured as a stopgap measure. Even though metal canteens were supposed

---

197. Vil'iam Pokhlebkin, *Istoriya vazhneyshikh pishchevykh produktov* (Moscow: Tsentrpoligraf, 2001), p. 272.

198. Tvardovskii, *Vasilii Terkin*, p. 5.

199. TsAMO RF, f. 208, op. 14703 c, d. 2, ll. 339–343, in Veshchikov *et al.*, *Tyl Krasnoi Armii v Velikoi Otechestvennoi voine 1941–1945 gg.*, p. 137. See also Krotkov, *Gigiena*, p. 92: "During the war all front and army sanitary inspectors unanimously demanded the replacement of glass canteens with metal canteens, most significantly aluminum, which resists well the influence of high and low temperatures, does not shatter on the march and while advancing and is almost three times lighter than glass"; see also ibid., pp. 118–119, for special instructions as how to keep canteens from freezing and thus bursting.

146   *Brandon Schechter*

to become the norm, over 4 million glass ones were ordered in the third quarter of 1942 and 5 million in the third quarter of 1943 alone.[200]

The army published norms for hydration as well as recommendations on what, when, and how to drink.[201] It was estimated that every soldier consumed 10–15 liters of water a day, drinking 3–4.5 liters and using the rest for preparing food and cleaning.[202] Medics were responsible for testing all water sources, which were to be clearly marked as potable, useful for coolant, and so on, and manuals diagrammed and described a variety of purification methods that soldiers and medical personnel could devise.[203] In practice, water was not something that the army could always provide, and soldiers were officially tasked with finding or digging their own wells and building their own filtration systems.[204] The army discouraged soldiers from drinking water, as there was no way to ensure that water found would not prove harmful or lethal, given the presence of rotting corpses, living humans who needed to answer the various calls of nature, and a retreating enemy who was known to poison wells. However, troops often had to drink untested water, as the front line moved rapidly forward or backward or units became encircled. This could lead to creative ways of avoiding illness: "we drank the peaty muck after we ran it through gauze."[205] Occasionally, soldiers

200. RGASPI, f. 84, op. 1, d.83, l. 173; GARF, f. R5446, op. 44a, d. 9410, l. 13. There were constant problems with realizing these orders. For example, the Georgian SSR made 50,000 instead of its allotted 175,000 canteens for the Transcaucasian Front, citing the need to produce wine bottles (it was also supplying wine to units of that front); GARF, f. R5446, op. 44a, d. 9410, l. 28.

201. See Krotkov, *Gigiena,* pp. 49–50, 110–111, and Gurov, *Boets and otdeleniie na pokhode,* p. 23.

202. *Nastavlenie po polevomu vodosnabzheniiu voisk* (Moscow: Voenizdat, 1941), p. 6.

203. Ibid., pp. 3, 71.

204. While *The Experience of Soviet Medicine in the Great Patriotic War* describes a very well-developed system of supplying water at the front, it admits that "troops supplied themselves with water for the most part independently, from those sources on the territory they were located or the area of combat. Krotkov, *Gigiena,* p. 44. While the history describes a system of purification using chlorine and several methods of filtration, I have found few references to these by participants in the war, including memoirs by provisioning officers. See "Glava III: Vodosnabzheniie voisk," in ibid., pp. 36–121; *Nastaleniie inzhenernogo dela dlia pekhoty (INZh-43)* (Moscow: Voenizdat, 1943), pp. 7, 227–231.

205. Maria Zinov'ievna Bogomolova, Memoirs, at Ia pomniu, http://iremember.ru /svyazisti/bogomolova-mariya-zinovevna-2.html (Accessed 10 November 2013).

The State's Pot and the Soldier's Spoon

just took their chances, drinking from ditches or wherever else they could find water.[206] Thus the importance of tea in the paёk: issuing tea ensured that soldiers would be drinking water that had at least been boiled.[207]

There was a certain ambiguity about water as an object of provisioning. It was outside of the paёk, but it was also as a necessity. Water was to be scavenged, but not trusted, preferably converted into something else. Nonetheless, this non-issue liquid became a way for making up for extreme shortages of food, as Boris Slutskii recalled: "Not just Kazakhs and Uzbeks, but heads and commanders of MPVO [Local Anti-Aircraft Defense] in the artillery regiment added many liters of water to their kasha—so that at least something would slosh around in the belly."[208] A dismayed report from the starving winter of 1941 on the Leningrad Front noted this practice as well: "soldiers, in order to increase the size of liquid dishes [soups or kasha] add water to their mess-tins, which significantly reduces the taste and assimilability of the food."[209] Despite the army's attempt to control completely what soldiers consumed, at times what they ate and drank was entirely beyond its control and often a reaction to failed attempts at provisioning. Water all too often took the place of a soldier's "daily bread."

Bread was a highly valuable and emotionally charged component of a soldier's ration. A regiment (at full strength just over three thousand soldiers) would eat 2.6 tons of bread a day.[210] Whether freshly baked in mobile field ovens or dried for long-term use, bread made up half of the

---

206. Koshkarbaev, *Shturm*, p. 158. The author recalled drinking from a ditch in the ruins of Berlin: "The water in the ditch was dirty, but cool and had a refreshing effect; standing up to my waste in the water, I scooped it up by the handful and greedily drank it. I was instantly relieved."

207. Gurov, *Boets i otdelenie na pokhode*, p. 23. This manual also proscribes specific times and amounts to drink while at rest on the march.

208. Slutskii, *O drugikh i o sebe*, p. 29. See also Muzhikov, Interview, and Yakupov, *Frontovye zarisovki*, p. 30, who is more laconic and optimistic: "When you are hungry you drink a lot. You scoop out some clear rain water from a puddle with your helmet."

209. TsAMO RF, f. 217, op. 1305, d. 17, ll. 37, 38, in Veshchikov et al., *Tyl Krasnoi Armii v Velikoi Otechestvennoi voine 1941–1945 gg.*, p. 197. In fact, the dilution of the food would have had no effect on the absorption or assimilation of nutrients. The exception would have been if the soldiers diluted the food with contaminated water which then gave them diarrhea.

210. F. G. Krotkov, "Problemy pitaniia voisk v gody Velikoi Otechestvennoi voini," *Voprosy pitaniia*, no. 3 (1975): 6. Vorontsov, *Prodol'snvtnnoe snabzheniie*, pp. 24–25.

calories in a soldier's ration, was officially considered "the primary food-stuff," and, at 500–800 grams (17.6–28.2 oz.), was the largest portion of rations by weight. The wide gap in bread rations was one of the most palpable examples of the hierarchy of foodstuffs between the front and rear. In Russia, as in the West, bread occupied a psychological and cultural space symbolizing sustenance writ large.

At the front, soldiers' obsession with bread could seem absurd. Saushin recalled two instances of the close relationship soldiers had to bread. The first came from the dark times of 1941, when, after a prolonged period of being cut off from supply, soldiers received their rations. While crouching under fire, one man "held his rifle in one hand and a half loaf of bread in the other. It was uncomfortable for him to bend to the earth, and when necessary lie down and rise again. . . . 'Drop the loaf, you'll get yourself killed!' I yelled to him. . . . The Red Army man stopped for a second, and with surprise and fear looked at me. 'But it is bread! Don't you understand Comrade Commissar, bread.' . . . It seems that for him it was easier to take death than to throw away the leftovers of his loaf."[211] Saushin also recalled that during an inspection, General Shcherbakov, the head of the Political Department of the Red Army, was disturbed by how thinly the men sliced their bread. A soldier responded: "It's bread Comrade General! The thinner you slice it, the more there is. You see it's worth its weight in gold."[212] On the Leningrad front, there was reluctance to give the men their bread ration in one lump sum—they ate it too quickly, leaving themselves without provender.[213] Gabriel Temkin recalled that the young soldiers in his platoon were glad to be in the army as it was the place one could find bread and that they would save it for last as "bread is good by itself,"[214] However, due to the need to extend supplies in the army, bread was not always bread. One soldier complained that in 1941, "They gave us 600 grams [21.2 oz.] of bread, but it wasn't bread, it was a watery sticky mass."[215]

211. Saushin, Khleb i sol', p. 53.

212. Ibid., p. 52.

213. TsAMO RF, f. 217, op. 1305, d. 17, ll. 37, 38, in Veshchikov et al., Tyl Krasnoi Armii v Velikoi Otechestvennoi voine 1941–1945 gg., p. 197.

214. Temkin, My Just War, p. 115.

215. Kats, Interview. According to The Experience of Soviet Medicine in the Great Patriotic War, reducing the moisture in bread was a goal throughout the war; Krotkov, Gigiena, pp. 172–175.

Paëk: Discontent and Subversion

Soldiers often complained about their paëk. The soldier with whom Gabriel Temkin shared his mess-tin grumbled: "Two things . . . bread and tobacco, should be distributed according to needs, and not according to the silly equal stomach principle. Take bread, the food most important for a human being. Is it fair to give somebody, a big guy like myself and a small guy like you—no offense, Gavryusha—the same daily paëk?"[216] Appetites, metabolisms, and differences in body mass were outside the scope of paëk, to the resentment of some soldiers.

Station was a key factor determining what those in the service received. The paëk did not always seem fair, and interest in how comrades of other ranks or branches of service ate speaks to the moral economy of provisioning. Boris Slutskii recalled how enlisted men envied the rations received by officers.[217] When the army was approaching Berlin, a soldier in Rakhimzhan Koshkarbaev's platoon jokingly described pilots as "devilish aristocrats" for receiving cookies and chocolate while infantrymen had "forgotten the taste of sugar":

> "I am thinking about the future, Commander. When the war ends, and they start to write its history, some good for nothing descendant will put it into their head to define the extent of participation of a branch of service in battles by how well they were fed. And it turns out, that the poor infantry didn't play any role. Just try and prove later, that you trudged through half of Europe with your stomach."[218]

As we see from this quotation, soldiers tended to see rations in terms of paëk, and not norms. Was a pilot risking his life any more than an infantryman? Why did he deserve more and better rations than cannon fodder? Even if he needed more calories to fulfill his task, why did a pilot get them in the form of scarce cookies and chocolate? The fact that the state used calories and scarce goods as a measure of worth made these questions all the more sensitive.

Within a unit, hierarchies and sympathies could create a situation that reinterpreted paëk. One machine-gunner recalled how "A skilled,

---

216. Temkin, *My Just War*, p. 104. The spelling of "paëk" has been changed to Library of Congress format in this quotation.

217. Slutskii, *O drugikh i o sebe*, p. 28.

218. Koshkarbaev, *Shturm*, p. 81.

experienced machine gunner was always respected in the battalion. The *starshina* would organize an extra hundred grams [of vodka], and the cook wouldn't forget you, because you are the main firepower of the rifle company, and even if everyone runs away, you don't have that right, you have to cover the retreat."[219] Platoon commander Mikhail Loginov purposefully sent newly arrived soldiers to the field kitchen so that they could get something extra to eat.[220] Lieutenant Rafgat Akhmtiamov shared his officers' rations with an old friend who was an enlisted man under his command.[221] Khisam Kamalov (in an autobiographical novel) describes how an artillery battery would send the soldier who knew how to flirt with the (female) cook to get their rations, as she would pour them a thicker soup.[222] Romance, or simply the maintenance of norms between the sexes at the front, often involved food.[223] Interaction between the sexes was just one of many ways in which understandings of food as something more than calories interfered with the state's mission of nutrition.

Early in the war soldiers began to challenge the calorie principle of provisioning, and as the war dragged on and they were forced to live through "epochs" of one or another foodstuff that had been stock-piled, they began to complain about repetitive food. Pearl barley porridge was known as "shrapnel," and one prosecutor mused that the common expression denigrating women soldiers who lived with commanders, *PPZh*, *Pokhodno-polevaia zhena*, or "portable front-line wife," was allowed to enter into common usage because it distracted soldiers from a more demoralizing phenomenon—*PPS, postoiannyi perlovyi sup*, or "eternal pearl barley soup."[224]

219. Abram Efimovich Shoikhet, Interview by Grigory Koifman, Ia pomniu, http://iremember.ru/pulemetchiki/shoykhet-abram-efimovich.html (Accessed 10 November 2013).

220. Loginov, *Eto bylo na fronte*, pp. 9–10.

221. N. S. Frolov, ed. *Vse oni khoteli zhit': Frontovye pis'ma pogibshikh soldat, vospominaniia veteranov voiny* (Kazan': Tarikh, 2003), pp. 61–62.

222. Kamalov, *U kazhdogo—zhizn' odna*, pp. 203–204.

223. E.g., Bair Irincheev and Artem Drabkin, *"A zori zdes' gromkie": Zhenskoe litso voiny* (Moscow: Eksmo, 2012), p. 108.

224. Pyotr Fyodorovich Bazhenov, Interview by Iu. Trifonov, Ia pomniu, http://iremember.ru/pekhotintsi/bazhenov-petr-fedorovich.html (Accessed 10 November

The State's Pot and the Soldier's Spoon

Ethnic Difference and Military Cuisine

Complaints about rations occasionally arose from the way in which provisioning utterly (and, given severe shortages and the state's aims to limit the power of religion, logically) ignored the identities of some of the men in the ranks. The Great Patriotic War was the first conflict in which large numbers of several traditionally Muslim ethnic groups (Kazakhs, Uzbeks, Tadjiks, Turkmen, and others) were mobilized into the Red Army. Culinary practices within the army often varied dramatically from what these men had eaten in the prewar world.

The meeting of different ethnicities at the front could lead to an expansion of culinary horizons, as Uzbeks ate borsch for the first time and Ukrainians ate *plov* (pilaf). Vil'iam Pokhlebkin claims that the war introduced many people from east of the Urals to the potato for the first time.[225] One Azerbaijani draftee (who would die defending the Brest' Fortress) complained on the eve of the war, "I can't eat the local food."[226] Nikolai Inozemtsev made several references to the *chebureki* (fried meat, cheese, or potato pies common in the North Caucasus and Crimea) that his comrade Akhmetov made on special occasions.[227] An article from the newspaper *Za Rodinu* describes how a Yakut, Ukrainian, and Russian all prepared national dishes for their comrades.[228]

Paëk could bring together or alienate soldiers from different ethnic backgrounds. The Red Army's Political Department was particularly disturbed when some soldiers refused to share tobacco with anyone other than their co-ethnics, interpreting this act as a danger to the "Friendship of the Peoples," the rhetoric of harmonious coexistence among the many

---

2013); Yakob Aizenshtat, *Zapiski sekretaria voennogo tribunala* (London: Overseas Publication Interchange, 1991), p. 116. Soldiers also complained about yellow pea soup. See NA IRI RAN, f. 2 razdel I op. 16 d. 1 l. 1260b.

225. Pokhlebkin, *Kukhnia veka*, pp. 227–228. As Collingham reminds us, "Potatoes became the food of the Second World War." Collingham, *The Taste of War*, p. 70.

226. *1941: Poslednie pis'ma s fronta* (Moscow, Voenizdat', 1991), pp. 31–32.

227. Inozemtsev, *Frontovoi dnevnik*, pp. 107–108, 195. Interestingly, Akhmetov was a Crimean Tatar who was not deported, but served through the end of the war.

228. D. D. Petrov, ed., *Frontovaia pechat' o voinakh iz Iakutii* (Iakutsk: Iakutskoe Knizhnoe Izdatel'stvo, 1982), pp. 40–41. They all turned out to be variations of dumplings.

ethnicities of the Soviet Union, which served as a cornerstone of the Soviet system.[229] Top political officers also discussed the importance of tea
for some ethnicities in 1943: "Things are bad with hot tea. This question
is particularly sharp in non-Russian units. Uzbeks and Kazakhs especially love tea. If one of them gets a medal they all go to drink tea with
him. But here we hit the question—where can they drink tea?"[230] Some
commanders improvised places for their Central Asian comrades to drink
tea. One officer recalls how he and his men greeted a new column of
soldiers from Central Asia:

> We tried to cheer them up in at least some way. We carved out a pavilion, called
> it a *chaikhana* [tea house] and even procured some *pialy* [Central Asian style tea
> cups] for tea time! We had in the division a DOP [Division Exchange Point], its
> director was a homeboy from Georgia. He gave Mel'kadze [a Georgian] a small
> sack with rice and carrots. The cook boiled *plov* with horsemeat for the soldiers.
> You cannot understand now, how happy our comrades in arms—Kazakhs and
> Uzbeks—were at that moment.[231]

Another officer was less sympathetic to the culinary habits of those
under his command, noting that "They grew up in a different climate, a
different attitude towards life, a different mentality. We were fed with
whatever was on hand, for example, borscht with pork. They spit it out,
didn't eat it. I don't think they all did this, some ate it."[232] Given, the
ubiquity of hunger, such behavior could seem criminal. In the army everyone was forced to eat things that they found less than appetizing, but
for some, the food available challenged fundamental conceptions of
themselves, which could occasionally lead to choosing hunger over be-
traying deeply held beliefs or to eating unfamiliar foods that their bodies
did not always accept.[233] Even as provisioning improved and the army

229. RGASPI, f. 17, op. 125, d. 85, l. 60.
230. RGASPI, f. 88, op. 1, d. 958, l. 7.
231. Adamskii, Interview.
232. Mikhail Fyodorovich Borisov, Hero of the Soviet Union, Interview by Artem
Drabkin, Ia pomniu, http://iremember.ru/artilleristi/borisov-mikhail-fedorovich-
geroy-sovetskogo-soiuza-artillerist.html#comment-963 (Accessed 10 November 2013).
233. Astaf'ev, *Prokliati i ubity*, p. 82, described how Kazakhs in his unit slowly came
to eat pork, first soup, then meat. All of this began when the most senior soldier among
the Kazakhs, Talgat cried: "'*Saitin algyr!* [The devil take you!] Eat it all! Eat! Allah
permits it because of the difficulty of the moment. You'll get weak, you'll be like

The State's Pot and the Soldier's Spoon

began to emphasize variety and such amenities as tea houses, offering an alternative to pork, as could be expected, was not something that interested the state. The war instead "taught" people how to eat anything.[234]

From Hunger to Feast

By mid-1943, the organization of the rear area became noticeably better and the resources available to the army, richer.[235] Aleksandr Lesin's diary is marked by constant references to food and hunger in 1942, but by the summer of 1943, food became less of a concern, and he rarely mentioned it through the remainder of the war. Rafgat Akhtiamov, who had written his parents several times in 1941 and 1942 to send food, wrote home in 1943: "Don't worry about me. Now all is well with food."[236] When soldiers mention food in interviews and memoirs, 1943 (and occasionally 1944) is remembered as the year in which quality and quantity noticeably improved.[237] This trend continued, raising expectations among the troops. As an artillery officer interviewed in March of 1945 stated,

> We are fed very well, as guardsmen. . . . We have enough to smoke. People have become so finicky, that they say: "I don't want a pig, I want suckling pigs, goose."

them,'—he pointed his spoon to the crowd of *dokhodiag* [an insulting term for those suffering from starvation], waiting for their food. Giving in, crying, the Kazakhs ate the soup with pork. Eating their full, they cried out *'Astaprala!'* and ran from the table to corner of the canteen to vomit." *Dokhodiagi* are discussed in more detail by Rebecca Manley in this volume.

234. Genatullin, *Strakh,* pp. 11–12.

235. Slutskii states that this had to do with the Red Army reaching "full, sly [*lukavaia*] Ukraine, which the Germans had not succeeded in totally robbing." Slutskii, *O drugikh i o sebe,* p. 29.

236. N. S. Frolov, *Vse oni khoteli zhit',* pp. 38–39, 43, 63.

237. Slutskii, *O drugikh i o sebe,* p. 30. This is not to say that there were no problems with food after 1943, as a variety of sources attest (e.g., TsAMO RF, f. 240, op. 2824, d. 123, ll. 62–65, in Veshchikov et al., *Tyl Krasnoi Armii v Velikoi Otechestvennoi voine 1941–1945 gg.,* p. 471), but generally the picture becomes more pleasant, and no one expects to go hungry for long periods of time after this shift. Saushin, *Khleb i sol,* p. 121, noted that the rise in expectations was palpable from the perspective of those provisioning. It should be noted that soldiers could still land in tight spots where provisioning was impossible. A political officer in the elite 8th Guards Rifles Division, recalled that in March of 1945, when his unit was cut off in Courland, for "18 days people had nothing to eat, we ate horsemeat, crow." NA IRI RAN, f. 2, razdel I, op. 28, d. 33, l. 12.

> There is enough of it there. People have gotten so fat that they are like peaches. So much free time, *narkomskiie sto gramm* ["the People's Commissariat of Defense's hundred grams"—a slang term for vodka], and we have a good appetite.[238]

In a similar vein, Vasily Grossman noted in 1945: "Soldiers don't eat issue food—pork, turkey, chicken is their fare. Among the infantry rosy, plump faces have appeared, which never happened before."[239] Beginning in January 1945, troops were allowed to send packages home to their families, from five to fifteen kilograms (11–33 lbs.) per month, according to rank.[240] The situation of 1941 had been reversed on all fronts.

With this new abundance came new responsibilities. Lesin called for the public execution of anyone stealing from the local population in Latvia, specifically citing that the army was now so well fed.[241] By the end of the war, food had become sufficient enough that it could be wasted, as Slutskii recalled: "In the winter of 1944–1945 all around the infantry overran kitchens, knocking mountains of kasha into the dirty snow—even though in the kasha they heaped six hundred grams of meat per person, and not thirty seven and a half grams of noble egg powder."[242]

CONCLUSION

The Great Patriotic War was both expected and unexpected by the Soviet peoples and the party-state that mobilized them. It had been propagandized before the invasion as a conflict that would take place on enemy territory with little loss of Soviet lives and resources. Instead, the Soviet state and peoples were confronted with a total war that saw immense loss of territory and life, one in which hunger and deprivation spread far and wide throughout the Union. The conflict that ensued saw the state press

238. NA IRI RAN, f. 2, razdel I, op. 30, d. 23, l. 4.

239. Grossman, *Gody voiny,* p. 444.

240. RGVA, f. 4, op. 11, d. 78, ll. 491–498, in Barsukov et al., *Prikazy narodnogo komissara oborony SSSR 1943–1945gg.,* pp. 344–345.

241. Lesin, *Byla voina,* p. 287.

242. Slutskii, *O drugikh i o sebe,* p. 30.

its resources to the limit and experiment with spreading thin reserves as far as possible while trying to maintain total control over the most fluid and easily consumable of those resources—paëk.

The way that the Bolsheviks imagined the war could not be divorced from resources, especially food. Nazi planning imagined the Soviet space as a place of extraction; occupation policies made these imaginings into reality. Placing food near the center of its concerns, the Soviet state reexamined its relationship with its citizens, categorizing those defending it on a higher plane under conditions in which the possibility of starvation was very real. The implementation of this relationship created hierarchies, which stated in quantifiable terms whose life (or function) the state valued above others. While many aspects of provisioning would be reconsidered, these hierarchies remained intact and were indeed refined in the course of the war, as a variety of elite formations and specializations saw privileges added to their status. In addition to creating new hierarchies, invested with real benefits, this system had the potential to efface identities that had existed before being drafted into the army.

The army as an institution was not interested in accommodating the culinary norms of the variety of peoples who comprised its ranks; it was concerned with the much more vital function of keeping people fed. Muslims would be issued lard or salt pork or stewed pork alongside atheists and Orthodox Christians. In dire straits, Russians would learn to eat horse from their Turkic comrades. If the cook of a unit happened to be Uzbek, men from European Russia might find themselves eating *plov* (with horse) for the first time. The army became a place where large numbers of men and women from a variety of ethnic and regional backgrounds came to share something like a common culinary culture. Despite the fact that provisioning was so localized, everyone in the army was likely to have received similar portions of *shchi*, borsch, and kasha. Everyone experienced the same periods of feast and famine, shared while dipping their spoons into the state's pots. They would use similar tactics to survive when the state failed to provide and reinterpret paëk in ways that better suited them. It would be nearly impossible for these soldiers not to appreciate how much better their rations were than those of their

156   *Brandon Schechter*

families in the rear. The shared experience of suffering and improvisation, alongside the shared experience of feasting and victory, is part of what made the Great Patriotic War such a central event in Soviet history. Food could unite and divide men and women in the ranks.

By the war's end, the abundance enjoyed by the army came from a much better organized apparatus with access to more and more resources.[243] And while the state would continue to draw on local resources wherever the army went (which could potentially alienate the locals, especially once the army stepped onto foreign territory), the army began to play an important role in feeding civilians as it advanced into friendly, neutral, and then enemy territory.

Everywhere it went, the army established a monopoly on foodstuffs, and in areas ravaged by war, the army was often the only source of provisions for both civilian and military personnel. In Berlin, in the course of May of 1945, the Red Army was feeding two million of its own soldiers and four million German civilians.[244] The concern for quality as well as quantity was immediate: Antipenko recalls being censured for providing ersatz coffee for the residents of Berlin at the end of the war.[245] The Red Army fed entire enemy cities, incorporating enemy civilians into military provisioning via ration cards.[246] Once the provisioning system was fully functioning, the mutual obligations of paëk came to encompass former enemy civilians and prisoners of war. In return for recognizing Bolshevik sovereignty, former enemies were provided with sustenance.[247] The army had come a long way from the dark days of 1941–1942, and its

243. Graft remained a problem late in the war, however; see, e.g., GARF f. R5446, op. 46a, d. 7395, ll. 20–21, 26–28. Holidays in particular were periods when officers illegally used rations for banquets.

244. N. A. Antipenko, *Front i tyl* (Moscow: Znanie, 1977), p. 59.

245. Antipenko, *Na glavnom napravlenii*, pp. 283–285.

246. TsAMO RF, f. 236, op. 2719, d. 76, ll. 62–65, in Veshchikov et al., *Tyl Krasnoi Armii v Velikoi Otechestvennoi voine 1941–1945 gg.*, pp. 674–675.

247. Slutskii, *O drugikh i o sebe*, p. 30: "When in Budapest and Vienna field kitchens doled out a kasha ration [*paikovaia kasha*] to the locals, this wasn't just because of pity towards our little enemies [*vrazheniatam*], not just because it was impossible to gorge yourself in front of the starved children of a blockaded city, but because of the plenty which had come to rule among the provisioning officers."

ability to provide for an organization of such scale moving so quickly was deeply impressive. In the course of the war, despite failings, the state demonstrated its ability to feed its army and later its enemies, thus extending its sovereignty into East Central Europe and reaffirming it in the everyday lives of its citizens.

THREE

QUEUES, CANTEENS, AND THE POLITICS OF LOCATION IN DIARIES OF THE LENINGRAD BLOCKADE, 1941–1942

Alexis Peri

> When two strangers meet and do not really talk, then they [talk about] the
> weather. It was always this way, everywhere, but now in Leningrad there is
> something else: "What kind of card do you have?" "What kind of ration are
> you on?" "Where do you eat?" "Got enough bread?"[1]

IT WAS JANUARY 1944 WHEN NINA KLISHEVICH, AN EIGHTEEN-year-old theater student, recorded this observation. At that time the severe famine that had gripped Leningrad was ending, but life in the blockaded city still revolved around food. Leningrad was surrounded by German and Finnish troops for 872 days between 1941 and 1944. During this, one of the longest and deadliest sieges of modern history, roughly 800,000 civilians perished, the vast majority of them from starvation and illnesses related to it. On August 29, 1941, the Wehrmacht severed the last railway line that connected Leningrad to the rest of the Soviet Union and thus to outside food supplies. Inside "the ring," as the encircled city was called, Leningraders struggled to survive without electricity, running water, fuel for heat, motorized transport, or adequate food. During the worst months of the famine, between autumn 1941 and spring 1942, most of the city's inhabitants received miniscule rations, which fell to as little as 125 grams of bread a day.[2]

---

1. "Blokadnyi dnevnik Niny Nikolaevny Erokhanoi," entry for January 26, 1944, GMMOBL, f. RDF, op. 1L, d. 490, l. 61. She used her maiden name, Klishevich, during the war.

2. On starvation-related illnesses, see chapter 5 of this volume. In late December 1941 and mid-January 1942, rations were raised to 200, then 250 grams of bread for most Leningraders, but these increases were unable to stave off the tide of death, which peaked in early 1942. Although it is difficult to tabulate the exact number of civilian

Queues, Canteens, and the Politics of Location

Food, as Nina Klishevich observed, became the dominant social currency in blockaded Leningrad. It recast social norms, hierarchies, and interactions, both intimate and mundane. "Whenever one encountered two or three people," the doctor Anna Likhacheva echoed, whether "at work, on duty, or in line, the conversation was only about food. What they were giving out based on ration cards, which norms, what one was able to receive, etc.—this was the cardinal, vital question of everyone."[3] Current scholarship has provided a detailed picture of how famine seized Leningrad and how local authorities distributed the city's meager food resources in an effort to combat it.[4] But how did hunger and the politics of food distribution alter Leningraders' visions of themselves and their community? How did the *blokadniki* (or people of the blockade) perceive and navigate the new social order created by the famine?

This chapter tackles these questions by highlighting the wartime writings of Leningraders who—despite extreme hunger and fatigue— diverted much of their energy away from immediate physical survival and toward documenting the city's social transformation. This study is based on 120 blockade diaries: one hundred diaries located in the archives, and twenty that have been published.[5] Due to space constraints, this

---

deaths, most scholars put it between 800,000 and 1 million. Reliable estimates can be found in David M. Glantz, *The Siege of Leningrad, 1941–1945: 900 Days of Terror* (London: Cassell Military Paperbacks, 2001), pp. 78–79; William Moskoff, *The Bread of Affliction: The Food Supply in the USSR during World War II* (Cambridge: Cambridge University Press, 1990), p. 196; Richard Bidlack and Nikita Lomagin, *The Leningrad Blockade, 1941–1944: A New Documentary History from the Soviet Archives* (New Haven, Conn.: Yale University Press, 2012), pp. 270–271.

3. "Iz dnevnika Likhachevoi Anny Ivanovny," entry for May 16, 1942 in: *Oborona Leningrada 1941–1944: vospominaniia i dnevniki uchastnikov* (Leningrad: Nauka, 1968), p. 684.

4. This chapter draws on the following scholarship on the history of Soviet wartime rationing: for the early Soviet era, Lars T. Lih, *Bread and Authority in Russia, 1914–1921* (Berkeley: University of California Press, 1990); for the Stalin period, Elena Osokina, *Our Daily Bread: Socialist Distribution and the Art of Survival in Stalin's Russia, 1927–1941* (Armonk, N.Y.: M. E. Sharpe, 2001), pp. xv, 69, 83, 197; for World War II, Moskoff, *The Bread of Affliction*; on rationing and food crimes in blockaded Leningrad, Bidlack and Lomagin, *The Leningrad Blockade*, a work to which the author owes a special intellectual debt.

5. These diaries formed the basis of the author's doctoral dissertation (Alexis Peri, "Minds under Siege: Rethinking the Soviet Experience inside the Leningrad Blockade,

chapter refers to only a handful of diaries, but with the goal of highlighting the themes and concerns that unite the larger corpus of texts. The journals discussed below represent a range of ages, social backgrounds, and political attitudes; they include youths, pensioners, industrial workers, intellectuals, and party members. Even so, this sample cannot be considered representative of the some three million people who inhabited Leningrad during the war. Moreover, diaries are, by their nature, highly subjective and individualized. But it is their particularity that provides useful data for this study.

This chapter uses diaries to investigate Leningraders' visions of the evolving social order for several reasons. First, as a genre, the diary traditionally chronicles the events and exchanges of everyday life through which the social is constructed. Second, aware that they were experiencing a crisis of world historical magnitude, many Leningraders kept journals in order to chronicle life inside "the ring" for posterity. They became eager documentarians of besieged society, using their journals as conceptual spaces where they could work through the physical, emotional, and societal tumult created by the blockade. Third, the diary provided an intimate space in which Leningraders articulated views and confessed to acts that they would have been loath to discuss in public. Of course, no journal can be considered entirely private or a direct reflection of its author's thoughts and experiences. Its contents are shaped by self-censorship, the processes of narrative construction, and the anticipation of audience. However, compared to public conversations, petitions, or party reports (*svodki*), they offer relatively intimate and candid perspectives on the politics of hunger and notions of distributive justice, which were not crafted for purpose of achieving a political goal or performing a public role. These diarists rarely sought restitution for the injustices

---

1941–1945" [University of California Berkeley, 2011]). In addition to the diaries, the dissertation incorporates other sources such as letters, newspapers, magazines, and internal party documents, some of which have been skillfully analyzed by other scholars. See John Barber, "War, Public Opinion, and the Struggle for Survival, 1941–1945: The Case of Leningrad," in Silvio Pons and Andrea Romano, eds., *Russia in the Age of Wars, 1914–1945* (Milan: Feltrinelli Editore, 2000), pp. 265–276; Richard Bidlack, "The Political Mood in Leningrad during the First Year of the Soviet-German War," *Russian Review* 59, no. 1 (January 2000): 96–113.

Queues, Canteens, and the Politics of Location

they described. For the majority of them, the historical, emotional, and epistemological motivations that drove their diary practices superseded more strategic ones.[6]

This chapter focuses on the worst period of the famine, between 1941 and 1942, and it makes two main arguments. First, it contends that the diarists' visions of the social imaginary were highly spatialized and embedded in locales that were essential to survival. The chapter examines two such settings, food lines and canteens.[7] During the winter and spring of 1941–1942, spaces and forms of social interaction were circumscribed greatly. Leningraders avoided leaving their apartments or even coming out from under the bedclothes in order to conserve energy and warmth. However, they did regularly go out to redeem their rations at food stores or eat in canteens. For the diarists, these sites came to represent the social order. They saw them as microcosms of society at large. In truth, the queue and canteen did not offer unified or consistent pictures of the social order. Rather, the different configurations of and logics undergirding queues and canteens fostered very different perspectives of blockade society. Moreover, the diarists read these spaces based on their own personal experiences within them and in conjunction with the heritage of Soviet socialism. This included ideological tenets, practices of

---

6. An exception is the diarist Elizaveta Aleksandrovna Sokolova, discussed later in this chapter, who did petition the party organization for larger rations. In past decades, scholars have demonstrated a wide variety of other methodological approaches to diary analysis, including the study of subjectivity, wherein the diary provides a locus of identity-formation or self-fashioning. Leading scholarship in this field includes Jochen Hellbeck, *Revolution on My Mind: Writing a Diary under Stalin* (Cambridge, Mass.: Harvard University Press, 2006); Igal Halfin, *Terror in My Soul: Communist Autobiographies on Trial* (Cambridge, Mass.: Harvard University Press, 2003). Shelia Fitzpatrick and Stephen Kotkin among others have offered approaches to the importance of public identity and the self-presentation in the Soviet self. See Shelia Fitzpatrick's notion of "the useable self" in *Tear Off Masks! Identity and Imposture in 20th-Century Russia* (Princeton, N.J.: Princeton University Press, 2005), and *Everyday Stalinism: Ordinary Life in Extraordinary Times, Soviet Russia in the 1930s* (New York: Oxford University Press, 1995). Also see Kotkin's notion of "speaking Bolshevik" in *Magnetic Mountain: Stalinism as Civilization* (Berkeley: University of California Press, 1995). For a summary of scholarly approaches to the diary, see Irina Paperno, "What Can Be Done with Diaries?" *Russian Review* 63, no. 4 (October 2004): 561–573.

7. This chapter focuses on canteens and queues for the sake of brevity, but other spaces, like markets and bathhouses, also were critical to the diarists.

distribution, and social norms from the prewar period. Together, particular features of each space and the larger social milieu informed how the diarists mapped the social geography of the blockade in their journals.[8]

This chapter's second argument pertains to the politics of location operating within this social landscape. Food was not only the city's main social currency; it was also the major source of stratification. While they stood in lines or ate in canteens, the diarists mapped various subgroups that made up the hierarchy of blockade society. In particular, they fixated on the disparities they saw between their own portions, behaviors, and attitudes and those of elites. All of the diarists studied here, regardless of their personal background or ration category, suspected that they were starving precisely because others illegally manipulated or unfairly benefited from the food distribution system. Nearly all of them attributed the blame for their suffering locally, to other Leningraders, instead of to the German besiegers.

Of course, the diarists knew that the military blockade created the famine, but in their journals they hardly mentioned this fact. Instead, they fixated on how food was allocated in the city—legally and illegally—

---

8. Leading social theorists and spatial geographers, including Henri Lefebvre, Michel de Certeau, and David Harvey, have demonstrated how social spaces and economic systems are not natural or fixed entities, but are produced through practices of everyday life. Lefebvre particularly emphasized that revolutions and class struggles are spatial in nature. See de Certeau, *The Practices of Everyday Life* (Berkeley: University of California Press, 1988); Lefebvre, *The Production of Space* (Oxford: Blackwell, 2005). See also Harvey, *The Condition of Postmodernity: An Enquiry into the Origins of Cultural Change* (Oxford: Blackwell, 1989), and "Space as a Key Word," in Noel Castree and Derek Gregory, eds., *David Harvey: A Critical Reader* (Oxford: Blackwell Publishing, 2006), pp. 270–275. Harvey focuses on the spaces produced by capitalism; recently, social geographers and anthropologists have produced insightful studies of the spaces produced by Soviet socialism. See Bruce O'Neill, "The Political Agency of Cityscapes: Spatializing Governance in Ceausescu's Bucharest," *Journal of Social Archaeology* 9, no. 92 (2009): 92–109; James H. Bater, *The Soviet City: Ideal and Reality* (Beverly Hills, Calif.: Sage Publications, 1980); R. A. French and F. E. Hamilton, eds., *The Socialist City: Spatial Structure and Urban Policy* (Chichester: John Wiley and Sons, 1979); David Crowley and Susan E. Reid, eds., *Socialist Spaces: Sites of Everyday Life in the Eastern Bloc* (Oxford: Berg, 2002).

Queues, Canteens, and the Politics of Location

and questioned whether the beneficiaries of these practices deserved such advantages. To use the economist Amartya Sen's classic formulation, they presented the famine as a problem of distribution more than of supply.[9] The "elites" they spotted in the canteens and lines eclipsed the Germans as the immediate adversaries who stood in the way of survival. Perhaps the diarists found it easier to direct their frustrations at the people around them rather than at a distant army; perhaps they fixated on municipal policies instead of the overall circumstances of war because the former seemed more likely to change. Even though the diarists consistently attributed blame locally, the primary cause of their starvation was the shortage of food reaching the city, not Soviet mishandling of it. While administrative blunders and corruption certainly played a role, it was the blockade of the city and the bombardment of its storehouses, delivery trucks, and food barges that made it impossible to feed everyone adequately.[10] Still, the purpose of this chapter is not to judge or justify the diarists' social inquiries and explanations. It is to explore perceptions, not actual causes, of the famine and to illustrate how the spaces and milieu of besieged Leningrad helped to foster the diarists' specific notions of distributive justice.

A key element of this milieu was the practice of food distribution in the prewar period. The diarists struggled to make sense of the longstanding tension between social equality and stratification that colored Soviet

9. Based on his study of the 1943 Bengal famine, Amartya Sen distinguished between the conditions of not having enough food versus there not being enough food to argue that more modern famines are caused by inequalities in entitlement than by shortages. Amartya Sen, *Poverty and Famine: As Essay on Entitlement and Deprivation* (Oxford: Claredon Press, 1981). There is a useful analysis of famines vis-à-vis Sen's thesis in Michael Ellman, "The 1947 Soviet Famine and the Entitlement Approach to Famines," *Cambridge Journal of Economics* 24 (2000): 603–630.

10. Recently, scholars and researchers have argued that starvation in Leningrad as well as across the Soviet Union was primarily a problem of supply, although the experience of the famine, as this chapter argues, was shaped by the practice of unequal distribution. See John Barber and Mark Harrison, "Patriotic War, 1941 to 1945," *The Cambridge History of Russia*, vol. 3, *The Twentieth Century*, ed. Ronald Grigor Suny (Cambridge: Cambridge University Press, 2006), p. 227; Lizzie Collingham, *The Taste of War: World War Two and the Battle For Food* (New York: Penguin Press, 2011), pp. 321, 331.

rhetoric and shaped practices of allocating foodstuffs, routinely in short supply. As Brandon Schechter discusses in his contribution to this volume, the Soviet state's commitment to feed its people was a core tenet of its social(ist) contract.[11] The Bolsheviks rose to power with the promise that they would solve the wartime food crises that occurred under the tsars and the Provisional Government. At the same time, their revolutionary mission was predicated on privileging certain classes over others. The new Soviet regime called on everyone to work and sacrifice for the building of socialism, but they fed certain strata of society more than others. While popular resentments about unequal resource distribution were common throughout the 1920s and 1930s, they came to a head during World War II when both the level of scarcity and the expectation of sacrifice were at a premium. As blockade survivor Lidiia Ginzburg put it, there was a blending of "the old (bureaucratic) forms and new content (people dying of hunger)" in besieged Leningrad.[12] But rather than question the premises of Soviet socialism, the diarists wielded the rhetoric of class warfare and their own understandings of socialist ethics to critique the food distribution system. They identified for themselves who was worthy or unworthy, deserving or undeserving of privilege based on their labor, behavior, or political commitment. In this way, the diarists remind us that Soviet concepts of legitimacy and entitlement were not just matters of state policy or ideology, but were actively formulated and reformulated by the public in the course of daily practices of consumption. In blockaded Leningrad, lines and canteens provided the critical frameworks for their formation.

11. For a discussion of this theme in Civil War–era Leningrad and in post–World War II Leningrad, see, respectively, Lih, *Bread and Authority in Russia;* and Christine Varga-Harris, "Forging Citizenship on the Home Front: Reviving the Socialist Contract and Constructing Soviet Identity during the Thaw," in Polly Jones, ed., *The Dilemmas of De-Stalinization: Negotiating Cultural and Social Change in the Khrushchev Era* (London: Routledge, 2006), pp. 101–116. I borrow the "social(ist) contract" formulation from this piece.

12. Lidiia Ginzburg, "Vokrug 'zapisok blokadnogo cheloveka,'" in A. S. Kushner and E. A. Polikashin, eds., *Zapisnye knizhki. Vospominaniia. Esse* (St. Peterburg: Iskusstvo, 2002), p. 725. English translation from Lidiya Ginzburg, *Blockade Diary*, trans. Alan Myers (London: Harvill Press, 1996), p. 81. Parentheses appear in the original quotation.

GOVERNING HUNGER: AN OVERVIEW OF
THE FOOD DISTRIBUTION SYSTEM

The mass starvation that afflicted Leningrad was an extreme case of the widespread hunger that affected Soviet people as a whole, whether they were at the front, in the rear, or under occupation. Especially with the majority of the Soviet Union's best agricultural land under German occupation, the Kremlin was aware that it could not adequately feed the population through rationing. As Wendy Goldman discusses in chapter 1, across the USSR, party leaders encouraged state, party, trade, and labor organizations to establish gardens and conclude food contracts with local producers in order to increase the food supply. The state was relatively lenient regarding the black market in urban areas and factory yards. This was true in Leningrad as well. The Second Party Secretary A. A. Kuznetsov noted that "independent action on society's part" was necessary to "help to save people without additional measures."[13] Trapped inside their city, however, Leningraders could not access regional farm produce and far-reaching supply lines as other communities could, nor could they plant "victory gardens" until after six months of famine had passed. With far fewer ways to supplement their diet, Leningrad Food Commissioner Dmitrii Pavlov explained, "the sole means of receiving food was through the ration card."[14]

Leningraders redeemed ration coupons at food stores, bakeries, and canteens. Although rationing was nothing new to Soviet society, Leningrad's Food Commission initially was ill equipped to deal with mass and prolonged hunger. In the first months of the war, ten different agencies issued ration cards based on slightly different policies. This gave rise to disorderly bookkeeping and allowed illegal practices, like the fabrication

---

13. Quoted in John Barber, "War, Public Opinion," 272. Jeffery W. Jones has also discussed this phenomenon in his study of wartime and postwar Rostov in "A People without a Definite Occupation: The Illegal Economy and 'Speculators' in Rostov-on-the-Don, 1943–48," in Donald J. Raleigh, ed., *Provincial Landscapes: Local Dimensions of Soviet Power, 1917–1953* (Pittsburgh, Pa.: University of Pittsburgh Press, 2001), pp. 236–254.

14. D. V. Pavlov, *Leningrad 1941: The Blockade*, trans. John Clinton Adams (Chicago: University of Chicago Press, 1965), p. 69. Here, Pavlov may have meant to imply that there were no illegal means of obtaining food, which was inaccurate.

and reuse of coupons, to flourish.[15] Moreover, at first Leningraders spent their coupons at any shop, but this policy led to chaos and panicky "runs" on stores rumored to be well stocked. The ballerina Vera Kostrovitskaia speculated that city leaders deliberately cultivated this confusion to mask chronic shortages: "city authorities did not attach each person to an individual store, knowing after all that they were in no condition to give out full norms to the population."[16] As a result of the disorganization, in December 1941, city authorities required Leningraders to reregister for ration cards frequently and to use them only in certain stores located in the district of the city where they lived.

Few municipal canteens operated during the first months of the siege. Instead, most canteens were linked to institutions like schools, factories, or hospitals, and one had to be associated with that organization in order to eat there. One also typically had to "pay" for the watery soup and a small portion of kasha that one received at canteens with ration coupons. The city eventually expanded the networks of both municipal and institutionally affiliated canteens, but this took place mostly after the winter and spring of 1941–1942, the period on which this chapter focuses.[17] Moreover, as the city's staggering death toll attests, access to a canteen was necessary, but not sufficient for survival. Like bakeries and food stores, canteens had long lines and regularly ran out of provisions.

Shops and canteens distributed food by ration categories similar to the ones used during the first Five-Year Plans. As in most other combatant countries, soldiers received the lion's share. Civilian rations were based on a combination of criteria including biological need, caloric expenditure, labor contribution, and social standing. Some special provisions were made for pregnant women, infants, and children under twelve as

15. Stephanie P. Steiner, "The Food Distribution System" (M.A. thesis, San Jose State University, 1993), pp. 45–49.

16. TsGALI, f. 157, op. 1, d. 28, Vera Sergeevna Kostrovitskaia, entry "September, October, 1941," "Leningrad-blokada. 1941–1943. Dnevnik," 2. Some of this diary may have been typed up and later reworked by Kostrovitskaia.

17. On the expansion of canteens and food stores, see the following issues of *Leningradskaia Pravda* (*LP*): October 26, 1941, p. 4; May 7, 1942, p. 2; May 17, 1942, p. 2; September 26, 1942, p. 2; January 8, 1943, p. 4; November 20, 1942, p. 4; April 21, 1942, p. 4.

Queues, Canteens, and the Politics of Location

well as for political and intellectual elites.[18] Employment, however, was the main determinant of how ration categories were assigned because it conveyed both one's caloric expenditure and labor contribution.

The ration categories used in Leningrad mirrored the ones used across the country, but they provided much smaller norms. Officially, there were five categories, one for each of the following groups: workers, technicians, and engineers in engineering and technical fields (known as ITR specialists), workers in war-related industries, white-collar employees (which also included some workers in light industries as well as clerical employees), adult dependents, and children under age twelve. However, beginning on November 13, 1941, and continuing through January 1942, the bread ration for the last three groups was identical. As for other foodstuffs, the actual amounts of cereals, meat, sugars, and fats that were allocated to white-collar employees, adult dependents, and children were very similar—save for the effort to provide children with more sugars and fats. In light of the fact that the different categories offered the same norms, Leningraders tended to consolidate the five groups into three: Category I for "workers" laboring in war-related industries, Category II for all other workers, and Category III for dependents. During the worst period of the famine, Category I workers received twice the amount of bread given to everyone else both because of the heavy nature of their labor and because they were contributing the most to the war effort.[19]

It is critical to note that none of these categories provided enough food for long-term survival, and hundreds of thousands of Leningraders

---

18. The Leningrad party organization's efforts to give pregnant women larger rations and to organize canteens for schoolchildren are discussed in "Protokol No. 50. Zasedaniia biuro Leningradskogo gorodskogo komiteta VKP(b)," January 3, 1942, TsGAIPD, f. 25, op. 2, d. 4408, l. 25; "Protokol No. 52," January 19, 1942, TsGAIPD, f. 25, op. 2, d. 4433, l. 6.

19. For food items other than bread, no distinction was made between categories of laborers. For detailed charts of the norms for all ration categories, including the gap between official and actual rations (for items other than bread), see Bidlack and Lomagin, *The Leningrad Blockade*, pp. 412–417. The diarists generally referred to ration categories by the bread norms associated with them because bread was the most reliably delivered. For a discussion of the similarities between prewar and wartime rationing in Leningrad, see Osokina, *Our Daily Bread*, pp. 153, 202–204; Moskoff, *The Bread of Affliction*, pp. 138–140.

from each category perished. Nevertheless, the categories did reveal the *relative* privileging of some groups over others within a hopeless situation. The diarists regarded the three main ration groups as the three rungs of the social ladder under siege. Although this system prioritized lives in a manner consistent with Soviet war aims as well as with prewar principles of distribution such as "each according to his labor" and "he who does not work, does not eat," the diarists strongly objected to this system by citing its ambiguities and inconsistencies or by painting the relatively advantaged groups as unworthy or undeserving.

In this way, the diarists tended to blame the food crisis on internal problems and adversaries rather than on external ones. Several factors help to explain this. First, the regime was not forthcoming about how it assigned ration categories. It gave special food parcels or Category I status to individuals who might otherwise not qualify. Second, the regime concealed the true severity of the famine from Leningraders. The main city newspaper *Leningradskaia Pravda* (*LP*) regularly discussed hunger *outside* of the USSR, but it buried information about food norms in the bottom, right-hand corner of the last page of selected issues. Also, the regime often neglected to adjust rations when there were dips in supply in order not to hurt morale or give the impression that it had miscalculated norms.[20] Leningraders were left to search for explanations for these regular shortfalls. The local press added fuel to the fire. It did not publicly reveal supply deficits or miscalculations, but it regularly condemned individuals for pilfering from the food supply, giving the impression that theft was the chief cause of the shortages.[21] This strategy gained credence from the fact that food theft was a real problem. Although the exact scale of food-related crimes and arrests is unknown, recent research by the leading siege scholars Richard Bidlack and Nikita Lomagin reveals that the NKVD arrested 17,000 Leningraders for theft between

---

20. Barber and Harrison, *The Soviet Home Front*, p. 81; Steiner, "The Food Distribution System," pp. 25, 72.

21. The press's silence regarding rationing was in no way unique to Leningrad, but extended all across the Soviet Union. See Karel Berkhoff, *Motherland in Danger: Soviet Propaganda during World War II* (Cambridge, Mass.: Harvard University Press, 2012), pp. 97–98, 102–103.

Queues, Canteens, and the Politics of Location

June 1941 and September 1942.[22] Outside of these arrests, there were plenty of violations of the ration system, as Leningraders from all strata turned to theft, corruption, and social networks in order to "self-provision." And for those trapped "inside the ring," such disparities and practices were especially visible in lines and canteens.

"WHO'S LAST?": THE PSYCHOLOGY OF A LINE

In the winter and spring of 1941–1942, Leningraders awoke well before dawn to stand in line at bakeries and food stores. Undeterred by air raids, social outbursts, or personal fatigue, the blokadniki waited for enormous stretches, sometimes days at a time, without knowing what goods the shops had to distribute and whether they had the right coupons to obtain them. Long queues preceded Leningrad canteens as well. Irina Zelenskaia, a manager at a Lenenergo power station, called one assembled crowd waiting for hours to enter a canteen "a procession of half-corpses so frightening that one cannot put it into words."[23] Indeed, blokadniki frequently died in line, and their gaunt remains silently reminded the others of how essential it was to reach the front. "An old woman, waiting for bread, slowly slides to the ground," the dancer Vera Kostrovitskaia wrote of a November 1941 queue, "but no one cares—she is dead or she will be trampled nevertheless. They [the line waiters] tilt their heads to see if her ration card has fallen on the ground, perhaps it is still tightly clutched in her boney hand." Such indifference to all but the prized ration card "is the only way to respond to death," she observed.[24] Lines were

---

22. Bidlack and Lomagin offer the most recent statistics on theft. They found that, between December 1941 and March 1942, when the over-water evacuation route (known as the "Road to Life") was active, 818 people were arrested for stealing from food trucks, 586 of them military personnel. In 1942, 359 railroad employees were accused of stealing (Bidlack and Lomagin, *The Leningrad Blockade,* pp. 161–162, 309–313).

23. Irina Dmitr'evna Zelenskaia, entry for January 6, 1942, "dnevnik," TsGAIPD, f. 4000, op. 11, d. 35, l. 49. There is a useful analysis of Soviet line culture (especially of notions of fairness among line-waiters in the late Soviet period) in V. G. Nikolaev, *Sovetskaia ochered' kak sreda obitaniia: Sotsiologicheskii analiz* (Moscow: Institut nauchnoi informatsii po obshchestvennym naukam, RAN 2000).

24. Kostrovitskaia, entry for "September, October 1941," TsGALI, f. 157, op. 1, d. 28, l. 2.

so pervasive that they extended into death. Not only did blokadniki perish in line, but corpses, as diarists like Elena Skriabina, Fyodor Nikitin, Nikolai Punin, and Mariia Konopleva observed, queued at mortuaries and cemeteries for burial.[25]

The diarists did not simply participate in these mournful processions; they studied them avidly. Many carried their journals with them so that they could jot down clues about Leningrad's social transformation as they waited. And they were not the only ones. Party informants also monitored lines for information about public attitudes, circulating rumors, and counterrevolutionary activity.[26] Recent research by Richard Bidlack and Nikita Lomagin confirms that Leningrad authorities received regular reports (*svodki*) of anti-Soviet sentiment brewing in line. Of course, as Bidlack and Lomagin warn, such informants had incentives—negative ones like blackmail and positive ones like Category I ration cards—to report certain levels of discontent, so their claims must be read cautiously.[27] The diaries must also be read with caution, but they do expand our perspective of blockade queues because their authors focused on different concerns than those highlighted in svodki. Informants tended to cast interactions in a state-versus-society framework with an eye to unrest, whereas the diarists monitored lines for insights about city demographics, collective psychology, and dynamics of social competition. And despite their individual variations, the diarists' readings are united by a common set of interests and discoveries regarding the line.

The diarists described the wartime line as both a peculiar and a representative social body. On the one hand, they likened the queue to a "many-headed monster" or a "long tapeworm," which took on a life of its

25. Fyodor Mikhailovich Nikitin, entry for November 21, 1941, "dnevnik," MNM, kniga postuplenii (k.p.) ("register of accessions") 6920, f. 1, d. 5580, l. 64; Mariia Konopleva, entry for December 25, 1941, "V blokirovannom Leningrade: zapiski," OR RNB, f. 368, ll. 12–3; Elena Skriabina, *V blokade: Dnevnik materi* (Iowa City: Herausgeber, 1964), pp. 42, 93. Skriabina reworked and republished her diary as *Gody skitanii: Iz dnevnika odnoi leningradki* (Paris: Piat' kontinentov, 1975); Nikolai Punin, entries for September 25, 1941, and November 20, 1941, "Blokadnyi dnevnik," *Zvezda* 1 (1994): 98.

26. Bidlack and Lomagin, *The Leningrad Blockade*, pp. 231–233. This work contains excerpts from these archival documents.

27. Ibid, pp. 246, 347. Bidlack and Lomagin point out that not all of the negative attitudes witnessed or overheard were anti-Soviet.

Queues, Canteens, and the Politics of Location

own.[28] On the other hand, they approached the line as a kind of microcosm, from which they tried to generalize about society as a whole. They scanned the assembled bodies for clues about the state of public health, and they compared the numbers of men and women in line to estimate demographic shifts.[29] The constancy, magnitude, and interminability of blockade queues added to the notion that they represented society in miniature. After all, they comprised the largest assemblies of living bodies inside the city, so they acquired additional significance—both socially and in terms of survival—for the blokadniki.

The diarists were eager to uncover what they termed "the psychology of the line."[30] Conversation was one point of entry into Leningraders' thoughts and attitudes. The diarists often recorded exchanges that they overheard or identified common topics of conversation. These included discussions about what food items were being given out and in what quantities, about deceased loved ones, about developments at the front, and about food-service workers who stole food and sold it at inflated prices.[31] Such speculation, discussed below, was widespread in Leningrad, as well as in the rear, as Wendy Goldman demonstrates in chapter 1.[32] The

28. Kostrovitskaia, entry for "September, October 1941," TsGALI, f. 157, op. 1, d. 28, l. 3; Elena Kochina, entries for December 4, 1941, January 13, 1942, and March 30, 1942, "Blokadnyi dnevnik," *Pamiat': istoricheskii sbornik,* vol. 4 (Moscow-Paris: YMCA Press, 1979–1981), pp. 167–168, 184, 204–205. Kochina's diary was published more than a decade after the Blockade, and so it may contain alterations introduced by the author.

29. Boris Apollonovich Lesin, entry for June 28, 1942, TsGAIPD, f. 4000, op. 11, d. 61, l. 15; Ivan Alekseevich Savinkov, entry for May 30, 1942, TsGAIPD, f. 4000, op. 11, d. 99, ll. 390b.–40.

30. Ginzburg, "Zapiski blokadnogo cheloveka," pp. 333–335. I modified the translation in Ginzburg, *Blockade Diary,* pp. 38–40. On line-waiting as a kind of imprisonment, see Richard C. Larson, "Perspectives on Queues: Social Justice and the Psychology of Queueing," *Operations Research* 35, no. 6 (November–December 1987), p. 897.

31. Esfir' Gustanovna Levina, entry for January 16, 1942, "dnevnik," TsGAIPD, f. 4000, op. 11, d. 57, l. 2. Additional examples are in Kochina, entry for January 9, 1942, "Blokadnyi dnevnik," p. 181; Vera Inber, entry for December 25, 1941, in *Pochti tri goda* (Moscow: Sovetskaia Rossiia, 1968), p. 4 (this particular entry does not appear in her diary manuscript).

32. See Wendy Z. Goldman, "Not By Bread Alone: Food, Workers, and the State" in this volume.

architect Esfir' Levina compiled this typical set of exchanges between line-waiters and nearby "speculators" during the winter of 1941–1942:

> I am returning to the bakery, I am standing in line. A group of women count their dead, some fellow suggests "and you will follow them if you are going to stand [in line]. Buy from me 300 grams for 90 rubles—it's really cheap." The policeman talks about [Chairman of the City Executive Committee Petr S.] Popkov's speech [about increasing rations and resuming evacuations].[33]

At least during the winter of 1941–1942, the diarists claimed to have gleaned little from these mundane, ritualistic exchanges. They found the tenor and frequency of line chatter more revealing. Irina Zelenskaia, for instance, noted the contrast between the muted tones Leningraders used in describing the deaths of family members versus the affectionate way they referred to food.[34] Many found that the silence of wintertime lines was more telling than the conversations. In her retrospective *Notes of a Blockade Person*, Lidiia Ginzburg discussed these "eerily quiet" lines, commenting: "Gripped by one all-consuming passion, they hardly uttered a word: with manic impatience they stared ahead over the next man's shoulder at the bread."[35] Ginzburg was a philologist and a keen student of human dialogue, but she analyzed mostly spring- and summertime lines because wintertime queues were so hushed.

Blokadniki felt compelled to wait even when they admitted that they had little hope of reaching the front before the shop ran out of provisions. The fourteen-year-old Dima Afanas'ev and the historian Georgii Kniazev noted this behavior in themselves as well as in others, admitting it was "not intelligent economy" to "waste away" in line, but that it gave the illusion of activity, which, Afanas'ev noted, was less depressing than stay-

---

33. Levina, entry for January 16, 1942, TsGAIPD, f. 4000, op. 11, d. 57, l. 2. This refers to Petr S. Popkov's speech of January 13, 1942, when he claimed "All of the worst is behind us," and promised larger rations and renewed evacuations.

34. Zelenskaia, entry for January 6, 1942, TsGAIPD, f. 4000, op. 11, d. 35, ll. 49–50. The examples she cites were not just diminutives for food, but diminutives that mimicked baby talk that an adult would use when feeding an infant or small child: "lovely little meatballs" (*kakleta*), is the way a child would mispronounce the actual word (*kotleta*) and *kashka* means "lovely little porridge." These forms are especially affectionate in tone.

35. Lidiia Ginzburg, "Zapiski blokadnogo cheloveka," pp. 333–339. I have modified the translation from that which appears in Ginzburg, *Blockade Diary*, pp. 38–46.

Queues, Canteens, and the Politics of Location

ing at home.[36] "It was psychologically impossible" to resist queuing, Ginzburg echoed, so the blokadniki "withstood all of the agonies of an hours-long line" even though they knew that "by ten or eleven in the morning the shop would be empty."[37] In these accounts, the psychology of a line centered on the private agony of isolated individuals doomed to wait irrationally, endlessly, and silently.

Other diaries stressed that queue psychology was rooted in the compulsive desire to size up other Leningraders in line in order to gauge one's social position relative to the others around them. The linear arrangement of the line encouraged this. These diarists classified and rank-ordered the waiting blokadniki not by gender, class, or education, but by location.[38] They divided them into two groups—the people standing in front and the people standing behind them. "The psychology of a line," the architect Esfir' Levina explained, "[is that] everyone is envious of the one in front and desires for 'all sorts of misfortunes' to befall them so that they will leave the line."[39] As Levina suggested, Leningraders often "compared upwardly" to those who stood in front of them in line—an act that bred resentment and jealousy. Social psychologists suggest that line-waiters typically compare downwards, pitying those behind them or at the end of a line. However, they have found that individuals in crisis, like the blokadniki, tend to fixate on those who stand ahead of them and thus are in relatively advantageous positions.[40]

---

36. Dmitri Vladimirovich Afanas'ev, entry for November 11, 1941, "dnevnik," in Tamara Staleva, *Vechnye deti blokady: dokumental'nye ocherki* (Moscow: The Author, 1995) p. 23. To verify the published text, I also consulted the unpublished manuscript of the diary loaned to me with permission granted by the diarist's wife, Natal'ia Aleksandrovna Afanas'eva; Georgii Kniazev, entry for February 8, 1942, in Daniil Granin and Ales Adamovich, *Leningrad under Siege: First-Hand Accounts of the Ordeal,* trans. Clare Burstall and Vladimir Kisselnikov (Barnsley: Military Pen and Sword, 2007), p. 171.

37. Ginzburg, "Zapiski blokadnogo cheloveka," pp. 333–336. Translation in Ginzburg, *Blockade Diary,* pp. 38–40.

38. On how the line makes all markers of privilege other than position irrelevant, see Erving Goffman, *Relations in Public: Microstudies of the Public Order* (New York: Basic Books, 1971), pp. 36–37. On the line as "a miniature social system," see Leon Mann, "Queue Culture: The Waiting Line as a Social System," *American Journal of Sociology* 75, no. 3 (November 1969), pp. 340–354.

39. Levina, entry for February 3, 1942, TsGAIPD, f. 4000, op. 11, d. 57, l. 6.

40. The diarists' observations resonate with scholarship on queue behavior, which suggests that a primary activity of line-waiters is self-evaluation via social comparison.

174   *Alexis Peri*

Although this advantage was temporary and fleeting, the diarists described those who made it to the front of the line as a kind of chosen people, destined to be saved by "the bread of their salvation." "The [line] manager, like the 'gatekeeper of paradise,' counted off the 'faithful souls' letting them inside ten at a time. I stood and gazed mindlessly at this 'procedure,'" the chemist Elena Kochina observed.[41] Conversely, line-waiters were "a little scornful of those behind," Levina explained.[42] The latter's less favorable position afforded them—albeit temporarily—lower status; those standing behind were expected to obey those standing in front and heed their calls to move back, keep quiet, stop shoving, and so on. They also deferred to the superior knowledge of those in front who had a better view of the proceedings. Even though this social pecking order was reshuffled every time a new line formed, the diarists were pre-occupied with assessing and improving their own positions each time they queued.

It is not surprising, then, that these long stretches of waiting together fostered not solidarity, but antagonism in the assembled crowd. Vera Kostrovitskaia explained that "only those who are lucky or who have the strength to push the more feeble people aside and snatch 200 grams of cereal from the salesperson get something [to eat]."[43] The musician Kseniia Matus put it more strongly, calling the blockade line "a raging ocean that will crush you and trample you to death. No one offers you so much

---

Leon Festinger, a pioneering scholar behind social comparison theory, found that people tend to compare themselves to people ahead of them, calling this the "unidirectional drive upwards" (Festinger, "A Theory of Social Comparison Processes," *Human Relations* 7 [1954]: 117–140). For research on why threatened people tend to compare downwards as a means of coping, see J. V. Wood, et al., "Social Comparison in Adjustment to Breast Cancer," *Journal of Personality and Social Psychology* 49 (1985): 1169–1183. On comparing downwards as a source of comfort, see Rongrong Zhou and Dilip Soman, "Looking Back: Exploring the Psychology of Queuing and the Effect of the Number of People Behind," *Journal of Consumer Research* 24, no. 4 (March 2003): 518.

41. Kochina, entry for December 4, 1941, "Blokadnyi dnevnik," pp. 167–168. English translation in Elena Kochina, *Blockade Diary*, edited with an introduction by Samuel C. Ramer (Ann Arbor, Mich.: Ardis Publishers, 1990), p. 49.

42. Levina, entry for February 3, 1942, TsGAIPD, f. 4000, op. 11, d. 57, l. 6.

43. Kostrovitskaia, entry for September, October 1941, TsGALI, f. 157, op. 1, d. 28, l. 2.

Queues, Canteens, and the Politics of Location

as a helping hand."[44] Sixteen-year-old Iura Riabinkin described the queue "a crush of people" with whom he had to "fight hand-to-hand combat" to keep his place.[45] This daily fight to improve one's position, physically and socially, became a more pressing battle than the one taking place at the Leningrad front, especially in the winter of 1941–1942, when the Luftwaffe curtailed its bombardment of the city. The line contained much more immediate adversaries. Matus, Levina, and others described how they waged this battle by cutting or cheating. Food stores often used lists of names or numbered tickets to keep order in line. This system, Levina explained, was easily manipulated. "At home, I prepare hundreds of numbers and give them out on the street before the store opens, keeping for myself a place in the first hundred. Every hour, there is a check. Rivals find themselves. They also arrived with numbers, and arguments take place over whose numbers are real."[46] Librarian Mariia Konopleva wrote in a tone of outrage, tinged with admiration, about the various tricks used to remove people from in line, such as spreading rumors about food deliveries at other stores or sounding fake air-raid sirens to summon people to shelters.[47]

The diarists also watched Leningraders vie for position in more amiable ways, working out systems for saving places, taking turns waiting, and so on. Some tried to forge temporary alliances through emotional appeals, sharing stories about their sick relatives or starving children to win the sympathy (and the place) of the person in front of them. Although these appeals may have worked on prewar lines, Levina noted that now blokadniki were impervious to sob stories: "In general, the public is self-restrained—nothing moves you. When one says that her husband is dying and her children lie there swollen, another answers that her husband has already died and of her three kids, two have died."

---

44. Kseniia Markianovna Matus, entry for December 26, 1941, "dnevnik," MNM k.p. 4153, f. 2, d. 2804, l. 16.

45. Iurii Riabinkin, entry for November 9–10, 1941, in Adamovich and Granin, *Leningrad under Siege*, p. 104.

46. Levina, entry for February 3, 1942, TsGAIPD, f. 4000, op. 11, d. 57, l. 6; Matus, entry for January 29, 1942, MNM k.p. 4153, f. 2, d. 2804, ll. 46–47 (where she mistakenly wrote "January 1941").

47. Konopleva, entry for January 19, 1943, OR RNB, f. 368, ll. 37–38.

176   *Alexis Peri*

Claimants competed to show who had suffered more to justify who deserved the better position in line. Such indifference to the plight of others had become so normalized that Levina wondered if it was an inherently Russian trait laid bare by the duress of war: "Where does this self-restraint come from—from Russian endurance, discipline, or hope?"[48] Leningraders remained so focused on their individual goals that they rarely took collective action. Nor did they intervene in others' disputes. When her bread was snatched out of her hands, the chemist Elena Kochina fought with the thief to get it back, while the bystanders simply dodged their blows and kept their eyes fixed on the bread counter.[49]

Kochina became so accustomed to strife in line that when a stranger gave up her place to her, she described it as a kind of marvel—an exception that proved the general rule of wartime queue behavior. Incidents of altruism and cooperation frequently appear in memoirs and interviews of blokadniki, but rarely in diaries.[50] The diarists documented unusual moments of spontaneous, voluntary cooperation between strangers, such as when line-waiters worked together to settle disputes or evict line-jumpers, or, when the pipes froze in January 1942, they passed buckets of water from the Neva River to the bakeries so they could make bread.[51]

48. Levina, entry for February 3, 1942, TsGAIPD, f. 4000, op. 11, d. 57, l. 6.

49. Kochina, entries for January 13, 1942, and January 27, 1942, "Blokadnyi dnevnik," pp. 184, 191.

50. There is no doubt that some acts of selflessness occurred between strangers, but these are not often reported in diaries. For an example of a memoir of solidarity in line, see *Dve sud'by v Velikoi Otechestvennoi voiny* (Moscow: Gumanitarnaia Akademiia, 2006), pp. 47–48. For scholarly claims of altruism, see Granin and Adamovich, "Everyone Had a Savior," *Blokadnaia kniga* (St. Petersburg: Pechatnyi Dvor, 1994), pp. 113–125; Bidlack and Lomagin, *The Leningrad Blockade*, pp. 323–327. Using diaries and memoirs, Bidlack and Lomagin argued that Leningraders continued to sacrifice for each other, perhaps because it enhanced their own sense of value and social utility and therefore worthiness to live. My research, while not devoid of examples of altruism, returned many more examples of competition and resentment. Similarly, John Barber found that Leningraders generally privileged their own survival over collective concerns (Barber, "War, Public Opinion," pp. 272–274).

51. Kochina, entry for January 25, 1942, "Blokadnyi dnevnik," p. 191. English translation in Kochina, *Blockade Diary*, p. 83. Kochina presented this bucket brigade as a popular initiative, but the Komsomol or city leaders may have organized it. The two other main examples of altruism that I have found in diaries are in N. Sudanova, entry for April 1, 1942, "dnevnik," TsGAIPD, f. 4000, op. 10, d. 1387, l. 7; Zinaida Sedel'nikova,

Queues, Canteens, and the Politics of Location

These moments of teamwork stemmed from the alignment of individual and collective interests, not from a spontaneous sense of solidarity, and they are overshadowed and outnumbered by incidents of competition recorded in the diaries. In this respect, the diaries offer a counternarrative to the postwar "myth" of the "blockade brotherhood," identified and analyzed by Lisa Kirschenbaum. Part of the legacy of the blockade has been the retrospective characterization of Leningraders as a "natural, harmonious community" marked by cooperation and unity.[52] What accounts for the disparity between the diaries and these postwar impressions? One might argue that the individual diarists studied here simply did not witness frequent moments of voluntary cooperation, or that such moments came into sharper focus for Leningraders after they were no longer caught up in the fight for survival. Both are possible. The diaries do not disprove that social cohesion existed in the city, but, as accounts of subjective experiences, they reveal that many individuals viewed Leningrad—represented by the wintertime lines—as a society divided. The diarists emphasized the "swearing, shoving, and cutting" in line, not camaraderie.[53]

At the same time, they recorded almost no mass riots or uprisings in line. Although NKVD files document a few attacks on lines and shops, queues do not appear to have been major sites of collective protest, as they were in Moscow in October 1941. Contemporary observers today may be struck by the surprising orderliness and stability of Leningrad's lines and canteens as well as its municipal infrastructure overall. Given the emotional turbulence of the diary accounts, one might expect that riots or more incidents of violence would have occurred than those reported by the NKVD.[54] Perhaps it was the exhaustion of hunger or the

---

entry for February 2, 1942, in *279 dnei voiny: blokadnyi dnevnik* (Volgograd: Volgograd-skii Komitet Popechati, 1995), p. 71.

52. Lisa Kirschenbaum, *The Legacy of the Siege of Leningrad: Myth, Memories, and Monuments* (Cambridge: Cambridge University Press, 2006), pp. 107, 242–243.

53. Matus, entry for January 19, 1942, MNM k.p. 4153, f. 2, d. 2804, ll. 41–42.

54. This topic remains a source of puzzlement for scholars. For helpful discussions of why Leningrad did not become a site of revolt, see John Barber, "War, Public Opinion," pp. 266–267, and John Barber, "The Moscow Crisis of October 1941," in Julian Cooper, Maureen Perrie, and E. A. Rees, eds., *Soviet History, 1917–1953: Essays in Honour of R. W.*

watchful eye of the police that prevented such outbreaks. It also seems likely that the isolation, atomization, and antagonism, which the diarists found in tension-filled lines and canteens, contributed to the apparent order and compliance in the city.

In sum, the diaries present the line as a condensed version of the social order, where thousands of social dramas and struggles were performed daily, and where the entangled processes of social comparison and self-evaluation were manifest. The line was only a temporary hierarchy, but this did not prevent the diarists from using it to generalize about city demographics, collective psychology, and the prevalence of social competition. Because they viewed the collective from their particular positions in line, their spatial maps of Leningrad contain both insights and blind spots. After all, many political and cultural elites did not have to wait in lines because they shopped at special stores with restricted access. These privileges, far more egregious, were outside the purview of most diarists.[55]

STATUS ON DISPLAY: THE BLOCKADE CANTEEN

After Leningraders braved the long lines and finally entered a canteen, they were presented with new opportunities for social comparison. The politics of location were different here. First, in the winter and spring of 1941–1942, there were few municipal canteens open to the general public, so the fact that the diarists discussed here had the necessary institutional affiliations for canteen access places them in a relatively privileged position. Second, in the linearly arranged world of the queue, society appeared highly stratified and bifurcated. In the canteen, social groupings were more numerous and intermixed. Fortunates and unfortunates could sit together and observe each other at length. Thus, depending on where and with whom they sat, the diarists documented various arrays of

---

Davies (Basingstoke: Macmillan, 1995), p. 201; Bidlack and Lomagin, *The Leningrad Blockade*, pp. 246, 261.

55. An exception appears in the diary of Nina Klishevich, who tried to shop at an NKVD store ("Blokadnyi dnevnik Niny Nikolaevny Erokhanoi," entry for November 4, 1941, GMMOBL, f. RDF, op. 1L, d. 490, l. 27). I noticed only one mention of party canteens that restricted access to elites; it is in the *LP*, March 31, 1944, p. 3.

Queues, Canteens, and the Politics of Location

subgroups and social types in the canteen. In line, the diarists classified Leningraders based on their proximity to the front. In the canteen, they categorized blokadniki using at least two criteria: how they behaved while eating and how much food they received.

During the first siege winter, social interactions were muted in canteens as in lines. Leningraders refrained from talking so that they could focus entirely on eating, chewing slowly to make the experience last longer. The actor Fyodor Nikitin described such deliberateness as good "economy" and demonstrating a newfound "respect" for food.[56] Conversations were sparse; sometimes they were composed of glances instead of words. "They eat their neighbor's plate with their eyes, 'are you going to eat that bit later?,' 'and how do you allocate your bread?' 'I have come to the belief that it is necessary to eat 200 grams in the morning,' " the architect Esfir' Levina observed, reviewing the verbal and nonverbal exchanges she witnessed.[57] In the winter and spring of 1942, many preferred silence and solitude instead of conversation; they savored eating as a private pleasure. This impeded social rituals like springtime romance. In the Architects' Union, Levina observed, "women sit separately from men (from those who have dystrophic eyes) who eye them as they eat. *Distrofiia* is preventing romance and love this spring (a very unusual spring) even though life has become more tolerable."[58] Here, Levina used the word *distrofiia* (formally, *alimentarnaia distrofiia,* or nutritional dystrophy), a term developed during the blockade to describe the symptoms and pathogenesis of starvation. One of its symptoms was a significant

---

56. Fyodor Mikhailovich Nikitin, entry for November 21, 1941, "dnevnik," MNM, k.p. 6920, f. 1, d. 5580, l. 67. More examples are in Levina, entry for September 5, 1942, TsGAIPD, f. 4000, op. 11, d. 57, l. 28; Zelenskaia, entry for November 13, 1941, TsGAIPD, f. 4000, op. 11, d. 35, ll. 30–31; "Iz dnevnika Leonida Gal'ko," entry for November 28, 1941, in *Oborona Leningrada, 1941–1944: Vospominaniia i dnevniki uchastnikov* (Leningrad: Nauka, 1968), p. 513.

57. Levina, entry for April 14, 1942, TsGAIPD, f. 4000, op. 11, d. 57, l.18. Additional examples are in Nikitin, entry for November 21, 1941, MNM, k.p. 6920, f. 1, d. 5580, l. 67; Zelenskaia, entries for November 18, 1941, December 12, 1941, and December 23, 1941, TsGAIPD, f. 4000, op. 11, d. 35, ll. 33, 42, 46–47.

58. Levina, entries for April 21, 1942, and August 5, 1942, TsGAIPD, f. 4000, op. 11, d. 57, ll. 18, 28. Both sets of parentheses appear in the original. She referred to the season as spring even though she wrote the entry in summer.

180   *Alexis Peri*

decline in libido.[59] In her contribution to this volume, Rebecca Manley
discusses the emergence of this term as well as the pathology of hunger
it denotes. Far more than a medical term, distrofiia was wielded by clinicians and nonexperts alike and laden with moral and cultural associations. Leningraders often used "dystrophy" and "moral dystrophy"
(*moral'naia distrofiia*) to describe not only the dying, but people who were
apathetic, antisocial, emotionally volatile, and unworthy of the extra food
that they were prescribed and authorized to receive from canteens and
clinics.[60]

Along with small talk, the diarists documented other prewar cour-
tesies that disappeared. Levina, Ginzburg, Liubovskaia, Zelenskaia, and
others worried that the decline of table manners indicated that Leningraders had been severely brutalized by war. Hunger led to callousness,
emotional instability, or rudeness. The hungriest blokadniki, those least
privileged and nearest to death, were the least able to control themselves
at table. Based on her observations in the Writer's Union canteen, Lidiia
Ginzburg created two composite types of Leningraders on the brink of
death, "A" and "B." At the smallest "trifle," "'A' fell into despair" and rushed
about creating disturbances in the dining room, while "B" could not
resist licking the dirty dishes of his fellow patrons.[61] They behaved, the
actor Fyodor Nikitin explained, like ravenous animals, who were to be
pitied and perhaps a bit despised for their coarseness.[62]

Irina Zelenskaia, a manager for the city's last functioning power plant
Lenenergo, confessed her own aversion toward those near death—whom
she called *distrofiki*—less for their emotional volatility than for their

59. Zelenskaia, entry for January 6, 1942, TsGAIPD, f. 4000, op. 11, d. 35, ll. 49–50.
60. In addition to Manley's chapter, see Peri, "Minds under Siege." On Soviet views
of *distrofiia* as a new and special "Leningrad illness" and "experimental pathology,"
see G. L. Sobolev, *Uchenye Leningrada v gody Velikoi Otechestvennoi voiny, 1941–1945*
(Moscow: Nauka, 1966), p. 68.
61. Ginzburg, "Zapiski blokadnogo cheloveka," p. 345.
62. Nikitin, entry for November 21, 1941, MNM, k.p. 6920, f. 1, d. 5580, l. 67. By
contrast, the radio worker Arkadii Lepkovich took pride in Leningraders' rough
manners as a sign of their warrior status. "The people have matured and they have become
unaccustomed to the politeness of the peacetime life; such a people is frightening and
ruthless to the enemy" (Arkadii Lepkovich, entry for December 13, 1941, TsGAIPD, f. 4000,
op. 11, d. 85, ll. 6–7).

Queues, Canteens, and the Politics of Location

numbness. She described eating in the station's canteen alongside an emaciated coworker, Vasia Mikhailov, who responded to her polite queries "soundlessly" and lifelessly. Mikhailov simply looked at her with a "senseless, careless smile on his lifeless face" that accentuated the "non-human sharpening" of his features. "You feel somehow hardened and losing human feeling," Zelenskaia admitted, in interacting with such distrofiki, but "strangely, I am still kind toward people . . . where a human spirit lives."[63] As Levina's and Zelenskaia's comments suggest, the canteen showcased the distrofiki as a kind of underclass of blockade society. Their small rations and lack of *kulturnost'* (the ability to exhibit self-control and propriety) marked them as outcasts, not unlike the "Muselmann" of the Nazi concentration camps or the *dokhodiaga* ("goner") from the Gulag.[64] Especially after the population began to eat better in late 1942, many diarists shunned the so-called distrofiki as distasteful reminders of the extreme suffering they experienced months before.

Such condemnations of impropriety occurred both on an individual level, among the diarists, as well as on a societal one. In late 1942, prewar etiquette was reinstated in Leningrad canteens, sometimes forcibly.[65] Levina observed how the leaders at the Architects' Union tried to restore good manners and hygiene in their workers in order to re-socialize them:

> Life is starting to be restored and the leaders of the Architects' Union are starting to teach their members: "blow your nose into a cloth, and do not wipe your fingers on the tablecloth, do not lick the plate with your tongue." In normal times, such remarks would be deemed offensive, but now are being obeyed. They are teaching people to live as one teaches invalids how to walk.[66]

63. Zelenskaia, entry for December 10, 1941, TsGAIPD, f. 4000, op. 11, d. 35, l. 40.

64. On "muselman" (also spelled "musselman" and "muselmann"), see: Primo Levi, *Survival in Auschwitz,* trans. Stuart Woolf (New York: Collier Books, 1986), p. 98. In *The Gulag Handbook,* Jacques Rossi listed *dokhodiaga* and *distrofik* as synonyms. See Rossi, *The Gulag Handbook: An Encyclopedia Dictionary of Soviet Penitentiary Institutions and Terms Related to the Forced Labor Camps,* trans. by William A. Burhans (New York: Paragon House, 1989), p. 103.

65. Aleksandra Pavlovna Liubovskaia, "Leningrad, 1941–1942: Zapiski zhitelia blokadnogo goroda," entry for May 17, 1942, p. 153. I was granted access to and permission to use this unpublished diary, held privately by the family, by the author's son, Igor' Liubovskii.

66. Levina, entry for October 17, 1942, TsGAIPD, f. 4000, op. 11, d. 57, l. 31. As the sociologist Norbert Elias classically argued, manners represent more than propriety;

According to Levina, manners were much more than niceties; they were tools of social rehabilitation and social control. The canteen, then, both reflected and regulated wartime norms of propriety. As the diarists observed how their fellow blokadniki behaved at table, they classified Leningraders as fortunate and unfortunate, normal and deviant, deserving and undeserving. And although they certainly remarked on the distrofiki around them, the diarists tended to compare upwardly in the canteen, as in the line. They focused on those who received larger portions than they did or whose bodies or decorum indicated a more robust diet.

Because portion sizes differed by ration category, the diarists' observations in the canteen often dovetailed with broader critiques of food distribution policies more generally. It is notable that the diarists tended not to analyze the ration system in the abstract, but situated their critiques within the context of the canteen. They devoted a great deal of energy toward documenting the elites whom they spotted there. These ranged from "new" elites, who gained power because of the famine, to more "traditional" elites like workers and party members, who were favored in the prewar period. The diarists often wielded the rhetoric of class struggle or of proletarian values to repudiate these groups' elite status and to justify the diarists' own claims of entitlement. Thus far, I have found only one instance wherein a diarist referred to herself using this framework. This was the librarian Aleksandra Liubovskaia, who joked that she and her children were "playing gentry" when they ate well.[67] The vast majority of diarists—regardless of ration category or privileges—presented themselves as victims of social inequality and stratification.

---

they display one's worthiness to belong to a particular society, class, or nation. See Norbert Elias, *The Civilizing Process: Sociogenetic and Psychogenetic Investigations* (Oxford: Blackwell, 2000), pp. 30, 42.

67. Liubovskaia, "Leningrad, 1941–1942," entry for January 20, 1942, p. 56. The diarists often evoked the category of class even though the elites they censured were status groups or social types rather than classes in a Marxian sense. Their tendency, however, reflects what Shelia Fitzpatrick called "the marriage" between "class and ascription" through which the regime and its citizens classified people for marginalization or privilege; see Fitzpatrick, "Ascribing Class: The Construction of Social Identity in Soviet Russia," *Journal of Modern History* 65, no. 4 (December 1993): 745–770; Jean-Paul Depretto, "Stratification without Class," *Kritika* 8, no. 2 (Spring 2007): 380.

Queues, Canteens, and the Politics of Location

NEW ELITES

Food-Service Workers

In lines and canteens, there was a critical divide between those who lined up in front of the service counter and those who occupied the coveted space behind it. The diarists reviled the cooks, servers, and delivery staff who were permitted to cross this threshold. As they waited for food in lines and canteens, the diarists scrutinized food-service workers—their actions and their bodies—and accused them of under-measuring portions, playing favorites, reselling stolen food in the black market, and generally feeding themselves at the expense of the population. After waiting in line from 7 a.m. to 9 p.m. for bread, the musician Kseniia Matus slandered the bakery workers: "Merry life! Bastards! How long can it possibly sustain us, unhappy, helpless people? If they could only go one day without gobbling everything up, if they could endure but one-hundredth of the lot we've endured."[68] Matus clearly saw the bakery workers as outsiders ("them") because, in her eyes, they did not undergo the profound suffering that united the blokadniki ("us"). Similarly, Irina Zelenskaia called lunch at the Lenenergo power station where she worked "a joke" and blamed the management for shortchanging deserving Leningraders. She described herself as one of the deserving ("us"), even though she herself held a management position. "We never get full portion at the canteen. For our own 250 people, 200 soups are given out, and not every day, and 80–100 second courses because of the fact that there are always horrible thieves."[69] Her suspicions became acute in spring 1942, when the regime increased norms but gave out less than the promised amounts. Zelenskaia, however, never questioned the norms as misleading or unrealistic—at least not in her diary. Instead, she blamed the staff that transported, cooked, and served food for the shortfall: "On the way to the eater an awful lot [of food] presses itself

---

68. Matus, entry for January 29, 1942, MNM, k.p. 4153, f. 2, d. 2804, l. 47. In the text she accidentally wrote "1941" instead of "1942."

69. Zelenskaia, entries for September 22, 1941, and December 3, 1941, TsGAIPD, f. 4000, op. 11, d. 35, ll. 18, 37–38.

184 *Alexis Peri*

into the hands of the canteen, the storehouse, and workers, not overseen by any kind of workers' inspection."[70]

Like Matus and Zelenskaia, most diarists declared with certainty that the disparity between what they and what food service personnel were eating was enormous. The actual scale of this discrepancy, though difficult to ascertain, seems more modest. Richard Bidlack and Nikita Lomagin have suggested that workers in the food industry had a 10 to 20 percent lower rate of starvation than the general public, which perished at roughly 37 percent during the first siege winter. Of course, mortality fluctuated greatly by institution. At certain bakeries and candy factories, for instance, 90 percent of food workers survived.[71]

Even diarists who benefited from their connections to such workers still blamed them for much of their hunger.[72] These personal exemptions and oversights underscore the severity of the food crisis as well as the particularity of the diarists' visions of it. One of these diarists was the engineer Ivan Savinkov. He managed a shop floor in the Molotov Factory, held a Category I card, received doctors' certificates for additional food, and occasionally got extras from the factory's canteen director, a friend of his.[73] Even so, Savinkov suffered from numerous hunger-related illnesses and was bed-ridden for several months. Rather than focus his rage on German bombardment of food trucks and barges slated for the

70. Zelenskaia, entry for May 21, 1942, TsGAIPD, f. 4000, op. 11, d. 35, ll. 810b–82.

71. Richard Bidlack, "Workers at War: Factory Workers and Labor Policy in the Siege of Leningrad," *The Carl Beck Papers in Russian and East European Studies*, no. 902 (Pittsburgh, Pa.: University of Pittsburg Press, 1991), p. 24; Bidlack and Lomagin, *The Leningrad Blockade*, pp. 272–273, 289. In the latter work, Bidlack and Lomagin reported that nearly all of the employees at the Krupskaia sweet factory and the Baltika Bakery No. 4 survived, as did 92 percent of workers at the Baltika Bread Factory. Of course, practices of pilfering from the food supply and the widespread knowledge and complaints about it are not unique to the war, but were a regular feature of Soviet life. For a discussion of this during the first Five-Year Plan, see Kotkin, *Magnetic Mountain*, pp. 250–269.

72. Similar critiques by other diarists who benefited can be found in Afanas'ev, entries for November 7, 1941, December 23, 1941, and January 3, 1942, *Vechnye deti blokady*, pp. 23–6; "The Diary of B. Kapranov," in V. E. Levtov and V. M. David, eds., *Budni podviga: blokadnaia zhizn' leningradtsev v dnevnikakh, risunkakh, dokumentakh, 8 sentiabria 1941–27 ianvaria 1944* (St. Petersburg: LIK, 2006), p. 42.

73. Savinkov, entry for February 25, 1942, TsGAIPD, f. 4000, op. 11, d. 99, l. 24.

Queues, Canteens, and the Politics of Location

city, Savinkov raged against those who handled the (few) deliveries of food that made it inside "the ring." "It is an interestingly organized affair," he remarked scornfully,

> whoever has a food service worker has a [illegible] staff member to carry food out of the canteen; the guards work together because they want to eat—this is the first small party of swindlers. The second is much larger: this is the acting assistant, the head cook, and the shopkeepers. Here, there is a much bigger game consisting of acts of damage, loss, evaporation, and concession; under the guise of filling the mess tins, terrible self-provisioning is taking place.[74]

Savinkov deduced two rings of conspiracy, one operated by those who prepared and served food and the other a more large-scale network of thieves, who stole from trucks and storehouses before the food ever made it to the canteen. The actor Fyodor Nikitin, who shared this supposition that theft was systematic and highly coordinated, called pilfering "our Russian plague" and likened the "bread ladies," bread cutters, and canteen directors to an enemy army, a "brotherhood in arms" that was closing ranks against blokadniki.[75] For Savinkov and Nikitin, internal adversaries loomed larger than the German besiegers. Of course, most Leningraders were not fully aware of the extent of the food crisis, which city authorities concealed from them, and they may have found it easier to blame these individuals, whom they confronted every day, instead of impersonal policies and circumstances.

According to the diarists, bakery and canteen workers did not conceal their guilt, but flaunted their ill-gotten gains. A kind of nouveau riche, these personnel adorned themselves in "gold rings and earrings" sold to them by desperate, hungry people in exchange for stolen bread.[76] Young children also displayed their privileged status conspicuously. In July 1942, the architect Esfir' Levina recorded a conversation she

---

74. Savinkov, entry for September 22, 1941, TsGAIPD, f. 4000, op. 11, d. 99, l. 9. More examples are in Riabinkin, entries for November 9–10, 1941, in *Leningrad under Siege*, pp. 102–103; Natal'ia Borisovna Uskova, entry for January 10, 1942, MNM, f. 1, 5577, k.p. 6518, l. 46.

75. Nikitin, entry for November 28, 1941, MNM, k.p. 6920, f. 1, d. 5580, l. 68. The NKVD did have some evidence of criminal rings coordinated between cooks, bookkeepers, and stockroom workers (Bidlack and Lomagin, *The Leningrad Blockade*, pp. 161–162, 309–313).

76. Nikitin, entry for November 28, 1941, MNM, k.p. 6920, f. 1, d. 5580, l. 68.

overheard between three little boys comparing their bodies on a street corner. "The winner" explained his victory by announcing: " 'I look better than all of you because my dad [works] at a bread factory.' "[77] Their superior wealth and health made them appear alien, not true blokadniki, but altogether different beings. While aboard an evacuation convoy with her husband, Dima, and daughter, Lena, in April 1942, Elena Kochina noted how the other passengers "present a homogeneous mixture" except for "only one young fellow and a girl [who] stand out":

> Both are robust and red-cheeked. They quickly sniffed one another out and got together. The guy jabbers on without stopping. Words fly out of his mouth, quickly running into one another. The result is a kind of leapfrog that is impossible to make out. But the girl evidently understands him perfectly. Throwing her head back, she scatters laughter throughout the car. Together, they raise quite a hullabaloo.

Kochina was struck not only by their impudence, but also by their distinct physicality and style of speech. Peculiar in its speed, energetic delivery, and mirth, this language was disturbingly human and incomprehensible to Kochina. The pair gravitated toward each other and ignored the other passengers until Dima Kochin interrupted them:

> "Somehow you don't look like you went hungry," Dima said tauntingly. "I didn't go hungry . . . my father works in Leningrad in supply. During the blockade we ate better than before the war. We had everything." "Then why are you being evacuated?" "I was bored in Leningrad. There wasn't anyone around to have a few laughs or go dancing with." [The girl] also spoke quite readily: "I work in the supply department at Lake Ladoga. We ate whole boxes of butter and chocolate." She said boastfully, "Of course, before the war I didn't see that." I felt indignation rising in me. Neither of them could begin to comprehend their tactlessness, telling this to the very people they had robbed.[78]

Such incidents helped Kochina to justify the times when her husband had stolen food from neighbors, shops, and storehouses. "After all," Kochina reasoned, "the salespeople are really robbing us blind. In return for bread they have everything they want. Almost all of them, without any shame at all, wear gold and expensive furs. Some of them even work

---

77. Levina, entry for July 21, 1942, TsGAIPD f. 4000, op. 11, d. 57, l. 27.

78. Kochina, entry for April 5, 1942, "Blokadnyi dnevnik," p. 206. English translation from Kochina, *Blockade Diary*, pp. 106–107.

Queues, Canteens, and the Politics of Location

behind the counter in luxurious sable and sealskin coats."[79] She viewed her family's thefts as necessary, but this accumulation of gold and other finery as sheer greed. Kochina's account provides a strong example of how many diarists' visions of the social order were linked to their personal claims of entitlement and exemption. It also underscores the extent to which illegal trade and theft became pillars of the blockade economy, fundamental to the practices of self-provisioning that Leningraders—and Soviet people across the country—relied on for survival.

Wives (and Husbands) of the Canteen

The diarists studied the emergence of another elite, also distinct in appearance and decorum. They called them the "canteen girls" (*devushka iz stolovoi*), or "wives of the blockade" (*blokadnaia zhena*), who traded sexual favors for food. Sex, along with food, became a major currency inside "the ring" as it did in other economies of scarcity, like the Gulag. "A new term even has emerged to explain this: 'blockade acquaintanceship' [*blokadnoe znakomstvo*]," Ivan Savinkov observed.[80] Although such transactions usually were kept secret, some diarists taught their potential readers how to spot this new social type. "Your eye," Zelenskaia remarked, "using a special sense, fishes out the healthy blooming faces":

> These are mostly young women and, if they are not in military uniforms, then of course one can suspect them of being "canteen girls," the only stratum of the population this winter that has preserved its normal appearance, although without much honor for themselves.[81]

The diarist's social observations were inextricably intertwined with her notion of distributive justice. Zelenskaia noted that military personnel had, she felt, a legitimate right to more food, whereas healthy-looking civilians were parasites that lived off of the rest of the population. In this way, she and other diarists underscored the reversal of cues and norms

---

79. Kochina, entry for November 23, 1941, "Blokadnyi dnevnik," p. 166. Translation in Kochina, *Blockade Diary*, p. 47.

80. Savinkov, entry for September 22, 1942, TsGAIPD, f. 4000, op. 11, d. 99, l. 59.

81. Zelenskaia, entry for entry for August 22, 1942, TsGAIPD, f. 4000, op. 11, d. 35, l. 96.

188   *Alexis Peri*

such that a healthy and feminine outward appearance indicated a kind of inner debauchery and unworthiness when it came to food. At the same time as she loathed these healthy bodies, Zelenskaia also admitted: "you are just happy to see fresh, healthy young faces, like these young ladies," rather than the "numerous walking skeletons" of the blokadniki.[82]

Most diarists gendered this social type female. Nina Klishevich depicted the "blockade wife" as "well-dressed, with hair done up in a wave, manicured, heavily made-up, in very high heels," antithetical to the androgynous blokadnitsa.[83] However, the male diarist Ivan Savinkov reversed the usual pairing of female prostitute and male patron and described how men also sold themselves to food-service workers. Savinkov called the female patrons of the sex trade "the new Leningrad female aristocrats [*aristokratki*]," or "the aristocrats of the stove"—class enemies of blockade society. However, like Zelenskaia and Klishevich, he vilified the women, not the men, as overly sexualized and brazenly materialistic. The main difference was that, unlike "blockade wives," these aristokratki were sexual predators, exuding gluttony through their telltale plump physiques and gold adornments. As Savinkov observed,

> Comparatively speaking, the workers connected to food can be separated out from all the rest of the people who live only on ration cards. This is first and foremost a fat, well-nourished carcass, dolled up in silk, velvet, stylish boots, and shoes. There is gold in her ears, heaps of it on her fingers, piles, and of course a watch, stolen and, depending on its grandeur, golden or plain. When this type of aristokratka chats with us, it is necessary for her to look at the watch, shaking her wrist for a long time and keeping it at eye level. Such an assured, insolent conversation—she thinks that for a plate of soup she can buy you for a night. And the conversation is only about food, about theft, [about] how and how much someone steals.[84]

82. Ibid. This discussion of the relationship between physicality and moral or ideological purity harkens back to debates over how party members (especially women) should look in the years following the 1921 famine. As Eric Naiman demonstrates, women who lacked strong secondary sexual characteristics were considered exemplars of sacrifice, discipline, and ideological purity. See Eric Naiman, *Sex in Public: The Incarnation of Early Soviet Ideology* (Princeton, N.J.: Princeton University Press, 1997), pp. 214–215. Thanks to Rebecca Manley for bringing this to my attention.

83. "Blokadnyi dnevnik Niny Nikolaevny Erokhanoi," entry for June 13, 1943, GMMOBL, f. RDF, op. 1L, d. 490, l. 57.

84. Savinkov, entry for September 22, 1942, TsGAIPD, f. 4000, op. 11, d. 99, l. 59.

Queues, Canteens, and the Politics of Location

189

For Savinkov, the canteen worker was a fat, "greasy" "carcass," a piece of meat more than a human being, who consumed food, valuables, and men with an insatiable appetite. So, while romance apparently faded in the canteen, sex remained central to the city's socioeconomic structure.

Interestingly, unlike other diarists, Savinkov characterized these sexual transactions as elite affairs that precluded junior engineers like him from participating. The aristokratki partnered with political and military elites who had less need of extra food, but probably were more physically desirable. He remarked, with both pride and bitterness, that the women had little to gain by choosing him:

> Such an "aristokratka of the stove" does not want a lowly engineer as her lover. My supervising engineer is proud of this. And so we enter into slavery under the cook, he goes [to her] in order not to die or freeze during winter. Such an acquaintanceship guarantees you food, firewood, and definitely a featherbed with a "fat lady in it." ... Sailors and definitely commanders hold the "aristokratka of the stove" in high esteem. Yes, this evil family will be damned for [each] plate of soup.
>
> I do not want to sell myself and therefore it is obvious that I am a distrofik and I have been ill for nine months of 1942 and in bed for five of them. Oh war! What are you doing to people![85]

Savinkov called himself a distrofik to indicate his physical deterioration, distasteful appearance, and marginal status—he was shunned and rejected. A highly malleable and politicized term, distrofiia connoted a mixture of physical, behavioral, and moral traits. Sometimes, it was wielded as an insult to condemn those who acquiesced to death, and sometimes Leningraders used it to indicate their true insider status as suffering blokadniki. By evoking distrofiia to explain the cook's rejection of him and his rejection of her, Savinkov achieved both. He criticized himself for being unappealing and unwilling to do anything—even sell himself—for food, while gesturing toward his moral purity compared to the aristokratka holding court in the canteen.

In sum, such vilification of food-service workers is a major theme of the journals, one that diarists framed through their experiences of lines and canteens. This theme also reverberated in other settings and was writ large on the pages of the LP, which was silent about administrative errors,

---

85. Ibid.

but published at least a dozen notices about food-service workers tried for theft.[86] The *LP* published twenty-five articles criticizing food-service workers for shortfalls and disorganization in the canteen, all but four of them between 1943 and 1944, after the famine was over (and after these diary entries were written).[87] These articles thus did not suggest to Leningraders that they should denounce food workers, but they did express the regime's partial and misleading explanations of the food supply, which had been circulating around Leningrad since the famine began.[88]

Beginning in 1943, as the famine subsided, this evasive strategy was revised. The *LP* began printing reports on the raids that the newspaper's staff was conducting on canteens in order to protect Leningraders' interests.[89] That same year, the *LP* also published—for the first time since the siege began—censorious "letters to the editor" complaining about the lack of food. In these "letters to the editor," the signatories legitimized their demands for better food and conditions by emphasizing their status as workers. They chastised food service staff for "not improving the lives of working people," and ordered them "to deliver to workers every gram that they are due."[90] Sometimes, irate workers denounced local labor and political leaders who "did not even bother to revise the schedule

86. See the following issues of the *LP* on the prosecution of food theft: November 20, 1941, p. 4; December 13, 1941, p. 4; January 13, 1942, p. 2; April 9, 1942, p. 2; June 2, 1942, p. 2; July 31, 1942, p. 4; August 5, 1942, p. 2; August 13, 1942, p. 2; September 15, 1942, p. 4; October 14, 1942, p. 3; September 15, 1943, p. 2. Karel Berkhoff argued that this practice of blaming local figures, not the rationing system occurred across the Soviet Union (Berkhoff, *Motherland in Danger*, pp. 98, 101–103).

87. These exceptional articles appeared in the *LP* on October 30, 1941, December 6 and 20, 1941, and in October 1942.

88. By contrast, in wartime and postwar Rostov, Jones argued that newspaper rhetoric not only shaped, but also suggested to readers how to place blame for high prices and food shortages (Jones, "People without a Definite Occupation," pp. 239, 242, 252–253).

89. *LP*, December 20, 1941, p. 2; *LP*, October 16, 1942, p. 4.

90. *LP* February 20, 1943, p. 2. Also see the letters to the editor and announcements in the following issues of the *LP*: November 24, 1942, p. 3; December 2, 1942 p. 2; January 19, 1943, p. 3; July 6, 1943, p. 3; September 3, 1943, p. 3; October 8, 1943, p. 3; November 25, 1943, p. 3; November 30, 1943, p. 3; December 10, 1943, p. 3; February 13, 1944, p. 3; March 31, 1944, p. 3; July 13, 1944, p. 3; July 29, 1944, p. 3; August 25, 1944, p. 3; October 12, 1944, p. 3; October 18, 1944, p. 3; November 29, 1944, p. 3.

Queues, Canteens, and the Politics of Location

breaks by shop floor, so that one can eat quickly without wasting precious working time."[91] According to NKVD reports, there were seventeen stoppages or slowdowns by aggrieved workers during the blockade.[92] Similarly, the first time that food shortages were openly discussed in the Soviet Information Bureau (Sovinformburo) reports, the discussion opened with the declaration that "the cafeterias ought to feed working people better."[93] The language of these grievances and declarations points to, and relies on the enduring assumption that workers were, or deserved to be, the privileged class in Soviet society.

TRADITIONAL ELITES

Workers and the Meaning of Labor

On the one hand, workers in war-related industries faced enormous, if not impossible, labor quotas. On the other hand, they enjoyed some advantages and relative material comforts. First, they had access to the canteens inside their factories and to occasional food parcels sent from the front. Some moved from their apartments into barracks at their work sites, in part to cope with the extended workday. However, this also allowed them to conserve energy and stay warmer. In addition, as of November 5, 1941, the Leningrad City Executive Committee slated workers at one hundred defensive plants to eat at their factories' canteens off-ration, meaning that they could redeem their coupons for additional food elsewhere.[94] These practices were justified pragmatically as well as ideologically. Workers in heavy industry expended a great number calories doing labor that was essential to the war effort. Moreover, as a class, they had long been favored—at least rhetorically—by a regime that had seized power and ruled in their name.

The division between Category I "workers in war-related industries" and Category II "white-collar employees" during the war was not new;

91. *LP,* February 25, 1943, p. 3.
92. Bidlack and Lomagin, *The Leningrad Blockade,* p. 346.
93. *LP,* October 6, 1944, p. 1. This was the first time food shortages were addressed on the first page of the *LP* since the siege began.
94. Bidlack and Lomagin, *The Leningrad Blockade,* p. 292.

it had been used when rationing was instituted in the prewar period. However, from the diarists' perspectives, the blockade raised the stakes of this distinction. None of the wartime rations provided adequate nutrition or calories for survival. Still, the differences between these two categories were notable.[95] First, during the worst months of the famine, those in Category I ate roughly twice as much as everyone else. Workers at the city's power plants, the Stalin Metal Works, and the Kirov Works, for instance, had a 20 percent lower death rate than the general population.[96] White-collar employees' rations approximated those of dependents and children who did not work and whose norms were so small that their ration card was nicknamed the *smertnik,* or death certificate.[97] Second, the "worker" designation was given to a smaller portion of the population during the blockade—just 34 percent in the winter of 1941–1942.[98] It excluded workers in lighter or non-war-related industries. At the same time, it included some elites from the party and intelligentsia, who petitioned to have Category I "worker" status.[99]

Initially, some diarists applauded the ration system as "necessary," "logical," and good for "discipline" because it supported both the war

95. For a discussion of these categories and Leningraders' complaints about them in the mid-1930s, see Bidlack and Lomagin, *The Leningrad Blockade,* pp. 29, 33–41. Fitzpatrick noted that the service worker category was particularly nebulous because it did not align with Marxian class categories, but still was used and in a pejorative sense (Fitzpatrick, "Ascribing Class," p. 751).

96. Bidlack, "Workers at War," pp. 20–25. Bidlack noted that the data from other factories is sparse and that figures might be skewed by the fact that most workers were men, who died at higher rates during the first winter.

97. Aleksandr Boldyrev, entry for March 29, 1942, in *Osadnaia zapis': blokadnyi dnevnik* (St. Petersburg: Evropeiskii Dom, 1998), p. 78.

98. Pavlov, *Leningrad 1941,* p. 77. Similar disputes over "workers'" rations also took place in Germany and occupied France, where workers were subdivided into "very heavy" laborers and lesser categories. Laborers in the lower strata lobbied to be recognized with "workers" cards. See Kenneth Mouré, "*Réalités Cruelles:* State Controls and the Black Market in Occupied France," in Ina Zweiniger-Bargielowska, Rachel Duffett, and Alain Drouard, eds., *Food and War in Twentieth-Century Europe* (Farnham: Ashgate, 2011), pp. 173–174; Collingham, *The Taste of War,* p. 367.

99. On these petitions and the fluctuations of Category I recipients, see Bidlack and Lomagin, *The Leningrad Blockade,* p. 297.

Queues, Canteens, and the Politics of Location

effort and Soviet tenets.[100] A Category II worker, Zelenskaia acknowledged that this system of "supporting all those who were able-bodied" and "not feeding those who are dying" was "cruel" but "acceptable" in light of the immediate goal of winning the war.[101] However, as the famine became more severe, most diarists grew critical of the workers who were privileged. They objected to this new, ration-based definition of worker in part because it devalued the work done by Category II workers and in part because Category I workers did not seem to work enough to warrant rations that were twice as large. In their eyes, the regime's claim that food was distributed to "each according to his labor" was dubious.

This perceived inactivity stood in sharp contrast to workers' industriousness at the start of the war. At that time, Leningrad was the Soviet Union's second most important industrial center. After the German invasion, city authorities extended the workday and raised production quotas, as well as strengthening the punishments for absenteeism.[102] As a result of these harsh policies, Leningrad's industrial output increased dramatically in summer and fall of 1941. However, by late November 1941, the lack of electricity, raw materials, and manpower began to cripple factories. Industrial productivity ground to a halt during the winter of 1941–1942 when the city soviet closed down 270 factories. Roughly half of the city's workers stopped going to work, and those who did go occupied themselves with other tasks—heating, repairs, chores, or reading. Aleksandra Liubovskaia was a librarian, translator, and Category II employee at a milling machine factory on the Petrograd side of the city. She described a typical day at the factory this way:

100. "Dnevnik i drugie materialy Anisima Prokof'evicha Nikulina," entry for July 1–10, 1941, TsGAIPD, f. 4000, op. 11, d. 80, ll. 1–2.

101. Zelenskaia, entry for March 19, 1942, TsGAIPD, f. 4000, op. 11, d. 35, l. 70. Here, the diarist's statement that the regime was "not feeding those who are dying" is hyperbolic, as the Food Commission allocated small rations as well as small amounts of additional food (known as *lechebnoe pitanie*) that was prescribed to those diagnosed with distrofiia. Her statement accurately implies that these measures did little to save the dying.

102. Bidlack and Lomagin, *The Leningrad Blockade*, pp. 188–189; Bidlack, "Workers at War," pp. 16–23, 29. David Glantz argued that factory production was substantial through the end of December 1941 (Glantz, *The Siege of Leningrad*, pp. 79–80).

> No one is seriously working. The head of the department, it is true, punctually comes to work at 8 a.m. and literally sits with his hands folded on the table for about an hour and then leaves. . . . Others sit for two hours at our tables and then go to lunch. With this, their working day ends because they go home early.[103]

Without sufficient resources or electricity, laborers crowded into the library to read newspapers, study maps, and discuss the war, turning the reading room into—as Liubovskaia put it—"some kind of a club."[104] Yet, during the six months or so that much of the industrial sector was inoperative, workers still received Category I ration cards.[105] Natal'ia Uskova, a philology student who took a job in a munitions factory in order to obtain Category I status, echoed this point: "Right now it [the factory] is not working because of the lack of electric energy. But all who have remained alive come to the office like it's their duty. . . . The big motivation is the canteen. Lunch is from 1 to 2 o'clock, but already at 12 o'clock a line forms on the stairwell and extends to the second floor. Here they feed us every day, despite the fact that the factory is not working."[106] As Daniil Granin and Ales' Adamovich noted in their classic *Book of the Blockade*, "work" acquired a new meaning; the factory became a place to eat. The most desirable jobs were nominal, but included canteen access. A rare moment of celebration appears in the homemaker Elena Skriabina's diary when her son Dima started "working"—that is, eating—in a plant that had not opened yet.[107]

In light of such inactivity, diarists in Category II insisted that the work they did was comparable to those in Category I. As she sat in the

---

103. Liubovskaia, entry for November 16, 1941, "Leningrad, 1941–1942, pp. 11–12. Interestingly, some factories may have ordered their workers to take up reading as a substitute for mental idleness. Bidlack and Lomagin cited the rules of one factory that made reading—along with shaving and fetching water and wood—mandatory as a survival tactic (Bidlack and Lomagin, *The Leningrad Blockade*, p. 52, fn. 86).

104. Liubovskaia, Epilogue, "Leningrad, 1941–1942, p. 200.

105. Bidlack and Lomagin, *The Leningrad Blockade*, pp. 294–296. Glantz, *The Siege of Leningrad*, p. 81.

106. Uskova, entry for March 15, 1942, MNM, f. 1, 5577, k.p. 6518, ll. 49–50.

107. Skriabina, entries for November 6, 1941, and January 15, 1942, *V blokade*, pp. 42–43, 65. Also see Punin, entry for November 20, 1941, "Blokadnyi dnevnik," pp. 100–101; Richard Bidlack, "Survival Strategies in Leningrad," in Robert W. Thurston, ed., *The People's War: Responses to World War II in the Soviet Union* (Urbana: University of Illinois Press, 2000), pp. 90–95; Granin and Adamovich, *Blokadnaia kniga*, p. 267.

Queues, Canteens, and the Politics of Location

canteen at the Architects' Union, Esfir' Levina fumed that engineers were fed substantially more than architects like herself, even though, she claimed, the differences in their jobs were negligible.[108] Similarly, Irina Zelenskaia initially praised the ration system, but soon felt "undeservedly wronged" by it, insisting that little separated her, a Category II worker, from the manual laborers at Lenenergo.[109] "We work or do nothing to the same extent," the newly minted party member exclaimed. "I am feeling like a victim of injustice. These horrors weaken one's will and what is worse, one's principles."[110]

Under the ration system, worker status was determined less by the labor one performed than by how much food one received. This prompted many diarists to reflect upon what it meant to be a worker. Drawing on a wide range of criteria—including political consciousness, industriousness, discipline, and the like—some diarists claimed that Category I workers lacked the proletarian values to warrant such privilege. Here, the journals of Ivan Savinkov (a Category I worker and critic of the party) and Irina Zelenskaia (a Category II employee and party member) are instructive because they raise similar objections despite the diarists' very different circumstances. Between September 1941 and January 1943, Savinkov kept a detailed record of inactivity at the Molotov Factory, as shortages, deaths, and evacuations made regular productivity impossible.[111] But what Savinkov found more upsetting than the inactivity was the realization that discipline, camaraderie, and communalism were fading among his fellow workers. Between February and March 1942, Savinkov reported a string of murders, thefts, and fights between workers in his brigade, which lowered morale and productivity to new depths. "Who would believe that my engineering work would be reduced to this?" he marveled. The factory canteen became a battleground where his coworkers fought each other for every bowl of soup.[112]

---

108. Levina, entry for August 3, 1942, TsGAIPD f. 4000, op. 11, d. 57, l. 25.

109. Zelenskaia, entry for October 9, 1942, TsGAIPD, f. 4000, op. 11, d. 35, ll. 102–103.

110. Zelenskaia, entry for April 9, 1942, TsGAIPD, f. 4000, op. 11, d. 35, ll. 73.

111. Savinkov, entry for October 14, 1941, TsGAIPD, f. 4000, op. 11, d. 99, l. 5.

112. Savinkov, entries for February 15, 1942, March 27, 1942, March 30, 1942, and September 24, 1942, TsGAIPD, f. 4000, op. 11, d. 99, ll. 22, 28, 59–60.

Irina Zelenskaia suggested that the lack of proletarian values should disqualify workers from privileges. Lenenergo was the city's last remaining power plant. In December 1941, it nearly ran out of coal, and therefore was unable to consistently deliver adequate power to the industrial sector.[113] But in the summer of 1942, when Lenenergo should have been fully operational, Zelenskaia claimed that Category I workers lacked the discipline and the commitment to labor to be considered "true" proletarians. Even those who lived at the station overslept and missed their shifts. Work at the station started two hours late and lasted only five hours total. When city authorities declared that May 1 and May 2—traditionally holidays—were mandatory workdays, the diarist remarked: "it is true with our doubtful discipline that, instead of two working days, we have five non-working days."[114] In her view, these workers' proletarian status was further diminished by their indifference to the party mission. As a member of the Lenenergo party committee, Zelenskaia tried to create equal enthusiasm for visiting "red corners" as for visiting the canteen, but without success. Red corners were special areas in a home or institution, where revolutionary memorabilia, like red banners, portraits of party leaders, or copies of Lenin's writings, were exhibited. They replaced the religious corners from the pre-revolutionary period, where icons were displayed. "We have been unable to organize something like the canteen in the red corner," Zelenskaia dismayed, "The workers themselves talk less about these external conditions but always talk about whether or not there will be food."[115]

Zelenskaia's disdain for her Category I coworkers grew stronger when she became part of Lenenergo's canteen personnel in late September 1941. Now on the other side of the food counter, she leveled the same accusations against workers that she had once lodged against food-service personnel.[116] In the canteen, she was "surrounded by swindlers," both workers and upper management, both vying for extra plate of soup.[117] Where

113. Bidlack and Lomagin, *The Leningrad Blockade*, p. 48.

114. Zelenskaia, entry for May 2, 1942, TsGAIPD, f. 4000, op. 11, d. 35, l. 780b.

115. Zelenskaia, entry for September 27, 1941, TsGAIPD, f. 4000, op. 11, d. 35, l. 20.

116. Zelenskaia, entry for September 24, 1942, TsGAIPD, f. 4000, op. 11, d. 35, l. 18–19.

117. Zelenskaia, entry for November 18, 1941, TsGAIPD, f. 4000, op. 11, d. 35, l. 33.

Queues, Canteens, and the Politics of Location

were the "heroes," she asked? What had happened to the "inner strength" of the Soviet people?[118]

These canteen wars eclipse the war in Zelenskaia's account. In October 1941, one month into her position, she described the canteen as the site of a "battle" or a "siege" (*osada*), where she was surrounded and out-numbered.[119] An "onslaught" of "blows pour onto me," she despaired; "I practically have to engage in hand-to-hand fighting."[120] Leningraders on both sides of the food counter drew on the rhetoric of class warfare in staking their claims. Workers wielded Soviet slogans against Zelenskaia, threatening, " 'right now they are squeezing us, but there will come a time when we shall squeeze them.' But who is considered 'they' and who is considered 'we'? The bosses? The communists?" Zelenskaia asked. The categories of "us" and "them" were fluctuating as each and all battled to prove their status as insiders and proletarians. When she and her fellow food-service personnel tried to defend themselves, explaining that the German blockade was to blame for the shortages, one party member retorted: " 'what does the war have to do with it?' "[121] "The people are becoming my personal enemies," Zelenskaia proclaimed; "my work could make you a misanthrope."[122] Here again, the canteen provided that critical setting in which, according to the diarist, Leningraders tried to distinguish friend from foe, proletarians from class enemies, even though these categories and their meanings were in flux.

The Challenge to Party Privilege

If, in the eyes of many diarists, Category I workers did an insufficient amount of manual labor, then party officials did even less. Even so, they often received Category I cards and access to special canteens and stores

118. Zelenskaia, entry for October 18, 1941, TsGAIPD, f. 4000, op. 11, d. 35, l. 22.

119. Zelenskaia, entries for October 8, 1941, October 24, 1941, and November 1, 1941, TsGAIPD, f. 4000, op. 11, d. 35, ll. 22–26.

120. Zelenskaia, entry for December 23, 1942, TsGAIPD, f. 4000, op. 11, d. 35, ll. 46–47.

121. Zelenskaia, entry for November 1, 1941, TsGAIPD, f. 4000, op. 11, d. 35, l. 26.

122. Zelenskaia, entries for September 23, 1941, and September 24, 1941, TsGAIPD, f. 4000, op. 11, d. 35, l. 18.

because of their leadership on the ideological front. The most elite avoided the monstrous lines that devoured Leningraders' time and energy. Based on NKVD records, Nikita Lomagin and Richard Bidlack have found that 70 percent of party members received Category I rations and that during the deadly winter months of 1942, party members died at a rate of 15.1 percent. They compared this to Nadezhda Cherepenina's recent estimate that more than double that figure, roughly 37 percent of Leningraders overall, died during the first eleven months of the siege.[123]

Most diarists, of course, had no sense of the numbers, but they recorded popular rumors that at Smolny (Leningrad's party headquarters) "they are eating cake." A few got a more detailed glimpse of its canteen. In January 1942, the diarist Kseniia Matus heard from Zina, a fellow musician and friend, what fare was like in the Smolny canteen. Zina had been invited there as part of musical ensemble, and she told Kseniia of the "600 grams of bread and three-course meal" that they shared with First Party Secretary Andrei Zhdanov.[124] The journal of Nikolai Ribovskii offers a rare peak into elite party canteens. Ribovskii was a union official from Vyborg, a seaport town 130 kilometers from Leningrad. He fled to Leningrad in the summer of 1941 to escape the approaching German army. A refugee with no job, he received a dependent's ration, and his health rapidly deteriorated that autumn. Ribovskii's fortune changed in December, however, when he became a political instructor for the Leningrad city soviet. He was given a Category I card and access to party canteens. At a time when two to three thousand Leningraders died daily, Ribovskii ate butter, goose, ham, turkey, and even caviar—most of it "off-ration."[125] After eating too much, too quickly, he spent a week recovering in the party's medical clinic, where the meals continued to be substantial. Ribovksii described this clinic as "just a seven-day vacation house," where "the war hardly makes itself felt":

---

123. Bidlack and Lomagin, *The Leningrad Blockade*, pp. 29, 272, 299–301. The death rates of Leningraders by ration category still are unconfirmed.

124. Matus, entry for January 18, 1942, MNM k.p. 4153. f. 2, d. 2804, l. 40.

125. Ribovskii's diary is in Natal'ia Kozlova, ed., *Sovetskie liudi: stseni iz istorii* (Moscow: Evropa, 2005), pp. 264–267. Also see Bidlack and Lomagin, *The Leningrad Blockade*, p. 301.

Queues, Canteens, and the Politics of Location 199

> Yes, only under the Bolsheviks, only under Soviet power is it only possible to
> have such rest under the conditions of war, of a prolonged siege of a city. . . .
> What could be better? We eat, drink, stroll about, sleep or we simply have
> nothing to do.[126]

This party clinic, with its lavish canteen and relaxed atmosphere, transported Ribovskii physically and psychologically far away from the hardships of war, which he had felt so acutely only months before. Ribovskii documented this without shame or moral reflection; perhaps his sense of relief trumped all other emotions. His response, although extreme, mirrors that of other diarists who frequently disputed the advantages of others without questioning or acknowledging their own.

Few diarists experienced party canteens first-hand as Ribovskii did, but they often sat near party members in canteens at their places of work and noted the disparities in the portions they received. Both diarists inside and outside of the party questioned whether their political leaders deserved Category I cards if they denigrated Soviet values. Here again, the similarity between Irina Zelenskaia's and Ivan Savinkov's diaries is revealing. Zelenskaia—an enthusiastic new party member in Category II—painted the station's party elite as "sluggish, indifferent, and uninspired people." They ate twice as much as she did, but were far less committed to their professional and political duties. While the staff helped to prepare the plant for a second siege winter, Zelenskaia predicted that "we will get the classic picture: the management will secure as much comfort for themselves as possible, while the rest will do what they can."[127] As she sat next to them in the canteen, Zelenskaia noted how their idleness was rewarded with larger, thicker bowls of soup. The diarist spoke up about the lack of productivity and enthusiasm during a meeting of Lenenergo's party committee, but as a result, she was given the absurd task of waking the station's party secretary at 7:55 in the morning so that he could begin work on time.[128]

Similarly, Savinkov declared that the Komsomol (Communist Youth League) workers at the Molotov Factory had the lowest levels of morale

---

126. Ribovskii, entry for March 5, 1942, in Kozlova, *Sovetskie liudi*, pp. 268–269.
127. Zelenskaia, entry for September 5, 1942, TsGAIPD, f. 4000, op. 11, d. 35, l. 98.
128. Zelenskaia, entry for August 17, 1942, TsGAIPD, f. 4000, op. 11, d. 35, ll. 95–96.

and discipline and the highest rates of absenteeism of workers under his charge.[129] Komsomol members were reputed to be model workers and tasked with over-fulfilling industrial quotas by 200 percent. Instead, according to Savinkov, they "killed the initiative to work" and abandoned their duties. Savinkov scribbled angrily: "I, however, demand more severe requirements for party members and Komsomol members, including more discipline. But they are just the opposite, they demand amnesty for their position. They need to go." Their willingness to abandon the plant, he noted, marked a reversal in Soviet priorities: "Now, the personal is taking precedent over the societal."[130] Individualism seemed to trump collectivism in the city of Lenin.

A more unusual critique of party privilege appears in the diary of Elizaveta Sokolova. Sokolova served as the interim director of the Institute of Party History, an organization that encouraged Leningraders— including Zelenskaia and Savinkov—to keep diaries for its collections. Sokolova was a strong proponent of party privilege. Her objection was that she herself had not been granted access to its canteens and stores. In her diary, Sokolova documented how tirelessly she worked so that she and her staff could eat at a party canteen. "Until nine in the evening yesterday I had to make telephone calls in order to obtain a decision of the higher party organs," the diarist explained. "It requires a lot of nerve to overcome various bureaucratic loopholes."[131] Once this access was granted, Sokolova cautioned her staff to behave like model party workers in the city party committee canteen lest there was any doubt that they deserved to eat there.[132] This echoed the observations of Levina, Nikitin, and others about the importance of etiquette as a marker of status and worthiness in blockade canteens.

In November and December of 1941, Sokolova set her sights on obtaining Category I rations for her staff, arguing that their scholarly work was essential to the lifeblood of the party.[133] When Nikolai Shumilov,

---

129. Bidlack and Lomagin, *The Leningrad Blockade*, pp. 188–189.

130. Savinkov, entry for October 25, 1941, TsGAIPD, f. 4000, op. 11, d. 99, ll. 8–9.

131. Elizaveta Aleksandrovna Sokolova, entries for October 27, 1941, and November 1, 1941, TsGAIPD f. 4000, op. 11, d. 109, ll. 3–25.

132. Sokolova, entry for December 24, 1941, TsGAIPD f. 4000, op. 11, d. 109, l. 35.

133. Sokolova, entry for November 28, 1941, TsGAIPD f. 4000, op. 11, d. 109, l. 32. The debate over whether party members should receive extra rations (and so remain

Queues, Canteens, and the Politics of Location   201

the city party committee's (*gorkom*) chief of propaganda and an editor of
the *LP*, refused her, saying (according to her paraphrase), "that it is forbidden to do that, that in Leningrad there is only enough bread for two days
and that half a thousand people die from hunger every day," she coun-
tered that she would not ask for him to bend the rules if he were not
already doing so: " 'If you did not give [Category I cards] to anyone,' I said,
'then we would not demand [them], but since you give them to local
party committee workers, it is possible for us to be supported too.' " From
this unfolded a frank discussion about the legitimacy of party privilege,
wherein Sokolova and Shumilov accused each other of being self-interested
rather than party-minded. Sokolova reconstructed their conversation
this way:

> "Well, there she goes again, [wanting] everything for herself," Shumilov said
> discontentedly; "workers in the district party committee (*raikom*) are our
> foundational cadres, and if we do not given them [Category I] cards, then who
> will carry out the party work? We will have no one to rely on." "But," I said, "our
> workers also carry out great party work for the masses according to the line of
> the party *raikom* . . . the *raikom* values our work and it is surprising and outrageous
> that you cannot help arrange Category I [cards] for us."[134]

By casting doubt on Shumilov's support of the Institute of Party History, Sokolova succeeded in obtaining Category I cards for her workers. This scene underscores the ration system's bureaucratic flexibility
as well as the moral flexibility it bred.[135] Sokolova would have been
considered a savior by her coworkers, but a thief by others. Indeed,
once when Sokolova was in a bomb shelter, a Category II worker confronted her about her relatively healthy appearance. The diarist retorted: "Why are you whining? What, [do you think] that others have
it better or something? The distribution of goods applies to everyone

---

strong leaders) in times of war or receive the same as other citizens (a symbol of their
sacrifice) recalls the period after the 1921 famine. At that time, the question of whether
or not asceticism "proved that you are a communist" was hotly debated in the press and
in party circles (Naiman, *Sex in Public,* pp. 211–214).

    134. Sokolova, entry for December 24, 1941, TsGAIPD f. 4000, op. 11, d. 109, l. 35.

    135. In his own account of the Blockade, Shumilov championed "the exceptional
role" played by the party, including the Institute of Party History. When naming
members of its heroic staff, he did not mention Sokolova. See Nikolai Shumilov, *V dni
blokady* (Moscow: Mysl', 1974), pp. 28–29, 50.

equally."[136] Sokolova recorded this assertion guilelessly even though her previous entries reveal her intimate knowledge of how to manipulate the rules. And after the "all clear," she left this shelter and sped to the party canteen, where she was disappointed to receive only soup and two portions of kasha. "And this is a special canteen!" she exclaimed, wondering how much less was given out at ordinary ones.[137]

Queues and canteens had long been fixtures of Soviet life. But during the horrific winter of 1941–1942, when thousands of blokadniki died daily, they became essential to Leningraders' survival and to their visions of the social imaginary. Isolated from the rest of the Soviet Union and from their own community, the diarists hungered for insights about the city's changing demographics, hierarchies, and norms. They also were eager to gauge their own position within the evolving social order. Moreover, as spaces of everyday life, canteens and lines were especially conducive to the diarists' ethnographic energies.

Although the diarists tried to generalize about blockade society from their encounters in lines and canteens, their accounts underscore the personal and particular nature of their perspectives. The diarists' impressions, recorded in any given entry, depended upon whether they stood in the front or back of the line or next to whom they ate in the canteen. The journals also illuminate the diarists' blind spots, be they misunderstandings about the famine or moral exemptions that the diarists made for their own behaviors. Moreover, the logic and configuration of each locale heavily informed the diarists' visions of the social. In the queue, blockade society seemed linear and bifurcated. The canteen, however, displayed a spectrum of social types—from distrofiki to food-service workers—whose social standing was revealed by their etiquette, portions, and physicality.

The politics of location and of consumption meld together in these accounts. The diarists studied lines and canteens in dialogue with several

---

136. Sokolova, entry for November 28, 1941, TsGAIPD f. 4000, op. 11, d. 109, l. 30. This echoes Shumilov's own statement that "communists, like all residents, endured the deprivations and hardships of the Blockade" (Shumilov, *V dni blokady*, p. 109).

137. Sokolova, entry for November 28, 1941, TsGAIPD f. 4000, op. 11, d. 109, l. 32.

Queues, Canteens, and the Politics of Location

factors including spatial dynamics, policies of food distribution, and Soviet tenets and practices, which had belonged to the milieu of prewar Leningrad. They reactivated prewar debates about class, equality, and entitlement, bringing them to bear on wartime disputes over the same issues. In this way, the food crisis seemed both to transform and magnify existing tensions within Leningrad.

During a famine, hunger becomes a zero-sum game. Every combatant country in World War II had to make difficult choices when allocating its limited food supplies to feed its population and support its war effort.[138] Faced with such extreme scarcity, it was impossible for Soviet authorities to feed all people equally and adequately. In this regard, Leningrad was an extreme case of the devastating starvation, the necessary self-provisioning, and the entitlement debates that characterized most war-torn communities in the Soviet Union. Leningrad is also an instructive case of how the ration system fostered within these communities a powerful sense of injustice and deprivation.

Regardless of whether they held a Category I, II, or III card or a party card, the diarists were consumed with suspicion that others unfairly received more than they did, either legally or illegally. None of the diarists studied here called for "equal shares" across all strata of the population. However, nearly all of them claimed that some of the groups and individuals who were relatively privileged by the ration system were unworthy of such advantages.[139] The fact that starving Leningraders complained about how food was distributed is hardly surprising, but *how*

138. For recent comparative studies of how the major World War II combatants allocated food, see Collingham, *The Taste of War*; Frank Tretmann and Flemming Just, eds., *Food and Conflict in Europe in the Age of the Two World Wars* (New York: Palgrave Macmillan, 2006).

139. Not unique to Leningrad, similar debates transpired in Great Britain and in Germany during World War II. Ina Zweiniger-Bargielowska and Mark Roodhouse have demonstrated that, while most Britons rejected the black market and its participants as unethical, they made moral allowances for themselves to sell and trade there. See Zweiniger-Bargielowska, "Fair Shares? The Limits of Food Policy in Britain During the Second World War," in Zweiniger-Bargielowska, Duffett, and Drouard, eds., *Food and War in Twentieth-Century Europe*, p. 125; Mark Roodhouse, "Popular Morality and the Black Market in Britain, 1939–1955," in Tretmann and Just, eds., *Food and Conflict in Europe in the Age of the Two World Wars*, pp. 243–265.

they complained is telling. They wielded their own understandings of the social(ist) contract and of Soviet values to discern who was deserving and worthy of the most food. Moreover, isolated within the confines of "the ring," these diarists fixated on internal adversaries, rarely mentioning the city's besiegers. These journals provide a counternarrative to the Leningrad party boss Andrei Zhdanov's claim that the blokadniki did "not fight with their stomachs" or with each other, but stayed fixed on the hated German enemy.[140] Of course, the diarists knew that the German blockade created the food shortages, but they seldom reflected on this during the time of greatest scarcity, the winter of 1941–1942. This was also the period when, because of brutally cold temperatures, German pilots stopped flying over the city, which made the enemy appear even more distant to Leningraders. But even when aerial bombardment resumed, the enemy remained impersonal to the diarists. Most Leningraders did not see German soldiers from the Leningrad front until they were paraded through the city as prisoners of war in 1944. By contrast, they confronted food-service workers and other patrons at the canteens on a daily basis. The search for internal enemies was a well-established practice in Soviet society, and the insularity of the blockade conditions only exacerbated this tendency. Moreover, the regime's tight control over information about the famine and its strategy of shifting blame onto individual thieves and away from administrative mistakes reinforced the diarists' tendency to attribute blame locally.[141]

In this way, the diaries do not indicate that the famine spurred Leningraders to reject Soviet socialism. They reviled local food or party workers, but rarely defamed Stalin or dismissed ideological principles altogether. On the contrary, diarists used such tenets to critique the in-

140. Zhdanov's statement of April 14, 1944, is cited in a variety of sources including Shumilov, *V dni blokady,* p. 135.

141. Research on the postwar years suggests that Leningraders continued to attribute blame locally as they faced major employment, housing, and food shortages, and other crises. See Robert Dale, "Rats and Resentment: The Demobilization of the Red Army in Postwar Leningrad, 1945–1950," *Journal of Contemporary History* 45, no. 1 (2010): 132–133; Elizabeth White, "After the War Was Over: The Civilian Return to Leningrad," *Europe-Asia Studies* 59, no. 7 (2007): 1145–1161; Christine Varga-Harris, "Forging Citizenship on the Home Front," pp. 101–116.

Queues, Canteens, and the Politics of Location

equalities that they perceived inside "the ring." And because Soviet practices and tenets of resource distribution had been inconsistent in the prewar era, they could be used to challenge ration policies as much as to justify them. Canteens and lines showcased the uneasy coexistence of multiple principles of distribution that operated in blockaded Leningrad and had operated in Soviet society before the war, including: "he who does not work, does not eat," and "first come, first served," "each according to his labor, each according to his need."

The diarists not only reconstructed wartime lines and canteens on the page; they documented the perceived social geography of the siege. Henri Lefebvre famously observed that revolution produces its own space.[142] War also creates its own geography. The diarists' descriptions reconstruct blockaded Leningrad of 1941–1942 as an embattled landscape of stratification, atomization, and resentment. Their social readings are imbricated in notions of distributive justice. The diarists studied here demanded these entitlements on the page only. In the postwar and post-Soviet periods, however, Leningraders—like soldiers and civilians from across the Soviet Union—would wield notions of entitlement, suffering, and worthiness to claim material compensation for all that they had suffered during the war.[143]

---

142. Lefebvre, *The Production of Space,* p. 54.

143. Entitlement was a central theme of the oral histories of siege survivors and their children, collected by a team of scholars at the European University in Saint Petersburg. See M. V. Loskutovoi, ed., *Pamiat' o blokade: Svidetel'stva ochevidtsev i istoricheskoe soznanie obshchestva* (Moscow: Novoe izdatel'stvo, 2006).

FOUR

NUTRITIONAL DYSTROPHY: THE SCIENCE
AND SEMANTICS OF STARVATION
IN WORLD WAR II

Rebecca Manley

During the war it was permitted to call hunger "hunger."

Varlam Shalamov, "Perchatka"[1]

IN THE TERRIBLE WINTER OF 1942, AS THE RESIDENTS OF
Leningrad succumbed to famine, Vera Inber recorded scenes of starvation in her diary. Among the figures she described on the city's streets
was a man with an awkward gait, being led by two women, who looked
as if he had been "gnawed by hunger." Inber subsequently identified the
man as a *distrofik,* adding in parentheses that "we only learned this word
here."[2] *Distrofik* was in fact a new term, not simply introduced to Leningrad during the blockade but invented there. It was derived from another
new term, a term that figures not only in Inber's diary, but in her poems:
"nutritional dystrophy" (*alimentarnaia distrofiia*). In "Pulkovo Meridian," the 1943 poem that would earn her a Stalin Prize after the war, Inber
described the illness that afflicted so many of the city's residents as "that

1. Epigraph from Varlam Shalamov, "Perchatka," in I. Sirotinskaia, ed., *Sobranie
sochinenii v shesti tomakh* (Moscow: Terra, 2004), vol. 2, pp. 283–311.

2. Vera Inber, *Leningrad Diary,* trans. Serge M. Wolff and Rachel Grieve (London:
Hutchinson & Co., 1971), p. 40. My translation. Note that the term "dystrophy" and the
parenthetical are not in her original manuscript, but were added to the 1968 Russian
edition. I thank Alexis Peri for pointing this out to me. Inber's phrase, while added later,
is nonetheless consonant with contemporary usage. Aleksandr Boldyrev, for example, in
a diary entry dated February 10, 1942, described a corpse he saw on the street as a "dead
distrofik. This is how the starving [*istoshchennykh*] are now officially called." A. N. Boldyrev,
Osadnaia zapis': blokadnyi dnevnik, ed. V. S. Garbuzova and I. M. Steblin-Kamenskii.
(St. Petersburg: Evropeiskii Dom, 1998), p. 55.

206

Nutritional Dystrophy

which in scientific language doctors refer to as 'nutritional dystrophy' but which those who are not latinists or philologists identify with the Russian word 'hunger.'"[3] Inber was well-positioned to understand both the "scientific language" of doctors and the specific term "nutritional dystrophy." Married to Il'ia Davidovich Strashun, head of Leningrad's First Medical Institute, she was intimately connected with the medical world: she attended lectures on the medical effects of starvation, the details of which she duly recorded in her diary, and she also spent time in the morgue.[4] Even as Inber composed the poem, moreover, her husband was helping organize conferences devoted to "nutritional dystrophy," conferences that would result, only a couple of years later, in an important publication on the topic.[5] And yet such specialized knowledge and intimate connections to the world of medicine were hardly needed in 1942 to make sense of "nutritional dystrophy." By the time Inber completed her poem, the term had become ubiquitous in Leningrad, an integral part of the wartime lexicon not only of "latinists and philologists," but of the population at large.

Nutritional dystrophy was defined, in the medical literature of the day, as "an illness that develops as a result of insufficient food."[6] The term has often been regarded by historians as a euphemism, a term invented to "mask mortality from famine" and to "soft-pedal civilian starvation."[7] While "nutritional dystrophy" did recast hunger in medical

---

3. Vera Inber, "Pulkovskii meridian," in A. Notkina, ed., *Sobranie sochinenii v chetyrekh tomakh* (Moscow: Khudozhestvennaia literatura, 1965), vol. 1, p. 483.

4. Inber, *Leningrad Diary*, pp. 45–46.

5. I. D. Strashun and E. L. Venderovich, eds., *Alimentarnaia distrofiia i avitaminozy* (Leningrad: Gosizdatel'stvo Meditsinskoi literatury, 1944).

6. See, for a typical formulation, E. M. Gel'shtein, *Narushenie obshchego pitaniia* (*osobennosti ikh vozniknoveniia i lecheniia vo vremia voiny*), vol. 28 of *Opyt sovetskoi meditsiny v Velikoi Otechestvennoi voine 1941–1945 gg.* (Moscow: Medgiz, 1951), p. 9.

7. These phrases can be found in V. F. Zima, "Medical Expertise and the 1946–47 Famine: The Identification and Treatment of a State-Induced Illness," in Frances L. Bernstein, Christopher Burton, and Dan Healey, eds., *Soviet Medicine: Culture, Practice, and Science,* (Dekalb: Northern Illinois University Press, 2011), p. 182; Lisa A. Kirschenbaum, "'The Alienated Body': Gender Identity and the Memory of the Siege of Leningrad," in Nancy M. Wingfield and Maria Bucur, eds., *Gender and War in Twentieth-Century Eastern Europe* (Bloomington: Indiana University Press, 2006), p. 225. See also the comments of Jacques Rossi cited below.

terms, I would argue that the term represented not an obfuscation of something previously known as "emaciation" or "starvation," but rather a new understanding of that condition. The widespread usage of the term, moreover, signaled a new openness within state institutions: for the first time since the early 1920s, hunger became a legitimate object of medical research and an acknowledged cause of death. This chapter addresses what the adoption and circulation of the terms *dystrophy* and *distrofik* can reveal about the distinctiveness of the Soviet encounter with hunger in World War II, its legacy, and the relationship between medical science and broader popular conceptions of hunger, the body, and the mind.

THE FACES OF WARTIME HUNGER

During the war, hunger haunted the pages of the central press, but the term was almost never used to describe the suffering of Soviet citizens themselves. For readers of the Soviet press, hunger was the preserve of occupied territories, inflicted on the peoples of the Soviet Union and Europe by the Nazis. As Lisa Kirshchenbaum notes, "even in Leningrad itself, where by the end of 1941 the reality of starvation was plain to see, and where the blockade afforded the local media unprecedented freedom from central control if not the local party's authority, the newspapers and radio rarely mentioned the word *golod* (famine) while it was occurring."[8] Beyond Leningrad, there was even less public discussion of hunger, and references to the heroic fortitude of the city's residents made no mention of the famine.

There was one domain, however, in which starvation figured prominently: a specialized body of medical literature on "nutritional dystrophy" that sought to identify the unique pathologies of the hungry body and mind. Articles, conference reports, and books on the topic began to appear as early as 1943, and constituted the almost exclusive preserve of discussions of hunger in the Soviet press. Between the covers of medical books, readers could find graphic descriptions of hunger's effects and in

---

8. Lisa Kirschenbaum, *The Legacy of the Siege of Leningrad: Myth, Memories, and Monuments* (Cambridge: Cambridge University Press, 2006), p. 52.

Nutritional Dystrophy   *209*

some cases even photos of emaciated or swollen bodies.[9] This literature did not attempt to obscure the etiology of the illness it described. As Mikhail Vasil'evich Chernorutskii, chairman of the Leningrad Society of Physicians, noted on the very first page of his first publication on the topic, "the cause behind the development of nutritional dystrophy, its etiology, is entirely clear: it is an insufficient supply of food to the population."[10] It is surely telling that Leningrad scholar Dmitrii Likhachev, doubtful that "the truth about the Leningrad blockade" would ever be published and dismissive of Inber's "Pulkovo Meridian" as nothing more than "pap" (*siusiuk*), singled out the medical literature as the one domain in which "something resembling the truth" had nonetheless appeared in print.[11] To be sure, this literature was not easily accessible and eschewed discussion of the most grizzly aspects of blockade life (it was, in Likhachev's terms, "proper"). Nonetheless, the medical reports emerged as a privileged site for documenting one of the war's defining features: starvation.

Hitler's "hunger plan" had made starvation a key component of his occupation policies in the East. Well before German forces came to occupy large swathes of previously Soviet territory, Nazi officials had enunciated their intention to starve the subject populations. The "city dwellers," an official in the Reich Ministry for Food and Agriculture stated, "will have to suffer great famine. . . ."[12] Hunger was an integral element not only of Nazi occupation policies, but also of their euthanasia

9. See M. V. Chernorutskii, ed., *Alimentarnaia distrofiia v blokirovannom Leningrade* (Leningrad: Medgiz, 1947).

10. M. V. Chernorutskii,, "Problema alimintarnoi distrofii," *Raboty leningradskikh vrachei za god Otechestvennoi voiny*, no. 3 (1943): 3.

11. Likhachev singled out Garshin's reminscenses (V. G. Garshin, "Tam gde smert' pomogaet zhizni," *Arkhiv Patologii* 46, no. 5 [1984]: 83–88, initially published in a slightly abridged version in *Zvezda* in 1945), as well as "the closed" (quotation marks are his) medical literature, and concludes: "very little and all 'proper.'" Dmitrii Sergeevich Likhachev, *Vospominaniia* (St. Petersburg: Izd-vo "Logos," 1995), p. 344.

12. Quoted in Karel C. Berkhoff, *Harvest of Despair: Life and Death in Ukraine under Nazi Rule* (Cambridge, Mass.: Belknap Press of Harvard University Press, 2004), p. 45. On the Nazi hunger plan, see Christian Gerlach, *Kalkulierte Morde: Die deutsche Wirtschafts und Vernichtungspolitik in Weissrussland 1941 bis 1944* (Hamburg: Hamburger Edition, 1999), and Alex J. Kay, *Exploitation, Resettlement, Mass Murder: Political and Economic Planning for German Occupation Policy in the Soviet Union, 1940–1941* (New York: Berghahn Books, 2006).

programs. Before gas chambers, hunger was relied on to do the work of killing the "racially unfit." It was likewise wielded against Soviet prisoners of war. Put on starvation-level rations, their mass death was a foregone conclusion.[13] Hunger was also a defining experience of the war in unoccupied territory, nowhere more so than in Leningrad. Leningrad, encircled and cut off from the mainland, was deliberately deprived of food. Ration levels hit their all-time low in late November 1941, when workers were reduced to a daily ration of 250 grams of bread, while dependents had to subsist on half that. Despite a meager increase in bread rations in late December, the food situation remained, in the words of Dr. Chernorutskii, "extremely difficult."[14] While the famine in Leningrad was by far the most extreme case of civilian starvation on unoccupied territory, it was by no means the only one. The Gulag saw starvation on a mass scale, and even beyond the Gulag, far from the frontlines, Soviet civilians died from starvation during the war, as Donald Filtzer's chapter in this volume makes clear.

Published medical literature on the topic presented the geography of starvation in carefully circumscribed terms. The research of Leningrad doctors, presented in a series of publications beginning in 1943 and continuing through 1947, was undoubtedly the most frank. The articles and reports issuing from Leningrad clearly situated the illness within the blockaded city and outlined the starvation-level rations on which Leningraders either subsisted or died. In charting the evolution of nutritional dystrophy over time, moreover, doctors constructed a narrative of the ravages wrought by hunger in the city under siege. Dr. Chernorutskii, who laid out the most comprehensive periodization of this kind, described the conditions that prevailed during that first blockade winter as "akin to complete starvation."[15] He even used the term "famine" (*golod*),

13. According to official statistics, starvation and tuberculosis (what Donald Filtzer in his contribution to this volume refers to as the Starvation-Tuberculosis complex) together accounted for approximately half of all deaths among Soviet POWs in 1943. See P. M. Polian, *Zhertvy dvukh diktatur: ostarbaitery i voennoplennye v Tret'em Reikhe i ikh repatriatsiia* (Moscow: "Vash vybor TSIRZ," 1996), pp. 257–258.

14. M. V. Chernorutskii, "Alimentarnaia distrofiia u vzroslykh," in Chernorutskii, ed., *Alimentarnaia distrofiia v blokirovannom Leningrade*, p. 36.

15. M. V. Chernorutskii, "Khod razvitiia alimentarnoi distrofii, ee klinicheskaia kartina i techenie," in Chernorutskii, ed., *Alimentarnaia distrofiia v blokirovannom Leningrade*, p. 194. In the absence of data on the sheer number of deaths, hospital

Nutritional Dystrophy

although not without the precautionary measure of a footnote to a published speech by the city's party leader.[16]

Beyond Leningrad, the geography and scope of wartime hunger were presented with considerably less precision. Although research on nutritional dystrophy was conducted in a host of Soviet cities ranging from Ulianovsk to Tashkent, studies published in the rear tended to emanate from evacuation hospitals, where the focus was on soldiers rather than civilians. By and large, mainstream medical literature passed over starvation in the rear in silence.[17] An article in the semi-popular *Fel'dsher i akusherka* (*Paramedic and Midwife*) published in 1943 located the phenomenon squarely in occupied territory, among soldiers who had fallen into encirclement and civilians under enemy occupation, while a piece on the topic in *Vrachebnoe delo* (*Medical Practice*) published two years later made no mention of the geography of the illness, the profile of the patients, or the conditions that gave rise to their illness (except to note that the illness was "brought on by insufficient and low quality food").[18]

---

mortality statistics were marshaled to demonstrate the extraordinary spike in deaths from starvation beginning in December 1941. Mortality data on the civilian population at large was incomplete and was not accessible to most doctors. On periodization and hospital mortality statistics see ibid., pp. 194–204; O. D. Isserson, "K voprosu o letal'nosti ot alimentarnoi distrofii v Leningrade s noiabria 1941 g. do noiabria 1942 g.," in Strashun and Venderovich, *Alimentarnaia distrofiia i avitaminozy*, pp. 96–100. On mortality statistics, see Nadezhda Cherepenina, "Assessing the Scale of Famine and Death in the Besieged City," in John Barber and Andrei Dzeniskevich, eds., *Life and Death in Besieged Leningrad, 1941–44* (Basingstoke: Palgrave, 2005), pp. 28–70.

16. Chernorutskii, "Alimentarnaia distrofiia u vzroslykh," p. 36. The speech, by P. S. Popkov, was published in *Leningradskaia Pravda* on March 3, 1944, when the blockade had already been lifted.

17. One notable exception is the work of the department of pathological anatomy in Molotov, which presented their research on two hundred cases of nutritional dystrophy with the note that the material "relates mainly to the civilian population, evacuated from Leningrad and other places, and partly to the population of the city of Molotov and places of imprisonment." E. Ia. Gertsenberg, "Patologicheskaia anatomiia i patogenez alimentarnogo istoshcheniia," in M. V. Kostylev, ed., *Trudy Molotovskogo gosudarstven-nogo stomatologicheskogo instituta* (Molotov, 1943), p. 146.

18. I. S. Shnitser, "Alimentarnaia distrofiia," *Fel'dsher i akusherka*, no. 3 (1943): 32. M. M. Gubergrits, "Ob alimentarnoi toksicheskoi distrofii," *Vrachebnoe delo*, no. 11–12 (1945): 547.

While published medical reports thus provide only a very partial picture of the scope of wartime hunger, they offer a detailed description of what quickly emerged as one of the war's chief pathologies, responsible for more deaths on a global scale than gunshot wounds, infectious diseases, or bombing.[19] In recent years, these reports have attracted increasing scholarly attention for their capacity to help elucidate the suffering of Leningrad's residents during the siege.[20] But the studies can also be read as part of an attempt to document and conceptualize hunger's effects. The doctors who penned them had, as Vera Inber wrote of pathologist Vladimir Garshin, "peered into the very insides of blockaded Leningrad."[21] In their reports, they struggled to find adequate ways to describe and explain the transformations they observed among their compatriots in the city's medical clinics and morgues. In the process, they contributed to a "science of starvation" emerging across Europe at this time, and conferred a new name on an age-old affliction— hunger—that nonetheless seemed to present itself in a new guise.[22]

HUNGER AS AN OBJECT OF STUDY

On November 20, 1941, a closed meeting of doctors and scientists was convened in Leningrad to develop "a registration method, diagnosis, terminology and therapy" to deal with a new category of sick people: people whose illness manifested itself in the form of "general weakness, the presence of edemas on the face and extremities and even emaciation

19. See Lizzie Collingham, *The Taste of War: World War Two and the Battle for Food* (New York: Penguin Press, 2011), p. 1.

20. Barber and Dzeniskevich, *Life and Death in Besieged Leningrad, 1941–44*; Pavel Vasilyev, "Alimentary and Pellagra Psychoses in Besieged Leningrad," in Ina Zweiniger-Bargielowska, Rachel Duffett, and Alain Drouard, eds., *Food and War in Twentieth Century Europe*, (Farnham: Ashgate, 2011).

21. Thus did Inber address Garshin in her inscription of his copy of Pulkovskii Meridian, dated July 4, 1942. T. S. Podzdniakova, ed., *Peterburg Akhmatovoi: Vladimir Georgevich Garshin* (St. Petersburg: Nevskii Dialekt, 1994), p. 42.

22. On the European "science of starvation" see Dana Simmons, "Starvation Science: From Colonies to Metropole," in Alexander Nützendel and Frank Trentmann, eds., *Food and Globalization: Consumption, Markets and Politics in the Modern World* (Oxford: Berg, 2008), pp. 173–191.

Nutritional Dystrophy

to varying degrees, evidently resulting from insufficient food and hard work."[23] A couple of weeks later, they issued the following statement, which was subsequently approved and disseminated to all the relevant health authorities: "We propose that the clinical complex of symptoms observed at present in connection with malnutrition (*narushenie pitaniia*) be designated by the term: nutritional dystrophy (*distrofiia alimentarnaia*)."[24] While death by starvation was nothing new in the Soviet Union, dystrophy was indeed, in the words of the head of the Leningrad Health Division, "a new cause of death."[25] As Nadezhda Cherepenina notes, "dystrophy did not appear as a disease and a cause of death in the classifications of the People's Commissariat of Health and the Central Statistical Office of the USSR State Planning Commission."[26] Nor could one find references to "nutritional dystrophy" in the existing medical literature. As a review of the extant European literature on starvation prepared in the final year of the blockade noted, before the war "this sickness did not have an established name. It was most commonly referred to as 'edema disease' in accordance with the symptoms. Otherwise it was called 'hunger edema,' 'epidemic edema,' 'wartime edema,' [or] protein-deficiency edema . . ."[27]

As the range of terms suggests, there was no unified picture of hunger as a medical condition on the eve of the war. The first studies of starvation in Russia, as in Europe, aimed to understand the response of the body to conditions of complete starvation. The paradigmatic subject of such studies were animals in the laboratory or hunger

23. P. F. Gladkikh, *Zdravookhranenie i voennaia meditsina v bitve za Leningrad glazami istorika i ochevidtsev, 1941–1944 gg.* (St. Petersburg: Dmitrii Bulanin, 2006), p. 28.

24. "O terminologii i lechenii alimentarnykh rasstroistv," December 7, 1941, in TsGASPb, f. 9156, op. 4, d. 317, l. 4.

25. Report to Leningrad City Soviet, January 5, 1942, in TsGASPb, f. 7384, op. 3, d. 45, l. 277.

26. Nadezhda Cherepenina, "Assessing the Scale of Famine and Death in the Besieged City," in Barber and Dzeniskevich, *Life and Death in Besieged Leningrad, 1941–44*, p. 39.

27. S. L. Gaukhman, "Massovye narusheniia obshchego pitaniia ('otechnaia bolezn'): Istoriko-literaturnyi ocherk. Obzor literatury 1915–1935 gg.," in Chernorutskii, ed., *Alimentarnaia distrofiia v blokirovannom Leningrade*, pp. 9–10.

artists, professionals who made a spectacle of fasting.[28] Interestingly, the famine of 1891, though central to an evolving public consciousness of hunger, left little mark on the scientific study of starvation. That famine had transpired far from the reach of the country's scientific centers and laboratories. While society mobilized to aid the famished, medical attention concentrated primarily on infectious diseases and the study of acceptable food substitutes.[29] Indeed, when V. V. Pashutin, head of the Imperial Military-Medical Academy, turned to the issue of starvation in the second volume of his magisterial survey of general and experimental pathology, he dismissed real-life cases of starvation as "poorly suited to the study of starvation" and maintained that "conclusions about people can be made, without fearing inaccuracies, on the basis of experiments on starving animals."[30]

The twentieth century brought an end to the laboratory study of starvation, as starvation became a pervasive European reality, and hunger was brought to doctors' doorsteps. Studies of what were variously referred to as "edema disease," "hunger edema," and "epidemic edema" proliferated in Germany during World War I as a result of the blockade. In Russia, the deprivation of the years of war and revolution generated a small but rich body of literature on the physiological effects of starvation as scholars such as sociologist Peterim Sorokin, starving himself, came to appreciate the differences between "the laboratory conditions of

28. The first Russian study of starvation, based on experiments conducted on animals in a laboratory, was V. A. Manassein, *Materialy dlia voprosa o golodanii* (St. Petersburg: Tipografiia Imperatorskoi Akademii Nauk, 1869). While there were no hunger artists in Russia, Russian physiologists were well apprised of the European and American studies of this phenomenon, and regularly cited studies of hunger artists in their discussions of hunger's effects. See, for example, F. F. Erisman, "Pitanie golodai-ushchikh," *Russkaia Mysl'*, no. 4 (1892), 4–5.

29. See, for example, A. A. Lipskii, "Golod i vyzyvaemye im bolezni: Publichnaia lektsiia" (St. Petersburg: Tipografiia Doma Prizreniia Maloletnikh Bednykh, 1892). Tellingly, Erisman, in a published lecture he delivered on the famine, addressed the medical effects of starvation not on the basis of the observation of starving peasants, but on the basis of laboratory studies conducted prior to the famine and studies of European and American hunger artists. The only laboratory studies undertaken during the famine itself were of food substitutes and their suitability for human consumption. F. F. Erisman, "Pitanie golodaiushchikh," 128–155.

30. V. V. Pashutin, *Kurs obshchei i eksperimental'noi patologii (patologicheskoi fiziologii)*, vol. 2 (St. Petersburg, 1902), ch. 1, p. 10.

Nutritional Dystrophy

fasting" and "forced starvation." As Sorokin observed in 1922, "starvation in laboratory conditions is not typical. The simple fact that a person starves for research, that he is protected from any harm, that he will not die of hunger, that all of this is done for science, plus the abstention from intensified labor, from the normal pace of life, etc.,—all of this sharply changes the picture of psycho-physiological processes and behavioral reflexes of the starving person in the laboratory."[31]

In the following years, however, attention was turned almost entirely to the problem of vitamin deficiencies. Deficiency diseases had long been a mainstay of European colonial research, which had defined, according to historian Dana Simmons, "conventional medical wisdom on hunger illnesses" before the world wars.[32] In this period, in the wake of the recent discovery of vitamins, studies of specific deficiencies proliferated: pellagra, which resulted from a deficiency of the B vitamin niacin, scurvy, the product of vitamin C deficiency, and other avitaminoses.[33] Even when they occurred against a backdrop of starvation, vitamin deficiencies were generally treated as a problem of the quality of food rather than the quantity.

The famines of 1932–1933 furnished doctors in the affected areas with ample evidence of starvation's devastating effects, but discussion of the famine was strictly forbidden, and in an era in which "feigning hunger" was cast as a crime, there was little support for doctors to document its effects. As a doctor in the famine zone reportedly remarked, "we do not write memoranda about death from famine because we are afraid that we doctors may be accused of some kind of wrecking."[34] Indeed, despite

31. P. A. Sorokin, *Hunger as a Factor in Human Affairs* (Gainesville: University Presses of Florida, 1975), pp. 84–85.

32. Dana Simmons, "Starvation Science," p. 185.

33. For one of the first investigations into vitamin deficiencies in Russia, see A. V. Palladin, "Sovremennoe polozhenie voprosa o 'vitaminakh,'" in K. N. Georgievskii, K. M. Kogan, and A. V. Palladin, eds., *O golode* (Khar'kov: Izdatel'stvo Nauchnaia mysl', 1922), pp. 79–94. On the development of the field in Russia and the Soviet Union, see B. A. Lavrov, "Ocherk razvitiia vitaminologii v sovetskom soiuze," *Voprosy pitaniia* 7, no. 1 (1938): 30–47.

34. Reported on by the OGPU and quoted in R. W. Davies and Stephen G. Wheatcroft, *The Years of Hunger: Soviet Agriculture, 1931–1933* (New York: Palgrave MacMillan, 2004), p. xiv. On the crime of "feigning hunger," see J. Arch Getty and Oleg V. Naumov, *The Road to Terror: Stalin and the Self-Destruction of the Bolsheviks, 1932–1939* (New Haven, Conn.: Yale University Press, 1999), p. 69. The doctors in Leningrad who were

the terrible toll that famine exacted in the early 1930s, there were few studies produced in the decade to document it. One notable exception was a 1933 study of edemas among seventy-two patients in Kiev, undertaken by celebrated physician N. D. Strazhesko at the city's Institute of Experimental Biology and Pathology. The article sought to compare different types of edemas, only some of which were due, in the words of the author, to "insufficient food and cachexia," and said nothing about hunger.[35] Given this, it is perhaps not surprising that standard prewar medical texts devoted little attention to the problem of starvation. Indeed, a textbook of internal medicine published on the very eve of the war presented "mass partial starvation," a phenomenon that "was well known in Tsarist Russia," as the current preserve of "the proletarian sectors of the population in capitalist countries and in their colonies." Tellingly, moreover, this text attributed edemas not only to starvation, but to a deficiency of vitamin B1, a view that the author, G. F. Lang, then head of the Leningrad Society of Physicians, would soon feel compelled to correct.[36]

When doctors in Leningrad turned to the medical literature for guidance, the most relevant literature they could find had thus been produced some two decades earlier. A library administrator in Leningrad later recalled how doctors and military specialists came to replace the regular patrons of the library. Among the list of literature searches performed by the library during the war were searches into "the treatment and cure of dystrophy" and "hunger edema."[37] In fact, as I suggested above, there

---

confronted with starvation in 1941, moreover, would have had little exposure to the condition, as Leningrad was well beyond the famine zone.

35. N. D. Strazhesko, "K voprosu o patogeneze otekov," *Vrachebnoe delo*, no. 6–7 (1933): 321–326.

36. G. F. Lang, *Uchebnik vnutrennykh boleznei: Bolezni pochek, apparata neiro-endokrinnoi regulatsii i obmena veshchestv, avitaminozy, ostryi revmatizm, bolezni sustavov i otravleniia promyshlennymi iadami*, vol. 2, no. 2 (Leningrad: Medgiz, 1941), p. 267. Lang drew attention to this mistake and corrected it in G. F. Lang, "Klinika alimentarnoi distrofii," in I. M. Rybakov, ed., *Trudy pervoi terapevticheskoi konferentsii* (Gor'kii, 1943), p. 423.

37. Lilia Solomonovna Frankfurt, in Cynthia Simmons and Nina Perlina, eds., *Writing the Siege of Leningrad: Women's Diaries, Memoirs, and Documentary Prose* (Pittsburgh, Pa.: University of Pittsburgh Press, 2002), pp. 163–169.

Nutritional Dystrophy

were no references to "dystrophy" in the extant literature, and relevant studies were published not only under the title of "hunger edema," but also of "epidemic edema," "protein-deficiency edema," and "wartime edema." As the variety of terms suggest, well into the First World War, there were some who thought the symptoms were a product not of hunger, but infection—hence the term "epidemic edema." While this view had been by and large refuted by the end of the war, edemas continued to be treated as a distinct illness, qualified by a range of adjectives alluding to their etiology. More pointedly, perhaps, hunger itself was not conceived in terms of a specific pathological unity.

The selection of a novel term in 1941 reflected doctors' dissatisfaction with the existing terminology and conviction that the range of symptoms they observed—including both edemas and emaciation, previously treated as separate, as the terminology above suggests—were in fact manifestations of one illness. Their observations confirmed something that studies from the First World War and, in Russia, the Civil War, had only suggested: that when it came to hunger, it was possible "to talk about one sickness, with a distinct nosological unity and its own etiology, pathogenesis, and clinical picture."[38] What was at issue, then, was not a syndrome or a condition, but a distinct disease.

That a novel term was needed seemed clear to all concerned. What that term should be, however, was a matter of debate. As Dr. M. V. Chernorutskii later recalled, "in Leningrad almost from the very beginning of the development of this pathology two terms came into equally widespread use to designate it: 'nutritional dystrophy' . . . and 'nutritional

---

38. Gaukhman, "Massovye narusheniia obshchego pitaniia," p. 10. This seems to have been the conclusion of most doctors who wrote on the topic during the war. I have found only one dissenting voice in the Soviet medical literature, that of the head physician of the administration of evacuation hospitals in the Georgian Republic, who wrote in 1944 that "the question of whether it constitutes a nosological form of an illness or a syndrome, accompanying other forms of illness, in my opinion, has not yet been fully resolved." G. I. Mateshvili, *Alimentarnaia distrofiia, ee klinicheskie formy, patogenez i lechenie* (Tbilisi: Gruzmedgiz, 1945), pp. 5–6. Doctors in the Warsaw Ghetto came to a similar conclusion, as did some of the Scandinavian doctors who treated the populations of liberated Nazi camps. On this dawning realization among doctors in Warsaw and Europe more broadly, see Simmons, "Starvation Science."

emaciation.'"[39] The latter was the term of choice in the sanitary division of the army on the Leningrad Front. And, as even its detractors conceded, from a morphological perspective, it was perhaps the more accurate term, for it aptly designated the atrophy of organs and tissues that was such a characteristic marker of the starving body. But it was the term "nutritional dystrophy" (often shortened simply to "dystrophy"), favored by Leningrad's civilian medical establishment, that came to define both the medical literature and the popular conceptualization of hunger. "Dystrophy" first appeared in a Russian language dictionary only in 1937 (notably in a dictionary of foreign terms). Derived from the Greek term for nourishment (*trofia*), it was defined, following standard international usage at the time, as "impairment in the nourishment of tissues or organs, a disorder in the metabolism."[40] Nutritional dystrophy was thus meant to denote disorders of this nature caused by lack of food (as opposed to a genetic disorder, for instance). In Chernorutskii's view, the term "dystrophy" was more appropriate than "emaciation," for it gestured to the "functional disturbances in the organism" in a way that "emaciation," which described only morphological changes, did not.[41]

39. Chernorutskii, "Alimentarnaia distrofiia u vzroslykh," p. 37. Terminology was among the objects of contention at the first city-wide medical conference devoted to the condition, convened in Leningrad in December 1942, and the relative merits of nutritional dystrophy and nutritional emaciation remained a topic of debate in the medical literature through 1943. On the conference, see TsGASPb, f. 9156, op. 4, d. 315, ll. 31–32. The term "hunger disease" (*golodnaia bolezn'*) does not appear to have been discussed in 1941. "Hunger disease" had been used on only a few occasions in the Russian and Soviet medical literature and was almost certainly derived from German studies produced during the First World War, only a distinct minority of which classified the illnesses they observed as "Hungerkranheit."

40. *Slovar' inostrannykh slov*, ed. F. N. Petrov (Moscow: Ogiz RSFSR, 1937), p. 193. The term "dystrophy" appears to have entered Soviet medical discourse in the early 1930s. One of the first works to use the term, in the context of a study of tuberculosis, noted that whereas "atrophy" denoted a quantitative decline, dystrophy encompassed both quantitative and qualitative changes in tissue metabolism. Note that dystrophy in the prewar literature had no relation to starvation (denoting impairment in the nourishment of cells rather than lack of food). V. M. Kerner, ed., *Problema belkovykh distrofii v patologii i klinike tuberkuleza* (Moscow: Biomedgiz, 1935), p. 61.

41. Chernorutskii, "Alimentarnaia distrofiia u vzroslykh," p. 37. A similar point was made in Lang, "Klinika alimentarnoi distrofii," p. 406. Dr. Gel'shtein, one of the principal proponents of the term "nutritional emaciation," argued that "dystrophic changes occur

Nutritional Dystrophy

The blockade generated a new conception of hunger as a unified illness and produced unique conditions for the study of hunger. In his preface to a study of nutritional dystrophy published in 1944, Dr. Strashun noted that "in the fall of 1941 the experimental animals disappeared, as there was insufficient food, and experimental work ceased."[42] Even as traditional experimental work was rendered impossible by the siege conditions, however, the city itself was being transformed into a giant laboratory. Those scientists and doctors who were not evacuated from the city (or who chose not to leave) became participants and actors in what Dr. Chernorutskii referred to in 1943 as "an enormous and cruel experiment, a kind of experimentum crucis belli."[43] Vladimir Garshin, the city's chief pathologist, referred to the siege in similar terms: it was an "uncommon 'experiment, formulated by life itself.' "[44]

While Leningrad doctors frequently invoked the metaphor of the experiment, the analogy has its limits. Dana Simmons has argued that war marked a shift to a "colonial model" of medicine, featuring "coercive selection" and mass experimentation upon human subjects, who were studied rather than treated. This applies most pointedly to the studies conducted in concentration camps, where Jews and Soviet prisoners of war found themselves the unwilling subjects of scientific studies of "famine disease" directed by German doctors. It is also an apt description of the studies conducted by French doctors in institutional settings such as prisons, asylums, and internment camps. But it does not apply to Leningrad, which much more closely approximated the case of the Warsaw Ghetto, in which doctors themselves were part of the subject population and produced what Simmons aptly terms "self-reflexive famine reports."[45]

---

only in the later stages of suffering" and could actually be avoided if treatment were provided on time. TsGASPb, f. 9156, op. 4, d. 315, l. 32.

42. I. D. Strashun, "Vmesto predisloviia: nauchnaia rabota 1 LMI im. akad. Pavlova za 2 goda," in Strashun and Venderovich, eds., *Alimentarnaia distrofiia i avitamonizy,* p. 4.

43. Chernorutskii, "Problema alimintarnoi distrofii," p. 12.

44. V. G. Garshin, "Tam gde smert' pomogaet zhizni," *Arkhiv Patologii* 46, no. 5 (1984): 85.

45. Simmons, "Starvation Science," pp. 173, 181–185. The report of the Warsaw doctors was translated into English in Myron Winick, ed., *Hunger Disease: Studies by Jewish Physicians in the Warsaw Ghetto,* translated from the Polish by Martha Osnos (New York: John Wiley & Sons, 1979).

In Leningrad, scores of researchers and doctors perished from starvation, and among those who went on to make signature contributions to the literature on nutritional dystrophy, many had experienced it first hand. Vladimir Garshin is a case in point. Diagnosed with dystrophy, Garshin spent much of the blockade in hospitals, both as a patient and a pathologist. Georgii Fedorovich Lang, head of the city's Society of Physicians before his evacuation in the spring, reportedly recorded the dropping weight of his family members on his office wall.[46]

More significantly, perhaps, the Soviet doctors were not merely observers; nor were they engaged in the instrumental project of discovering the bare minimum that life could survive on, or what was required to keep a workforce alive. While their therapeutic capacity was sharply constrained by the conditions of the blockade and they operated within the constraints of a political system that encouraged them to return people to the workforce, they nonetheless saw their mission in therapeutic terms. However limited their capacity to heal, and however imperfect the medical service they provided, they had no interest in withholding treatment.[47]

The laboratory-like conditions evoked by these doctors stemmed not from an experimental design, then, but rather from the devastating precision with which it was possible to "account," in Chernorutskii's terms, for "almost all factors of fundamental importance."[48] In this sense, the famine in Leningrad was distinct from previous famines. Indeed, while some Leningraders drew parallels to the hunger of 1918 and the Civil War, most saw the two experiences as incommensurate.[49] Lidiia Ginzburg

---

46. Garshin lost his wife to starvation, as well as several colleagues. See T. S. Podzdniakova, ed., *Peterburg Akhmatovoi: Vladimir Georgevich Garshin* (St. Petersburg: Nevskii Dialekt, 1994). On Lang, see V. I. Borodulin, *G. F. Lang* (Moscow: Meditsina, 1976), p. 95.

47. For an excellent discussion of the way medical care in the Blockade was apprehended by *blokadniki*, including some medical practitioners, see Alexis Peri, "Minds under Siege: Rethinking the Soviet Experience inside the Leningrad Blockade, 1941–1945" (PhD dissertation, University of California Berkeley, 2011), pp. 138–154. Peri argues that "the Blockade exposed the limitations of medicine—both as a body of knowledge and a method of healing." Ibid., 138.

48. Chernorutskii, "Problema alimintarnoi distrofii," p. 12.

49. On this see Kirschenbaum, *The Legacy of the Siege of Leningrad*; Alexis Peri, "Revisiting the Past: History and Historical Memory during the Leningrad Blockade,"

Nutritional Dystrophy

later reflected that "during the civil war years it had been a different kind of starvation, elemental and chaotic (especially in the provinces). The siege starvation was a well-organized one. People knew that they would receive from someone invisible the minimum ration, at which level some lived and some died—which it was, depended on the organism."[50] As Irina Sandomirskaia notes, for Ginzburg "the hunger of besieged Leningrad is radically different: survival is completely dominated by the routines and practices of administration."[51] The very system of food distribution, what Ginzburg refers to as its "organized" quality, rendered the city's inhabitants ideal participants in the terrible experiment and transformed the blockade into a unique opportunity to study the effects of hunger on the human organism. As Chernorutskii noted, "In these conditions the mechanics and dynamics of change observed in the human organism, their pathogenesis, acquired almost experimental nakedness."[52]

The "experimental nakedness" Chernortuskii referred to inhered not only in the conditions in the city, but in the very nature of the illnesses doctors observed. Hunger appeared to doctors in a new guise, a "pure" form. Even as late as the famine of 1921–1922, the primary cause of death in times of famine in Russia was not starvation per se but infectious diseases.[53] Typhus and cholera had long been regarded in Russia as the "companions" to famine.[54] Leningrad marked a turning point in this

---

The Soviet and Post-Soviet Review, no. 38 (2011): 105–129. Peri in particular emphasizes the way in which people saw the experience as incomparable.

50. Lidiya Ginzburg, *Blockade Diary*, translated by Alan Myers (London: Harvill Press, 1996), pp. 57–58.

51. Irina Sandomirskaia, "A Politeia in Besiegement: Lidiia Ginzburg on the Siege of Leningrad as Political Paradigm," *Slavic Review* 69, no. 2 (2010): 319.

52. Chernorutskii, "Problema alimintarnoi distrofii," p. 12.

53. According to Serguei Adamets, approximately half of the victims of the famine of 1922 died from "eleven infectious diseases—typhus, relapsing fever, abdominal fever, cholera, smallpox, whooping cough, scarlet fever, measles, dysentery, diphtheria, and malaria." Serguei Adamets, "Famine in Nineteenth and Twentieth-Century Russia: Mortality by Age, Cause, and Gender," in Tim Dyson and Comac Ó Gráda, eds., *Famine Demography: Perspectives from the Past and Present* (New York: Oxford University Press, 2002), p. 171.

54. See, for instance, the remarks made by the Zemstvo medical authority Ivan I. Molleson in Saratov in 1892 in Charlotte E. Henze, *Disease, Health Care and Government*

222   *Rebecca Manley*

regard: like the wartime famines in Athens, the Netherlands, and the Warsaw Ghetto, it represented what economist Cormac Ó Gráda has termed a "modern" famine, in that the number of deaths due to contagious diseases was significantly fewer than those due to starvation itself.[55] Doctors in Leningrad marveled at the striking absence of cases of infectious disease, and could not but conclude that the "main, if not the only cause of the high mortality rates in the first quarter of 1942 is dystrophy."[56] As Dmitrii Pavlov, the official charged with managing Leningrad's food supplies during the war, later reflected, "Leningrad's experience proves that hunger need not be accompanied by the inseparable fellow travelers, infectious diseases and epidemics."[57] Pavlov's comments were intended to celebrate the successful sanitary measures applied by the city, and they echoed the evaluation of the situation offered by the Leningrad Health Division in early 1942.[58] Others explained the absence of epidemics in rather darker terms. Dr. M. D. Tushinskii, who noted with more than a touch of irony that "the streptococcus has been evacuated from Leningrad," attributed the absence of infectious diseases to the city's isolation.[59]

---

in *Late Imperial Russia: Life and Death on the Volga, 1823–1914* (New York: Routledge, 2011), p. 81.

55. Cormac Ó Gráda, *Famine: A Short History* (Princeton, N.J.: Princeton University Press, 2009), pp. 113–116. Whether this was already the case in the famines of 1932–1933 is difficult to evaluate, as the causes of death in the countryside, where the vast majority of deaths occurred, were not recorded. The general point with respect to Leningrad holds true if one does not count pneumonia and dysentery, both of which were listed as complications in a significant number of cases.

56. Report by V. S. Nikitskii, the head of the Leningrad Health Division, in the spring of 1942, in TsGASPb, f. 7384, op. 3, d. 45, ll. 231, 234–236.

57. Quoted in Ó Gráda, *Famine: A Short History*, p. 111.

58. In a report dated January 5, 1942, Nikitskii reported that "despite the decline in sanitary conditions, the adoption of immediate measures by healthcare authorities succeeded not only in preventing the outbreak of infectious diseases, but even in reducing their incidence." TsGASPb, f. 7384, op. 3, d. 45, l. 287. This congratulatory tone is notably absent from subsequent reports, and Nikitskii's successor, Mashanskii, who like Pavlov celebrated the absence of disease, nonetheless recognized that "one can argue about the reasons for [their] absence." GARF, f. A-482, op. 47, d. 1095, l. 6.

59. On Tushinskii's claim to this effect, see Inber, *Leningrad Diary*, 46. Tushinskii's ironic comment is reported in Borodulin, *G. F. Lang*, p. 94. Isolation was also the explanation of choice for Leningrad doctors writing about the absence of measles during

Nutritional Dystrophy 223

Whatever the cause, hunger did present itself in a new, purer guise. To be sure, the absence of hunger's traditional companions did not mean an absence of complications. Dystrophy was often observed in conjunction with diseases such as colitis, dysentery, or pneumonia, diseases that were considerably harder to detect against a backdrop of starvation. While some doctors contested the widespread view "that in the period of dystrophy other illnesses receded, diminished, lost their mass character,"[60] and diagnoses were admittedly difficult given "the lack of light, heat, [and] the closure of radiography and laboratory facilities," the influence of dystrophy was overwhelming. As the head of the Leningrad Health Department put it, citing the results of autopsies, "across all the material runs the red thread of 'starvation.' "[61] Medical practitioners in Leningrad sought to understand not only the diseases that accompanied hunger, but the workings of hunger upon the body in what the Jewish doctors in the Warsaw Ghetto, who were engaged in a very similar endeavor, referred to as "clean cases," cases not complicated by other diseases.[62]

THE PHYSIOLOGY AND PSYCHOLOGY OF HUNGER

During the siege, doctors observed and analyzed the effect of hunger on every aspect of the body and bodily functions. Patients were observed, vital processes were measured, and blood was analyzed. Pathologists weighed and examined the organs of patients who died. As Garshin later wrote, "Careful specimens, extremely fine cuts from human tissues . . . We needed to study all the changes in the structure of the organs, the cells."[63] Doctors recorded the weight loss, the sensation of hunger, the slight weakening of muscles, the muscle pain, and the excessive urination that were among the early symptoms of the disease in what Leningrad

---

the siege. On this see Donald Filtzer, *The Hazards of Urban Life in Late Stalinist Russia: Health, Hygiene, and Living Standards, 1943–1953* (Cambridge: Cambridge University Press, 2010), pp. 280–281.

60. TsGASPb, f. 9156, op. 6, d. 18, l. 13.

61. TsGASPb, f. 7384, op. 3, d. 45, ll. 229–230.

62. Winick, *Hunger Disease*, p. 13. Doctors in Leningrad, despite the deprivation, worked in considerably better conditions than their colleagues in Warsaw and also studied the complications that sometimes accompanied dystrophy.

63. Garshin, "Tam gde smert' pomogaet zhizni," p. 85.

doctors soon came to identify as its first stage. In this so-called ambulatory phase, patients could still work and move around. Stage two signaled a sharp change in this regard: patients spent more and more time in bed, and work was no longer possible. The atrophy of muscles accelerated and weight loss, fatigue, and excessive urination all continued. This stage also saw changes in the skin, which typically became dry and flaky. Body temperature dropped, as did the heart rate and levels of protein and sugar in the blood. It was also in this second stage that edemas, which might appear fleetingly in stage one, could emerge with more permanence, particularly on the face and on the body's extremities. In fact, Leningrad doctors distinguished two forms of stage two dystrophy: edematous and non-edematous. In Leningrad, where starvation was severe, the non-edematous or "dry" form was the more common. The third and final stage in the typology developed by the Leningrad medical establishment was often fatal. By this point, all the body's fat reserves had been used up, and even therapeutic feeding could often not reverse the irreparable damage that had already occurred.[64]

While the symptoms of nutritional dystrophy were certainly recognizable, researchers and clinicians struggled to determine when a case passed from simple hunger to an actual illness (nutritional dystrophy), and to determine the presence of complicating factors such as dysentery or pneumonia.[65] The pathogenesis of the condition was regarded as particularly complex. Definitively rejecting suggestions from the First World War that a reduction in fat or carbohydrates was the activating

64. The three stages of dystrophy were not defined uniformly in the literature. There was some debate about whether the stages should be defined in relation to clinical manifestations, pathophysiological data, or some combination. Doctors were quick to acknowledge, moreover, that dividing the illness into three distinct stages was "entirely relative." They nonetheless insisted on the importance of such divisions for the establishment of "a unified approach to patients." The description of the stages presented here is drawn from the instructions approved by the People's Commissariat of Health in June 1943, in GARF, f. 8009, op. 5, d. 235, ll. 2–4; E M. Gel'shtein, *Metodicheskie ukazaniia po raspoznavaniiu i lecheniiu alimentarnogo istoshcheniia* (Leningrad, 1942), p. 2; Lang, "Klinika alimentarnoi distrofii," pp. 410–411; M. I. Khvilitskaia, "Diagnoz," in Chernorutskii, ed., *Alimentarnaia distrofiia v blokirovannom Leningrade*, pp. 188–189.

65. Chernorutskii, "Alimentarnaia distrofiia u vzroslykh," p. 38. M. I. Khvilitskaia, "Simptomatologiia," in Chernorutskii, ed., *Alimentarnaia distrofiia v blokirovannom Leningrade*, p. 128.

Nutritional Dystrophy

feature, research in Leningrad confirmed the key role played by proteins. Protein deficiency was, in the words of Dr. Eliazar Markovich Gel'shtein, head physician of the Leningrad Front, "the fundamental pathogenic factor of nutritional dystrophy."[66] Insufficient food, the research suggested, did not simply deplete the body of fat and lead it to consume its own tissues and organs, but led to fundamental changes in the metabolism, the endocrine system, and the nervous system.[67] It thus transformed the body's regulatory mechanisms.

The severity of the condition depended not only on food intake, but on a variety of other factors. Cold weather and heavy manual labor, both of which were all too common in Leningrad, increased the body's need for food, and were known to exacerbate the onset and progress of starvation. More complicated to assess was the role of gender. On one level, hunger seemed to efface the differences between men and women; as women's bodies became more androgenous, they ceased menstruating, and both men and women lost their sexual urges.[68] At the same time, however, hunger drew a sharp distinction between men and women. Indeed, during the early period of the Leningrad famine, for every one hundred patients with nutritional dystrophy, only two to five were women.[69] As Dr. Gel'shtein noted in his discussion of the etiology and pathogenesis of nutritional dystrophy, "in Leningrad, from December 1941 until January 1942, nutritional dystrophy was exclusively a male phenomenon; among women this sickness began to appear only after two to three months."[70] In this "later stage," Gel'shtein commented at a conference in late 1942, in response to questions about "why mortality was higher among men," "it was as if men got their revenge."[71] The very terms suggest just how much the experience of extreme hunger divided

---

66. E. M. Gel'shtein, ed., *Narushenie obshchego pitaniia (osobennosti ikh vozniknoveniia i lecheniia vo vremia voiny)*, vol. 28 of *Opyt sovetskoi meditsiny v Velikoi Otechestvennoi voine 1941–1945 gg.* (Moscow: Medgiz, 1951), p. 51.

67. See Chernorutskii, "Alimentarnaia distrofiia u vzroslykh," p. 48.

68. On the population's perceptions of this process, see Kirschenbaum, "'The Alienated Body,'" p. 27, and Peri, "Minds under Siege," p. 27.

69. Lang, "Klinika alimentarnoi distrofii," pp. 409–410.

70. Gel'shtein, *Narushenie obshchego pitaniia*, p. 21.

71. TsGASPb, f. 9156, op. 4, d. 315, l. 31.

men from women. Women, it seemed, were better able to bear the sustained lack of food. Leningrad doctors were by no means the first to observe this. V. A. Manassein and V. V. Pashutin had made similar observations in early laboratory studies of hunger conducted in Russia, as had German doctors during the blockade of the First World War, but there had been little clinical data, as many of the paradigmatic studies of starvation had transpired among prisoners of war and in the army, in which the populations affected and studied were exclusively male.[72] This perhaps explains why some Soviet studies conducted in the rear, in evacuation hospitals, failed to note the striking gender divide: I. S. Schnitzer, for instance, wrote that "men, women and children suffer equally from this illness."[73] With some notable exceptions, however, the medical literature was quite clear: women's bodies took longer to succumb.

Explanations for women's greater resilience varied. American researchers who had organized a "starvation experiment," using American conscientious objectors as their subjects, read the results of the Leningrad studies with great interest, and paid particular attention to the comments on gender, an issue that their own studies could not address. They attributed the difference to the fact that "women were subject to less physical exertion than men" and had greater stores of body fat.[74] While Soviet doctors also pointed to body fat as a likely explanation, they were under no illusion about women's work: as Lang noted of the phenomenon in Leningrad, the "enormous difference" in starvation rates could "hardly be explained" by differences in work, as the blockade had all but eliminated such distinctions.[75] Indeed, even within the same unit, in a group of men and women "undertaking the same level of physical labor," nutri-

---

72. Isserson notes the finding in German studies, and the lack of clinical data, in O. D. Isserson, "K voprosu o letal'nosti ot alimentarnoi distrofii v Leningrade s noiabria 1941 g. do noiabria 1942 g.," in Il'ia Davidovich Strashun and E. L. Venderovich, eds., *Alimentarnaia distrofiia i avitaminozy* (Leningrad: Narkomzdrav sssr, Gosudarstvennoe Izdatel'stvo Meditsinskoi literatury, Leningradskoe otdelenie, 1944), p. 97.

73. Shnitser, "Alimentarnaia distrofiia," p. 32.

74. Josef Brožek, Samuel Wells, and Ancel Keys, "Medical Aspects of Semistarvation in Leningrad (Siege 1941–1942)," *American Review of Soviet Medicine* 4, no. 1 (October 1946): p. 74.

75. Lang, "Klinika alimentarnoi distrofii," p. 410.

Nutritional Dystrophy 227

tional dystrophy afflicted numerous men and not a single woman.[76] The body fat explanation enjoyed support among doctors, and seems to have been the explanation of choice among the population at large. As Elena Skriabina noted in her diary, "Women are generally hardier. They have a greater supply of fat under their skin. However, they have begun to fail too."[77] Doctors, however, rarely rested simply at body fat. Gel'shtein, addressing the issue at the 1942 conference, commented that "I don't know the precise scientific explanation, but I think that it is mainly connected to the peculiarities of the metabolism that separate the female from the male organism." Gel'shtein posited that women's lower metabolic rate enabled them to better endure hunger, and that the "endocrine apparatus" might also play a role.[78] Similar hypotheses were advanced by G. F. Lang and M. M. Gubergrits, founder and chair of the Kiev Medical Institute's department of the propaedeutics of internal medicine, who spent the war working on dystrophy, among other things, in an evacuation hospital in Cheliabinsk.[79]

In their studies of nutritional dystrophy, Leningrad doctors observed and recorded the effect of hunger not only on the body, but on the mind. Clinicians and psychiatrists debated the effect of dystrophy on the nervous system, and charted its effects on human conduct. Observers frequently noted two poles of behavior: those diagnosed with dystrophy were characterized either as "listless" and "apathetic" or as "excitable" and "irritable."[80] A study, for example, of one hundred patients with nutritional dystrophy in 1942 (based on a combination of clinical observation and an analysis of their diaries and letters) revealed that nearly two thirds were "listless, sullen, indifferent," while almost a third were

76. Gel'shtein, *Narushenie obshchego pitaniia*, p, 21.

77. Elena Skriabina, *Siege and Survival: The Odyssey of a Leningrader* (Carbondale: Southern Illinois University Press, 1971), p. 62.

78. TsGASPb, f. 9156, op. 4, d. 315, l. 31. Only after referencing the metabolism did he note the "tendency to accumulate a layer of fat under the skin."

79. Lang, "Klinika alimentarnoi distrofii," p. 410. M. M. Gubergrits, "Ob alimentarnoi toksicheskoi distrofii," *Vrachebnoe delo*, no. 11–12 (1945): 553.

80. See, for instance, G. B. Abramovich and S. S. Mnukhin, "Klinika alimentarnoi distrofii: Izmeneniia psikhiki," in Gel'shtein, ed., *Narushenie obshchego pitaniia*, pp. 117–118.

described as "irritable."[81] Others presented these same traits as distinct stages in the evolution of the distrofik. M. I. Khvilitskaia described the way those suffering from nutritional dystrophy became "aggressive, prone to get into fights, stubborn, and rude," and the way that "their intellectual interests narrow, becoming defined, in the main, by their need for food." As the disease progressed, many became "indifferent," their sense of shame disappeared, and their behavior became "egocentric." In effect, the personality was "flattened" as individuals' "moral level" declined and all their thoughts were redirected to "the acquisition of food."[82]

Whether conceived as separate stages or as two poles of behavior, there was remarkable unanimity regarding the distrofik's defining psychological traits. There was not a study or report that failed to mention the distrofik's indifference. Indifference could manifest itself in lack of concern for loved ones, as in a study that reported on a twenty-year-old who, despite having always loved his father, found himself unmoved when the latter died, and in disregard for one's own safety, exemplified in the oft-reported cases of people ignoring air-raid warnings.[83] It could even, in the later stages of dystrophy, manifest itself as a refusal on the part of the distrofik "to undertake those small efforts required to ingest food."[84] At the same time, distrofiks were almost universally described as egocentric. Psychiatrist Raisa Iakovlevna Golant, for example, noted how those who were ill with dystrophy "became more rude, more egotistical: comradely and familial relationships were ruined. The ill committed acts that were not at all characteristic for them."[85] Khvilitskaia, who described

81. E. K. Iakovlevna and N.V. Oparina, "Izmeneniia lichnosti pri alimentarnoi distrofii," in Skliarchik, "Konferentsiia Leningradskogo obshchestva psikhiatrov i nevropatologov," p. 80.

82. Khvilitskaia, "Simptomatologiia," pp. 163–165.

83. E. K. Iakovleva and I. V. Oparina, "Izmeneniia lichnosti pri alimentarnoi distrofii," in TsGANTD SPb, f. 313, op. 2, d. 347, l. 4l; V. N. Miasishchev, "Nervno-psikhicheskie zabolevaniia alimentarno-avitaminoznogo proiskhozhdeniia," in V. N Miasishchev, ed., *Nervno-psikhicheskie zabolevaniia voennogo vremeni (po materialam Leningradskikh konferentsii 1942–1943 gg)* (Leningrad: Gosudarstvennoe izdatel'stvo meditsinskoi literatury Leningradskoe otdelenie, 1945), p. 9.

84. R. Ia. Golant, "Psikhozy pri alimentarnom istoshchenii i avitaminozakh," in *Nervnye i psikhicheskie zabolevaniia voennogo vremeni* (Moscow: Medgiz, 1948), p. 219.

85. R. Ia. Golant, "O nekotorykh psikhicheskikh narusheniiakh v usloviiakh voennogo vremeni na osnovanii Leningradskogo opyta dvukh voin," in R. Ia Golant

Nutritional Dystrophy

the indifference and the egoism in some detail, noted only at the end that they also observed cases of "genuinely human traits of stoic selflessness," of "principled, ethical" behavior and that "in these cases, the personality was preserved."[86] While Khvilitskaia concluded on an upbeat note, most did not. Hunger, in the words of Chernorutskii, led to a "degradation of the person."[87]

Interestingly, one of the stock victims of famine in the medical and broader popular imagination—the person who was mad from hunger— made few appearances during the siege. Psychiatrists at the Bekhterov Institute repeatedly remarked on the absence of cases of true psychosis.[88] Many concluded that the psychoses previously thought to be a result of hunger were in fact a result of pellagra, an avitaminosis, which, because it appeared in Leningrad only in the spring of 1942, could now be properly distinguished from starvation.[89] Other psychic manifestations were attributed to preexisting conditions that were exacerbated by the lack of food.[90] By the end of the war, few specialists would contest the conclusion reached by V. N. Miasishchev that "experience has shown that the vast majority of people ill with nutritional dystrophy and even those who died from it did not have a nervous disorder or psychosis."[91] While popular references to people going "mad from hunger" were not uncommon, the archetypal victim of famine, as he emerges from the medical literature, is not mad but degraded.[92]

---

and V. N. Miasishchev, eds., *Nervnye i psikhicheskie zabolevaniia v usloviiakh voennogo vremeni* (Leningrad: 9aia tipografiia Upravleniia Voennogo Izdatel'stva MVS SSSR, 1948), p. 15.

86. Khvilitskaia, "Simptomatologiia," p. 165.

87. Chernorutskii, "Problema alimintarnoi distrofii," p. 5.

88. See Abramovich and Mnukhin, "Klinika alimentarnoi distrofii: Izmeneniia psikhiki," p. 118; E. S. Averbukh, "Psikhicheskie narusheniia pri istoshchenii na pochve golodaniia," TsGANTD SPb, f. 313, op. 2-1, d. 15, ll. 26–27.

89. See the comments to this effect in Golant, "Psikhozy pri alimentarnom istoshchenii i avitaminozakh," p. 217.

90. E. S. Averbukh, "Psikhicheskie narusheniia pri istoshchenii na pochve golodaniia," TsGANTD SPb, f. 313, op. 2-1, d. 15, ll. 26–27.

91. Miasishchev, "Nervno-psikhicheskie zabolevaniia alimentarno-avitaminoznogo proiskhozhdeniia," p. 3.

92. See Vasilyev, "Alimentary and Pellagra Psychoses in Besieged Leningrad," p. 118. On popular conceptions of hunger psychosis see Peri, "Minds under Siege," pp. 175–180.

As doctors recorded the transformations wrought by hunger upon the human body and mind, they sought to improve diagnoses and to find new ways to treat patients and minimize suffering. Such efforts began in earnest in the spring of 1942, when doctors had themselves begun to recover from the illnesses they were studying. Across the city, medical institutions and societies resumed their activities with meetings and talks devoted to one principal topic: nutritional dystrophy. Even the Institute of Experimental Medicine, acclaimed for its theoretical work before the war, turned exclusively to the problem of dystrophy, bringing together biochemists, physiologists, clinicians, and pathologists to study the illness from fifteen different angles.[93] In the fall of 1942, the city health division established a research commission under the leadership of Chernorutskii to study "dystrophy and avitaminoses." The task was of practical and immediate significance: as Chernorutskii put it in his remarks at the first citywide conference convened by the commission, it was "to heal the sick and ease their suffering."[94]

With time, thanks in large measure to their exchanges at conferences such as this one, doctors came to be able to better recognize the complications that often accompanied dystrophy and to thus improve the provision of care. As Vladimir Garshin observed in 1944, "under the influence of the work of the conferences and commissions, clinical diagnoses improved."[95] The conferences brought clinicians and pathologists together and enabled them to probe the way hunger transformed and often masked other illnesses. Pneumonia, for instance, lacked many of its standard symptoms in the distrofik, and its detection in autopsies prompted clinicians to refine their diagnoses. Similar advances occurred in the diagnosis of dysentery. The findings and expertise accrued in clinics and conferences were distilled into an instructional film in 1943, prepared with the collaboration of Garshin, Gel'shtein, and other specialists, to ensure that newly trained medical cadres remained abreast of the latest developments.[96]

93. See the report on the institute's work delivered in Moscow on July 1, 1943, in GARF, f. 8009, op. 2, d. 542, l. 4.
94. TsGASPb, f. 9156, op. 4, d. 315, l. 11.
95. Garshin, "Tam gde smert' pomogaet zhizni," p. 86.
96. Podzdniakova, Peterburg Akhmatovoi, p. 48.

Nutritional Dystrophy

The conferences also provided doctors with an opportunity to compare notes on their efforts to treat dystrophy, an endeavor that was severely hampered by the dire lack of supplies. Leningrad doctors were well aware of the starving body's need for protein, but given the absence of milk, meat, and eggs, they were forced to turn to other sources.[97] At a meeting of the Leningrad health division held in 1942 devoted to the diet of distrofiks, doctors advocated the use of "albumin [dried egg white] and casein, from which you can make various dishes." They also noted the "usefulness" of soy and dried cabbage, although they warned against the free distribution of dried cabbage "as the population will not be able to use it as it should."[98] Doctors thus played a crucial role in the introduction of food substitutes such as casein and yeast that would help offset the ravages of hunger.[99]

Proper treatment, however, was not only a matter of finding food. Reflecting back on the experience at the end of the war, Khvilitskaia noted that given "the clear etiology of this illness," one could easily think, "at first glance," that "one need only provide the patient with the appropriate food and the illness will go away by itself."[100] In reality, however, treatment was substantially more complex. For a start, as doctors discovered through a process of trial and error, food had to be carefully measured out. Indeed, Professor Tur, a prominent pediatrician from Leningrad, presented what he characterized as "maximal feeding," or a tendency to "from the very first day, feed, feed and feed . . ." as a "gross therapeutic mistake." Speaking to a conference in Moscow in 1944 and

97. Interestingly, initial reports by the Leningrad health division stressed their attempts to use vitamins "to prevent the development of dystrophy." TsGASPb, f. 7384, op. 3, d. 45, l. 285. Subsequent reports contained no mention of vitamins, reflecting perhaps the absence of vitamin preparations in the city, but more importantly, I think, the realization that vitamins were not the issue. Once protein was recognized as the crucial etiological factor in the development of dystrophy, treatment plans all focused on assuring sufficient quantities of protein in the diet.

98. TsGASPb, f. 9156, op. 4, d. 91, l. 18.

99. The introduction of casein is widely attributed in the medical literature to S. M. Ryss and O. G. Sviatoslavskaia. See, for example, Gel'shtein, *Narushenie obshchego pitaniia*, p. 129.

100. M. I. Khvilitskaia, "Lechenie," in Chernorutskii, ed., *Alimentarnaia distrofiia v blokirovannom Leningrade*, p. 215.

reprising arguments he had made earlier in Leningrad, he noted that "unfortunately, this mistake occurred and continues to occur even today. . . . The negative consequences of such a regime are more lethal the more severe the degree of emaciation and the more the functions of the digestive system and metabolism are destroyed."[101] In place of maximal feeding, Tur cautioned that "in the first two or three days of treatment the diet of severe distrofiks must be limited in terms of quantity and qualitatively." They should be given only easily digestible food in small but frequent installments, and the diet of the patient should not be overloaded with proteins and fats.[102] Over the course of the blockade, doctors would thus work to refine not only the basic elements of a therapeutic diet, but the quantities and the manner in which they were to be administered. In addition to a therapeutic diet, doctors also emphasized the importance of providing the ill with warmth and quiet, and recommended a host of other treatments, including intravenous glucose, amphetamines, and blood transfusions, the efficacy of which was subject to some debate.[103]

This is not to suggest that blockade medicine was effective. Indeed, notwithstanding their increasingly sophisticated understanding of dystrophy, doctors' capacity to heal was limited. Particularly in the first blockade winter, doctors had access to little that could improve the lot of their patients. What they required most—food—was the material in shortest supply. Nor is it to suggest that diagnoses were a strictly medical affair. As Alexis Peri has convincingly demonstrated, diagnoses were malleable during the blockade, shaped by the imperative to maintain the labor force; the desire to help people by keeping them at work or giving them respite from work, depending on the moment; and (widely suspected) corruption.[104] Medicine clearly did not operate in isolation from political and social constraints. In their medical research, however, doctors faced few of the dilemmas they confronted in the clinic. Their conferences and reports, which became increasingly frequent as medical practitioners

101. GARF, f. 8009, op. 2, d. 629, l. 45.

102. Ibid. Gel'shtein made a similar point in his instructions issued on the Leningrad Front. See Gel'shtein, *Metodicheskie ukazaniia po raspoznavaniiu i lecheniiu alimentarnogo istoshcheniia*, p. 7.

103. See, for example, Khvilitskaia, "Lechenie," p. 224.

104. Peri, "Minds under Siege," pp. 146–148.

Nutritional Dystrophy

themselves began to recover from the illness they described, served not only to improve diagnoses and treatment, but also, in the words of Vladimir Garshin, to "renew our capacity to work," to "renew the power of our souls."[105] Garshin's letters to his son bear powerful witness to the new significance the pathologist attached to his work. In his letters from that spring, he repeatedly noted that "I cannot abandon my work," that "I am needed here."[106] Reflecting on the differences between his prewar and current research, he noted that "before I was somehow unaware of the connection between my work and the common cause (*obshchee delo*)."[107] In place of his traditional academic work, he was now engaged with pressing questions that required immediate answers. Indeed, his descriptions of the conferences suggest just how out of the ordinary they were: "almost the whole 'medical world' of the city gathered together. . . . These were striking meetings. We rushed to communicate to each other our findings, our experience. The reports were delivered in some kind of particularly trembling manner."[108] The conference proceedings suggest that doctors were indeed eager to share their findings, and despite initial fears that the conference might be "boring," numerous participants affirmed that it was "to the contrary very interesting."[109]

The conferences satisfied the need of the participants to work, to be useful, to contribute. They also satisfied a powerful urge to document the changes they observed around them. From the outset, Chernorutskii underscored the importance of publishing the results.[110] Indeed, the research reports constitute an important documentary record of the siege. While some have seen the reports on dystrophy as part and parcel of an attempt to sanitize wartime hunger, for those who could read them, the materials presented by Leningrad doctors provided dramatic witness to the devastation wrought by hunger. Vladimir Garshin's reflections are instructive. As a pathologist, he worked with slides, "the most slender slices from human tissues, beautifully colored." He had been trained to

105. Garshin, "Tam gde smert' pomogaet zhizni," p. 86.
106. Podzdniakova, *Peterburg Akhmatovoi*, 37–39.
107. Ibid., 39–40.
108. Garshin, "Tam gde smert' pomogaet zhizni," p. 86.
109. TsGASPb, f. 9156, op. 4, d. 315, l. 11.
110. Ibid., l. 12.

approach his material analytically, "with a cold heart." But alongside this habitual approach, "learned through dozens of years of experience and work, something else emerges and grows. These beautiful pictures cry out about the drama, cry out about the organism's futile struggle. These beautiful pictures speak about the destruction, the collapse of the main vital structures."[111]

Garshin's comments underscore the unique nature of the reports on dystrophy: they were at once standard scientific reports, the product of "cold analysis," and moving documentary records of the siege. It is telling, I think, that when the Leningrad Division of the Institute of Experimental Medicine presented its wartime research to colleagues in Moscow and to the Presidium of the all-Union Medical Soviet in 1943, their presentation produced, in the words of one professor present, "disturbing sensations. It is an altogether unusual report, as we are talking about absolutely unusual circumstances of work." Indeed, only one participant cast the value of the Institute's work into doubt, questioning whether it was "worth it" to "expend so much energy on the study of nutritional dystrophy, that is, that great misfortune of Leningrad, which is typical neither for our people nor for our existence? This misfortune was a result of the blockade, therefore why should we study it thoroughly for several years? Is it worth dissecting nutritional dystrophy, which we have already become sick and tired of?" Her remarks proved by far the most controversial of the session. By way of rejoinder, other participants stressed the significance of the research reports not only for the future evolution of science, but for the historical record. As the director of the institute put it, "nobody can diminish the significance of the works undertaken, for example, by Garshin and our physiologists. We had to reflect in history everything that happened." Another doctor, a member of the Medical Soviet, criticized the suggestion that nutritional dystrophy should no longer be studied. "I think that this is a significant fact; our comrades in Leningrad observed it and how one can claim that it should not be studied I cannot imagine." Professor A. N. Sysin, a prominent figure in the country's public hygiene establishment, likewise saw no choice in the matter: the theme of dystrophy was unavoidable, in his view, chosen not

111. Garshin, "Tam gde smert' pomogaet zhizni," p. 85.

Nutritional Dystrophy   235

by the institute but by the events of the war itself. Like other participants, he stressed the documentary value of the studies: "a mass of facts were not lost; they have been studied and will remain in the historical record."[112]

FROM THE CLINICS TO THE STREETS

The urge to document the transformations wrought by the siege was evident not only among doctors, but the population at large. As individual residents set about the difficult task of describing the effects of hunger upon the body and mind, they drew on medical terminology and practice in notable ways. While the principal publications about nutritional dystrophy were produced for a specialized audience of medical professionals, medical terminology and practice did not exist in isolation. Within weeks of the adoption of the new terminology, "nutritional dystrophy" began to appear in individual diaries and popular speech. It became, as Leningrad health official F. I. Mashanskii remarked in 1943, "a term of the streets and of homes."[113] Clinics were organized to treat those suffering from the illness, and individuals were diagnosed with it, compelling people to see their affliction as a case of dystrophy. Thus did Olga Epshtein record in her diary in mid-May 1942, "I have been diagnosed with dystrophy in the first stage."[114] Like doctors, residents of Leningrad came to see hunger not simply as a condition defined by insufficient food, but as an illness, a medical state with distinct stages.[115] The term "hunger" was in this sense insufficient, for it failed to distinguish between

112. GARF, f. 8009, op. 2, d. 542, ll. 16, 14, 15.

113. GARF, f. A482, op. 47, d. 1095, l. 9.

114. Entry of May 13, 1942, in Ales' Adamovich and Daniil Aleksandrovich Granin, *Blokadnaia kniga* (St. Petersburg: Pechatnyi dvor, 1994), p. 148.

115. Vera Inber, for example, noting the establishment of centers of "intensified nutrition" in May 1942, described those whom they were intended to serve as "Pale, exhausted, weak people (dystrophy, second degree)" and "people who can't walk any more, can't even move (dystrophy, third degree)." Inber, *Leningrad Diary*, p. 86. Elena Kochina likewise referred to the stages of dystrophy, although her stages were not, in fact, those identified by doctors. "Some have swollen up and shine as if they are covered with lacquer—the first stage of dystrophy. Others have dried up—the second stage." Elena Kochina, *Blockade Diary*, ed., with an introduction by Samuel C. Ramer (Ann Arbor, Mich.: Ardis Publishers, 1990), p. 52.

those who were hungry (virtually everybody) and those who were ill. How else can one make sense of the question that an obviously hungry boy posed to his teacher in February 1942: "What are the signs of dystrophy?"[116]

While Leningraders continued to use the word "hunger," "dystrophy" became increasingly common as a way of identifying the terrible changes that the lack of food wrought on the human body and mind. The centrality of the new term to naming hunger is cast into sharp relief by a rumor that Ol'ga Berggol'ts, temporarily in Moscow in March of 1942, recorded in her diary. A friend named Irina, who had just arrived from Leningrad, reported that "the word 'dystrophy' has now been banned— death results from other factors, but not from hunger!"[117] Her comments point to the way that "hunger" and "dystrophy" had become virtually synonymous in the city. Far from an attempt to obscure hunger, "dystrophy" was perceived by Berggol'ts and her friend as way of naming it.

Every resident became an observer of the effects of hunger. Diaries penned during the blockade document the transformations wrought by hunger upon the body, behavior, and mind, as Alexis Peri's contribution to this volume suggests.[118] Among the most notable signs recorded by the population in their diaries were weight loss and changes in the skin. "I have acquired the appearance of a genuine distrofik," Liubov' Shaporina noted in her diary. Her weight had dropped over sixty pounds over the winter, her skin hung in folds on her shoulders, and her face had become "alien," covered in wrinkles and discolored "such that it resembles the faces of all the other emaciated Leningraders."[119] The "genuine distrofik" was similarly identified and described by another diarist (this time observing a friend rather than herself) as "emaciated," with "sunken

116. K. V. Polzikova-Rubets, *Oni uchilis' v Leningrade* (Leningrad: Detgiz,1948).

117. Entry of March 23, 1942, in Ol'ga Berggol'ts, *Ol'ga. Zapretnyi dnevnik*, ed. N. Sokolovskaia and A. Rubashkin (St. Petersburg: Azbuka, 2011), p. 82.

118. A fuller treatment can be found in Peri, "Minds under Siege." On the body more specifically, see also Polina Barskova, "The Corpse, the Corpulent, and the Other: A Study in the Tropology of Siege Body Representation," *Ab Imperio*, no. 1 (2009): 361–386, and Kirschenbaum, " 'The Alienated Body.' "

119. Entries of April 28, May 2, and May 6, 1942, in L. V. Shaporina, *Dnevnik*, ed. V.N. Sazhin and V. F. Petrovaia. (Moscow: Novoe Literaturnoe Obozrenie, 2012), pp. 321–322.

Nutritional Dystrophy

eyes" and "grey skin."[120] Leningraders further recorded the appearance of edemas (swelling), most commonly on the face or on the feet. "Today for the first time I have a genuinely dystrophically swollen physiognomy," noted Aleksandr Boldyrev in his diary in February 1942.[121] Others described the distinctive gait of people suffering from dystrophy. Of her own body, Elena Skriabina wrote that it was "like a skeleton. Blue veins stand out on my hands. My feet are swollen. I move with great difficulty."[122] Not all described their bodies. Some simply did not have the strength. Nikolai Punin noted in his diary, "If there was a bit of peace, perhaps, I would describe the state of my body, the hungry body."[123]

Almost invariably, descriptions did not rest with these purely physical attributes, as the changing usage of the term "distrofik" suggests. The term appears to have come into circulation very quickly: by the end of December 1941, an official decision of the executive committee of the Leningrad city soviet addressed the issue of the medical treatment of "distrofiks."[124] A few weeks later, the celebrated specialist of social hygiene Zakharii Grigor'evich Frenkel' noted in his diary that he was being admitted to a hospital "for distrofiks" in the hotel Astoria.[125] It was not long before people began to refer to themselves and others using the same terminology. "'Distrofik'—I saw the word in the mirror," the teenager Sasha Nesterov reportedly remarked.[126] Punin reflected in the fall of 1942 that in his final weeks in Leningrad he had been unable to continue his diary: "I couldn't write: I was a hunger distrofik."[127]

---

120. Entry of February 14, 1942, in G. K. Zimnitskaia, "Blokadnye budni (dnevnik Leningradskoi devochki)," in S. E. Glezerov, ed., *Blokada glazami ochevidtsev: dnevniki i vospominaniia* (St. Petersburg: Ostrov, 2012), p. 58.

121. Entry of February 20, 1942, in A. N. Boldyrev, *Osadnaia zapis': blokadnyi dnevnik*, ed. V. S. Garbuzova and I. M. Steblin-Kamenskii. (St. Petersburg: Evropeiskii Dom, 1998), p. 62.

122. Skriabina, *Siege and Survival*, 62.

123. N. N. Punin, *Mir svetel liubov'iu: dnevniki, pis'ma*, ed. L. A. Zykov (Moscow: Artist. Rezhisser. Teatr, 2000), p. 351.

124. In Gladkikh, *Zdravookhranenie i voennaia meditsina v bitve za Leningrad*, p. 60.

125. Entry of January 17, 1942, in Z. G. Frenkel, ed., *Zapiski i vospominaniia o proidennom zhiznennom puti* (St. Petersburg: Nestor-Istoriia, 2009), p. 494.

126. In Adamovich and Granin, *Blokadnaia kniga*, p. 358. For a similar usage, see Shaporina, *Dnevnik*, p. 322.

127. Punin, *Mir svetel liubov'iu*, p. 359.

The Russian language had a rich array of terms to denote the person suffering from hunger: a dictionary of Russian popular sayings lists several, including *golodai, golodan', golodar'*, and *goloden'*.[128] It is telling that none of these emerged in Leningrad as ways of designating the victims of the famine. Traditionally, words denoting the hungry were overlaid with other meanings. The hungry were the destitute, the poor. The word *golodai*, to take but one example, denoted a starving person, but it could also mean a poor person.[129] The Second World War transformed the cultural geography of hunger. During the siege, an urban population suffered a famine in which the entire population was affected. Lidiia Ginzburg describes the reaction of the city's younger generation of intellectuals: "they understood that there might be famine in the country, especially in the desert, complete with camels and mirages, when a man doesn't have anything to eat for days on end and dies in agony from that. But they knew nothing of dystrophy and didn't believe that the inhabitants of a large city could die a hungry death."[130] Death from insufficient food, she suggests, was, for many urban intellectuals in Leningrad, simply incomprehensible. Herein lay, perhaps, the appeal of the term "distrofik": its novelty made it seem only appropriate to designate a state of being that was utterly unfamiliar, something that seemed so different from the plight of the poor or of starving villagers.[131] The medicalized nature of the term, moreover, may have heightened its appeal. It is surely telling that Ginzburg likened "the hunger that we experienced" to "a chronic illness."[132]

"Distrofik" came to denote not merely a person in a state of starvation, but a whole way of being, and became an integral term in the city's wartime lexicon. In Lidiia Ginzburg's wartime prose, the terms *golodnyi*

128. *Slovar' russkikh narodnykh govorov*, vol. 6 (Leningrad: Nauka Leningradskoe otd-nie, 1970), pp. 314–315.

129. Ibid., p. 314.

130. Ginzburg, *Blockade Diary*, p. 59. Modified translation based on the original.

131. Ginzburg notes in *Den' Ottera*, written in the war's final years, that the standardized quality of hunger in Leningrad "sharply distinguished it psychologically from the hunger of poverty." Lidiia Ginzburg, *Prokhodiashchie kharaktery: proza voennykh let; Zapiski blokadnogo cheloveka*, ed. E. Van Buskirk and A. Zorin (Moscow: Novoe izdatel'stvo, 2011), p. 241.

132. Ibid., p. 240.

Nutritional Dystrophy

(hungry) and *golodaiushchii* (starving) were used to denote a person who did not have sufficient food (or who experienced feelings of hunger), but "distrofik," and its adjectival form "distroficheskii" denoted not merely an absence of food and the physiological state that resulted, but an entire range of patterns of behavior as well as a unique psychological outlook. The distrofik is described in Ginzburg's prose as "indifferent" and apathetic, characterized by a lack of will and of "initiative." Ginzburg repeatedly described the "dystrophic indifference to the life and death of one's family and friends" and the "dystrophic greed" that were characteristic traits of those suffering from starvation. The worldview of the distrofik was characterized by "waiting for death, fatal indifference, and deadly egoism."[133] In her reflections on dystrophy and the distrofik, Ginzburg noted the way hunger degraded people, made them cruel, and incapable of sacrifice. "Dystrophy, the emaciated pharaonic cow, devoured everything—friendship, ideology, cleanliness, shame, the intelligentsia habit of not stealing whatever is lying out. But more than everything love. Love disappeared from the city, much like sugar or matches."[134] "Dystrophy," she writes, "destroyed [the person] much earlier than death."[135]

It was precisely these behavioral and moral associations, overlaid on the purely physical connotations of the term, that made "dystrophy" such a resonant term in Leningrad during the blockade. The Leningrad philologist V. S. Liublinskii wrote to his wife in late July 1942 that

> in the past six months the intonation and meaning of the term "distrofik" has changed. Initially (in January–February) it had a ring of pointed compassion to it; it signified a victim of hunger, it summoned help and compassion or perhaps some kind of exemption; then it started to acquire more ironic notes, people began to speak of "moral" and "moderate" distrofiks—and not only with regard to those who had debased themselves or, under the very real pretext of lack of strength, turned away from their duties [*obiazannosti*] (even to themselves); finally, over the past several months, as the number of two-legged distrofiks has

---

133. Ibid., pp. 272, 275. On the place of the distrofik in Ginzburg's writing and thought see also Emily S. Van Buskirk, "Varieties of Failure: Lydia Ginzburg's Character Analyses from the 1930s and 1940s," in Emily S. Van Buskirk and A. L. Zorin, eds., *Lydia Ginzburg's Alternative Literary Identities: A Collection of Articles and New Translations* (Oxford: Peter Lang, 2012), pp. 153–157; Sandomirskaia, "A Politeia in Besiegement."

134. Ginzburg, *Prokhodiashchie kharaktery*, pp. 272–273.

135. Ibid., p. 25.

240   Rebecca Manley

diminished, the term has come to acquire a purely disparaging meaning; increasingly, it conveys disdain (people use it to refer to a low-power enterprise [*malomoshchnoe predpriatiie*] or an overly small piece of something)."[136]

Liublinskii's observations are borne out by a wide range of contemporary sources, which underscore the varying uses to which the term "distrofik" was put. At times, "distrofik" could be employed self-deprecatingly, as when a colleague told Liubov Shaporina, concerned that she was submitting her work late, "don't worry, we are all distrofiks."[137] More commonly, however, it was used to denigrate. Diarists frequently noted how "distrofik" had become a term of "mockery," "insult" and had acquired a "contemptuous, abusive connotation."[138] "'Distrofik' has become a swear word at work, on the streets, in trams," Aleksandr Boldyrev noted in a diary entry in the fall of 1942. "Distrofiks are despised, tormented."[139] As Boldyrev's comments suggest, the term's metamorphosis into an insult reflected the increasingly hostile view of distrofiks among blockade residents. By the summer of 1942, the distrofik was no longer an object of compassion but one of contempt. Distrofiks were resented, in the words of Sof'ia Ostrovskaia, "because they have not gotten well on time or because they have not died on time." They were regarded as "former people . . . walking to their death."[140] This conception of the distrofik has led a number of scholars to note its affinity with the "Muselmann," a term

136. Letter of July 29, 1942, in V. S. Liublinskii, "Blokadnye dnevniki. Vospominaniia. Stikhi. Pis'ma," in Ts. I. Grin, G. V. Miheeva, and L. A. Shilov, eds., *V pamiat' ushedshikh i vo slavu zhivushchikh: Pisma chitatelei s fronta, dnevniki i vospominaniia sotrudnikov Publichnoi biblioteki, 1941–1945* (St. Petersburg: Rossiiskaia natstional'naia biblioteka, 1995), p. 180. See the similar observations made by V. I. Vinokurov in his diary in S. Bernev and S. V. Chernov, eds., *Blokadnye dnevniki i dokumenty, Arkhiv Bol'shogo Doma* (St. Petersburg: Evropeiskii Dom, 2004), p. 282.

137. Shaporina, *Dnevnik,* p. 384.

138. See, respectively, entry of July 27, 1943, in V. Bazanova, "Vchera bylo deviat' trevog," *Neva,* no. 1 (1999): 143; entry of July 9, 1942, in P. N. Luknitskii, *Leningrad deistvuet . . . Frontovoi dnevnik,* vol. 2 (Moscow: Sovetskii pisatel', 1964), p. 259; entry of August 1942 in G. A. Kulagin, *Dnevnik i pamiat'* (Leningrad: Lenizdat', 1978), p. 285.

139. Diary entry of September 22, 1942, in Boldyrev, *Osadnaia zapis',* p. 164.

140. Cited, respectively, in Peri, "Minds under Siege," p. 166; P. Barskova, "Avgust, kotorogo ne bylo, i mekhanizm kalendarnoi travmy: razmyshleniia o blokadnykh khronologiiakh," *Nezavisimyi filologicheskii zhurnal* 116 (2012), http://magazines.russ.ru/nlo/2012/116/b10.html.

Nutritional Dystrophy

used in Auschwitz and other Nazi concentration camps and later defined by survivors as the "living dead," "the drowned," "the prisoner who was giving up and was given up by his comrades, . . . a staggering corpse."[141] It is in many ways an apt analogy. Yet even as the figure of the distrofik came to resemble, in popular usage, the "drowned" of the concentration camp universe, perceptions of the distrofik in Leningrad were shaped by moral, social, and political values that imbued his or her behavior and the term itself with other shades of meaning.

Among the changing connotations of "distrofik" outlined by Liublinskii, the addition of the qualifier "moral" merits special attention. The phrase "moral dystrophy" entered into widespread circulation in 1942. While it could be used simply to denote the general moral degradation that accompanied dystrophy, it was commonly used to deride specific forms of behavior, particularly at the workplace.[142] Moral distrofiks were people who whined and complained. As a production director at the Kalinin factory noted of a colleague in a letter to his wife in the summer of 1942: "something has happened to him, he is no longer himself, he is a whiner [nytik]), a 'moral distrofik,' as we call such people."[143] The term was also commonly applied to people who reneged on their duties "under the cover" of starvation. This was the way Kseniia Polzikova-Rubets used the term in the spring of 1942 to describe friends who had decided to

---

141. These characterizations come from Aldo Carpi, Primo Levi, and Jean Amery cited in Giorgio Agamben, *Remnants of Auschwitz: The Witness and the Archive* (New York: Zone Books, 1999), pp. 41, 44. On the figure of the Muselmann in Nazi camps, see ibid., pp. 41–86. On the increasing hostility toward distrofiks and the affinity of the distrofik with the Muselmann, see Peri, "Minds under Siege," pp. 166–167; Barskova, "Avgust, kotorogo ne bylo." On hostile attitudes see also S. V. Iarov, *Blokadnaia etika: Predstavleniia o morali v Leningrade v 1941–1942 gg.* (St. Petersburg: Nestor-Istoriia, 2011), pp. 245–247.

142. Lidiia Ginzburg used the term in the first sense. In all her blockade-related writing, the phrase "moral dystrophy" appears only twice. I would argue that the minor place the phrase occupies in Ginzburg's prose reflects her belief that moral degradation was an integral part of dystrophy itself, something that could be avoided only by those who were fortunate enough to escape starvation. Ginzburg, *Prokhodiashchie kharaktery*, pp. 69, 246. On moral dystrophy see also Peri, "Minds under Siege," pp. 168–170.

143. V. M. Samoilov, letter of June 21, 1942, in Inessa Lomakina, *Nasha biografiia: Ocherki istorii proizvodstvennogo ob'edineniia 'Zavod imeni Kalinina,' 1869–1989,* ed. G. A. Kapitonova (Leningrad: Lenizdat, 1991), p. 312.

leave the city. Bitter about their claims that they were unable to return a bed to her due to "dystrophy," betrayed by their failure to try to bring her with them, and indignant that people who were "needed" (she was a doctor) would depart at all, she summed up their behavior with one short phrase: "moral dystrophy."[144] The phrase was deployed in a similar fashion by the second in command in the city's party leadership, who charged that the endless conversations "about the people's hunger, about emaciation, about how it is impossible to do anything" were but an attempt by party members to "mask [their] own inactivity and lack of desire to organize anything. . . . We call these kind of people 'moral distrofiks,' that is, people whose moral spirit has cracked."[145] From this vantage point, moral distrofiks were, as Ol'ga Berggol'ts put it in a radio address in early 1943, people who "find a thousand excuses to shirk from the common work."[146] In all these cases, the term had a sociopolitical valence and was used to denigrate people who hid behind their physical emaciation (actual, or as the blockade progressed, allegedly ostensible), using it as an excuse for inactivity. This was precisely the way the term was deployed by the director of the Leningrad documentary film studio at a meeting of front-line film directors in May, 1942: speaking of one of his Leningrad colleagues, he noted that "he was a coward, he was afraid of shots, he did everything he could to weasel his way out of work. We had dystrophy, an illness from starvation. But some had moral dystrophy. That's what he had."[147]

As these examples suggest, the very concept of "moral dystrophy" was premised upon the belief that the distrofik could and should rise above the apathy, egoism, and indifference that many doctors and residents described as integral elements of the condition. It served at once to disparage those who had manifestly failed in this regard, and to

---

144. Note that Polzikova-Rubets used the term *nravstvennaia* rather than the more common *moral'naia* to denote "moral dystrophy." Polzikova-Rubets, *Dnevnik uchitelia blokadnoi shkoly*, pp. 58–59.

145. A. A. Kuznetsov, cited in Nikita Lomagin, *Neizvestnaia blokada*, vol. 1 (St. Petersburg: Neva, 2002), p. 110.

146. Ol'ga Berggol'ts, *Dnevnye zvezdy; Govorit Leningrad* (Moscow: Pravda, 1990), p. 240.

147. V. I. Fomin, ed., *Kino na voine: dokumenty i svidetel'stva* (Moscow: Materik, 2005), p. 174.

Nutritional Dystrophy

reassure: the concept of moral dystrophy implied a choice. It suggested that the degradation of the person was not inevitable; that bravery, self-sacrifice, and devotion could coexist with mass starvation; and that what Khvilitskaia described as "principled, ethical" behavior was indeed possible. The concept allowed party leaders and poets alike to cast the survivors of the siege (those who had not succumbed to "moral dystrophy") as "heroic defenders" of the city. It also served as an important foil against which those who had suffered the travails of starvation were able to assert their continued humanity: they had been distrofiks, but had not, as Liubov Shaporina noted of friends, "morally dystrophied" or, as Liublinskii wrote of himself, "become a moral distrofik."[148] In many ways, it was the concept of "moral dystrophy," with its suggestion that moral degradation was a matter of individual spirit or moral fiber, that made it possible to conceive of the blockaded city, where almost everyone had suffered from starvation, as a preserve of "moral purity" and of spirited resistance to the Germans.[149]

Having entered into popular speech, "dystrophy" acquired a range of meanings that built on but also went beyond its medical usage. Depending on the context, "dystrophy" served not only to describe a physical or psychological condition or to diagnose an illness, but also to excuse, to insult, or to indict. Even as the term came to be applied to objects as diverse as disorderly rooms, halting trams, and meager cigarettes, dystrophy and the figure of the distrofik continued to stand at the center of reflections on hunger.[150] In both medical circles and among the population at large, they remained powerful ways of talking both about the transformations wrought by hunger upon the human body and mind and

---

148. On these usages see the diary entry of July 17, 1943, in Shaporina, *Dnevnik,* pp. 402–403; and Liublinskii in a letter to his wife dated July 29, 1942, in Liublinskii, "Blokadnye dnevniki," p. 179.

149. On the retrospective construction of the blockaded city as a realm of moral purity see Kirschenbaum, *The Legacy of the Siege of Leningrad,* pp. 107–108.

150. See A. I. Vinokurov in Bernev and Chernov, *Blokadnye dnevniki i dokumenty,* p. 282. M. V. Mashkova, "Iz blokadnykh zapisei," in Ts. I. Grin, G. V. Mikheeva, and L. A. Shilov, eds., *V pamiat' ushedshikh i vo slavu zhivushchikh: Pisma chitatelei s fronta, dnevniki i vospominaniia sotrudnikov Publichnoi biblioteki, 1941–1945* (St. Petersburg: Rossiiskaia natstional'naia biblioteka, 1995), p. 110.

244   *Rebecca Manley*

about the relationship between hunger and questions of morality, fortitude, and patriotism.

BEYOND LENINGRAD

Nutritional dystrophy is inextricably linked to the siege of Leningrad,
yet it also points to the way the experience in Leningrad informed conceptions of hunger beyond Leningrad and the Leningrad Front. The term
came into use in the Soviet rear as early as the summer of 1942, when
regional statistical bureaus started to petition the central statistical administration for feedback on how to categorize death from emaciation,
which was not, at the outset of the war, afforded its own category in mortality statistics. As officials in the Molotov statistical bureau, who had
thus far lumped deaths from emaciation into the "other" category, wrote:
"Because this diagnosis is frequently made, especially in recent months,
we ask whether we are correctly situating it?" After consulting with the
commissariat of health, a decision was made to record such deaths in a
category of their own: nutritional dystrophy.[151]

Although statisticians in Leningrad failed to comply with the new
ruling, and the number of deaths from nutritional dystrophy there thus
went unrecorded, both the term and the condition it sought to describe
clearly emanated from Leningrad. The sharp spike in deaths from starvation observed in Molotov and in Vologda, from which a similar request was issued, was in no small measure due to the influx of evacuees
from the besieged city. Soon, however, what some referred to as a "Leningrad disease" would expand beyond the borders of Leningrad and its
evacuated diaspora. Within a year, "nutritional dystrophy" began to
appear in NKVD and party reports on cases of starvation in the Soviet
rear that had nothing to do with Leningrad. In the spring of 1943, for
instance, the director of the Amur railway line reported a "rise in

---

151. Cherepenina, "Assessing the Scale of Famine and Death in the Besieged
City," p. 40. The decision was disseminated to all regional statistical bureaus in a letter
of July 20, 1942, with the injunction that the number of deaths due to "avitaminoses
and dystrophy," allotted the number 83a in the cause of death charts by the People's
Commissariat of Health, be included in the overall statistics on the number of deaths,
but be recorded separately in a secret addendum. RGAE, f. 1562, op. 329, d. 805, ll. 162–65.

Nutritional Dystrophy 245

sickness from elementary [*sic*] dystrophy," adding in parentheses "edemas caused by malnutrition [*nedoedaniia*]."[152] By 1944, peasants and workers in far-flung regions of the Union were being entered on registries as victims of "nutritional dystrophy" or increasingly, simply "dystrophy."[153]

The emergence of cases of "nutritional dystrophy" deep in the Soviet interior clearly reflected the difficult material conditions of the time: as Donald Filtzer demonstrates in his contribution to this volume, 1943 saw a spike in cases of starvation in the rear. The fact that these cases were being recorded under the heading of "dystrophy," however, underscores just how central the experience in Leningrad was in defining medical terminology and practice in the Soviet Union as a whole. By the summer of 1943, the term from Leningrad was already sufficiently widespread to figure prominently in a set of instructions issued by the Commissariat of Health on "the diagnosis and treatment of general malnutrition." Whereas the initial version of the instructions, issued in June 1943, presented the illness resulting from insufficient food as one "known by the name of edema disease, protein-deficiency edema or nutritional dystrophy," an amendment to the instructions issued later that year referred only to "nutritional dystrophy," inserting the other terms in parentheses as "previous names."[154] The change in emphasis is telling: by the end of 1943, "nutritional dystrophy" had emerged, in the words of one contemporary publication, as "the generally accepted term" to denote an illness that was no longer simply a concern in Leningrad, but had become an all-Union medical issue.[155] As a doctor put it at a conference held in Moscow in 1944, "there is not a corner in our Soviet Union where material did not accumulate on the various manifestations of the dystrophic process."[156] Hence the need for instructions on the topic.

---

152. Report to the Central Committee, April 21, 1943, in A. I. Livshin and I. B. Orlov, eds., *Sovetskaia povsednevnost' i massovoe soznanie 1939–1945* (Moscow: ROSSPEN, 2003), pp. 188–189.

153. See, for example, reports in G. Kessler and G. E. Kornilov, *Kolkhoznaia zhizn' na Urale, 1935–1953* (Moscow: ROSSPEN, 2006), pp. 419, 449.

154. See GARF, f. 8009, op. 5, d. 235, l. 2, and ibid. op. 2, d. 589, l. 4.

155. Shnitser, "Alimentarnaia distrofiia," 32.

156. GARF, f. 8009, op. 2, d. 629, l. 92.

The instructions, drawn up by the Institute of Nutrition and building on similar instructions issued by the Sanitary Division of the Red Army the previous year, were penned "with the goal of establishing the correct diagnosis and therapy" for illnesses resulting from insufficient food. They aimed to standardize and disseminate what doctors had learned in the city under siege and to redress the "hazy" ideas about dystrophy currently in circulation. As Miron Semenovich Vovsi, chief physician for the Red Army, put it at a meeting of the Scientific Medical Soviet convened to approve the instructions, "[they] are the fruit of the tragedy that befell us, and especially Leningrad, where we unfortunately acquired a lot of experience in questions of malnutrition. It seems to me, given that similar illnesses have been encountered in various places and that, as long as the war continues, this suffering may appear again, doctors should have an understanding of it."[157]

Vovsi was not the only one to recognize the broader relevance of the Leningrad research. Indeed, his proposal to the Medical Soviet came just one week after it had convened to discuss the work of the Leningrad Institute of Experimental Medicine in a meeting that affirmed the value and relevance of its research. When one member of the soviet had questioned whether it was "worth it" to pursue the study of dystrophy, those present had rushed to dystrophy's defense, citing not only the documentary, historical value of the research, discussed above, but also its relevance to the postwar period. By way of a rejoinder, one participant approvingly related a recent conversation with a member of the institute, who reportedly said: "comrades, let's not forget the postwar. . . . In the occupied regions that are liberated, what do you think we will find? Do you think that children and adults are eating well there?" The research of the institute would, it stood to reason, not only contribute to "the history of science" but be "directly brought into the postwar era," put to use in treating the populations of liberated territories. The subsequent two speakers made similar points, noting that the "data collected in Leningrad" would enable doctors in the Red Army to develop "practical mea-

---

157. Ibid., d. 543, l. 13. Vovsi had spent time on the Leningrad Front and had been among the consultants for the instructional film on nutritional dystrophy prepared in the city only shortly before this meeting.

Nutritional Dystrophy

sures of aid" in liberated territories, and affirming that "this misfortune must be a fortune for others."[158] Similar views were articulated in Leningrad itself by health professionals who, as early as December 1942, projected that the city's encounter with "the bony hand of hunger" would furnish Soviet doctors with the knowledge necessary to treat the populations of liberated territories, victims of the Fascists' murderous policy of "killing people with hunger."[159]

While there was general agreement about the relevance of dystrophy research to liberated territories, where the enemy sought to "kill [the population] with hunger," there was considerable discomfort about its application deep in the Soviet rear, far from the enemy's reach. At the meeting of the Medical Soviet noted above, even those who heartily endorsed the study of dystrophy in Leningrad expressed unease about its study in the rear. Professor Rakhmanov, for instance, praised the heroic work of doctors in Leningrad, but was sharply critical of its study in the rear. "Now when this phenomenon is studied in many rear institutions, in the deep rear, where the phenomenon of dystrophy does not exist and where this study is unnecessary and can be explained only as a fashion [*moda*]—against this kind of study one must object."[160] Even Dr. Vovsi, who shepherded the instructions intended for distribution in the rear through the approval process, betrayed a certain apprehension about the public dissemination of information on the topic. Noting that "there is of course nothing secret here," he nonetheless sought to limit the diffusion of the instructions by making them "for office use only." When Professor Sysin, a longtime proponent of sanitary education, questioned the wisdom of this limitation, Vovsi replied that "we don't want this to be for sale in every kiosk."[161] Dystrophy thus remained a sensitive topic.

158. Ibid., d. 542, ll. 19, 21.

159. N. D Nikiforov, at a conference of Leningrad doctors, in TsGASPb, f. 9156, op. 4, d. 315, l. 38. Dr. Tur articulated a similar view in 1944 at a conference in Moscow. See GARF, f. 8009, op. 2, d. 629, l. 55.

160. Ibid., d. 542, l. 17.

161. Vovsi also justified the need for the instructions with reference to the "undoubted tendency to exaggerate the purity and intensity of nutritional disorders." GARF, f. 8009, op. 2, d. 543, l. 13.

Despite the reservations, however, the Soviet medical establishment, represented by the People's Commissariat of Health, the Medical Soviet, the Institute of Nutrition, and the Sanitary Division of the army, worked together to render the findings from Leningrad and the Leningrad Front accessible to the doctors who would need them, who were located not only in the yet to be liberated territories, but deep in the Soviet rear. The instructions mentioned above and other specialized publications were only one venue through which this took place. The medical terminology and expertise accrued in Leningrad and on the Leningrad Front were further diffused to the rest of the country through the evacuation of Leningrad doctors to the rear, chief among them the esteemed physician Georgii Fedorovich Lang, whose relocation to Moscow and appointment as Chairman of the All-Union Society of Physicians made him particularly influential. It was Lang who had recommended Dr. Vovsi's appointment as head physician for the Red Army, and Lang's first few months in Moscow were spent in the apartment of his colleague and friend.[162]

Medical conferences further ensured the diffusion of the Leningrad research. Researchers from Leningrad presented their findings to colleagues in Moscow on a number of occasions, and specialized conferences organized by the People's Commissariat of Health brought researchers from different cities, including Leningrad, together to address the problem of dystrophy.[163] Such was the importance accorded the illness that the first wartime conference of physicians, held in Gor'kii in January, 1943, devoted an entire day to questions of nutritional dystrophy and avitaminoses. Dr. Lang, in what was effectively a keynote address, made a determined case for the use of the term "dystrophy" and offered what the chairman Dr. Strazhesko described as "an exhaustive description of the clinical picture" of dystrophy "based on his own observations in Leningrad."[164] Among the participants were Dr. Vovsi, who would go on to

162. Borodulin, G. F. Lang, pp. 96, 98.

163. On the role of the People's Commissariat of Health in organizing conferences, see GARF, f. 8009, op. 2, d. 629; and Dr. Iu. A. Mendeleva in Simmons and Perlina, Writing the Siege of Leningrad, p. 159.

164. Lang argued that "we must once and for all settle on the term 'nutritional dystrophy' as the most appropriate." Lang, "Klinika alimentarnoi distrofii," p. 406. N. D. Strazhesko, Trudy pervoi terapevticheskoi konferentsii (Gor'kii, 1943), p. 510.

Nutritional Dystrophy

issue the instructions on dystrophy several months later, and representatives from twenty-five different provinces as well as the front.

At conferences such as this, doctors working in the rear contributed to the growing body of knowledge about dystrophy, drawing on their experiences in cities ranging from Moscow to Tashkent, from Erevan to Sverdlovsk. In the rear, the diagnosis of dystrophy could sometimes be more complicated than in Leningrad. In Leningrad, it was the universal affliction. In the rear, as one doctor noted, "nutritional dystrophy creeps up in an underhanded way. . . . The patient usually cannot say when the illness began. Most frequently patients talk about general weakness and especially weakness in the legs that make moving hard. People who pay little attention to their sensations sometimes only notice the illness when edemas appear."[165]

While in Leningrad dystrophy was a matter of life and death, and fell squarely within the domain of doctors, in the rear dystrophy was treated not only as a medical problem, but as a problem of workplace productivity. Across the country, factory management was confronted with alarming declines in productivity as workers had to be given often repeated work relief. It was in this context that the Sverdlovsk Institute of Labor Hygiene and Professional Illness turned to the issue of dystrophy in the fall of 1943. Labor hygienists presented the war as a kind of perfect storm for the development of dystrophy in its combination of inevitable food shortages with a heightened demand for more intensive work. As N. A. Vigdorchik, who had been evacuated to Sverdlovsk from Leningrad, put it at a conference devoted to the topic, given the efforts required to defeat the enemy, "one cannot think about a short work day, about sufficient breaks at work, about a normal work regime."[166]

For labor hygienists, the risk of developing dystrophy was correlated not with gender or age, but rather with the nature of the work performed.[167] Heavy labor invariably made workers more likely to develop dystrophy,

165. GARF, f. A428, op. 47, d. 1408, l. 10.
166. Ibid., l. 7.
167. On this and the conference proceedings more broadly see Filtzer, *Hazards*, pp. 181–182.

and labor hygienists warned that "wartime conditions have made some previously light jobs much harder." For labor hygienists, then, food was only one element in the development of dystrophy. Equally important was the type of labor performed, the length of the walk to work (of 116 patients who were asked about this, the vast majority spent one and a half hours or more getting to and from work, and some as much as four), and the state of heating in factories and dormitories. Vigdorchik stressed that initially, many distrofiks could continue to work, mobilizing their "energy reserves" by sheer force of "will, spirit, and conscious effort." Nonetheless, he warned that ultimately, without treatment, no amount of effort or will would be able to overcome the "energy deficit" and that the individual would find himself unable to work. Vigdorchik recommended that diagnoses must be given in the earliest stages of the illness and that treatment involve not simply respite from work, but also, crucially, additional food. He also cautioned against short stints on the sick list: they almost invariably led to patients cycling in and out of work, never fully recovering.[168]

Vigdorchik's recommendations were incorporated into the revised version of the People's Commissariat of Health's instructions on the diagnosis and treatment of nutritional dystrophy in November 1943. From the outset, the instructions had embodied the key principles of diagnosis and treatment elaborated in Leningrad. Thus the section on treatment emphasized the importance of proteins, recommending the use of yeasts as well as preparations such as casein, and counseled that feeding should be frequent and in small quantities, "not less than five to six times a day."[169] Now an entire section on "prophylactics" was added stressing the need to "diminish the energy expenditures at work" of patients suffering from dystrophy, and recommending a host of measures, some of which, as Wendy Goldman's contribution to this volume makes clear, were already in effect, most notably "the organization of subsidiary agriculture at the workplace, as well as individual gardens."[170] As these rec-

168. GARF, f. A428, op. 47, d. 1408, ll. 7–9, 11, 14–15.

169. GARF, f. 8009, op. 5, d. 235, l. 8.

170. Other measures, to be sure, were alas far from the norm, such as "the provision of workers with vegetables, especially ones rich in vitamins, the preparation of yeasts in quantities sufficient to include them in the daily ration of workers; the preparation of

Nutritional Dystrophy 251

ommendations suggest, the Soviet medical establishment was well aware that the principal cause of nutritional dystrophy was insufficient food. Labor hygienists, moreover, addressed not only the pathology of starvation, but the broader social context in which it developed. Dystrophy never acquired nearly the same cultural resonance in the rear as it did in Leningrad. Nonetheless, it became an important term in the lexicon of sanitary inspectors and state officials. While the ability to provide for the ill was sharply constrained, sanitary inspectors and trade union officials regularly mobilized the new vocabulary to insist on better rations for the ill and proper treatment.[171]

It is perhaps not surprising, given the dire conditions, that "nutritional dystrophy" also emerged as an important term in the lexicon of the Gulag during the war. Conditions in the camps deteriorated dramatically in the first two years of the war. The workday increased even as food supplies dwindled. In 1942, the hardest year of the war, one quarter of all inmates perished from hunger and disease. By war's end, over 800,000 had died.[172] Many of them had died, at least according to official statistics, of "nutritional dystrophy."

"Nutritional dystrophy" was sufficiently central to the lexicon of the Gulag that Jacques Rossi included it in his "Gulag handbook." Rossi mistakenly presents "dystrophy" as a "term, incomprehensible to the uninitiated, invented by the administration of the Gulag in the mid- 1930s to replace the old formulation 'from emaciation' in mortality statistics."[173] A more revealing account of the genealogy and significance of the term appears in the work of Gulag survivor Varlam Shalamov. "Nutritional

---

pine extracts and extracts from herbs; oversight of cafeterias and the composition of rational menus, over the correct use of food items." GARF, f. 8009, op. 2, d. 589, l. 6.

171. See, for example, GARF, f. A-482, op. 47, d. 2370, l. 1; GARF, f. 5451, op. 43, d. 236, ll. 218, 220, 240–42.

172. Steven A. Barnes, "All for the Front, All for Victory! The Mobilization of Forced Labor in the Soviet Union during World War Two," *International Labor & Working-Class History,* no. 58 (Fall 2000): p. 242. See also V. N. Zemskov, "Smertnost' zakliuchennykh v 1941–1945 g.g.," in *Liudskie poteri SSSR v period vtoroi mirovoi voiny. Sbornik statei* (St. Petersburg: BLITs, 1995), pp. 174–177.

173. Jacques Rossi, *Spravochnik po Gulagu: Istoricheskii slovar' sovetskikh penitentsiarnykh institutsii i terminov, sviazannykh s prinuditel'nym trudom* (Moscow: Prosvet, 1991), p. 102.

dystrophy," remarks Doctor Kuz'menko in one of Shalamov's tales, "is a terrible thing. Only after the Leningrad blockade was it called by its real name in the camps. Before that the diagnosis was avitaminosis, pellagra, emaciation from dysentery."[174] In this story and others, Shalamov rightly traces the origins of the term not to the Gulag but to the Leningrad blockade. More significantly, in Shalamov's account, the label "dystrophy" serves not to mask the plight of the starving, but to acknowledge it, to name it. As he notes of the diagnosis of nutritional dystrophy in another story, "during the war it was permitted to call hunger 'hunger.'"[175]

The term appears to have come into circulation in the Gulag in late 1943, when the NKVD distinguished dystrophy as a distinct illness, and a short pamphlet on nutritional dystrophy and pellagra was made available to camp medical personnel.[176] The pamphlet was penned by Dr. Iosif Abramovich Kassirskii, who served as head physician of the medical-sanitary division of the Commissariat of Transportation during the war and who spent part of the war on the Leningrad Front. The preface, by the head of the Gulag Sanitary Division, D. M. Loidin, insisted on the importance of distinguishing nutritional dystrophy from pellagra and other avitaminoses. The pamphlet rehearsed the etiology, clinical picture, complications, pathological anatomy, and treatment of nutritional dystrophy. Over two thousand copies were made, and

174. Shalamov, "Shakhmaty doktora Kuz'menko," p. 394. Shalamov himself was diagnosed with the condition in 1944, and spent several months in a Gulag hospital. See Lesniak, "Moi Shalamov."

175. Shalamov, "Perchatka," p. 288. See also Varlam Shalamov, "Veismanist," in *Sobranie sochinenii v shesti tomakh*, ed. I. Sirotinskaia (Moscow: Terra, 2004), vol. 1, pp. 538–545. Former Gulag inmate Iulii Margolin likewise presents the diagnosis of nutritional dystrophy as an acknowledgement of "a hungry death." Iu. B. Margolin, *Puteshestvie v stranu Ze-ka* (New York: Izd-vo im. Chekhova, 1952), p. 297.

176. Dystrophy makes its first appearance in the Gulag's annual reports on cause of death and illness only in 1944. In the two preceding years, the statistics seem to subsume all deficiency- related illnesses under the catch-all of "pellagra." That said, the term "dystrophy" appears to have come into use for clinical and administrative purposes in 1943. On cause of death statistics in 1944, see GARF, f. 9414, op. 1, d. 2796, ll. 92, 177; on 1942 and 1943, see GARF, f. 9414, op. 1, d. 2771, ll. 50, 60; Ibid, d. 2784, ll. 89–90, 106; and on administrative uses of the term, see GARF, f. 5446, op. 44, d. 9553, l. 7.

Nutritional Dystrophy

it was to be distributed widely across the medical facilities of the Gulag.[177]

The production and circulation of this pamphlet suggest the ways in which research generated in Leningrad and on the Leningrad Front was imported into the Gulag. Notably, the Gulag was not itself conceived as an experimental laboratory. Beyond a handful of studies examining the effects of labor therapy, which ranged from the exploitative to the more properly therapeutic, hunger was not an object of organized study within the Gulag. Indeed, the studies of starvation conducted in Nazi concentration camps by German doctors had no parallel in the Soviet Gulag, despite the large number of starving inmates.[178] "Nutritional dystrophy" entered the Gulag as part of an attempt to improve the medical services there, and to endow Gulag medical practitioners with the capacity to name and to treat the afflictions resulting from insufficient food. This is not to suggest that their aims were purely therapeutic. Gulag medicine sought to maximize prisoner productivity within the constraints posed by limited foodstuffs, extreme cold, and grueling physical labor. Nonetheless, the diagnosis of nutritional dystrophy opened up new opportunities for Gulag doctors, and thus helped shape the course of Gulag medicine. It is telling that when Moshe Prywes, a Polish doctor imprisoned in the Gulag at the start of the war, discovered the pamphlet by Kassirskii and Loidin among a stack of papers in the Gulag hospital where he worked, he was overjoyed: the pamphlet allowed him to identify the illness that afflicted his fellow prisoners (in this case pellagra) and devise more

---

177. I. A. Kassirskii, "Alimentarnaia distrofiia i pellagra (diagnostika, klinika i terapiia)," (Izdaniie GULAGa NKVD SSSR, 1943), in GARF, f. 9414, op. 2, d. 164, ll. 1–17. My information on Kassirskii himself comes from http://kassirsky.ru/.

178. I am grateful to Dan Healey for drawing my attention to these experiments and for sharing his unpublished work on Gulag medicine with me. On attempts to study the effects of labor on dystrophy patients in the late war and postwar years, see Dan Healey, "Combatting 'Enforced Idleness' in Gulag Hospitals: Labour as 'Therapy' in Stalin's Forced Labor Camps, 1943–1953," paper presented at the Russian and Soviet Cultural and Social History Seminar, University of Oxford, January 23, 2013. On the relative paucity of research into nutritional deficiencies, see Dan Healey, "Medical Investigations in Stalin's Gulag: A Research Culture behind Barbed Wire, 1930–1956," paper presented at the Munk Centre for Global Affairs, University of Toronto, February 3, 2011.

254   *Rebecca Manley*

effective treatments for dystrophy, pellagra, and other vitamin deficiencies. Many years later, as an established doctor in Israel, Prywes still had his copy of the pamphlet.[179]

As diagnoses of dystrophy multiplied in the camps, it became common to speak not only of dystrophy, but also, as in Leningrad, of distrofiks. The figure of the distrofik became a symbol of the afflictions of camp inmates, and of the way that the organized hunger of the Gulag laid waste to the human body and transformed the mind. To be sure, the term "distrofik" never acquired the currency in the Gulag that it had in Leningrad. By the time the war broke out, the Gulag had already generated its own term to designate those who were on their last legs, wasted away by hunger—the *dokhodiaga*.[180] Definitions of the dokhodiaga bear striking resemblances to the Muselmann of the Nazi camps, a similarity that Primo Levi commented on after reading Solzhenitsyn: the Muselmann, he wrote, "is mirrored exactly, even in its cynical irony, by the Russian term dokodjaga, literally 'come to an end,' 'concluded.'"[181] While "distrofik" had a distinctly medical valence in the Gulag, it nonetheless came to be used synonymously with "dokhodiaga," supplementing though never displacing the older and more pervasive term.[182]

179. Prywes and Chertok, *Prisoner of Hope*, pp. 136–137.

180. The term *dokhodiaga* features prominently in the testimonies of survivors and is included in every dictionary or lexicon of Gulag terminology. The first published instance of the term I have found dates to 1940, and is in a book written by a former inmate who made his way to China. In the glossary that accompanies his book, he defines the *dokhodiaga* as someone who "intends to get all the way to socialism," "a person who is wasted away due to insufficient food and excessive work." Igor' Volkov, *Solntse vskhodit na vostoke*, vol. 2 (Kharbin: Izd. Monarkhicheskago ob'edineniia, 1940), p. 301. A similar etymology was noted by another former inmate in emigration after the war. Vladimir Volkov, *It Happens in Russia: Seven Years Forced Labour in the Siberian Goldfields* (London: Eyre and Spottiswoode, 1951), p. 181. Note that the term *dokhodiaga* would not have been known to the population of Leningrad during the war, although there is some evidence that it came to be used among Russian POWs in German camps. See Vasily Grossman, *Life and Fate*, trans. Robert Chandler (New York: New York Review Books, 2006), p. 33, and V. S. Varshavskii, *Sem' let: Povest'* (Paris: self-published, 1950), p. 198.

181. Primo Levi, *The Drowned and the Saved* (New York: Vintage International, 1989), p. 98.

182. As one memoirist put it, *dokhodiaga* "is the social designation of my status as a human being. There is also a medical designation—distrofik." V. Belousov, *Zapiski*

Nutritional Dystrophy

As the Red Army marched toward Berlin, Red Army doctors brought their knowledge of nutritional dystrophy with them. Red Army medical staff identified distrofiks among the liberated populations of Nazi camps and accorded them a special diet, building on knowledge gained by their experience in and around Leningrad and in evacuation hospitals in the rear.[183] At the same time, nutritional dystrophy entered into Soviet public discourse as a signature Nazi crime, the product of a deliberate starvation plan that was graphically communicated in the press through photographs of emaciated bodies. Medical and forensic expertise was marshaled to document the number and severity of cases for the Extraordinary Commission on Nazi Crimes, and the results of these reports were disseminated in the press. An article in *Pravda* entitled "German Doctors . . . Killed Soviet Prisoners of War with Hunger" described how "nutritional dystrophy in both its cachetic and edematous forms" had resulted from the inadequate camp rations.[184]

Nutritional dystrophy also figured among the evidence marshaled of Nazi crimes at Auschwitz. Indeed, the Soviet forensic medical commission at Auschwitz presented "nutritional dystrophy" as the "principal sickness" among the camp's survivors.[185] Its report devoted an entire section to the illness, and followed what its authors referred to as "the existing classification schemes," treating the "dry" and edematous forms separately and conforming to the three-stages formula first developed

---

dokhodiagi (Ashkhabad: Turkmenistan, 1992), p. 3. Jacques Rossi lists *dokhodiaga* as a synonym for *distrofik* under his treatment of the latter term. Rossi, *Spravochnik po Gulagu*, p. 102. In *The Gulag Archipelago*, Solzhenitsyn generally uses the term *distrofik* in explicitly medical contexts, but on occasion he uses the terms synonymously. See Aleksandr Solzhenitsyn, *Arkhipelag GULag*, vol. 3 (Paris: YMCA Press, 1975), p. 122.

183. The Sanitary Division of the Red Army issued its own directives on the diagnosis and treatment of nutritional dystrophy. These drew on the experience in and around Leningrad, although they also contained their own specificities (such as weight-loss measures to determine the stage of dystrophy), and were adapted to frontline conditions. See, for example, "Ukazaniia po raspoznavaniiu i lecheniiu rasstroistv obshchego pitaniia i avitaminozov," (Moscow: Medgiz, 1942); "Ukazaniia po raspoznavaniiu, lecheniiu i profilaktike alimentarnoi distrofii i avitaminozov," (Tashkent, 1944).

184. *Pravda*, August 3, 1944, p. 3. A photo of an emaciated Soviet prisoner of war accompanied the article.

185. GARF, f. 7021, op. 108, d. 18, l. 14.

in Leningrad.[186] Dystrophy figured in Soviet press descriptions of the survivors,[187] and in 1946 was showcased on an international stage as part of the proceedings at Nuremberg, where cases of "elementary [sic] dystrophy" among survivors of Auschwitz were presented as evidence of Nazi crimes.[188] Far from a euphemism, then, "nutritional dystrophy" served in these articles and legal proceedings to name the illness that resulted from the Nazi hunger plan, and to lend medical authority to claims of Nazi crimes. The term was sufficiently central to Red Army descriptions of the state of starving inmates at Auschwitz that when Soviet authorities commissioned Primo Levi and a fellow Italian Jewish survivor of Auschwitz, the physician Leonardo de Benedetti, to write a report on medical conditions in the camp, they presented their analysis of starvation under the rubric of "nutritional dystrophy."[189]

Given the centrality of the term in the Gulag, it is not surprising that German prisoners returning home in the years following the war brought the term "nutritional dystrophy" with them. "Dystrophy" became a key term, in the words of Frank Biess, in "the diagnostic arsenal of the German medical and psychiatric professions."[190] While German studies of dystrophy were based primarily on observations of returning POWs,

186. Ibid., l. 15. The genealogy of both the term and the three stages classification is openly acknowledged in a report of the Polish Commission charged with investigating Nazi crimes. In its description of a camp survivor at Auschwitz, the report's authors note that she had "the illness that doctors call *dystrophia alimentaris*. Following the terminology of Soviet doctors who base themselves on the experience from the era of the Leningrad blockade, it is nutritional dystrophy of the third degree." Archives Nationales de France, 736Mi/1, p. 2. I thank Nathalie Moine for sharing this material with me.

187. An article on the camp published only days before the war's end noted that over one quarter of the children were diagnosed with "nutritional dystrophy (extreme emaciation)." The article on "the murder of children" appeared in a two-page spread on the findings of the Extraordinary State Commission on German-Fascist Crimes at Auschwitz in *Pravda*, May 3, 1945, p. 3.

188. The Russian original was *alimentarnaia distrofiia*, but the translator rendered it as "elementary."

189. Primo Levi and Leonardo de Benedetti, *Auschwitz Report*, trans. Judith Woolf, ed. Robert S. C. Gordon (New York: Verso, 2006), pp. 47–49. On Levi's experiences at this time see Levi, *The Truce: A Survivor's Journey Home from Auschwitz* (London: Bodley Head, 1965).

190. Frank Biess, *Homecomings: Returning POWs and the Legacies of Defeat in Postwar Germany* (Princeton, N.J.: Princeton University Press, 2006), p. 71.

Nutritional Dystrophy

considered the paradigmatic victims of the affliction, they also drew in important ways on wartime research.[191] *Die Dystrophie,* for instance, by the Hamburg professor Dr. Heinrich Berning, was largely based on the experiments he conducted on Soviet prisoners of war in German captivity.[192] The work underscores the complexity of the postwar circulation of ideas and medical terminology. Hungry bodies traversed Europe during the war and its immediate aftermath, carrying not only the increasingly recognizable markers of starvation, but also new terms to name it. "Dystrophy" emerged as a potent way to name the affliction that seemed to characterize so many of the war's victims, but the term was used in different ways in different contexts. In postwar Germany, the term came to denote less the ravages of starvation than the peculiar apathy that characterized the former prisoners of war. According to Frank Biess, the diagnosis of dystrophy served to shift attention away from soldier's experiences of war to their experience in Soviet captivity, thus helping to fuel the discourse of German victimization.[193] It was also used to draw parallels between the plight of Germans in the Soviet Union and the plight of the victims of Nazism.[194]

In the immediate postwar years, the terms "dystrophy" and "distrofik" entered into more general circulation. Both terms were included in Ozhegov's Russian dictionary of 1949, marking "dystrophy's" passage from the more rarified world of foreign terms to mainstream Russian

191. Alice Autumn Weinreb, "Matters of Taste: The Politics of Food and Hunger in Divided Germany 1945–1971," (PhD dissertation, University of Michigan, 2009), p. 166.

192. Biess, *Homecomings,* p. 74. There were other notable postwar studies with a similar genealogy. See ibid. and Weinreb, "Matters of Taste," pp. 113–114.

193. Biess, *Homecomings,* pp. 72–73.

194. In postwar Germany there were heated debates about whether the victims of Nazi concentration camps should be considered under the umbrella of "Dystrophie" (like the returning German POWs) or whether they in fact suffered from their own affliction. The first volume to address the afflictions of camp inmates and Nazism's victims included a Soviet contribution, which detailed the findings of Soviet doctors during the war. See Goukassian, "Hungerdystrophie," in Max Michel, ed., *Gesundheitsschäden durch Verfolgung und Gefangenschaft und ihre Spätfolgen. Zusammenstellung der Referate und Ergebnisse der Internationalen Sozialmedizinischen Konferenz über die Pathologie der Ehemaligen Deportierten und Internierten, 5.–7. Juni 1954 in Kopenhagen, und ergänzender Referate und Ergebnisse* (Frankfurt am Main: Röderberg-Verlag, 1955), pp. 133–134. On the volume more generally see Weinreb, "Matters of Taste," pp. 166–172.

speech, and subsequently in a Dictionary of Contemporary Russian Literary Language.[195] The diffusion of literature about the siege of Leningrad undoubtedly played a role in this process. When Ol'ga Berggol'ts traveled to Moscow in the spring of 1942, she was shocked to find that Muscovites "had not heard anything about an illness called dystrophy. They asked me: is it fatal?" Such questions were unimaginable only a few years later. Early literary accounts of the blockade translated "dystrophy" into laymen's terms for the reading public: one might consider Inber's "Pulkovo Meridian," cited in the introduction to this chapter, or Aleksandr Fadeev's account of his visit to the blockaded city, published in 1944, in which he pauses at the first mention of the word: "It was the first time I heard this word 'distrofik,' derived from the word 'dystrophy,' signifying a terrible illness—starvation [*istoshchenie*]."[196]

The postwar diffusion of the term, however, also reflected other developments. In 1946, large swaths of the Soviet Union suffered from a devastating harvest failure. "Nutritional dystrophy" was used by doctors and officials in the Soviet Union to describe the state of the starving during the famine that ensued. Few of the doctors who spoke about the relevance of their research during the war could have imagined that it would need to be applied in the postwar period so close to home. The knowledge accrued during the war was quickly redeployed to treat the latest victims of starvation. In early 1947, for example, Dr. Kassirskii, head physician for the sanitary division of the Ministry of Transportation, prepared an abbreviated version of the directives he had drawn up in 1943 for use in the Gulag, on the basis of his experiences on the front, for use in the ministry's network of hospitals and clinics. Issued in mid-February

195. *Slovar' russkogo iazyka*, ed. S. I. Ozhegov and S. P. Obnorskii (Moscow: Gos. izd-vo inostrannykh i national'nykh slovarei, 1949); *Slovar' sovremennogo russkogo literaturnogo iazyka*, vol. 3 (Moscow: Izdatel'stvo Akademii nauk SSSR, 1954). p. 811. In these entries, "dystrophy" was defined in much the same way as in the prewar dictionary of foreign terms, with the notable addition of the term "emaciation" (or "malnutrition") in the literary dictionary. Moreover, the dictionaries included the term "distrofik," absent in the prewar dictionary and presented in the literary dictionary as a colloquial way of designating someone suffering from dystrophy.

196. Letter to G. P. Makogenko dated March 8, 1942, in Berggol'ts, Ol'ga. *Zapretnyi dnevnik*, p. 204; Aleksandr Fadeev, "Leningrad v dni blokady," in *Sobranie sochinenii v semi tomakh* (Moscow: Izdatel'stvo Khudozhestvennaia Literatura, 1969), vol. 4, p. 113.

Nutritional Dystrophy

1947, the directives were designed to ensure prompt and appropriate treatment of nutritional dystrophy and pellagra, with a view to "liquidating" the "isolated" cases and curing those who were already ill.[197] A mere one week later, a concise, twenty-two page overview of nutritional dystrophy penned by Dr. Gel'shtein was sent off to the press with a printing run of ten thousand. One might easily think that the short booklet was simply Gel'shtein's attempt to ensure that the research dimension of his wartime work was not lost for posterity (his previous publications, after all, had been in collected volumes or for internal medical use only). The timing of the publication, however, along with the fact that it was edited by Dr. Kassirskii, suggests that like Kassirskii's own directives, it was intended to meet more immediate needs.[198]

The famine of 1946–1947 also afforded some doctors an opportunity to complete research begun during the war: as Dr. Gubergrits explained in a letter to a ministry of health official, he had begun his research on dystrophy in Cheliabinsk during the war. At the time, convinced through trial and error that the depleted body was not always able to process the proteins it so desperately needed, he and his colleagues sought to find alternative ways to make proteins readily available. In wartime conditions, the only viable option was blood transfusion. What they really wanted to try—giving patients amino-acids, essentially proteins which had already been broken down—was simply not technically feasible at the time. By 1946, the technical obstacles had been overcome, and the postwar famine provided Gubergrits and his colleagues with renewed experimental possibilities. While at first the preparation was administered only to dogs, when these experiments proved successful, he extended them to the human population.[199] As he put it to the ministry official, "as you know, last year and in the first half of this year in Ukraine, such patients could be found." Dr. Vovsi was sufficiently impressed with his research that he recommended that the Medical Council "popularize" his results,

---

197. V. Zakharchenko and I. Kassirskii, *Ukazaniia po raspoznavaniiu i lecheniiu obshchikh rasstroistv pitaniia i avitaminozov* (Moscow: Transzheldorizdat', 1947), p. 6.

198. Gel'shtein, *Alimentarnaia distrofiia*. The same does not appear to be true of an important collection of Leningrad research on dystrophy published the same year. Chernorutskii, *Alimentarnaia distrofiia v blokirovannom Leningrade*.

199. GARF, f. 8009, op. 2, d. 1111, ll. 42, 8–11.

260   *Rebecca Manley*

and stressed their significance for the treatment of dystrophy along with a range of other illnesses.[200]

CONCLUSION

The war heralded a new openness about hunger's medical effects, and provided an opportunity to openly discuss afflictions that doctors had previously hardly dared write about: at the conference held in Gork'ii in early 1943, some participants explicitly compared what they were witnessing to 1933, and in the concluding remarks to the conference, N. D. Strazhesko, head of the Ukrainian Institute of Experimental Medicine and member of the Soviet Academy of Sciences, offered a corrective to some of the day's proceedings, drawing "in part on secondary literature, and in part on my own observations and research, conducted in the Ukraine in the hungry years [*golodnye gody*]."[201] Mention of these "hungry years" would have been unthinkable before the war, and even though Strazhesko himself published an article on edemas at the time, it was a lone exception. In 1932–1933, genuine research on starvation was simply not possible. Some fifteen years later, this was no longer the case. Between the famines following collectivization and the famines of 1946–1947 stood the war, which had transformed hunger into a legitimate arena of research. To be sure, starvation remained a sensitive subject, and the postwar famine was passed over in silence in the press. Nonetheless, under the heading of "dystrophy," it was now possible to identify the victims of starvation and even to treat them.[202] Researchers, moreover, could engage in genuine scientific debate. While discussion of hunger's causes was off limits, its consequences were not.

200. GARF, f. 8009, op. 2, d. 1111, ll. 42, 2--3.

201. In his contribution to the discussion at the 1943 Gor'kii conference, R. I. Zak noted, for instance, that wartime pellagra manifested itself quite differently from the pellagra he observed among civilians in 1933. *Trudy pervoi terapevticheskoi konferentsii* (Gor'kii, 1943), p. 504. See also N. D. Strazhesko's comments in the same volume, p. 510.

202. Aid for the starving was woefully inadequate, but not altogether nonexistent. See V. F. Zima, *Golod v SSSR 1946–1947 godov: Proiskhozhdenie i posledstviia* (Moscow: Institut Rossiiskoi Istorii RAN, 1996), pp. 129–144; Nicholas Ganson, *The Soviet Famine of 1946–47 in Global and Historical Perspective* (New York: Palgrave Macmillan, 2009), pp. 27–46.

Nutritional Dystrophy 261

Hunger thus emerged from the war as a genuine medical condition. Once seen by the Russian medical profession primarily as a problem of public hygiene, hunger had now become an illness in its own right. In this sense, the advent of "nutritional dystrophy" did indeed signal a medicalization of hunger. Any argument about medicalization, however, must be carefully qualified. At no time did physicians doubt that the causes of the illness they observed around them lay in a shortage of food. Nor did they believe that medicine offered a solution to hunger. Often starving themselves, doctors recognized that the only viable *solution* to the illness lay tragically beyond their reach: an improvement in the food supply. Beyond this, they could only hope to deepen their knowledge and improve treatment in an effort, in the words of Vladimir Garshin, to make "death help life."[203]

Wartime medical research on hunger sought not only to better understand its medical effects, but to document, in Chernorutskii's words, "life at the limit." Lidiia Ginzburg's *Notes of a Blockade Person,* begun in 1942 (and subsequently rewritten and rearranged), constituted another attempt to document the physiological and psychological effects of starvation. Ginzburg's work stands as an important testament to the way that the dire food shortages of the Second World War prompted new forms of reflection upon hunger. Like the city's doctors, Ginzburg used the term "dystrophy" not to mask the transformations wrought upon the "siege person," but to highlight them.

Chernorutksii, in his conclusion to an article about nutritional dystrophy, drew a contrast between "the limitless strength of our people's spirit, on the one hand, and the limits of the endurance of the human organism," both of which had been cast into sharp relief by the experience of the blockade.[204] Indeed, it was precisely the difficult material conditions that set the true strength of the "people's spirit" into relief. Wartime discourse celebrated the capacity of Soviet citizens to dedicate themselves to a higher moral plane. In this patriotic discourse, as in

---

203. This was the title of Garshin's memoirs of the blockade, which he completed in February 1944 and dedicated to his deceased wife. Garshin, "Tam gde smert' pomogaet zhizni."

204. Chernorutskii, "Problema alimintarnoi distrofii," p. 12.

Bolshevik discourse more broadly, excessive preoccupation with food was seen as a mark of inferiority.[205] An ability to rise above one's stomach was seen as an essential element of the truly patriotic citizen.

Lisa Kirschenbaum, in her work on "the legacy of the siege of Leningrad," has traced the evolving discourse of sacrifice and heroism into which Leningraders embedded their narratives of the siege.[206] Even Lidiia Ginzburg wrote that "the people of besieged Leningrad worked (while they could) and saved (if they could) both themselves and their loved ones from dying of hunger. And in the final reckoning that was also essential to the war effort, because a living city barred the path of an enemy who wanted to kill it."[207] Ginzburg imbues the very act of survival with a higher meaning: "on that other, historical scale, his will to self-preservation is serving the vast complex of a whole country at war."[208] In the medical literature, frequent references were made to the resilience of the Soviet people. A piece on changes in the psyche, for instance, concluded by drawing attention to the relative rarity of cases of psychosis, which, in the eyes of the authors, stood as testimony to the way Soviet citizens' "moral character, their heightened sense of duty, their limitless devotion and love for the motherland, and hatred of those who dare encroach upon their freedom and independence" all contributed to the "resilience of the nervous system."[209] The head of the Leningrad Health Department, F. I. Mashanskii, similarly attributed the absence of what

205. Consider, for instance, the terms in which Aleksandr Sheliubskii, a political officer in the Red Army, denigrated the enemy: "The Germans don't know how to endure hunger. Our Russian soldier was always able to endure hunger, not only in this Patriotic War but also during the Civil War and all other wars. The Germans don't know how to deal with hunger. When they fight, they are used to stuff themselves like pigs. I can prove this on the basis of their letters. It's really creepy—all they talk about is food. . . . Eating for them comes first. All that they have in their brain is grub." Quoted in Jochen Hellbeck, "'The Diaries of Fritzes and the Letters of Gretchens': Personal Writings from the German-Soviet War and Their Readers," *Kritika: Explorations in Russian & Eurasian History* 10, no. 3 (2009): 600–601.

206. Kirschenbaum, *The Legacy of the Siege of Leningrad*.

207. Ginzburg, *Blockade Diary*, p. 3.

208. Ibid., p. 94.

209. Abramovich and Mnukhin, "Klinika alimentarnoi distrofii: Izmeneniia psikhiki," p. 118.

Nutritional Dystrophy 263

he took to be some of the characteristic psychological effects of hunger to Leningraders' higher devotion to the cause.[210]

At the same time, the figure of the distrofik seemed to negate the very possibility of purposeful sacrifice. In his "indifference" and all-consuming focus on food, the distrofik seemed to be incapable of committing himself to a higher cause. Descriptions of the distrofik and of the effects of hunger repeatedly returned to the moral degradation that accompanied dystrophy. Cruelty and humiliation figure in many written records of the siege, and are key attributes of the distrofik in Lidiia Ginzburg's portrait of the siege person. Elena Kochina later wrote that "we came to know a hunger that degraded and crushed us, that turned us into animals." In a similar vein, Olga Freidenberg described her soul as a "siege person" as "desecrated."[211]

As these comments suggest, the experience of hunger was central to wartime myths, but also threatened to destabilize them. Since the war itself, hunger has stood at the nexus of divergent narratives of the war, narratives of solidarity and sacrifice on the one hand (epitomized by the willingness to endure hunger and to share one's bread), and of breakdown and betrayal on the other (epitomized by stories of cannibalism and theft). Cases of dystrophy were marshaled by Soviet authorities as proof of Nazi atrocities, but when they occurred among Soviet soldiers or on Soviet territory, they threatened to turn the charges of "death by starvation" back upon Soviet power.

Dystrophy and the figure of the distrofik served to medicalize one of the central forms of wartime suffering: starvation. At the same time, as this chapter has tried to suggest, dystrophy became a powerful means of denoting an age-old affliction that had appeared in a new guise, displaced from its traditional domain in the geographic imagination—the countryside—and separated from its traditional companions—typhus, cholera, and typhoid fever. Coined in Leningrad, and to some degree forever a "Leningrad illness," the term nonetheless came to denote the suffering not only of the city under siege, but also of the Gulag, the POW camps, and even Auschwitz. Dystrophy entered into widespread

---

210. In Gladkikh, *Zdravookhranenie i voennaia meditsina v bitve za Leningrad*, p. 80.
211. Cited in Kirschenbaum, *The Legacy of the Siege of Leningrad*, pp. 62, 63.

circulation at the moment when institutionalized, organized starvation reached its apogee. While the bodily transformations wrought by hunger were nothing new (edemas had, after all, been described by the ancients), the experience of war generated a new conceptualization of hunger as an illness and generated a powerful urge to document and understand the nature of life "at the limit."

FIVE

STARVATION MORTALITY IN SOVIET HOME-FRONT INDUSTRIAL REGIONS DURING WORLD WAR II

Donald Filtzer

The high intensity of work at the factory and the inadequacy of the food make it a matter of urgency that [workers receive their rightful days off], as witnessed by the frequency with which workers are dropping dead from emaciation right on the job. On some days you see several corpses in the shops. During the two months December 1942 and January 1943, they observed 16 bodies just in the factory shops. Those dying from emaciation are mainly workers doing manual labor.

> *Shliaev, Chief Prosecutor of Cheliabinsk province, to Bochkov,*
> *Prosecutor General of the* USSR, *March 29, 1943, concerning*
> *the refusal of the management at the giant Kirov works in*
> *Cheliabinsk to grant its workers the two days off a month*
> *stipulated in wartime labor regulations.*[1]

OF THE THREE PRINCIPAL BELLIGERENT COUNTRIES WHOSE domestic populations endured critical threats to their food supply, only the Soviet Union witnessed mass civilian deaths from starvation.[2] Here

1. Epigraph found in GARF, f. 8131, op. 37, d. 1436, l, 48.
2. See the introduction to this volume. We also wish to provide a brief note on terminology. As Rebecca Manley explains in her chapter, Russians used the single term *alimentarnaia distrofiia* (often shortened to just *distrofiia*) to describe what we refer to in this chapter variously as "semistarvation" or "starvation." Within the Soviet Union the term *distrofiia* took on considerable scientific, social, and political meanings, and it is in these terms that Manley analyzes its usage. In this chapter we have chosen not to use *alimentarnaia distrofiia* because its English translation ("nutritional dystrophy") is not part of the English medical lexicon. Here we are following the practice adopted by Josef Brožek, Samuel Wells, and Ancel Keys in their early postwar article on starvation during the Leningrad siege, "Medical Aspects of Semistarvation in Leningrad (Siege 1941–1942)," *American Review of Soviet Medicine* 4, no. 1 (October 1946): 70–86. When we use the term "semistarvation," we are referring to the earlier, milder phases of severe

first and foremost we think of the millions who died in the siege of Leningrad or who died of starvation in the territories under Nazi occupation. This chapter analyzes a less well-known phenomenon: the widespread morbidity and mortality from starvation in Soviet home-front cities and towns. During 1943 and 1944, starvation and tuberculosis—a disease that was endemic to the USSR and is highly sensitive to acute malnutrition—were between them the largest single cause of death among the non-child civilian population.

To understand why this was so we should look back at the discussion on rationing in this book's introduction. The USSR did not have enough food to feed both its military and its civilians, even with the arrival of Lend-Lease food aid. The state therefore had to engage in a grim calculus and decide how it could most efficiently use its limited resources—that is, how many calories and grams of protein it could allocate to different groups. In these circumstances it was inevitable that some people would not obtain enough to eat and many would die. No matter what regime had been in power in the USSR—Stalinist, Trotskyist, Menshevik, or capitalist—it would have faced the same set of choices. If the state had provided more food to dependents or those in nonessential occupations, there would have been less food for workers in defense factories. The military and economic consequences of such a choice would have been fewer weapons, tanks, and munitions, which might in turn have led to more casualties at the front, a prolongation of the German occupation, and more civilian deaths in the occupied territories. These were horrible choices to have to make, and any regime, no matter how democratic or how faithful to pre-Stalinist socialist principles, would have had to make them.

Although the deprivation was felt most acutely by those with the smallest entitlements, defense workers on higher rations were by no means immune to its effects. After laboring for extended hours on spare rations for two or three years, starvation took its toll on them as well. If they

---

under-nutrition, where timely and appropriate intervention could still reverse the condition. When we use the term "starvation," we refer to a more serious stage where even medical intervention and re-feeding could not always avert death. Doctors in the Warsaw Ghetto termed this "Hunger Disease."

Starvation Mortality in Soviet Industrial Regions 267

suffered lower levels of morbidity and mortality than others in the general population, this was only by degree. Their experience highlights yet again one of the central themes of this book: the endurance of a population that, no matter how cold, weak, and sick, persevered and persisted at its labors, and produced just enough of the wherewithal needed to defeat the invaders.

ASSESSING THE SCALE OF STARVATION IN HOME-FRONT TOWNS AND CITIES

Our knowledge of starvation mortality in hinterland regions has heretofore been based largely on anecdotal and eyewitness accounts. William Moskoff's interviewees, for example, recited tales of starvation deaths in Kuibyshev, Central Asia, and the Urals; Victor Kravchenko, a former party member and factory director in the Urals (and during the period covered by his memoirs, an anti-Stalinist socialist), remarked that during the winter of 1942–1943, "the sight of men and women falling dead of starvation on Moscow streets became too commonplace to attract crowds."[3] Archival documents are replete with similar anecdotal accounts, one of which we quote at the head of this chapter. Yet quantitative estimates of the scale of civilian starvation have remained difficult for a number of reasons.

For the urban population, statistical records exist from which, ostensibly, we could estimate both the magnitude of starvation deaths and their incidence by age and gender. Every year, local city and provincial statistical administrations filled out what was known as "Form 5," which listed causes of death by age and gender. These, however, provide data only for the urban population. The Soviet Union did not record causes of death for the rural population until the mid-1950s, primarily because rural medical services were too sparsely distributed and inadequately staffed with trained physicians to make reliable data collection feasible.

---

3. William Moskoff, *The Bread of Affliction: The Food Supply in the ussr During World War II* (Cambridge: Cambridge University Press 1990), pp. 227–229; Victor Kravchenko, *I Chose Freedom: A Personal and Political Life of a Soviet Official* (London: Robert Hale, 1947), p. 413.

268   *Donald Filtzer*

For this reason, rural wartime starvation mortality will probably forever remain a mystery.

Where the towns are concerned, demographic historians have been loath to attempt quantitative estimates of wartime hunger mortality because of a directive ordering local statistical administrations to conceal deaths from malnutrition under the opaque category of "other" causes of death.[4] Because of this, they assumed that the magnitude of wartime starvation deaths was unknowable.

If we are trying to assess the total number of starvation deaths for the USSR as a whole, this assumption appears to be true, not because such deaths were concealed in the vital statistics, but because we lack the aggregated demographic data needed to make these estimates. We return to this point at the end of the following section on methodology. The Soviet Union used a number of different forms for recording and reporting vital statistics, of which Form 5 was just one. Although we have not yet found reliable longitudinal records of Form 5 for the whole of the unoccupied USSR, or even the RSFSR, for all of the war years, close examination of these forms from Russia's major industrial cities and regions reveals a great deal about starvation mortality at the local level. These forms yield two important findings. First, not all localities obeyed the directive to hide deaths from starvation. A number of them continued to list deaths due to starvation (*alimentarnaia distrofiia*) and acute vitamin deficiency (avitaminosis) separately. Second, even when local statisticians did adhere to the new rules, it is possible to assess the general order of magnitude of starvation deaths by comparing the relative weights of "other" causes of death before and during the war. Prior to the war, "other" causes accounted for a very small fraction of urban deaths; in 1943, they accounted for anywhere from a quarter to a third, depending on the locality. One of this chapter's hypotheses, therefore, is that the difference between the prewar and wartime "other" categories can serve as an indirect proxy for deaths due to starvation. To be sure, there are a

---

4. N. A. Aralovets and O. M. Verbitskaia, "Osobennosti smertnosti gorodskogo i sel'skogo naseleniia v tylu v 1941–1945 gg.," in *Naselenie Rossii v XX veke: Istoricheskie ocherki*, vol. 2, 1940–1959 (Moscow: Rosspen, 2001), pp. 106–107. We explain this more fully below in the section on methodology.

Starvation Mortality in Soviet Industrial Regions   269

number of caveats to this approach. What this chapter argues, however, is that even when the formidable methodological challenges are taken into account, the cause-of-death data remain accurate enough to allow us to discern the general contours of home-front starvation mortality and to determine which regions, age groups, and gender were most severely impacted.

The data, when taken together with figures on infant mortality and medical reports, show that the war produced two more or less distinct mortality crises in hinterland cities and industrial regions. The first ran from late 1941 throughout 1942, and its main victims were infants, small children, the elderly, and the ill and infirm. These groups quickly succumbed to the shocks of evacuation and to the two major epidemics— measles and typhus—that broke out in late 1941 and early 1942 and spread eastwards with the mass displacement of the population. Nineteen forty-two was a year of astronomically high infant mortality. In urban areas of the RSFSR, infant mortality leapt from 206 deaths for every 1,000 live births in 1941, to 345 deaths per 1,000 live births in 1942,[5] with rates approaching, or even exceeding, one out of every two live births in cities such as Ivanovo, Kazan', and Kirov.[6] The Form 5 data for 1942 are very incomplete, but those that we have suggest that many, although not all, localities also began to see increasing deaths from starvation in that year.

---

5. Data, together with sources, are in Donald Filtzer, *The Hazards of Urban Life in Late Stalinist Russia: Health, Hygiene, and Living Standards, 1943–1953* (Cambridge: Cambridge University Press, 2010), pp. 271–272.

6. RGAE, f. 1562, op. 20, d. 500, ll. 22, 26, 42. In some cities the rates were inflated by the arrival or transit of infant evacuees. The deaths of infants who died while passing through a city or town, or after reaching their final destination, would be registered where they died, not in their place of birth, and these deaths would enter into the calculations of that town's infant mortality rate. Thus, Vologda, where large numbers of children evacuated from Leningrad during the winter of 1942 perished, recorded 423 infant deaths between April and June 1942, many of them Leningrad evacuees. In that same period the city recorded 564 births, suggesting a quarterly infant mortality rate of 750 per 1,000 live births. Clearly three out of every four births to mothers native to Vologda did not die; many of the deaths were infant evacuees born elsewhere. RGAE, f. 1562, op. 20, d. 500, l. 12; GARF, f. A-482, op. 47, d. 685, ll. 170–172. Even taking the global infant mortality rate for the RSFSR does not fully overcome this statistical problem, since some of the infants who died on Russian territory were evacuated from Ukraine or Belorussia.

The real hunger crisis, however, erupted in 1943, and differed qualitatively from that of the previous eighteen months. Its main victims in the towns were not children or the elderly, but males between the ages of thirty and fifty-nine. For this group the main cause of death was either starvation or starvation in conjunction with other, often preexisting, malnutrition-sensitive diseases and conditions. The most important of these was tuberculosis.

The data for 1944 suggest a more complex picture. General mortality fell, but starvation and starvation-dependent diseases continued to be the main cause of death. What is more, there was greater geographical unevenness in the severity of starvation. Central Russia, Moscow, and the Volga showed a significant recovery. In the Urals, however, deaths from starvation remained high, while morbidity from the condition began to affect a far greater number of "cadre" workers in large defense factories than it had in 1943. By 1944, however, the regime had greater reserves of food, perhaps not enough to allow an across-the-board improvement in the diets of the general population, but sufficient to allow Urals factories to intervene and re-feed many starvation sufferers before they actually died.

Why did adult starvation deaths peak only in 1943 instead of 1942, and why did they affect the Urals more than other regions? There are three reasons. First, clinical starvation manifests itself over time as the human body depletes its energy and protein reserves. By 1943 the cumulative energy imbalance built up since mid-1941 finally began to take a heavy toll on the adult civilian population. Doctors in the Warsaw Ghetto, where, with the possible exception of Leningrad, food deprivation was far more extreme than anywhere on the Soviet home front, had already observed this phenomenon: patients whose calorie intake should have led to death within sixty to seventy-five days survived for several months, and in some case up to one year.[7] Doctors treating starvation patients in Saratov and Tashkent noted a similar, if less extreme pattern: many of

---

7. Emil Apfelbaum-Kowalski, Ryszard Pakszwer, Jeanne Zarchi, Ari Heller, and Zdzislaw Askanas, "Pathophysiology of the Circulatory System in Hunger Disease," in Myron Winick, ed., *Hunger Disease: Studies by Jewish Physicians in the Warsaw Ghetto*, translated from the Polish by Martha Osnos (New York: John Wiley & Sons, 1979), p. 127.

Starvation Mortality in Soviet Industrial Regions

the patients who came to their clinics had begun to develop symptoms of advanced clinical starvation many months, and sometimes a full year, before their condition reached the point where they had to seek medical help.[8]

Second, the Urals was the region where the specific determinants of starvation came together in most concentrated form. It had a harsh climate, and dormitories and factory shops were largely unheated. Workers frequently trudged long distances to and from work in extreme cold. Local food supplies were sparse because of the region's weak agricultural base, and the development of subsidiary agriculture produced only meager supplements. Moreover, the workload in its defense factories was intense. In other words, this was a region where the imbalance between energy intake and energy expenditure was particularly pronounced.

Third, under "normal" circumstances, we would expect morbidity and mortality from starvation to have shown a cyclical pattern over the course of 1943 and 1944. It would become progressively more severe until the autumn of 1943, after which the grain harvest and the harvesting of potatoes and other crops from workers' allotments and factory farms should have increased food stocks. By early 1944, these stocks, especially the potatoes and vegetables from the private plots, would have been depleted and starvation once again would increase.[9] As heavy a toll as this cycle would have taken, it was made deeper by two factors. One was the poor grain harvest throughout the unoccupied USSR in 1943, which precipitated the across-the-board cut in rations of November of that year.

---

8. D. G. Abramovich, "Serdechno-sosudistaia sistema i ee otrazhenie v elektrokardiogramme pri alimentarnoi distrofii" (Candidate of Medical Sciences dissertation, Saratov, 1944), pp. 34–35, 122–253. Ashraf Khodzhaev, "Funktsiia zheludka pri alimentarnoi distrofii" (Candidate of Medical Sciences dissertation, Tashkent, 1946), pp. 50–72.

9. GARF, f. A-482, op. 47, d. 2213, ll. 66, 67 (Kirov province); op. 47, d. 2212, ll. 156, 156ob. (Ufa); op. 52s, d. 125, l. 253 (Cheliabinsk province). The scale of the problem can be gauged from figures from the iron and steel combine in Magnitogorsk, a relatively privileged factory where actual mortality from starvation appears to have been less severe than elsewhere in the Urals: during 1943 and early 1944 the factory assigned 7,000 workers—a full 14 percent of its overall establishment—to special rest homes and dining rooms set up to refeed workers suffering from semi- or full-fledged starvation. In one shop, nearly 40 percent of its 610 women workers were suffering from amenorrhoea. GARF, f. A-482, op. 47, d. 2210, ll. 15, 55–56.

272   *Donald Filtzer*

The other was specific to the Urals, where in Sverdlovsk province, and perhaps elsewhere in the Urals, much of the autumn 1943 potato crop was lost to blight.[10] Only at the end of 1944—perhaps thanks in part to Lend-Lease food aid–did starvation show a sustained decline, leading to its eventual disappearance, at least until the early postwar famine of 1946–1947, the last famine the country was to endure.

METHODOLOGY

The analysis of starvation mortality in this chapter is based on data from Form 5 returns compiled by provincial (*oblast'*) statistical administrations. These returns were sent to the Statistical Administration of the RSFSR (SU RSFSR), where they were checked, verified, and forwarded to the USSR Central Statistical Administration (TsSU). Form 5 listed eighty-two specific causes of death, distributing the totals for each cause by age and gender. These eighty-two causes included both diseases and events (fatal injuries or homicides, or, in the case of newborns, prematurity or failure to thrive at birth). Line 83 was labeled "other causes of death," and line 84, "illnesses and causes imprecisely determined or not included in the [official] classification." During the postwar famine of 1946–1947, deaths from starvation were hidden under both of these rubrics,[11] but during the war the bulk of them were entered as part of line 83, "other causes."

Statistical practice in this area took some time to evolve. Form 5 was compiled from the individual death certificates submitted to local registration bureaus, known as ZAGS (*Zapis' aktov grazhdanskogo sostoianiia*), on which the physician or paramedic attending the deceased entered onto the certificate the code number for the appropriate cause of death as listed on Form 5. Until mid-1942, there were no codes for deaths due to civilian wartime injuries (for example, victims of air raids, artillery bombardment, or gas attacks) or for deaths due to acute malnutrition (avitaminosis or cachexia). Following queries from at least two local statistical administrations, on July 20, 1942, the TsSU issued instructions

10. See below in the section, "The Changing Pattern of Starvation."
11. Filtzer, *Hazards*, pp. 218–223.

Starvation Mortality in Soviet Industrial Regions 273

to record deaths from war-related injuries using the code 40a (line 40 was for deaths due to non-work-related "mechanical injuries"), and deaths from starvation using a newly-created code 83a, adjunct to, but separate from, line 83 ("other causes of death"). These new codes were not, however, to appear on Form 5. Instead, the totals from each line would be included in the totals for lines 40 and 83, respectively, and the precise number of deaths from starvation would appear only in a secret appendix. In other words, no deaths were to be overtly attributed to starvation.[12]

If one goes to the archives, however, and examines the Form 5 sheets, it becomes clear that not all provincial statistical administrations adhered to the instructions.[13] Of the forms we have examined, Moscow province, Sverdlovsk and Sverdlovsk province (including Nizhnii Tagil, which reported separately), and the cities of Kuibyshev, Novosibirsk, Omsk, Stalinsk, Kemerovo, and Prokop'evsk, specifically enumerated deaths due to starvation. Some used the term *alimentarnaia distrofiia* and/or avitaminosis; others identified these deaths by the code 83a; others used a different coding, but it is clear that they refer to starvation. When the forms reached Moscow, the statisticians at the RSFSR's Statistical Administration drew a thin line through the figures for starvation deaths and added them back into line 83, but nonetheless they remained readable. Therefore, in these specific localities, the authorities provided what they considered to be accurate tallies of deaths due to starvation. On Forms 5 where no separate entry for starvation exists, it is still possible to make a rough estimate of the number of starvation deaths in the locality by comparing the ratio of "other" deaths to total deaths in 1940 with this same ratio for 1943. Roughly speaking, the share of "other" deaths in total mortality in 1943 is so vastly higher than in 1940, that it

---

12. Aralovets and Verbitskaia, "Osobennosti smertnosti gorodskogo i sel'skogo naseleniia v tylu v 1941–1945 gg.," p. 106. Nadezhda Cherepenina, "Assessing the Scale of Famine and Death in the Besieged City," in John Barber and Andrei Dzeniskevich, eds., *Life and Death in Besieged Leningrad, 1941–44* (Basingstoke: Palgrave, 2005), p. 40. The TsSU instruction and ensuing amendments are in RGAE, f. 1562, op. 329, d. 805, ll. 162, 165. I am grateful to Rebecca Manley for making this last reference available.

13. The sources for all the Form 5 data discussed in this chapter, including all figures, appear in appendix B.

274   *Donald Filtzer*

can be assumed, as a working hypothesis, that this excess is mainly due
to starvation.

The validity of this hypothesis can be tested in two ways. First, in
the city of Cheliabinsk, officials did not list starvation deaths on Form 5,
but the number of such deaths does appear in other documentation, and it
is possible to compare the figures in the two documents. In Cheliabinsk
in 1940, the two categories of "other" (line 83) and what may be termed
"non-classified" (line 84) deaths accounted for just 244 out of a total
7,007 deaths—3.5 percent. In 1943, however, these two categories accounted
for a staggering 5,768 deaths out of a total of 17,852—32.3 percent. Assuming that the incidence of genuinely "other" and "non-classified" causes
of death remained roughly the same in 1940 and 1943, and accounted for
the same percentage of total mortality in both years (around 3.5 percent),
the remaining deaths in lines 83 and 84 in 1943 would account for 28.8 percent of Cheliabinsk's total mortality. The contention here is that almost
all of these additional or extra deaths were the result of starvation. This
contention is confirmed by the city's own state sanitary inspectors. In
1943, the city's State Sanitary Inspectorate (Gosudarstvennaia Sanitar-
naia Inspektsiia, or GSI) reported 18,073 deaths (about 1.2 percent more
than the city's statistical administration recorded on Form 5), of which
5,346—29.6 percent—were from starvation (*istoshchenie,* which can be
translated variously as "exhaustion," but also more clinically precisely as
"emaciation" or even cachexia). The fit between the two sets of figures
is not exact, but it is extremely close.[14]

Second, it is possible to compare our indirect estimations of starvation deaths, for example, in Cheliabinsk, with the ratio of starvation
deaths to total deaths in cities, such as Sverdlovsk, which explicitly listed
starvation deaths on Form 5. In Sverdlovsk in 1940, lines 83 and 84
totaled 180 deaths, out of a city-wide total of 9,254—1.95 percent. In 1943,

---

14. GARF, f. A-482, op. 47, d. 2313, l. 147. A repeat of these calculations for 1944
gives a less good, but still acceptable fit. According to the GSI report, during 1944 both
total deaths and deaths from cachexia fell compared to 1943; total deaths declined by
37.9 percent, cachexia deaths less rapidly, by 33.7 percent. This left cachexia accounting
for 31.6 percent of all deaths in the city in that year. Using Form 5 for 1944 we would
arrive at a slightly lower number, with starvation (cachexia) accounting for 28 percent
of deaths in 1944.

Starvation Mortality in Soviet Industrial Regions

lines 83 and 84 totaled 707 deaths, out of a total of 15,665—4.5 percent. This is more than double their share in 1940, but still a very small figure, especially when we contrast it with the number of deaths attributed overtly to starvation. These came to 4,364—27.9 percent of all deaths in Sverdlovsk in that year, roughly the same order of magnitude we saw in Cheliabinsk.[15]

In theory it should be possible to use this method to arrive at a rough estimate of the number of starvation deaths in the Soviet Union as a whole. Unfortunately, the data do not allow us to do this. Causes of death among the rural population were not registered, so we have no way to assess the impact of starvation upon the largest subset of the Soviet population. For the towns we do not have longitudinal cause-of-death data for either the USSR or the RSFSR, home to the vast majority of the Soviet population living in unoccupied territory. The best we can do is estimate starvation mortality within the urban RSFSR for 1943, the year when starvation deaths peaked. In 1940, "other" causes of death accounted for approximately 3.8 percent of all deaths; in 1943 they accounted for 21.3 percent. The difference between the two magnitudes is 17.8 percent. If we take as a working hypothesis that this is a valid proxy for starvation, and apply this to the 761,000 deaths recorded in the nonoccupied urban areas of the RSFSR (*excluding* Leningrad) during 1943, this implies 135,000 deaths from starvation.[16] As we explain below, we have to allow for very large margins of error in these figures, mainly because of uncertainties surrounding the diagnosis and recording of deaths due to hunger. Moreover, without Form 5 for the RSFSR for 1942 and 1944, we cannot replicate even this crude calculation for the three full war years. Our local data suggest that, although the total number of deaths in Russian towns and cities fell in 1944, the percentage of those deaths due to starvation changed very little. About 1942, however, we know almost nothing, since even the local data are very incomplete, and in any case the instruction on how to record starvation deaths was issued only in the middle of that year. Can

15. Repeating the same arithmetical exercise for Sverdlovsk in 1944, we see that lines 83 and 84 accounted for 581 out of 12,766 total deaths, or 4.6 percent, versus 3,991 deaths attributed to starvation, or 30.6 percent of the total. Thus, although deaths as a whole in Sverdlovsk declined, the relative importance of starvation became even greater.

16. Total deaths are from GARF, f. A-374, op. 34, d. 1540, l. 19.

we at least make an educated guess about a lower boundary of starvation mortality? For the three years 1942–1944, the towns and cities of the unoccupied parts of the RSFSR (again, excluding Leningrad), recorded 2,277,000 deaths. If even 10 percent of these were due to starvation, this would give a total of 227,000 deaths. If the relative weight of starvation in 1942 were to turn out to be closer to its relative weight in 1943 and 1944, yielding a three-year average of, let us say, 15 percent, then we would be looking at around 340,000 deaths just in Russia's urban areas. This pales in comparison to the 4.1 *million* Soviet citizens estimated to have died from hunger, disease, and overwork in the occupied territories,[17] but even our lowest estimate signals a nutritional crisis on the Soviet home front of famine proportions.

Although accurate national estimates of starvation mortality are not possible, the local data are much more complete, and these tell us a great deal. We have used Form 5 data from twenty-two localities for which we have Form 5 returns for the years 1940, 1943, and 1944. In some cases, but unfortunately not all, it is possible to compare the metropolitan center with the urban areas of its provincial hinterland (for example, Sverdlovsk and Sverdlovsk province).[18] The amount of information, however, is far too large to show each locality individually. In order to simplify the pre-

17. John Barber and Mark Harrison, "Patriotic War, 1941 to 1945," in *The Cambridge History of Russia*, vol. 3, *The Twentieth Century*, ed. Ronald Grigor Suny (Cambridge: Cambridge University Press, 2006), pp. 226–227.

18. For 1942 we have sheets for only a few localities. For this reason, plus the fact that data collection and reporting during 1942 were badly disrupted, we have excluded 1942 from the discussion. In a number of regions we are able to use the data only for the metropolitan center, but not for the urban areas of the province as a whole. Excluded are: Moscow province because parts of it were briefly under German occupation; Kuibyshev, Omsk, and Saratov provinces and the Tatar ASSR because they were primarily rural; and provinces that underwent major boundary changes at various points during the war, rendering year-on-year comparisons impractical. These include Ivanovo and Iaroslavl' provinces, which in 1944 respectively lost what became Vladimir and Kostroma provinces; Novosibirsk province, which experienced two major wartime boundary changes (the Kuzbass was separated off into Kemerovo province at the end of 1942, and Tomsk became a separate province in late 1943); and Cheliabinsk province, from which Kurgan province was hived off in 1943. It would require fiendishly difficult computations to recalculate the yearly figures so that they covered the same territorial entities, but without this any assessment of wartime changes would be meaningless.

Starvation Mortality in Soviet Industrial Regions 277

sentation we have amalgamated the twenty-two localities into five distinct regions.[19]

1. Moscow.
2. Central Russia: the cities of Iaroslavl', Ivanovo, and Gor'kii.
3. Volga Region: the cities of Kuibyshev, Saratov, and Kazan.'
4. The Urals: Kirov city and Kirov province; Izhevsk; Molotov city and Molotov province; Sverdlovsk city and Sverdlovsk province (including Nizhnii Tagil, for which separate Form 5 returns exist); and the cities of Cheliabinsk, Zlatoust, and Magnitogorsk (we have used Zlatoust and Magnitogorsk as proxies for Cheliabinsk province). Geographically, Kirov and Izhevsk lie slightly west of the Urals, but their rapid growth as they received a large influx of defense factories, their precarious access to food supplies, and the general state of their public and environmental health made them socioeconomically far closer to the Urals than to any other region.
5. Western Siberia: the cities of Novosibirsk, Omsk, and the Kuzbass cities of Prokop'evsk, Stalinsk, and Kemerovo.

THE STARVATION-TUBERCULOSIS COMPLEX

This chapter does not examine starvation deaths alone, but rather what we call the "starvation-tuberculosis complex." There are two essential reasons for this: the close biological connection between starvation and tuberculosis; and the problems surrounding the accuracy of wartime diagnoses in the Soviet rear.

Let us look first at the medical side of the argument. In periods of crisis and acute dearth, starvation deaths are not limited to starvation alone. Protein-energy malnutrition (PEM) is closely associated with a

---

19. Using regional aggregates, whilst making the presentation of the data more manageable, does have two disadvantages. It obscures local variations within the individual regions, and we lose potentially revealing comparisons between the metropolitan centers of major provinces and the smaller industrial towns that made up their hinterland. Fortunately, however, among the 22 localities we find relatively few radical outliers; those that are important we have called attention to in the text.

278   *Donald Filtzer*

range of diseases and conditions that can themselves lead to increased
mortality, either directly or by exacerbating malnutrition to the point
where the sufferer dies. These malnutrition-related diseases, too, should
be included in any assessment of hunger mortality. The interaction between malnutrition and these diseases is quite complex, often involving
a vicious spiral from which it becomes impossible to distinguish cause
and effect. Malnutrition makes the sufferer vulnerable to infections, either by making an uninfected person more susceptible to a fresh infection, or, as in the case of tuberculosis, by rendering an already infected
person unable to fight off the disease-causing microorganism. In many
cases this leads directly to increased mortality. In others the result can
be acute or long-term morbidity.[20]

In the wartime Soviet Union, tuberculosis was the one nutrition-
dependent disease that dominated all others. Tuberculosis was endemic
in Russia and the USSR, and before the war had been the leading cause
of death among both males and females between the ages of five and
forty-nine. In the RSFSR in 1940, it accounted for 30 percent of all urban
deaths in this age range, dwarfing by far every other cause of death,
including pneumonia and gastrointestinal infections.[21] One important
characteristic of tuberculosis is that it is extremely sensitive to abrupt

20. In the modern Third World, where chronic PEM remains a major public health
issue, we see both of these problems. Malnutrition in these regions accounts for a high
percentage of child deaths and markedly reduces labor productivity, both directly and as
a contributing factor in debilitating conditions such as intestinal parasites. It still plays a
direct role in compromising infected persons' ability to withstand, and to survive, major
killer diseases, such as HIV/AIDS, malaria, tuberculosis, and measles. For a useful review
of the research on malnutrition and infection, see Ulrich E. Schaible and Stefan H. E.
Kaufmann, "Malnutrition and Infection: Complex Mechanisms and Global Impacts"
(Public Library of Science), *PLoS Medicine* 4, no. 5 (May 2007): 0806–0812, available at
www.plosmedicine.org. Under-five mortality has declined dramatically since the 1990s,
but it remains the case that over 8 million children under the age of 5 died in 2009, a
third of these either directly or indirectly because of malnutrition. *Levels and Trends in
Child in Child Mortality: Report 2010* (New York: United Nations Children's Fund, 2010),
pp. 1, 10. In the late 1990s debilitating intestinal parasites were estimated to afflict some
3 billion people worldwide, accounting for more debility than malaria. L. S. Stephenson,
M. C. Latham, and E. A. Ottesen, "Malnutrition and Parasitic Helminth Infections,"
Parasitology. 121, Supplement (2000): S23–24.

21. GARF, f. A-374, op. 11, d. 28, ll. 11, 110b. In this age range the three categories of
coronary artery disease, pneumonia and other respiratory diseases, and accidental

Starvation Mortality in Soviet Industrial Regions

falls in nutrition. The general pattern in countries with endemic tuberculosis was that infection rates among children and teenagers were high, but the vast majority of people did not become ill. Instead, their immune systems kept the disease in check, and the bacilli remained dormant, encapsulated in tubercles in the lungs. If, however, a person's immune system became compromised, then the disease could again become active, and the risk of mortality would increase. The extreme food shortages and nutritional deficiencies of the war years, the radical deterioration in general sanitation, and the decision by the Soviet authorities to close down much of their tuberculosis treatment and control apparatus at the start of the war created ideal conditions for a surge in tuberculosis deaths. Indeed, any marked increase in tuberculosis deaths would itself have been a strong indicator of a collapse in general nutrition.

With the war, tuberculosis deaths did indeed increase dramatically. In absolute terms, the number of urban tuberculosis deaths in the RSFSR among those aged five years and older leapt from 65,667 in 1940 to 85,094 in 1943,[22] a jump of 29.6 percent, although we cannot be sure of the rates per 10,000 population. However, a 1945 attempt to measure the increase in tuberculosis deaths per 10,000 population in major home-front cities between 1940 and 1943 showed, with only a few exceptions, striking increases. (See table 5.1.) Of the thirty-nine cities listed, nine showed increases in the tuberculosis death rate of between 18 and 40 percent; another nine showed increases of between 41 and 70 percent; and 11 showed increases of between 71 and 131 percent. In the seven cities that saw an actual decline in the tuberculosis death rate—in some cases a very substantial decline—the rate nevertheless was still very high.[23]

---

injuries between them accounted for 28.4 percent of all deaths; gastrointestinal infections accounted for a further 5.7 percent.

22. GARF, f. A-374, op. 11, d. 222, l. 20b. It is important to point out that tuberculosis rates fell back again in 1944. I have not shown the changes in table 5.1, but this will become obvious when we analyze the Form 5 mortality data in the next section.

23. The statisticians who made these calculations used statistical returns that for most cities reported somewhat larger numbers of tuberculosis deaths in 1943 than the numbers listed on their respective Forms 5; it is possible, therefore, that they overestimated the increase in tuberculosis mortality. Yet the increases in tuberculosis mortality rates are of such an order of magnitude that, even allowing for these discrepancies, there

Table 5.1. Tuberculosis deaths per 10,000 population, in major home-front cities of the RSFSR, 1940 vs. 1943

City	1940	1943	% change	City	1940	1943	% change
Kostroma	16.0	37.0	131.3	Kirov	36.4	50.7	39.3
Shuya	18.5	40.0	116.2	Prokop'evsk	34.0	46.0	35.3
Rybinsk	27.7	59.3	114.1	Nizhnii Tagil	24.0	31.6	31.7
Cheboksary	23.9	46.9	96.2	Molotov	37.2	46.2	24.2
Kizel	13.2	25.3	91.7	Saratov	26.5	32.6	23.0
Moscow	15.2	29.0	90.8	Stalinsk	29.4	36.1	22.8
Krasnoyarsk	35.0	64.7	84.9	Izhevsk	32.9	40.1	21.9
Kineshma	19.0	33.9	78.4	Gor'kii	24.0	29.1	21.3
Cheliabinsk	33.3	58.7	76.3	Anzhero-Sudzhensk	27.1	32.2	18.8
Ivanovo	13.9	23.9	71.9	Berezniki	26.5	29.0	9.4
Magnitogorsk	18.5	31.6	70.8	Novosibirsk	40.3	42.6	5.7
Omsk	34.7	57.1	64.6	Chkalov	38.0	38.7	1.8
Iaroslavl'	18.5	29.9	61.6	Kazan'	44.6	41.8	−6.3
Irkutsk	24.9	40.0	60.6	Barnaul	48.8	44.4	−9.0
Vologda	34.0	52.6	54.7	Tomsk	50.5	45.5	−9.9
Serov	38.6	58.0	50.3	Kemerovo	40.6	33.4	−17.7
Zlatoust	27.4	40.1	46.4	Arkhangel'sk	36.9	28.8	−22.0
Kuibyshev	32.9	47.9	45.6	Ul'ianovsk	36.2	25.7	−29.0
Tiumen'	32.6	46.0	41.1	Ufa	48.0	30.6	−36.3
Sverdlovsk	27.3	38.5	41.0				

Source: GARF, f. A-482, op. 52s, d. 130, ll. 28ob., 29, 29ob.

To what extent was the rise in tuberculosis deaths due to wartime malnutrition? The association of tuberculosis with malnutrition is an old one. Germany and Austria both saw large increases in tuberculosis mortality during the latter stages of World War I, when the food situation in both countries—and especially in Germany—had reached near-famine proportions.[24] During World War II, doctors in the Warsaw Ghetto and in besieged Leningrad noted the increased frequency and virulence of

---

can be no doubt that the advent of the war brought in its wake a sharp deterioration in the situation.

24. Ancel Keys, Josef Brožek, Austin Henschel, Olaf Mickelsen, Henry Longstreet Taylor, et al., *The Biology of Human Starvation* (Minneapolis: University of Minnesota Press, 1950), pp. 1017–1021.

Starvation Mortality in Soviet Industrial Regions 281

tuberculosis as acute starvation gripped their respective populations.[25] In both Warsaw and the wartime USSR, doctors attributed this link to the impact of starvation on the human immune system. These were prescient observations, which modern immunology and molecular biology were able to confirm only several decades later, although even now the exact mechanisms by which protein-energy malnutrition or deficiencies in specific micronutrients render people vulnerable to infection with tuberculosis are unclear.[26] What is clear is that the relationship between tuberculosis and malnutrition is complex. The two conditions are so closely interlinked that in most real-life situations where we see them both together it is impossible to distinguish primary causality. If severe malnutrition can precipitate the reactivation of tuberculosis, tuberculosis itself *causes* weight loss and cachexia. Moreover, during wars and famine, malnutrition is accompanied by an overall worsening of sanitation, medical care, and general living conditions, all of which are themselves risk factors for tuberculosis. During such crises the interaction of these myriad factors makes it impossible to attribute the increased frequency and virulence of tuberculosis to just one single cause.[27]

The close epidemiological link between tuberculosis and starvation also affected the accuracy of cause-of-death diagnoses. Starvation could present a number of clinical symptoms that could be confused with other

25. Brožek, Wells, and Keys, "Medical Aspects of Semistarvation in Leningrad (Siege 1941–1942)," p. 81.

26. J. P. Cegielski and D. N. McMurray, "The Relationship between Malnutrition and Tuberculosis: Evidence from Studies in Humans and Experimental Animals," *International Journal of Tuberculosis and Lung Disease* 8, no. 3 (2004): pp. 286–298. The human immune system consists of two components. One is the humoral immune system, where the body produces antibodies (also known as "immunoglobulins"), which are complex protein chains that attack and neutralize foreign agents (mainly viruses or bacteria) that enter the blood stream. The other is what is known as "cell-mediated immunity." The body contains a number of different types of cells—T- and B-lymphocytes, macrophages, dendritic cells, neutrophils—that hunt down and destroy invading infectious agents. It is this second type of immunity—cell-mediated immunity—that provides the primary defense when a person is infected by the tuberculosis bacterium, *Mycobacterium tuberculosis,* but it is also the part of the immune system that is most directly compromised by PEM.

27. Cegielski and McMurray, "The Relationship between Malnutrition and Tuberculosis," pp. 287–288.

diseases. Extreme weight loss could mimic not just the cachexia caused by advanced tuberculosis, but also cancer, although cancers were a relativity uncommon cause of death in this period.[28] The same held true of diarrhea and bloody stools, both a common symptom of starvation, but which could easily be confused with dysentery.[29] To a lesser extent this problem extended to deaths from apparent heart attacks or heart failure. Without an autopsy it would be difficult, if not impossible, to tell if a sudden death due to what looked like a heart attack or heart failure was due to a person's heart having given out as a result of acute starvation, or if the person suffered from coronary artery disease, with starvation possibly (but not necessarily) an aggravating factor. Where tuberculosis was concerned, however, the difficulties in making an accurate diagnosis were extraordinarily difficult. Doctors in the Warsaw Ghetto found that patients whom they knew to have tuberculosis showed negative skin tests—something that later immunologists were able to explain as being due to the suppressed cell-mediated immune reactions caused by semi-starvation.[30] But they also found that patients who appeared to have died from starvation were found upon autopsy to have had pervasive tuberculosis.[31]

The doctors who carried out the Warsaw Ghetto studies were limited in what they could achieve by the circumstances in which they were working and the rudimentary nature of their available equipment. Yet they and their counterparts in Leningrad were well-trained physicians with a sophisticated grasp of the principles of rigorous research methodology and clinical observation. The local medical personnel who made

28. Thus at City Hospital No. 1 in Sverdlovsk, doctors attributed the death of a 32-year-old man to advanced tuberculosis and advanced starvation. An autopsy showed that the main cause of death was cancer of the rectum, which had metastasized to the lungs, liver, spleen, and brain. The patient developed bronchopneumonia, which was confused with tuberculosis, and his cachexia was caused by his cancer, not actual starvation. GARF, f. A-482, op. 47, d. 2124, l. 114. Similar examples can be found in GARF, f. A-482, op. 47, d. 2225, ll. 61, 62.

29. S. S. Vail', "O nekotorykh izmeneniiakh kishek, pecheni i podzheludochnoi zhelezy pri alimentarnoi distrofii," in I. M. Rybakov, ed., *Trudy pervoi terapevticheskoi konferentsii* (Gor'kii: no publisher, 1943), pp. 429–430, 433.

30. Winick, *Hunger Disease*, p. 65.

31. Anna Braude-Heller, Israel Rotbalsam, and Regina Elbinger, "Clinical Aspects of Hunger Disease in Children," in Winick, *Hunger Disease*, p. 52.

Starvation Mortality in Soviet Industrial Regions

determinations in the cause of death in the wartime USSR, however, were often poorly qualified and/or did not have the facilities to do proper post-mortems. The bulk of skilled and experienced Soviet physicians had either been mobilized for the front or reassigned to military hospitals in their own locality. Some larger hinterland cities, such as Sverdlovsk and Molotov, which had well established medical schools and research hospitals, managed to retain a basic infrastructure, although this did not necessarily mean they had access to trained pathologists. Other cities benefited from the arrival of medical institutes evacuated from Kiev and the western USSR, or managed to retain some senior staff too old to serve in the army. During 1943, the main city hospital in Cheliabinsk, for example, relied on doctors from the Kiev Medical Institute for over half its full-time staff.[32] In peripheral areas and in the smaller provincial industrial towns that accounted for a very large percentage of the Soviet workforce and the hinterland civilian population in general, medical resources, already inadequate before the war, were depleted even further, with virtually no access to trained pathologists or proper laboratories.[33] Even in the

---

32. GARF, f. A-482, op. 47, d. 515, l. 206. In general, home-front regions became heavily dependent upon doctors evacuated from the western USSR. By January 1943, physician evacuees made up between 40 and 60 percent of all doctors serving the civilian population in the cities and provinces studied in this chapter. GARF, f. 8009, op. 6, d. 1906, pp. 12–13, 19–20 (the file has only page numbers, not sheet numbers). We do not have comprehensive figures for the later war years, but in August 1944, between 60 and 80 percent of doctors in the industrial towns of Sverdlovsk province were evacuees, prompting the Provincial Health Department to express its alarm over what would happen when they were re-evacuated westward. Medical students awaiting graduation from Sverdlovsk's own Medical Institute had already been designated for assignment outside the province. In the document cited here, the province health authorities were hoping to make up the gap by receiving new graduates from medical schools in Irkutsk and Kazan'. GARF, f. A-482, op. 47, d. 2030, ll. 87, 87ob.

33. In Zlatoust, the second most important industrial city in Cheliabinsk province after Magnitogorsk, toward the end of 1942, the head of the internal medicine department at the city's main polyclinic was actually a paramedic (*fel'dsher*). Its laboratory had neither a doctor nor a trained laboratory technician. It notionally had a neurologist, but the latter did not see any neurology patients because he or she had been reassigned to the local draft board (*Voenkom*) to vet potential draftees. GARF, f. A-482, op. 47, d. 617, ll. 42, 42ob. It was common for physicians' posts in clinics and hospitals to be filled not by actual doctors, but by paramedics, many of whom had been rushed through short training courses (normally their training took three years). In August 1944, roughly a quarter of all doctors' posts in outpatient and polyclinics in the main

main cities, hospitals were too short-staffed and under-equipped to do autopsies on all who died.[34] Moreover, the overwhelming mass of people who died at home, in the streets, or on the factory floor would never have received a postmortem, and may not even have had a doctor to determine the cause of death. What held true for apparent starvation deaths held equally true for tuberculosis. If an analysis by tuberculosis experts in Novosibirsk province is in any way representative, the vast majority of tuberculosis death notifications were filled out not by specialists, but by general practitioners, whose knowledge of tuberculosis was usually poor. The forms were replete with basic errors, such as the date of death, a clear indication of the cause, and full biographical data on the deceased. All of these call into question the accuracy of the tabulations of tuberculosis mortality.[35]

Finally, Soviet doctors, like their Western counterparts, had little clinical experience observing mass starvation. Of course people, including Europeans, had been starving from famines and wars for thousands of years, but in the era of modern Western clinical medicine starvation had been something confined to Europe's colonies. The closest it had come to Europe was the famine in Tsarist Russia at the close of the nineteenth century, and then the great hunger that afflicted German cities during the winter of 1917, followed by the Soviet famines of 1920–1921 and 1932–1933. This meant that unless Soviet doctors were old enough to have observed famine cases first-hand during 1920–1921 or 1932–1933, they were unlikely to know the clinical signs of starvation. As Rebecca Manley shows in chapter 4, doctors caught in the siege of Leningrad embarked on a very rapid learning curve, accumulating a large amount of clinical data in a very short time, and disseminating their findings to military and civilian medics throughout the country. The very newness of the phenomenon, the similarity of starvation symptoms to those of other diseases, and the inexperience of many home-front doctors added yet another layer

---

industrial towns and cities of Sverdlovsk province (excluding Sverdlovsk itself) were staffed by paramedics. GARF, f. A-482, op. 47, d. 2030, l. 95.

34. GARF, f. A-482, op. 47, d. 2124, l. 440b. (Children's Clinic, Molotov Medical Institute), and 112–1140b. (Sverdlovsk City Hospital No. 1).

35. GARF, f. 8009, op. 28, d. 15, ll. 11, 23. The report is from 1944 and refers to the situation in 1942. There is no indication as to whether or not reporting accuracy improved during 1943 and 1944.

Starvation Mortality in Soviet Industrial Regions

285

of imprecision to mortality records and statistics.[36] Given these various complications and imprecisions in accurately determining cause of death, we take as the basis of our analysis not a comparison of prewar and wartime totals of the "other" and "non-classified" categories, but rather a comparison of changes in what we call the "starvation-tuberculosis complex." We include in this category for 1940, 1943, and 1944 all deaths from tuberculosis, "other" causes, and "non-classified" causes. When starvation deaths were listed directly on Form 5, we still include the "other" and "non-classified" categories, because even in such cases, there would have been considerable error and uncertainty in the attribution of deaths.

A PROFILE OF STARVATION MORTALITY

The data on hunger mortality reveal seven important trends:

1. There was a pronounced rise in mortality among the non-child population, that is, persons aged five years and older.
2. Among the non-child population, the age distribution of mortality shifted downward, with the main burden moving

36. The Soviet clinical literature on this topic is truly vast, and reveals a large amount of debate, if not confusion, among doctors concerning the mechanisms, the physiology, and the course of starvation: how it affected the body's chemistry and internal organs, how the condition progressed, what physical symptoms it displayed at different stages of progression, how these changes showed up in blood and urine chemistry or histological samples, and how best to treat a sufferer. A relatively late and well-developed schema on how to recognize the symptoms of starvation, drawn up for the use of military doctors, is reproduced in *Opyt sovetskoi meditsiny v velikoi otechestvennoi voine, 1941–1945 gg.,* vol. 28, *Narusheniia obshchego pitaniia (osobennosti ikh vozniknoveniia, techeniia, preduprezhdeniia i lecheniia vo vremia voiny),* ed. E. M. Gel'shtein (Moscow: Medgiz, 1951), p. 126. On starvation and colonial medicine, see the provocative little article by Dana Simmons, "Starvation Science: From Colonies to Metropole," in A. Nützendel and Frank Trentmann, eds., *Food and Globalization: Consumption, Markets and Politics in the Modern World* (Oxford: Berg, 2008), pp. 173–191. My thanks to Rebecca Manley for calling this article to my attention.

A further, but less serious, complication in the statistics is that even where acute malnutrition was the real cause of death, not all such deaths were due to cachexia (*istoshchenie*) or acute starvation more broadly defined (*alimentarnaia distrofiia*). Scurvy and pellagra, caused respectively by a lack of vitamin C and vitamin B_3 (niacin), could both prove fatal. Yet apart from Moscow province, we know of no local health department that recorded such deaths separately from those attributed to starvation.

from the most elderly toward adults, primarily men in late middle age and "middle" middle age—that is, toward people still of working age, or even of prime working age.

3. The extent of this shift varied by region. It was sharpest in the Urals, where the greatest percentage of deaths fell upon men in their thirties and forties.

4. The largest single cause of death was the starvation-tuberculosis complex.

5. As with general mortality, the primary victims of starvation were men in their thirties, forties, and fifties.

6. Women were relatively protected from starvation. Overall, they died in far smaller numbers than men in the same age group, despite their increased share of the working-age population, and constituted only a very small percentage of starvation victims.

7. There were marked regional variations in these patterns. These did not, however, follow a simple pattern of concentric circles, with mortality increasing the further a region was from Moscow. People in Iaroslavl' fared slightly worse than people in nearby Ivanovo. People in the Urals fared worse than those in Western Siberia (Novosibirsk, the Kuzbass, somewhat less markedly also Omsk), perhaps because the latter were able to provide more food from their personal plots. While such efforts could attenuate starvation mortality, they could not eliminate it. In the Kuzbass, potato consumption made possible a very large increase in average daily calorie intake; nonetheless the region registered a significant number of starvation and tuberculosis deaths in 1943, although the number declined markedly in 1944.

The Shift in the Burden of Mortality toward Adult Males of Prime Working Age

The mortality data on Form 5 tell us only the total number of deaths by age group, gender, and presumed cause. Were the total size, age composition, and gender composition of the population stable from one year to the next, it would be possible to make reasonable assumptions about

Starvation Mortality in Soviet Industrial Regions

changes in mortality within each age and gender group simply by comparing the number of deaths. During the war years, however, the size, age, and gender compositions of urban populations changed rapidly and significantly. A few major cities, most notably Moscow, experienced a fall in population, as women, children, defense personnel, and government staff were evacuated to the east, and men were mobilized for the front. Other cities, however, saw their populations increase, generally very substantially, due to the influx of evacuees and workers mobilized to work in defense industries.

In theory it should be possible to track changes in mortality trends by looking at crude mortality rates (CMR), that is, deaths per 1,000 population, as these would take account of fluctuations in population size. In a "normal" year (of which there were relatively few in the USSR prior to the 1950s) the bulk of deaths would be concentrated in two age groups: children aged between zero and four years and the elderly. In contrast, older children, teenagers, and young adults would account for only a small proportion of total deaths. Quantitative changes in the size of a population would not affect the CMR if the age composition of the population remained the same, since the CMR compares not the absolute number of deaths, but the number of deaths per unit of population. By the same token, if the age structure did not alter and we then observed significant shifts in the CMR, this would be an important indicator of major changes in the population's general state of health.

For the war years, unfortunately, such extrapolations and inferences are nearly impossible. All assessments of civilian wartime mortality come up against the absence of adequate population data. Soviet demographic and medical statisticians did, in fact, prepare estimates of the crude mortality rate in each major city and province,[37] but their estimates of the size of each locality's population were far from precise.[38] For 1940

---

37. "Al'bom diagramm o rozhdaemosti i smertnosti naseleniia RSFSR za gody otechestvennoi voiny," prepared by the Scientific-Methodological Bureau of Sanitary Statistics, Narkomzdrav RSFSR in 1945; in GARF, f. A-482, op. 52s, d. 188.

38. They were not, however, total guesswork either. The authorities had records of births and deaths (known in Russian as "natural population movement") and what they thought was a reasonably accurate record of registrations of people moving into and out of each city (so-called "mechanical population movement").

they relied on the results of the 1939 census, which we can take as reasonably accurate, although most cities would have experienced a small amount of population increase during 1940. For 1943, they appear to have used a set of population estimates as of January 1, 1944, which can be found in the files of the USSR Central Statistical Administration.[39] Even if we accept their calculations as accurate, the information they impart is still limited because the age and gender composition of cities changed so dramatically. The most important factor was the precipitous decline in the size of the sub-group of the population that, prior to the war, had made the largest single contribution to overall mortality—infants and very young children. Exceptionally high infant mortality in 1942, combined with a collapse in the birthrate, meant that in subsequent years this cohort accounted for a far smaller percentage of urban populations and thus a correspondingly smaller contribution to overall urban mortality. The makeup of urban populations changed in other important ways, as well, as a result of the mass influx of evacuees and mobilized workers, the outflow of young males into the Red Army, and the inflow of teenagers mobilized through the Labor Reserves system. Other groups streaming into the cities included civilians deemed not physically fit to serve in the military and mobilized for work via the State Defense Committee (GKO) and the Committee for the Accounting and Distribution of Labor Power; Central Asians (primarily male collective farmers) mobilized to work in the factories and mines of the Urals; and prison and semi-prison laborers under the control of the NKVD. Under normal circumstances, the influx of teenagers and young adults, groups among whom mortality was generally very low, ought to have lowered overall mortality. Yet there is no way to assess how much the size of these cohorts changed—whether, for example, the outflow of those going into the army was greater or less than the inflow of mobilized workers in these same age groups. Moreover, the young people mobilized into the army tended to be the healthiest sector of the population, whereas the people who replaced them, even if they were the same age, were by definition physically unfit for military service and thus more vulnerable to the adverse living and working conditions of home-front cities. For all of these

39. RGAE, f. 1562, op. 20, d. 484.

Starvation Mortality in Soviet Industrial Regions 289

reasons, any comparison of crude death rates from the prewar and war years would be highly misleading.

Demographers in countries with reasonably accurate census data generally circumvent these various problems by calculating standardized mortality rates, which adjust for the age and gender breakdown of the population under analysis. Such a calculation for the wartime Soviet Union is simply unthinkable, since no such population data exist. We have tried to circumvent this difficulty at least partially by comparing deaths among only a subset of the general urban population: those people aged five years and older. The justification for this should be obvious from the following figures. The prewar Soviet Union had high levels of infant and child mortality. In 1940, for the urban RSFSR as a whole, deaths of children aged between zero and four years accounted for 54.9 percent of all urban deaths; in 1943, they accounted for just 19.7 percent. In the city of Cheliabinsk, deaths in this age group were an astronomical 68.4 percent of all deaths in 1940, but just 16.8 percent in 1943 and 16.6 percent in 1944. In Magnitogorsk, which had a relatively young population, deaths of infants and small children accounted for 73.1 percent of all deaths in the city in 1940, then fell to 21.0 percent in 1943 and 20.6 percent in 1944.

Figure 5.1 shows the deaths of children aged zero to four years as a percentage of all deaths in each region.[40] With the exception of Moscow, the results are remarkably similar from one region to the next. Child deaths dropped from between 55 and 60 percent of total mortality in 1940 to less than 20 percent in 1943, with a small further decline during 1944 in the Volga, Urals, and Western Siberia, and small increases in Central Russia. The reasons for this shift were four-fold: (1) very high infant mortality in 1942, which dramatically reduced the number of infants surviving as toddlers into 1943 and 1944; (2) a collapse in the birthrate in 1942, so that very few babies were born during the remaining years of the war; (3) an improvement in infant mortality rates from 1943 onward, so that a much smaller percentage of those babies who were born died; and (4) a very large increase in adult deaths.

Figures 5.2a–5.2c show the distortion that arises if we include the under-fives in our calculations. The figures look at the major hinterland

40. The sources of the data for all figures in this chapter are given in appendix B.

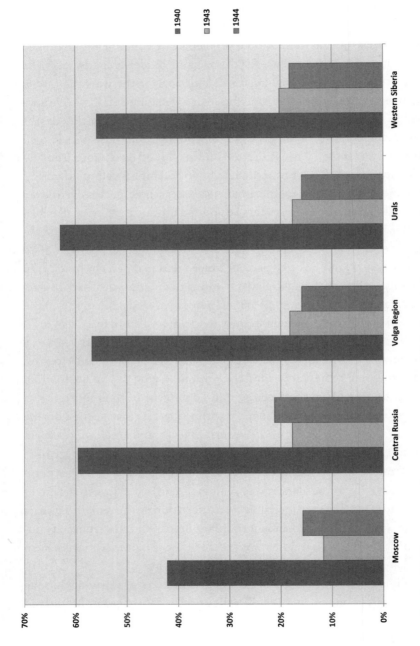

5.1. Deaths of children 4 years and younger as a percentage of all deaths, major home-front regions, 1940 and 1943–1944.

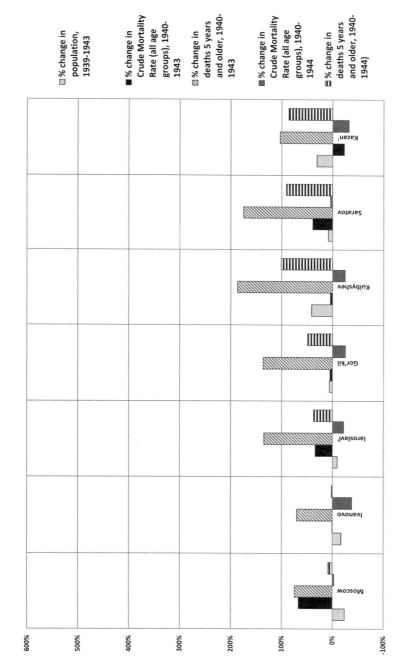

5.2a. Percentage changes in population, 1939–1943; the crude mortality rate, 1940–1944; and the number of deaths of persons aged 5 years and older, 1940–1944, in major home-front cities.

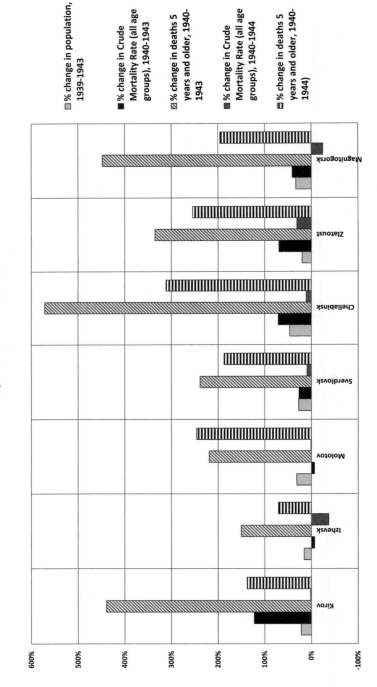

5.2b.

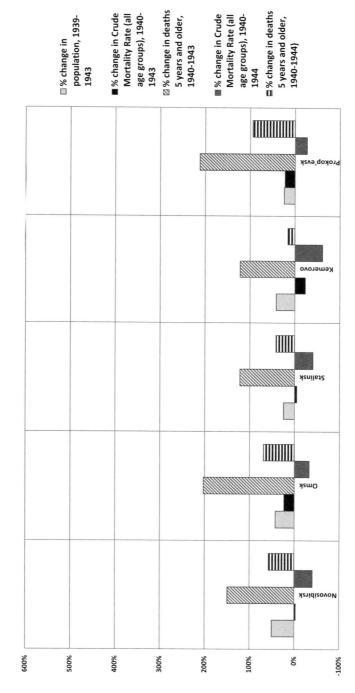

cities for which we have found both 1939 census data and population estimates for January 1, 1944, and compare *percentage changes* in three variables during the period 1940–1944: population; the crude mortality rate; and the number of deaths of persons aged five years and older. Each city has five bars. Reading from left to right, the first bar shows the percentage change in population between the 1939 census and December 31, 1943, the second bar shows the percentage change in the crude mortality rate (CMR) between 1940 and 1943, and the third bar, the percentage change in the number of deaths among people aged five years and older between these same two years. Bars 4 and 5 show the same percentage changes in comparing 1944 with 1940. In cities where bars 2 and 4 appear to be missing, as in Ivanovo, this is because the changes in the CMR were close to zero and are not visible on the graph.

What do figures 5.2a—5.2c tell us? During the war, Soviet home-front cities saw simultaneous increases in the size of their populations and the number of people who died. Was the greater number of deaths due simply to the larger number of people? One way to try to find out is to look at the crude mortality rate (CMR), that is the number of deaths per 1,000 population. If the increase in population sees the CMR remain more or less stable, this suggests that the conditions affecting mortality have not fundamentally altered, and the larger absolute number of deaths is simply in line with the greater number of people. This is indeed the picture that seems to emerge if we look at the CMR in home-front towns and cities. Cities that recorded very large increases in the total number of deaths during 1943 show either very small increases in the crude death rate (Gor'kii, Kuibyshev), or even an actual decline (Kazan', Izhevsk, Molotov, Novosibirsk, Stalinsk, Kemerovo). An even larger number of cities shows a fall in the crude mortality rate during 1944 (Moscow, Ivanovo, Iaroslavl', Gor'kii, Kuibyshev, Kazan', Izhevsk, Novosibirsk, Omsk, Stalinsk, Kemerovo, Prokop'evsk). Looking at the crude death rate alone gives the impression that wartime mortality in these cities either remained in line with changes in population or even improved. Such a conclusion would have very real political and historiographical implications—it would suggest that the USSR, and in particular its food distribution mechanisms and its public health system, had far greater success withstanding the ravages of the war than in fact it did.

Starvation Mortality in Soviet Industrial Regions 295

Yet this conclusion is incorrect. As soon as we strip out deaths among infants and young children and look only at the fates of those aged five and older, the picture changes significantly. Given the dramatic decline in the size of the under-five population and with it the number of under-five deaths, a stable, or even a modest decline in the CMR would mean that deaths among the non-child population had risen and were cancelling out the drop in infant and child deaths. Groups that in normal times had a lower propensity to die now saw their death rates go up. During 1943, deaths in the five-and-older age group, which traditionally accounted for fewer than half of all deaths, shot up by over 100 percent in Kazan', Stalinsk, and Kemerovo; by between 136 and 186 percent in Iaroslavl', Gor'kii, Kuibyshev, Saratov, Izhevsk, and Novosibirsk; by over 200 percent in Molotov, Sverdlovsk, and Prokop'evsk; and by a truly staggering 335 percent in Zlatoust, 439 percent in Kirov, 448 percent in Magnitogorsk, and 571 percent in Cheliabinsk. These rises so vastly outstripped both increases in population and changes in the crude mortality rate that they could not possibly be attributable to population growth alone. On the contrary, they point to a real and very marked increase in mortality among the five-and-older population and an unmistakable shift in the burden of mortality onto older age groups.[41] This conclusion holds valid even if we compare 1940 with 1944, when mortality in absolute terms fell by very large amounts. The percentage increase in deaths among those five and older compared to 1940 is much smaller than in 1943, but it still measurably outstrips changes in population and in the crude mortality rate.

Among the adult population the distribution of deaths within and between age groups, and between men and women, changed with the war.[42] With the exception of Moscow, we see three trends. Firstly, except for the very elderly, within each age group the gap between male and

---

41. The exception to this pattern was Moscow, which was partially depopulated as adults of prime working age exited the city for various reasons, leaving it with a large elderly population which suffered high mortality. Here the crude mortality rate and deaths among the over-fives increased more or less in step with one another—yet even in Moscow, deaths among the five-and-older population in 1943 increased by 75 percent over 1940.

42. The data are too detailed to provide here. What follows is a summary of what these data show.

female deaths widened. In other words, the extra deaths caused by the war fell most heavily on men, despite the greater proportion of females in the population. Secondly, there was a slight—and in some regions pronounced—downward shift in mortality toward younger age groups. The share of deaths among those over the age of sixty declined, and the share of deaths among those aged thirty to fifty-nine went up. Thirdly, there were marked regional differences in this process. Again, the most hard-hit region was the Urals, where the downward shift in the burden of mortality was especially sharp: in 1943 men aged thirty to forty-none (as opposed to thirty to fifty-nine) accounted for a full third of all deaths. In Kirov they made up 38 percent of all deaths, and in Cheliabinsk 41.7 percent.

Causes of Death: The Starvation-Tuberculosis Complex

Figures 5.3a–5.3b show the relative importance of the major causes of death among the population aged five and older in 1940, 1943, and 1944. Two classes of disease—gastrointestinal diseases (infections and conditions such as stomach ulcers), and pneumonia and other diseases of the respiratory system—showed relatively little fluctuation over the period. Some localities (Iaroslavl' and Ivanovo provinces in Central Russia, Molotov and Kirov provinces in the Urals) saw a spike in deaths from gastrointestinal infections during 1942, probably associated with the arrival or through-transit of evacuees, many of whom fell ill and eventually died due to the horrendous sanitary conditions on the trains that carried them eastwards.

The picture with coronary artery disease (in which we also include deaths from strokes) is more mixed. With the exception of Moscow, which retained a relatively large number of elderly inhabitants, deaths from coronary artery disease either remained stable or declined in importance. However, the regional aggregates conceal some measurable local deviations, namely in Kirov (where heart deaths fell markedly in line with the influx of young workers) and Kazan' (where coronary deaths rose following the arrival of elderly evacuees). In general the war should have brought a downward shift in the age profile of the non-child population which, all things being equal, should then have reduced the percentage

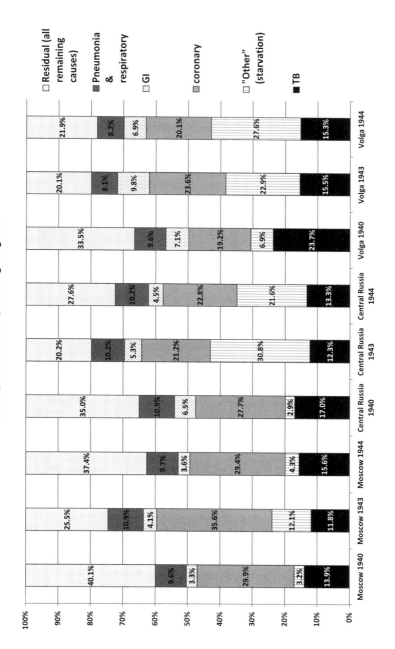

5.3a. Major causes of death of persons aged 5 years and older, home-front industrial regions, 1940 and 1943–1944.

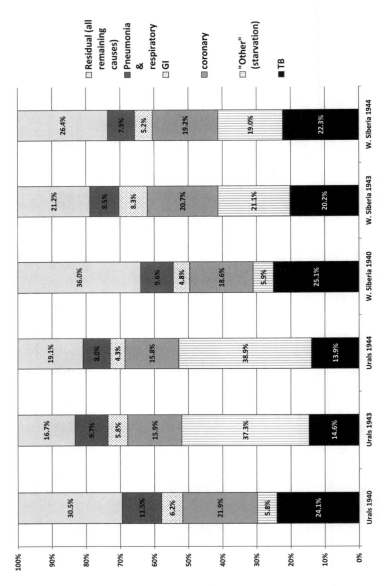
5.3b.

Starvation Mortality in Soviet Industrial Regions 299

of deaths due to heart disease. That these deaths stayed stable among a generally younger population is itself an indirect indicator of a marked deterioration in people's general health, the impact of extreme hunger, and the strains of an almost unbearable intensity of labor. However, without age-specific population data, this observation remains only conjecture. It is equally possible that local variations in coronary artery mortality had less to do with actual medical or social conditions than with local variations in the way the disease was diagnosed (or misdiagnosed) and identified as the probable cause of death.

Figures 5.3a–5.3b clearly show one cause of death that loomed above all others in its contribution to wartime mortality: the starvation-tuberculosis complex. Only Moscow, with its older population and high incidence of heart disease, did not reflect this trend. In the small number of cities and regions for which we have data for 1942, most show that death from the starvation-tuberculosis complex was already starting to rise, but the real surge came in 1943.[43] Within the TB-starvation complex, starvation was the major component, although for reasons already explained, we cannot be certain of the exact relative weights of the two factors. We can illustrate this with the columns for the Urals. Roughly speaking, the importance of starvation would fall within a range: its *minimum* contribution would be the difference between TB + "other" deaths in 1940 and TB + "other" deaths in 1943, a difference of 22 percentage points. Its *maximum* contribution would be the gap between TB deaths in 1943 and TB + "other" deaths in 1943, approximately 37.3 percentage points. If we take the maximum end of the range, in every region except Moscow, starvation became the most important cause of death among the non-child population. If we take the lower end of the range, the picture is somewhat more varied and open to conjecture. In Central Russia and, even more dramatically, the Urals, the role of starvation seems clear and unambiguous. In the Volga and Western Siberia—areas that had very high prewar rates of tuberculosis mortality—it is possible that starvation played a more secondary role.

---

43. The partial exceptions were Ivanovo province and more strikingly, Iaroslavl' province—in the latter case because of the large number of Leningrad evacuees who died of malnutrition while passing through the province.

300   *Donald Filtzer*

It added substantially to overall mortality, without itself becoming the dominant cause.

What is unambiguous, however, is the combined influence of tuberculosis and starvation. In the Urals, by far the worst-affected region, the starvation-tuberculosis complex accounted for 52 percent of all non-child deaths in 1943, and an almost unimaginable 72 percent in the city of Kirov. One way to visualize its effect is to look at the contribution that the starvation-tuberculosis complex made to the increase in all non-child deaths between 1940–1943 and 1940–1944. In other words, how many of the *additional* people who died in 1943 compared to 1940 died because of starvation or tuberculosis? We do this by taking the number of additional tuberculosis + "other" deaths in 1943 compared to 1940 (or respectively, 1944 versus 1940), and seeing what percentage it represents of all additional non-child deaths in these same years. We show this in Figure 5.4.

Figure 5.4 is particularly salient because it illustrates the persistence of the starvation-tuberculosis complex during 1944, when we would generally have assumed that the food situation was improving. Although there were some important local exceptions,[44] the absolute number of deaths in each region declined markedly during 1944, although it is likely that this improvement was confined to the second half of the year. Yet despite this decrease, starvation and tuberculosis combined continued to be the most important single cause of non-child mortality in every region but Moscow, and in some regions their *relative* importance even increased. Figure 5.4 shows that if we look only at the "extra" deaths that occurred in 1944 compared to 1940, the starvation-tuberculosis complex accounted for the vast majority of them, Moscow included.

---

44. Two major exceptions here were the cities of Molotov and Nizhnii Tagil. In Molotov, the number of deaths from tuberculosis and "other" and "non-attributed" causes among the five-and-older population increased from 3,851 in 1943, to 4,592 in 1944, an increase of 19.2 percent. Total deaths in this age group in the same period went up from 8,464 to 9,175, an increase of only 8.4 percent. In Nizhnii Tagil, a city where the authorities specifically identified deaths from starvation on Form 5, the disparity between the increases in starvation and general mortality was even larger: deaths from tuberculosis, "other" causes, "non-attributed" causes, and starvation went from 2,820 in 1943, to 3,288 in 1944, an increase of 16.6 percent; this compared to only a 1.4 percent increase in all deaths among the five-and-older population (5,652 to 5,730).

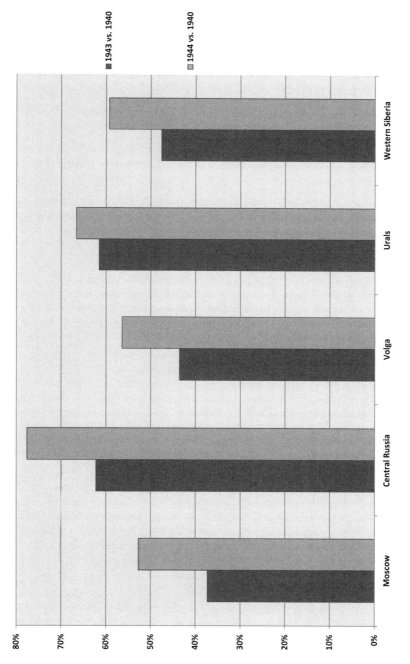

5.4. Percentage of extra deaths of persons aged 5 years and older attributable to TB and "other" causes, 1943 vs. 1940 and 1944 vs. 1940.

302   *Donald Filtzer*

Age and Gender

Another striking feature of wartime starvation is that its burden fell over-whelmingly on males between the ages of thirty and fifty-nine. The age gradient was less pronounced in some regions than in others, but the pattern was true everywhere. We show this graphically by disaggregating "other" deaths from the TB-starvation complex and showing the age and gender distribution of deaths in this category during 1943, the year that saw the highest number of starvation deaths.[45] The result is in figures 5.5a–5.5b. Two features stand out above all others: (1) very few women died of starvation, despite their high representation in the workforce;[46] and (2) among men, the most vulnerable were those aged thirty to fifty-nine. These two features were true in every region, including Moscow, but found their sharpest expression in the Urals and Western Siberia.

45. We have included here all age groups, in order to show the impact of starvation on very small children. While infants and toddlers did die of starvation, they were not its main victims. Conversely, the starvation-tuberculosis complex was not a major cause of death in this age group. In the Urals, the region worst affected by starvation, children aged 0 to 4 years accounted for 17.8 percent of all deaths in 1943, but only 7.4 per cent of starvation deaths. If we take deaths from starvation and tuberculosis together, their share rises slightly, to 10 percent, still well below their share of deaths from all causes. If these children died, they tended to die of other causes, primarily the traditional child-killers of gastrointestinal infections and pneumonia. Among Urals 3- and 4-year-olds, TB overtook pneumonia as the main cause of death in 1943, but these were large percentages of very small numbers of children. Overall, malnutrition cost surprisingly few child lives. But this applies only to urban children. We have no systematic information on mortality among the large number of young children in children's homes in rural areas.

46. We do not know the percentage of women within the urban population as a whole, but within industry, their percentage of the total workforce rarely exceeded 50 percent; they formed the overwhelming bulk of employed personnel only in those industries that had already been "feminized" before the war (food processing, meat and dairy, light industry, and textiles). See the data for December 1942 and October 1944 in RGAE, f. 1562, op. 329, d. 570 and 571 (1942), and d. 1144 and 1145 (1944). In the main branches of defense and defense-related industries they were a far higher percentage of nonindustrial personnel than they were of actual workers. In the service sector their percentage would have been far higher. From the point of view of the discussion here, we can be sure that they made up at least half the urban population, and perhaps considerably more than half. The far lower number of female deaths is therefore an important finding.

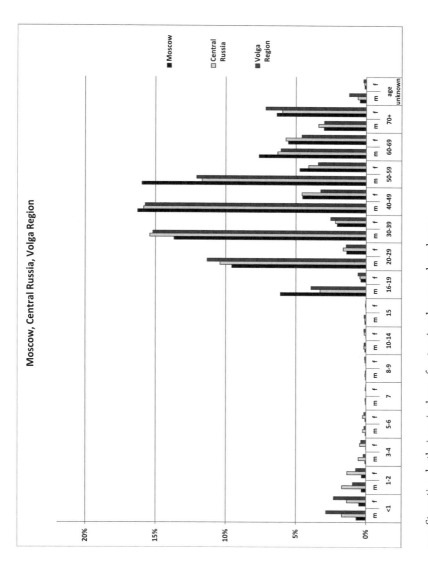

5.5a. Starvation deaths in major home-front regions by age and gender, 1943.

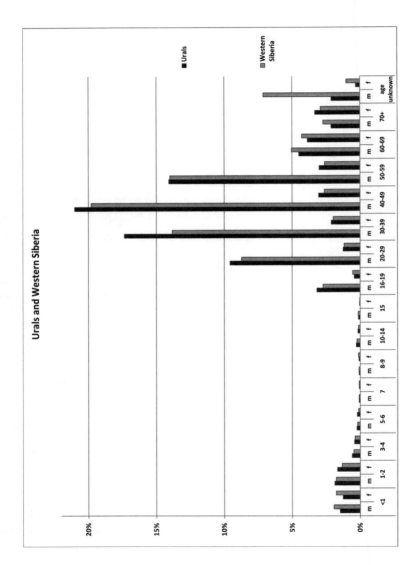
5.5b.

Starvation Mortality in Soviet Industrial Regions 305

The small number of female deaths was not unique to the Soviet Union in World War II. It is a general historical feature of famines that women have a "mortality advantage." What is surprising, however, is that its causes have attracted relatively little research or been plausibly explained.[47] Soviet women were hardly immune to malnutrition. Limited evidence shows that they suffered from amenorrhea, and that malnutrition was the largest single cause of illness-related work absence among women textile workers in Orekhovo-Zuevo in Moscow province during 1942.[48] Yet actual female mortality from starvation remained very low. One possible explanation is that women in any town or region were more likely to have been local. They were also more likely to have been in better health before the war and to have access to a personal plot and social networks through which they could find food. Men, on the other hand, whether mobilized from other parts of the USSR or native to the locality, would by definition have been physically unfit for conscription into the military, and thus would have been more vulnerable to malnutrition.[49] Men mobilized for factory work and shipped east seem to have fared particularly poorly. They were housed in earthen dugouts and makeshift barracks, with no sanitation, and no means to supplement their diets beyond what they received from the ration.

47. Kate Macintyre, "Famine and the Female Mortality Advantage," in Tim Dyson and Cormac Ó Gráda, eds., *Famine Demography: Perspectives from the Past and Present* (Oxford: Oxford University Press, 2002), pp. 240–259. Macintyre discerned three basic types of explanation for women's superior resistance to famines. One was that data collection was poor and the alleged female advantage was not confirmable. Two were biological explanations, which focussed on women's larger reserves of body fat and men's comparative leanness. Third were sociocultural explanations, which have identified factors such as women's responsibility for food acquisition and cooking and the tendency for men to migrate in search of food or work during times of dearth. In the latter case, the men would consume valuable energy and very possibly not find the food for which they were searching, while the women would have the social support of family and community, thus aiding their survival. I am not an expert on any of these topics, but Macintyre points out serious drawbacks to each of these theories, although the biological explanation remains the most plausible. Her main conclusion was that considerably more research is needed before we fully understand this question.

48. See the example of amenorrhea among women workers at Magnitogorsk cited above in n. 10. On Orekhovo-Zuevo, see GARF, f. 5451, op. 43, d. 236, ll. 85–850b., 97, 101, 198, 199.

49. Wendy Goldman, personal communication.

306   *Donald Filtzer*

BEHIND THE DATA: SOCIAL HIERARCHIES
AND TIME LAGS

Despite the large increase in starvation mortality, those who died were, in fact, a minority of all starvation sufferers. What do the data reveal about who died of starvation and who survived? Who was most vulnerable and who had greater access to the limited food aid that the state was able or willing to make available, that factories and local political authorities could grow themselves or wangle out of unofficial sources, or that workers could obtain from their private or collectively tilled allotments?

1943: Who Died of Hunger?

If we look back at table 1.2 in chapter 1, we can reorganize that table's four ration categories into six more refined categories: manual workers performing exceptionally heavy labor; core workers in strategically important industrial enterprises; workers in non-defense industry; white-collar employees; adult dependents; and children. In each group there was an energy tradeoff: at the upper end of the hierarchy, workers performing the most physically demanding jobs received the most food; at the lower end, white-collar employees (school teachers, clerks, low-level officials) and adult dependents used up fewer calories and received very little food. Teenaged children needed a lot of calories, but children had the lowest allocations—adult workers with families often curbed their own consumption in order to facilitate the survival of their children.[50] With the exception of those performing the most arduous labor, the ration alone was insufficient to ensure long-term survival.

Even this picture, however, is vastly over-simplified. Within industry—even defense industry—there were hierarchies of consumption. Younger teenage workers generally had their rations protected, and so they had reasonably good chances of survival. They suffered malnutrition and temporary (and in some cases permanent) growth retardation, but both the mortality data and factory medical reports suggest that they did not die, at least not in large numbers. Among adults, "native" workers with plots

---

50. GARF, f. A-482, op. 52s, d. 82, l. 123.

Starvation Mortality in Soviet Industrial Regions 307

and allotments from before the war had clear survival advantages over evacuees and mobilized workers, most of whom had no plots and were thus totally dependent on their enterprise for provisions.[51] This dependency placed mobilized workers and evacuees in an especially precarious position, because many of them were already in very poor health when they arrived, and it took only a small further deterioration to push them into serious debility or even death.

The position of adult workers is further complicated by uncertainties about who controled, and was responsible for feeding, the vast numbers mobilized to work in home-front industry, especially in the Urals. Virtually all large hinterland factories had construction units, most of which were under the control of the NKVD; the largest factories also employed prisoners directly on the shop floor alongside free workers. The NKVD controled two types of labor power: prisoners in the Gulag and the so-called "Labor Army." Mortality among Gulag prisoners was very high—roughly 20 percent in both 1942 and 1943. Morbidity was even higher: according to the historian V. N. Zemskov, 38.3 percent of all prisoners in the Gulag system in 1942 were so ill or malnourished that they could do only light work, while over a quarter could do no work at all.[52] The

---

51. Marina Vasil'evna Gontsova, "Povsednevnaia zhizn' naseleniia industrial'nogo tsentra v gody Velikoi Otechestvennoi voiny (na materialakh goroda Nizhnii Tagil)" (Candidate of Historical Sciences dissertation, Nizhnii Tagil, 2011), p. 89. All workers, irrespective of whence they came, in theory had the opportunity to earn extra food (so-called Stakhanovite rations) by over-fulfilling their production targets (norms). As Gontsova notes, factories not infrequently found themselves unable to provide these extra food entitlements.

52. V. N. Zemskov, "Smertnost' zakliuchennykh v 1941–1945 gg.," in N. A. Aralovets, A., O. M. Verbitskaia, V. B. Zhiromskaia, Iu. A. Poliakov, and A. I. Repinetskii, eds. *Liudskie poteri SSSR v period vtoroi mirovoi voiny. Sbornik statei* (St. Petersburg: Russko-Baltiiskii Informatsionnyi Tsentr, 1995), pp. 174–177. Zemskov gives figures for the number of prisoners and the number of deaths per calendar year, from which it is possible to calculate mortality rates. For the war period as a whole, average mortality among prisoners leapt from 6.9 percent in 1941 to 20.7 percent in 1942 and 20.3 percent in 1943, before falling back to 8.8 percent in 1944 and 6.7 percent in 1945. Gontsova notes that morbidity in Tagillag in 1942 was even higher than the Gulag average: in May of that year a full half of all prisoners were totally incapable of working ("Povsednevnaia zhizn' naseleniia industrial'nogo tsentra v gody Velikoi Otechestvennoi voiny [na materialakh goroda Nizhnii Tagil]," p. 99).

308   Donald Filtzer

deaths of prisoners, however, were not registered locally and were not included in the data on Form 5.[53]

The disposition of the Labor Army (*trudovaia armiia*—its members were known as *trudarmeitsy*) is more difficult to assess. A large part of the Labor Army was made up of Soviet Germans deported from various parts of the USSR, including soldiers of German ethnicity serving loyally in the Red Army. However, it also included prisoners released early from prisons and jails, workers of draft age mobilized from Central Asia and sent to industry, coal mining, and construction rather than into the Red Army, and young people of draft age considered physically unfit for military duty and dispatched to work in the rear.[54] Not all—not even a

53. The law on registration of Gulag deaths was set down in an order (*Prikaz*) of the NKVD of the USSR, "O poriadke registratsii smerti zakliuchennykh," June 11, 1939. GARF, f. 9401, op. 1a. d. 34, ll. 35–350b. I am grateful to Leonid Borodkin for giving me a copy of this order. The regulations stipulated that, when a prisoner died, the death was to be communicated to the ZAGS (registration office) in the locality whence the prisoner had originally come, although the cause of death and the location where the prisoner died were to be kept strictly secret. Although space does not allow us to show the calculations here, the number of starvation deaths among prisoners at Tagillag camps located within Nizhnii Tagil in 1943 exceeded by around one-third the number of starvation deaths recorded on the city's Form 5. Camp deaths could not, therefore, have been included in the Form 5 data. Calcuated from figures in Gontsova, "Povsednevnaia zhizn' naseleniia industrial'nogo tsentra v gody Velikoi Otechestvennoi voiny (na materialakh goroda Nizhnii Tagil)," p. 246, and data on the Nizhnii Tagil official website, www.history.ntagil.ru/7_19.htm.

54. There is now a substantial body of literature on the "Labor Army." The most important published works are the collection coauthored by V. M. Kirillov, P. M. Kuz'mina, N. M. Paegde, A. A. Permiakov, and S. L. Raznikov, *Gedenkbuch: Kniga pamiati nemtsev-trudarmeitsev Bogoslovlaga 1941–1946* (Moscow and Nizhnii Tagil: BIZ, 2008); and G. A. [Grigorii Aleksandrovich] Goncharov, *"Trudovaia Armiia" na Urale v gody Velikoi Otechestvennoi voiny* (Cheliabinsk: Cheliabinsk State University, 2006). For the problem of rejected draftees, see GARF, f. A-482, op. 52s, d. 82, l. 78.

The Central Asian workers—of whom over 160,000 had been mobilized by February 1943 (Goncharov, *"Trudovaia Armiia,"* pp. 118–119)—deserve special attention, which we cannot give to them here. Theirs was an especially sad tale. Known variously as *natsionaly* or *natsmeny* and coming not just from Central Asia, but also from Bashkiriia and Tatariia, they were horribly abused and neglected, not just by the factories, mines, and construction organizations that employed them, but by the selection commissions that rounded them up and despatched them in the first place. As a rule, they arrived at their destinations with only the clothes on their backs, many without shoes. They endured ice-cold barracks and, despite their hunger, could not, or would not, eat the

Starvation Mortality in Soviet Industrial Regions 309

majority—of mobilized workers were *trudarmeitsy,* but those who were came under the administration of the NKVD. We know from factory medical reports that it was common for them to work side by side with "free" workers. It appears, however, that the NKVD was responsible for feeding them, and mortality among them was also high. One source claims that in Sverdlovsk province during 1942–1943, some four thousand German *trudarmeitsy* died, half of them from starvation.[55]

The question here is, who registered their deaths, the NKVD or the local medical authorities, and do the mortality data from Form 5 include them? This is not a technical question—it greatly affects how we interpret the figures. For if their deaths were not included in Form 5, it means that the figures analyzed here reflect the full severity of starvation among the general population. If, on the other hand, their deaths are part of these data, it suggests a rather different picture—namely, that a certain, perhaps significant proportion of starvation mortality fell upon especially vulnerable groups of workers, and that the free civilian population had at least some degree of protection from the very worst effects of acute malnutrition, at least until 1944.

The probability is that boundaries between *trudarmeitsy* and free labor were blurred. Some, if not most, *trudarmeitsy* lived in NKVD camps and were clearly their property. But factory and province medical reports make it clear that this was not always the case, especially for workers mobilized from Central Asia and other non-Russian republics. Factory No. 76 in Serov, in Sverdlovsk province, reported that a large proportion of its workers suffered from malnutrition in 1943, yet relatively few were classed as suffering from clinical starvation—and of these, the vast majority were *trudarmeitsy* already suffering from the condition when they

---

unfamiliar food they were given. Their general state of health was so bad that a large percentage of them had to be sent back home, and death rates among them could be very high indeed: at one defense factory in Molotov province, 105 out of the 405 *natsmeny* arriving during 1943 died, primarily of starvation. Another 147 were returned to their native republic—an overall attrition rate of 62.2 percent. GARF, f. A-482, op. 52s, d. 80, ll. 2020b., 203. This may have been an extreme case, but it was typical of their experience throughout the Urals and elsewhere. For other accounts, see the series of reports from different localities in GARF, f. A-482, op. 47, d. 1430.

55. V. P. Motrevich, "Rabochie kolonny," http://www.ural.ru/spec/ency/encyclo paedia-16-1676.html.

310 Donald Filtzer

arrived at the factory.[56] City Hospital No. 1 in Sverdlovsk reported that of the 243 patients who died there of starvation during 1943, around 8 percent were from NKVD construction battalions, and a further 14.4 percent were *priezzhie,* that is, they had come to the city from elsewhere under one capacity or another.[57] Figures for 1944 from the Uralmash hospital in Sverdlovsk—which treated workers not just from Uralmash, but from a number of factories, together with their dependents—are harder to interpret. They show that roughly a quarter of the patients they treated in their internal medicine departments were mobilized workers, although we have no way of knowing how many of them were NKVD laborers or how many were treated for starvation.[58] We have somewhat firmer figures from M. Kirillov and colleagues, who provide estimates of the number of Germans attached to industrial enterprises during 1942–1944 and the estimated mortality rates among them, both in the Urals as a whole and in Sverdlovsk province. From the latter we can extrapolate that, during 1943, deaths among Labor-Army Germans living outside of NKVD camps could have contributed a maximum of 3.6 percent to all deaths of those aged five and older in Sverdlovsk province, although the real percentage could well have been lower.[59]

56. GARF, f. A-482, op. 52, d. 82, ll. 140, 217.

57. GARF, f. A-482, op. 47, d. 2124, ll. 120, 127a [*sic*].

58. GARF, f. A-482, op. 47, d. 2225, ll. 285, 290. Starvation was the single largest cause of deaths in the hospital in both 1943 and 1944, but the report does not give a social breakdown of those who died.

59. Kirillov, et al., *Gedenkbuch,* pp. 36, 65, 66. They draw their data from various sources, both primary and secondary. On January 1, 1944, there were 29,033 German *trudarmeitsy* in NKVD camps in Sverdlovsk province, plus 11,042 attached to industrial enterprises. In December 1942 the number of *trudarmeitsy* camp inmates had been 39,130, indicating a 25.8 percent drop in their numbers over the course of 1943. Assuming a similar fall in the numbers attached to enterprises, the mid-1943 number (from which we would calculate a mortality rate) would be approximately 12,960. The mortality rate among Labor Army inmates in Tagillag and Bogoslovlag during 1943 was roughly 7.4 percent. Assuming a similar mortality rate among Labor Army Germans working in enterprises (in reality, it was probably lower) implies 959 deaths among them, or 3.6 percent of the 26,518 urban deaths among those aged 5 and older in Sverdlovsk province for that year. These, of course, are extremely crude calculations, but it is unlikely that they distort the order of magnitude of the Labor Army's contribution to total mortality.

Starvation Mortality in Soviet Industrial Regions

All of these bits of evidence taken together suggest that the Labor Army and other sections of the compulsorily mobilized workforce made at least some contribution to the high number of *officially recorded* starvation deaths in those regions where they were heavily employed, but not enough to have greatly influenced overall mortality rates. Far and away the greatest share of the burden of starvation mortality fell upon the civilian population. More importantly, we should be careful not to confuse cause with effect: if starvation deaths were especially high in the Urals, this was not because the Urals had larger numbers of *trudarmeitsy*. On the contrary, *trudarmeitsy* died there because they encountered in more acute form the same conditions that produced high mortality among the population at large.

The other great imponderable is the contribution to mortality of those who did not work in defense plants: workers in industries deemed less essential to the war effort; white-collar employees; and dependents, including the dependents of workers. Despite the mobilization of all available resources for the war, these people made up a large percentage of the civilian population. Even in Nizhnii Tagil, an archetypal Urals factory town, dependents, school pupils, and children made up a full 41 percent of those receiving some form of rations; the other 59 percent consisted of workers, white-collar employees, teachers, and students in higher education (the latter two categories having been granted workers'-level rations in 1943). Many dependents, especially those native to the region, had garden plots, as well as other (not necessarily legal) sources of food, but on the whole they constituted a large reservoir of highly vulnerable people.[60]

---

60. Gontsova, "Povsednevnaia zhizn' naseleniia industrial'nogo tsentra v gody Velikoi Otechestvennoi voiny (na materialakh goroda Nizhnii Tagil)," p. 93. According to Gontsova (ibid., p. 57), in 1943 there were 112,865 private plots in the city, rising to a peak of 126,000 in 1944—nearly double the number there had been in 1942. This averaged out to roughly one plot for every two residents. In 1943, for Sverdlovsk province as a whole, private plots provided 38.4 percent of urban residents' needs for potatoes (ibid., p. 61, citing figures from A. N. Trifonov). Gontsova seems to consider this an impressive figure, but in fact, given the poor state supply of potatoes and vegetables, it further supports the picture shown by Nizhnii Tagil's mortality data: the city faced a huge nutritional gap that the private plots were unable to fill.

In the absence of data on the social origins of those who died,[61] we can only speculate about where the burden of starvation mortality fell most heavily. The documentation in the archives deals overwhelmingly with workers in defense industry. We know that malnutrition among them was rife, that it created high levels of morbidity which cost factories large amounts of lost work time, and that many workers died, sometimes right on the shop floor. However, the anecdotal evidence suggests that, despite the huge number of calories they expended, local workers, those mobilized from other regions and freely-hired, and those not under control of the NKVD were not the primary victims of starvation mortality. It is more likely that starvation mortality fell most heavily upon those who received the least: workers unable to meet their production quotas, and thus unable to claim extra meals; evacuees with no access to garden plots; Central Asians, many of whom arrived in the Urals already frail and malnourished, who could not cope with the Urals climate and the unfamiliar diet; members of the Labor Army; non-working dependents; and virtually anyone, whether in employment or not, whose state of health was already dangerously weak. In short, in 1942 and 1943, the weakest and least protected died first. In 1944, however, this picture showed a marked shift. The cumulative effects of overwork and inadequate nutrition penetrated deeper into the ranks of so-called "cadre" workers—that is, experienced workers, who were reasonably skilled, were either native to the town or city where they were now working or evacuated there with their prewar factories, and whose diets up until then had allowed them to carry on working.

1944: The Changing Pattern of Starvation

Even a cursory glance at figures 5.2a–5.2c shows that right across the USSR, 1944 saw a sharp fall in both the absolute number of non-child deaths and deaths from starvation. What the mortality data do not show

---

61. Up until the mid-1930s, the statistical authorities produced Form 5 returns for each social group (workers, white-collar employees, specialists, people who were economically independent), as well as aggregate records for each locality. The practice was then discontinued.

Starvation Mortality in Soviet Industrial Regions 313

is that in that same year the cumulate effect of overwork and prolonged malnutrition began to take a heavy toll not just on the most vulnerable sections of the population, but on core workers. The most serious problem it posed to the regime was not necessarily mortality, as great as it was, but its high cost in lost work time among the living. For the vast bulk of starvation sufferers did not die—if given rest and re-feeding most could survive. Economically, however, they were dead weight. They could not work, and thus contributed nothing to production, yet to save them required diverting scarce food resources that otherwise could have gone to provide energy to workers still on the job (or to the local elites for whom starvation was never a serious threat).

The main evidence here are not the mortality data, but figures for the sickness rate (*zabolevaemost'*)—that is, the amount of time workers were absent from work due to temporary disability through illness or injury. Soviet practice employed two different measures of sickness absence: the number of cases recorded per 100 workers, and the average number of days lost per 100 workers.[62]

It is worth noting that in recording the causes of lost work time, the Soviets used a totally different classification scheme from the one used for recording mortality. They were interested only in a relatively small number of problems, although recording practice varied from one factory to another. Thus they were very concerned with colds, "flu," and tonsillitis, but not with pneumonia (even though pneumonia was one of the greatest killers of adults after tuberculosis and starvation), in the

---

62. The quality of these data—compiled by both the trade unions and factory medical personnel—is not good. During 1942 in particular, record-keeping was chaotic, and many factories, especially those evacuated to the east, did not keep any records at all. Equally important, in mid-1942, the regime, alarmed at the rising number of days lost due to accidents and sickness, tightened up the rules on factory doctors issuing sick notes. Workers now had to be more seriously ill or injured in order to be granted time off from work. Thus any figures, even if scrupulously collected and presented, comparing the same factory in 1942 and 1943 were not using comparable standards of measurement. More significant from the point of view of the years we are discussing here (1943–1944), the sickness figures, as high as they were in most factories, do not fully reflect the huge toll that the war took on workers' health, not just because of the tight rules governing the issue of sick notes, but also because the data recorded only sick notes issued for three days or more.

314   *Donald Filtzer*

mistaken belief that high rates of "flu" were the result of the failure of factory managers to heat workshops and dormitories and protect workers from drafts.[63] They recorded time lost to acute gastrointestinal infections, but not dysentery (another major killer of adults), in the correct belief that they could cut the incidence of acute infections if they improved hygiene in their dining rooms and canteens. For obvious and legitimate reasons, they recorded time lost due to work and domestic injuries and to skin infections, none of which made any significant contribution to mortality.[64]

The main information we have on how starvation impacted on lost work time is from the Urals, and to a lesser extent from the Kuzbass. At most Urals defense enterprises, debility and morbidity (as opposed to mortality) from starvation were actually worse in 1944 than in 1943, as long working hours and protracted food deprivation finally reduced large numbers of cadre workers to a point where, despite their better general state of health and higher rations, they were physically unable to carry on.

---

63. Upper respiratory viruses thrive in cold conditions; the real problem was overcrowded barracks and workplaces, which facilitated their transmission.

64. Sickness rate data were collected, collated, and disseminated by VTsSPS, which used these main categories: "flu" and tonsillitis; skin infections; injuries (work and domestic); rheumatism; pulmonary tuberculosis; malaria; acute gastrointestinal infections; coronary artery disease; gynecological illnesses; and time lost by women caring for sick children or other dependents. All other causes of lost work time went into the "other" category, which could account for anywhere from one-third to one-half of all days lost. Factory doctors kept more precise records, and their quarterly and year-end reports also recorded time lost to chronic conditions (such as stomach ulcers), eye infections, and the major infectious diseases (dysentery, typhus, typhoid fever, brucellosis). Most factories concealed time lost to starvation in the "other category," but many did not, especially in the Urals, which is why we have the data we are discussing here.

Skin infections deserve special attention because both during and after the war they were one of the major causes of lost work time. The obvious cause of this was the poor state of work and domestic hygiene, including the almost total absence of soap, and during the war, also the shortage of bandages and materials for dressing wounds. Yet we should also keep in mind that both the incidence and severity of skin infections are sensitive to malnutrition. So here we see a class of nutrition-dependent diseases which, while not contributing directly to mortality, nonetheless was a major cause of morbidity. See Catherine J. Field, Ian R. Johnson, and Patricia D. Schley, "Nutrients and their role in host resistance to infection," *Journal of Leukocyte Biology* 71 (January 2002): p. 26.

Starvation Mortality in Soviet Industrial Regions   315

Hunger in these factories displayed a clear seasonal pattern. Its first peak was in mid-1943, it abated during the last three months of that year, and then suddenly worsened, in many factories dramatically, during the first six months of 1944, after which it steadily declined to very low levels. At first glance, such a pattern is more or less what we would expect. In the fall of 1943 workers and factories would have harvested food from the allotments and farms, mainly potatoes and vitamin-containing vegetables. Workers would have subsisted off these until stocks ran out. The sickness rate evidence suggests that in most places this happened sometime during early 1944, after which food supplies fell back to levels that no longer sustained workers' ability to work, or even their ability to stay alive. There are, however, at least two complications here, both of which make it harder to understand the apparent improvement in food supplies. The first is the poor harvest of 1943, in response to which the regime reduced ration allowances in November of that year. The second concerns the importance of potatoes, which in turn has two aspects to it. Growing potatoes and vegetables on an allotment, even where workers cultivated their plots collectively, comes at a cost in energy. Unless workers had a non-working family member who could tend the plot on a regular basis outside of winter time, they would have been performing their agricultural labor, much of which was physically demanding and quite arduous, on top of their already energy-sapping shifts on the shop floor. Therefore, the question was always whether the yields from the plots provided more energy than people expended cultivating them. Where yields were poor or harvested foods were lost because of poor storage, the energy balance could indeed by negative.[65] Second, as we have already noted, in Sverdlovsk and Sverdlovsk province, including Nizhnii Tagil, much of the 1943 potato crop, both on factory farms and on workers' allotments, was lost due to potato blight. The blight had so contaminated the soil that local agronomists even cautioned against planting a new crop in 1944.[66] The

---

65. During 1943, a number of aviation factories lost the bulk of their harvests due to poor plowing and failure to bring in the crops on time, so they rotted in the fields. GARF, f. 7678, op. 7, d. 154, ll. 27–28.

66. GARF, f. 5451, op. 43, d. 301, ll. 15, 41, 42, 420b. We have found no reference to this in the files of the People's Commissariat of Public Health, from which most of our knowledge of semi-starvation and starvation comes. It came to light because local trade

316   *Donald Filtzer*

impact of the potato blight in Sverdlovsk province is clear enough, but it is important to note that we still see large-scale semi-starvation in the other regions where we know, from table I.2 in the book's introduction, that potato yields did provide at least some—and often a substantial—addition to overall nutrition.

The scale on which clinical starvation advanced into the industrial workforce in the Urals was in many cases truly dramatic. An April 1944 report from the Sverdlovsk province NKVD to Beria, Stalin, and other members of the leadership, set out in striking terms just how serious the food situation had become. During early 1944, province defense plants reported critical shortages of protein, fats, and non-bread sources of carbohydrates. Supplies of potatoes at peasant markets had collapsed to barely 10 percent of what they had been just three months before (presumably because of the potato blight); the markets had little milk or butter for sale. Prices rose accordingly: a kilogram of potatoes (roughly one-day's consumption) cost 75 rubles; a kilogram of meat, 350 rubles; a kilogram of butter, 1,000 rubles. If we consider that an average worker earned roughly 450–500 rubles a month, we can see just how little privately purchased food workers could buy at these prices. The impact on workers' health was stark: as of April 1944, town and district medical units had registered 22,400 cases of starvation and semi-starvation, the "absolute majority" of whom were urban residents, and most of these were workers. The death toll was severe: in March 1944 alone there were 451 deaths from starvation in the city of Sverdlovsk, 428 in Nizhnii Tagil, and 112 in Serov.[67]

Factory No. 76, an ammunition factory in Serov, showed just how rapidly conditions deteriorated. The plant claimed to have had very few starvation cases among its non-mobilized workforce during 1943, but in

---

union officials in Sverdlovsk and Sverdlovsk province asked VTsSPS in Moscow to consult with Moscow agronomists to find out if the warning of the local agronomists was correct. We do not know how the matter ended. This file also contains a note from communications workers union officials in Sverdlovsk noting that at their factories there had been further crop losses due to widespread flooding, which had led to some 350 workers suffering from semi-starvation. Ibid., l. 49.

67. GARF, f. 9401, op. 2, d. 264, ll. 293–294, reproduced in http://www.alexander yakovlev.org/fond/issues/62057 as document No. 257. I am grateful to Brandon Schechter for providing me with a copy.

Starvation Mortality in Soviet Industrial Regions

1944, over 12 percent of its workforce lost time because of starvation.[68] During the nine months of January to September 1944, around 4.5 percent of the total workforce of Uralmash in Sverdlovsk either died or was granted permanent discharge because of ill health. During the half-year, January–June 1944, an additional 5 percent was placed on temporary sick leave because of starvation.[69]

The food crisis was not confined to Sverdlovsk province. In late 1943 and early 1944, the iron and steel combine in Magnitogorsk had seven thousand workers—roughly one out of every seven employees—spend time in special rest homes for re-feeding and recovery.[70] Another iron and steel works, Factory No. 700 in Molotov province, put over one thousand of its workers—one out of every fourteen—through similar programs during the calendar year 1944.[71]

The factory trade union committee at Factory No. 259, an ammunition factory in Zlatoust, noted in early February 1944 that 4,000 workers were diagnosed with clinical signs of starvation. According to the union's report, 200 were at stage 3, an advanced and usually terminal state of starvation; 600 were either at stage 2 or were borderline between stages 1 and 2—that is, seriously ill but able to recover with careful re-feeding and

---

68. GARF, f. A-482, op. 47, d. 2225, l. 106.

69. GARF, f. 8131, op. 37, d. 1841, l. 205. During 1944, Uralmash had an average establishment of around 18,600 workers. It had its own large farm, and many of its workers had private plots, from which they harvested 9,500 tons of potatoes in 1944—around half a ton per worker, or enough to provide a worker and his or her family 1,150 kilocalories of energy a day. Yet during January–June 1944 the factory lost a total 27,057 work days due to starvation. We do not know how many workers were actually affected, but we know from the clinical literature on starvation that workers signed off work because of it usually were off the job anywhere from as little as two weeks to more than two months. If the average time lost per patient was one month—an average of milder and more serious cases—this would imply that around 900 workers, or about 5 percent of the workforce, suffered from starvation during the first half of 1944. Remember, this figure is for just six months. Had the trend continued for the whole of 1944 (which it did not), the percentage affected would have been twice as large. This figure is over and above the 4.5 percent who died or whose health was so bad that it forced them to leave work altogether. Ibid., l. 208. We do not know how many of these cases were due to starvation or tuberculosis, but the number could not have been small.

70. GARF, f. A-482, op. 47, d. 2210, ll. 15, 55–56. See above, n. 9.

71. GARF, f. A-482, op. 47, d. 2214, ll. 106–107; the size of the factory's workforce is in RGAE, f. 8875, op. 46, d. 103, l. 30b.

318   *Donald Filtzer*

rest; and the remaining 3,200 were at stage 1, ill but with a good prognosis with medical intervention.[72] The local union described the situation:

> The workers' ration is very small, in the best case it consists of the basic ration and one extra ration ticket for those entitled to a Stakhanovite ration or extra nourishment [*usilennoe dietnoe pitanie*—UPD]: 100 grams of groats, 100 grams of meat, and 20 to 25 grams of fats. This basket of foods might be sufficient for just one meal a day, but if you take into consideration the working conditions at our factory—an eleven-hour day and the high intensity of labor—it is clear that the nutrition is inadequate.
>
> The failure of the city's vegetable harvest, its location far away from any agricultural districts, and the fact that the factory's Department of Workers' Provisioning [ORS] has no access to any decentralized sources of food procurement, make it impossible to improve workers' diets from these sources.
>
> All this explains the factory's high levels of sickness; in the shop headed up by comrade Zenikov, over 50 percent of the workers are suffering from semi-starvation [*distrofiia*]; in hot shops the number of workers being put out of action is especially high. Because of the poor level of nutrition, people's resistance to virtually every disease is low, in particular their resistance to influenza, acute gastrointestinal infections, skin infections, and others. Temporary disability due to pulmonary tuberculosis has risen from 0.06 percent [of the workforce] in 1943, to 0.08 percent.[73]

We can illustrate the larger trend through the example of the Vysokogorskii Machine Factory in Nizhnii Tagil, which during the war operated as an ammunition factory under the designation of Factory No. 63 (table 5.2). While we could have chosen several Urals factories, the value of No. 63 is that it allows us to trace the progression of days lost to starvation on a month-by-month basis over the entire course of 1943 and 1944. Row 2 of the table shows the total number of days lost to sickness and injury per 100 workers for each month in 1943; row 3 shows the number of days lost specifically to semi-starvation and starvation; and row 4 converts the raw figures in rows 2 and 3 into percentages, allowing us to measure starvation's relative importance among the various causes of workers' ill-health. Rows 5–7 repeat the same exercise for 1944.

Even in 1943, starvation cost this factory more days lost to sickness than any other factor except for skin infections, a category also sensitive

---

72. For a discussion of the different stages of semistarvation and starvation, see Rebecca Manley's chapter in this volume.

73. GARF, f. 5451, op. 43, d. 301, l. 31.

Table 5.2. Days lost to temporary disability, 1943 and 1944, Vysokogorskii Machine Factory, Nizhnii Tagil, including all days lost and days lost to starvation per 100 workers

	Jan.	Feb.	Mar.	Apr.	May	June	July	Aug.	Sept.	Oct.	Nov.	Dec.	Total
1943, all days	107.4	135.4	144.6	129.0	122.4	82.4	109.9	119.5	178.9	210.7	157.7	148.2	1646.1
starvation	3.0	10.0	12.0	16.6	16.7	18.2	21.3	19.6	46.7	40.0	27.2	20.5	251.8
% starvation	2.8%	7.4%	8.3%	12.9%	13.6%	22.1%	19.4%	16.4%	26.1%	19.0%	17.2%	13.8%	15.3%
1944, all days	192.6	150.3	155.9	128.8	137.7	197.4	240.6	152.3	134.4	130.8	75.9	88.4	1785.1
starvation	34.8	26.0	38.4	36.2	53.2	61.2	102.9	65.3	22.3	15.2	4.4	0	459.9
% starvation	18.1%	17.3%	24.6%	28.1%	38.6%	31.0%	42.8%	42.9%	16.6%	11.6%	5.8%	0.0%	25.8%

Source: GARF, f. A-482, op. 47, d. 2225, ll. 138, 139, 140.

320   *Donald Filtzer*

to malnutrition. In 1944, however, starvation reigned supreme, outstripping even the catch-all category of "other causes" of lost work time. More importantly, the table reveals the chronological progression of the problem. During the first three months of 1943 starvation was at very low levels, accounting for well under 10 percent of all days lost to sickness. In April 1943, it began to rise, and fluctuated at fairly high levels through September, after which it underwent a gradual decline. In January 1944, however, it began once more to rise, accelerating in both absolute numbers and as a percentage of all sickness, reaching a peak in July at a level more than twice as costly as July of the previous year, and 64 percent higher than 1943's worst month, September. In August 1944, it fell back to its June level, and then dropped sharply, and by December 1944 had disappeared altogether as a factor influencing workers' health.

Factory No. 63 was probably at the more extreme end of the spectrum in terms of the total number of days of temporary disability and the number of days attributed to starvation, but all the Urals factories for which we have collected medical reports showed the same general trajectory.[74]

Earlier, we discussed how the lack of trained physicians and their inexperience recognizing cases of starvation influenced the reliability of cause of death diagnoses. These same difficulties also beset factory doctors treating workers in defense industry. Because the condition usually progressed slowly, at least among non-prison workers, sufferers themselves did not necessarily understand the cause of their deteriorating health and seek medical assistance. At least up through 1943, factory doctors tended to mistake signs of advanced starvation—lethargy, inability

---

74. By the same token, there were other localities in an even worse state. Krasnoural'sk in Sverdlovsk province recorded 229 starvation deaths during January–May 1944, a full 45.8 percent of all recorded deaths. GARF, f. A-482, op. 47, d. 2030, l. 730b. The town had a population in 1944 of approximately 35,000, and had this rate of starvation deaths persisted over the entire year, it would have worked out to 157 deaths per 10,000 population. Compare that to the roughly 80.4 starvation deaths per 10,000 population that we can calculate for Sverdlovsk in 1943, when starvation mortality was at its highest. Sverdlovsk recorded 4,364 deaths specifically due to starvation during 1943; on January 1, 1944, its population was around 543,000. Sverdlovsk deaths are from Form 5, as given in appendix B. Population figures for both cities are from RGAE, f. 1562, op. 20, d. 484, ll. 34, 37.

Starvation Mortality in Soviet Industrial Regions

to stand, loss of vision, incontinence, bradycardia, and hypothermia—as symptoms of its earlier stages. Because they were already under pressure to avoid signing workers off work, when finding patients with these symptoms, they tended simply to place them on lighter work or assign them bed rest at home. This was insufficient, because at this stage of starvation, patients needed not just rest, but re-feeding. What this means is that many cases that in 1943 would have been treatable if detected early, instead led to long-term morbidity and/or death.[75] Conversely, by 1944, factory doctors understood the clinical manifestations of semi-starvation much better, picked up cases earlier, and prescribed remedial measures in time to prevent its more serious manifestations. And while this may account for some of the statistical increase in sickness absence due to semi-starvation, its main significance was clinical: because doctors were better at detecting cases, they could act promptly to assist recovery.

Such medical intervention would have been impossible, however, if factories had not had the resources—both the food and the replacement labor power—to allow them to place starving workers on re-feeding programs and minimize the case mortality rate. This became possible only in 1944, to some extent thanks to food aid from the United States.[76] In Magnitogorsk, for example, the level of starvation deaths in 1943 and 1944 was far, far lower than in either Cheliabinsk or Zlatoust (the other main iron and steel town in Cheliabinsk province). In Magnitogorsk during both of these years, roughly 30 percent of all deaths were due to the starvation-tuberculosis complex, compared to 53 percent of all deaths in Zlatoust in 1943 and 52 percent in 1944, and 50.1 percent and 49.4 percent, respectively, in Cheliabinsk. Magnitogorsk was a relatively privileged enterprise, and if, as already noted, it put seven thousand workers through re-feeding, this very probably goes a long way toward explaining the city's lower starvation death rate.[77]

---

75. GARF, f. A-482, op. 47, d. 1408, ll. 70b.–16. Even where cases were detected in time, hospitals and other inpatient units did not always have the food needed to effect refeeding. See also Filtzer, *Hazards,* pp. 180–183.

76. See the discussion of Lend-Lease food aid in the following section.

77. Toward the end of 1943, the iron and steel combine's medical department organized a system of early identification and diagnosis of sufferers. The least severe cases received extra food in their workshops; moderately severe cases went for re-feeding

Donald Filtzer

This trend was observable also in the Kuzbass, a region that differed from the Urals in that its workers were able to supplement their diets with large amounts of food that they grew themselves. Here, too, however, starvation and nutrition-dependent deaths in 1943 were far from insignificant.[78] Deaths from tuberculosis were very high, causing around 20 percent of all non-child deaths in each of the region's major cities (Prokop'evsk, Stalinsk, and Kemerovo). Deaths from "other" and "non-classified" causes, together with those directly attributed to starvation, made up another 15 to 25 percent of all deaths. This same pattern carried over into 1944, when the starvation-tuberculosis complex remained the largest single cause of non-child deaths, although in the Kuzbass, as elsewhere, overall mortality fell sharply. The medical reports for 1944 show that once sufferers were placed in an inpatient facility, case mortality became fairly low. In other words, there continued to be large numbers of badly malnourished adults in the Kuzbass, but far fewer of them now died. Thus of 45 starvation cases hospitalized in Stalinsk in 1944, not one died. Of 145 cases hospitalized in Prokop'evsk, only 28 died. Of 333 starvation cases hospitalized in the mining center of Anzhero-Sudzhensk,

---

to one of four newly set-up rest homes; and the most severe cases were admitted to a special inpatient facility. The latter was closed at the end of 1944 because it had no patients. GARF, f. A-482, op. 47, d. 2210, ll. 55–56. What is interesting is that despite these efforts, overall mortality in Magnitogorsk was not low. The city had an unusually high number of deaths from pneumonia. It is, of course, possible that doctors were deliberately falsifying their cause-of-death reporting and ascribing a significant proportion of their starvation deaths to pneumonia. The account of the measures taken at the iron and steel combine to combat starvation is sufficiently believable to doubt that this was the case.

78. Kemerovo province was somewhat unique in that, although its statistical administration openly listed deaths from starvation on Form 5, most deaths from starvation were clearly being hidden under the "other" and "non-classified" rubrics. In all other regions that cited starvation as a cause of death on Form 5, the number of such deaths was considerably in excess of those on lines 83 and 84. Here it was just the opposite. The 1943 returns for Prokop'evsk listed 98 deaths from starvation, versus 471 in the "other" and "non-classified" categories. In 1944 they listed 32 starvation deaths, versus 120 deaths from "other" and "non-classified" causes. In Stalinsk the corresponding figures in 1943 were 88 and 396, and in 1944, 3 and 172. Kemerovo claimed 166 starvation deaths in 1943, versus 315 from "other" and "non-classified" causes; in 1944 the respective figures were 24 and 150.

Starvation Mortality in Soviet Industrial Regions   323

at most 22 died, possibly fewer.[79] The fact was that the Kuzbass now had enough food to keep most of these people alive.

By the second half of 1944, the state had enough resources to devote extra food to the starving through re-feeding programs. Once food became available, it channeled it toward saving the starving even though they no longer made any contribution to production. We can perhaps better appreciate just how much the situation must have changed by looking at the calculus of re-feeding those who were starving. From the point of view of the efficient use of food stocks under conditions of extreme dearth, it was "better" for society if those with acute malnutrition simply died. If the deceased was a nonproductive dependent (that is, a dependent without a job and not growing food on a private plot), it was one less mouth to feed, and his or her death (probably his, because we know that few women died of starvation) freed up food, even if only small amounts, that could go to those at the front or working in industry. If the deceased was a worker, you "merely" needed to feed the person who came in to replace him, on a like-for-like basis. Such more or less was the situation in 1943. Over the course of 1944, however, the situation changed decisively. Factories could now remove the acutely malnourished from work, put them on high-calorie re-feeding programs, and *at the same time* feed at subsistence level the new workers who replaced them. Allowing workers to survive cost a factory more than twice as much in food than if a worker died, since it had to feed *both* the patient (and at a higher level of nutrition than when the patient had simply been a worker) *and* the patient's replacement. This was a choice the state was now able to make. In short, the calculus that governed food allocation became less invidious as the food situation improved.

---

79. GARF, f. A-482, op. 47, d. 2029, l. 12. The province health authorities claimed that the number of starvation cases treated in its various hospitals (as opposed to fatalities) was higher in 1944 than in 1943, a situation it blamed on the fact that the province had been sent "several thousand people 'mobilized' from the West [of the USSR], among whom up to 20 percent were already suffering from starvation." Ibid., l. 15. The fact that the word "mobilized" was in quotation marks raises the question of whether these were ordinary mobilized workers, or "special contingents" under the control of the NKVD. We strongly suspect the latter.

324   *Donald Filtzer*

THE CONTRIBUTION OF LEND-LEASE FOOD AID
TO SOVIET CIVILIAN FOOD CONSUMPTION

The obvious question that now arises is, if the harvest of autumn 1943 was so poor that it necessitated reductions in civilian rations, what were the sources of the improved food supply witnessed from mid-1944 onward? One factor was the movement of the front westwards. Eastern and central Ukraine had been liberated by mid-1944, and the rest of Ukraine and Belorussia by August. From that point onward, the Red Army was able to provision itself largely from food sources outside the USSR, thus freeing up more of domestic agricultural production for the civilian population. Against this, however, is the fact that the food situation in the liberated Soviet territories was itself dire: the increased numbers of Soviet citizens now back under Soviet control were so many more mouths whom the state had to feed.

Another source of food was Lend-Lease food aid. The vast majority of this came from the Unites States, with smaller amounts contributed by Great Britain and Canada. Just how important this food aid was has never been clear. Technically speaking, it was intended for use only by the Red Army, although in fact small amounts were diverted into the civilian food supply. From the point of view of the civilian diet, it did not matter who ate this food. If it went entirely to the Red Army, this in theory should have freed up an equivalent portion of domestic Soviet food production that could then go to civilians. William Moskoff added up the total amount of food despatched to the USSR from the United States and concluded that over the course of the war it would have given each Soviet soldier the equivalent of 10 ounces (280 grams) of food a day—in his view a relatively small amount, "although the meats and oils were a real addition to the diets of those who received them."[80] Moskoff's assessment was a welcome counter to Cold War notions that the USSR survived the war only thanks to the United States's largesse, but it neglected two essential points. First, the importance of 280 grams of food a day depends entirely on what type of food it is. Two hundred eighty grams of butter, for instance, provide well over 2,000 calories,

---

80. Moskoff, *The Bread of Affliction*, pp. 120–122.

Starvation Mortality in Soviet Industrial Regions 325

while 280 grams of cabbage provide fewer than 70. Second, it is wrong to average out Lend-Lease deliveries over the entire period of the war. As we shall note, most Lend-Lease food arrived after July 1943, and so its nutritional impact was more concentrated than a simple average would lead us to believe.

In 1996, the Russian historian M. N. Suprun attempted a more systematic assessment by calculating the actual caloric value of Allied food deliveries. These, he concluded, were enough to have fed the entire Red Army for 1,688 days, virtually the entire length of the war. This may seem a fairly startling result, but the conclusions Suprun drew from it were rather modest. By feeding the Red Army, Lend-Lease food allowed a comparable quantity of domestically produced food to go to the civilian population, without which starvation on the home front would have been much worse than it was.[81]

In fact, when doing his calculations, Suprun committed an unfortunate error: when using Soviet nutrition tables to find the calorie content of each food category, in most (but not all) cases he mistook kilojoules for kilocalories. Since there are 4.18 kilojoules to one calorie, his computations overestimated the energy value of Allied deliveries roughly by a factor of three.[82] This mistake does not, however, undermine the originality or simplicity of his idea. It is possible to repeat the calculations using the correct calorie values, and from this to try to draw some meaningful conclusions.[83] When we do this, we find that between June 1941 and May 1945, Allied food aid was sufficient to have fed the whole of the Red Army not for 1,688 days, as assumed by Suprun, but for 509 days. These calories, however, were not spread equally over the three years of the war. The bulk of Lend-Lease aid—nearly two-thirds—arrived after July 1943. We therefore need to measure its potential contribution to the Soviet diet within each subperiod of the Soviet Union's war against Nazi Germany. The results are summarized in table 5.3. A detailed explanation of how

81. M. N. Suprun, "Prodovol′stvennye postavki v SSSR po Lend-Lizu v gody vtoroi mirovoi voiny," *Otechestvennaia istoriia*, no. 3 (1996): 46–54.

82. Ibid., p. 50. For some major food items—wheat, flour, beans, and sugar—he listed the calorie content correctly; for all other items he used kilojoules. Hence his final calculation yielded a three-fold, rather than 4.18-fold, error.

83. We show how we have done the calculations in appendix A.

Table 5.3. Calories provided by Lend-Lease food aid, 1941–1945, by delivery period

Military personnel (March 1944)	Calorie value of daily ration (average assumed by Suprun)	Total calories consumed per day	Total calorie value of Allied food aid, October 1941–June 1945 (Canada, to December 1945)	Number of days Lend-Lease food aid supported
11,235,000	4,000	44,940,000,000	22,874,650,250,000	509

Delivery period and source	Metric tons	% of total metric tons falling within each delivery period	Days Red Army could be fed within each delivery period	Number of days in delivery period	Days fed as % of total number of days in delivery period	Calories per day this provided, assuming ration of 4,000 kcal/day
From USA, 6/22/41–6/30/42	313,836	6.4	33			
From GB, 6/22/41–6/30/42	154,452	3.2	16	71	374	19.0	760
From Canada, 6/22/41–6/30/42	211,938	4.4	22			
From USA, 7/1/42–6/30/43	1,013,748	20.8		106	365	29.0	1,162
From USA, 7/1/43–6/30/44	1,762,558	36.2		184	366	50.3	2,014
From USA, 7/1/44–5/12/45	1,175,891	24.2	123			
From Canada, 5/1/44–12/45	235,000	4.8	25	148	365	40.5	1,622
Total	4,867,423	100.0		509			

Sources: M. N. Suprun, "Prodovol'stvennye postavki v SSSR po Lend-Lizu v gody vtoroi mirovoi voiny," *Otechestvennaia istoriia,* no. 3 (1996), pp. 50–52; Roger Munting, "Soviet Food Supply and Allied Aid in the War, 1941–45," *Soviet Studies* 36, no. 4 (October 1984) p. 588; Charlotte Chatfield and Georgian Adams, *Proximate Composition of American Food Materials,* United States Department of Agriculture Circular no. 549 (June 1940) table 2, pp. 18–90.

Note: The explanation of the calculations appears in appendix A of this chapter.

Starvation Mortality in Soviet Industrial Regions 327

we made the calculations in this table appears in appendix A of this chapter.

During the first twelve months following the German invasion, Allied food aid, which during this early period came mostly from Britain and Canada, would have provided each Soviet soldier the equivalent of around 760 calories a day, or 19 percent of all the calories he or she consumed. This rose to 1,160 calories a day (29 percent of all calories) between July 1942 and June 1943; then to 2,010 calories a day (50 percent of all calories) between July 1943 and June 1944; and finally fell to 1,620 calories a day (40 percent of all calories) from July 1944 to June 1945.

The question is, what do these numbers mean? Lend-Lease made a significant contribution to available calories only from July 1942 onward. During all of 1942, 1943, and the first half of 1944, food consumption among the home-front civilian population was pushed right down to the lowest possible limit. Many people died of starvation; many more suffered serious morbidity or debility from malnutrition; virtually everyone was malnourished to some degree. The 1943 harvest was poor, and in November 1943, the regime reduced ration entitlements for everyone. As we have already noted, potato blight destroyed most of the 1943 potato harvest in Sverdlovsk province, and possibly elsewhere in the Urals, so workers were deprived of their most important source of compensatory nutrition. Therefore, the fact that the regime reduced rations at this crucial time implies that virtually all of the Lend-Lease food it received was going to the Red Army, without freeing up a portion of domestic food production to help the general population. Its contribution to soldiers' diets was so large that it would be safe to assume that the Red Army could not have fed its soldiers adequately without it.

As we have seen in this chapter, in the winter and spring of 1944, Urals defense factories began to place workers suffering from semi-starvation on re-feeding programs, and from the middle of 1944 to the end of the war, clinical starvation among defense workers virtually disappeared. Although starvation remained the major *cause* of death among urban adults in hinterland regions during 1944, the number of these deaths in *absolute terms* fell substantially, with most of that fall very probably coming during the second half of the year. In other words, it was only from mid-1944 onward that the Soviet regime could both feed the army and provide extra food to improve the health and well-being of civilians in the rear. It seems reasonable to assume that some of this extra food came from Allied food aid.

Just how this food was used we do not know. We can only speculate about alternative scenarios. In December 1944, there were approximately 67.7 million people receiving some form of rations. This is roughly six times the size of the military, so if all of the 1,620 calories a day freed up by Lend-Lease went to civilian consumption and was then distributed equally among everyone receiving rations, it would have boosted their diets by around 270 calories a day, equivalent to an extra 140 grams of bread or four or five small potatoes. This is not an insignificant quantity of extra calories, and it might well have saved the lives of some people at the very margins of survival, but its overall impact on the population as a whole would not have been great. However, we know from earlier discussion in this chapter that extra food was not distributed equally among everybody, but was targeted: it went to those suffering serious debility and/or in danger of dying, while those not at risk (or not yet at risk) remained on their allotted rations. Someone suffering from semi-starvation who was placed in an inpatient re-feeding unit was likely to be on a diet of around 3,200 calories a day. If the state used Lend-Lease aid to provide half of those calories, this could have treated 11.235 million sufferers— that is, the same number of civilians as there were soldiers in the Red Army. That is a substantial minority of the entire rationed population, and probably more than the number of people dangerously ill with malnutrition. Alternatively, the 1,620 calories for 11.235 million soldiers would have allowed 22.5 million of the most vulnerable civilians to boost their daily intake by 810 calories a day. This is a large amount of calories, and whilst it may not have fully eliminated their hunger, fatigue, or other serious but nonfatal effects of malnutrition, it would have reduced starvation mortality to very low levels and attenuated a great deal of starvation-related morbidity.

In sum, given what we know about the real food situation inside the country, it seems reasonable to conclude that during 1943, Lend-Lease did little to help the civilian population and went almost entirely to preventing hunger and malnutrition in the military. In 1944 the situation

Starvation Mortality in Soviet Industrial Regions 329

was different. Lend-Lease food aid provided critical assistance for those at the margins of debility or death. It kept many urban civilians from dying during the first half of the year and helped to eliminate starvation disease almost entirely from mid-1944 onward.

CONCLUSION

It is not possible to quantify the full extent of starvation mortality on the Soviet home front, even among the urban population. What we have shown here is that in the country's major industrial regions mortality among the non-child population increased dramatically, and that starvation in conjunction with tuberculosis (the most important starvation-dependent disease) was far and away its leading cause. Those most likely to succumb were men in their forties and fifties; women were badly malnourished, but relatively few of them died.

What caused the crisis was the German occupation of Ukraine and key agricultural lands in western and southwestern Russia. This left the Soviet regime in a position where it did not have adequate food supplies to feed both its civilian population and its army, and so it prioritized who would be fed and how much, depending on what was available at any given time. In this situation, it proved inevitable that certain groups among the civilian population would be more vulnerable than others. During the first eighteen months of the war children, nonworking dependents, and the elderly were the first to perish, whether directly from starvation, from infections picked up during evacuation, or from a lethal combination of the two. This was by no means a deliberate policy. On the contrary, the regime very quickly learned from experience and devised extensive measures to curb the spread of infections among those in transit, to provide them with food, and to contain the rise in infant mortality. If these measures were only partially, and often chaotically, applied, this was because the scale of the emergency was simply beyond the authorities' ability to control it.[84] As the evacuation process came to an end, those who could not find work in industry or as skilled specialists remained in a precarious position. The regime did not deny them rations,

84. Filtzer, *Hazards*, pp. 151–156.

330   *Donald Filtzer*

but the ration on its own was not enough for them to survive. Worse still, in many localities people found it impossible to redeem their ration cards and obtain even the meager calories to which they were notionally entitled.[85] Some groups, however, very clearly were deemed expendable, in particular Gulag prisoners and *trudarmeitsy*. There was no policy to starve them to death, but they were at the bottom of the hierarchy for the receipt of scarce food, and so mass deaths were inevitable. As already noted, mortality in the camps leapt from around 7 percent of all inmates in 1941, to just over 20 percent in both 1942 and 1943, before dropping sharply to around 9 percent in 1944.[86] Although the magnitude of deaths among prisoners was far greater than among the civilian population, the pattern of increase and decrease in mortality was the same: as soon as the regime disposed over-sufficient food supplies, mortality in the camps fell.[87] *Trudarmeitsy* living outside the camps, and mobilized workers in general, were

85. This is a separate story that affected both individuals and institutions, from factories to children's homes. Children fell into two categories. The so-called "organized contingent" of children consisted of those with some attachment to a state institution—a children's home, a boarding school, a pediatric hospital or sanatorium, or children attending primary or secondary school—from which they were supposed to receive the major part, and sometimes all, of their nutrition. Especially during the first two years of the war, these institutions faced inordinate difficulties obtaining in full the allocations notionally assigned to them. Gontsova notes that even here there were sharp gradations: in Nizhnii Tagil, at least, children's establishments (nurseries, kindergartens) attached to defense factories faired considerably better than those that received provisions from the local department of trade—although the situation was further complicated by embezzlement of the children's food by childcare staff and even the syphoning off of children's food stocks by factory managements to provide extra food rewards to Stakhanovites and other workers who over-fulfilled their targets. Gontsova, "Povsednevnaia zhizn' naseleniia industrial'nogo tsentra v gody Velikoi Otechestvennoi voiny (na materialakh goroda Nizhnii Tagil)," pp. 70–72. Far more vulnerable still was the "unorganized contingent" of children who relied solely on the individual ration allowance, and in some cases workers undermined the rationale of these hierarchies by sharing their rations with their children, even at the cost of becoming acutely malnourished themselves. GARF, f. A-482, op. 52s, d. 82, l. 123.

86. See above, the section, "1943: Who Died of Hunger?," and n. 52.

87. The trend among *trudarmeitsy* appears to have been somewhat different. If the camps in Sverdlovsk province can be taken as a general indication, mortality among the *trudarmeitsy* living in camps controled by the NKVD peaked in 1942 at just over 7 percent in Tagillag and just under 12 percent in Bogoslovlag, but afterward fell steeply. Kirillov, et al., *Gedenkbuch*, p. 65.

Starvation Mortality in Soviet Industrial Regions   331

in a better position, but on the whole their plight was desperate. Mortality among them was high, including from starvation.[88]

The general situation, therefore, was for scarce food to be targeted toward those deemed most "valuable" for the war effort, which meant first and foremost "free" workers in defense industry. The strategy was partially successful, in that it kept the vast majority of workers alive and able to function, but their health continued to deteriorate to such a point that, by 1944, starvation inside the factories had become a mass phenomenon.

As more food became available in 1944, the policy did not become one of increasing the consumption of everyone. Rather, food was targeted on the basis of perceived need; where workers in the defense industry

---

88. A number of major factories tried to divert food to improve the diets of prisoner-workers. Prison laborers working in industrial enterprises had their own ration allowances, lower than those for "free" workers. According to Gontsova ("Povsednevnaia zhizn' naseleniia industrial'nogo tsentra v gody Velikoi Otechestvennoi voiny [na materialakh goroda Nizhnii Tagil]," p. 100), the ration for prisoners and *trudarmeitsy* was set at the level of dependents. From 1943 onward, prisoners *inside* the camps could earn extra bread allowances—but only bread—for exceeding production targets. We do not know if this same "privilege" extended to prisoners working inside factories, but we do know that the ration allocations of the latter were strictly limited and that it was against the law for factories to exceed them and provide them with extra food. Yet managers at some of the country's most important defense enterprises were willing to defy these regulations. One interesting case arose in 1943, when the management of the Gor'kii motor vehicle works (GAZ) diverted food officially allocated for extra meals to workers who over-fulfilled their output targets (norms) and used it to supplement the diets of the 1,000 to 2,000 Gulag prisoners placed at the factory by the NKVD. When challenged as to why they did this, the management replied that, had they not provided the extra food, the workers would have "refused" to work. This is extremely improbable. Far more likely is that they were too malnourished to work. It seems that GAZ was not alone in this practice. Factory No. 615 in Moscow, part of the electrical industry, was accused of breaking the law in the same way. GARF, f. 5451, op. 43, d. 236, ll. 116–117. An equally striking case was the Kirov works in Cheliabinsk, where in 1942 management supplemented the diets of its 2,000 prisoners by diverting food from the stocks assigned for ordinary workers. The food situation at this factory was serious, and some of its workers did indeed die of starvation, but the amounts of food redirected in this way when averaged out over the entire workforce would have had little impact on these outcomes. They did, however, provide the 2,000 prisoners with significant amounts of extra calories, including from fats. If this might appear to have been an act of pragmatic altruism on the part of the factory's management, let us remember that this was the same factory that was pilfering workers' food stocks to provide relatively lavish rations for its technical specialists and managers. GARF, f. 5451, op. 43, d. 187, l. 131.

were concerned, this meant those showing clinical signs of semi-starvation. Workers as a whole continued to receive just enough to enable them to continue working. Only when they fell ill did the regime intervene and provide the food needed to keep them from dying. In this way the regime could avoid "squandering" food on those who, from a biological point of view, might be able to carry on without it, and reserve it for those who manifestly could not. It is perfectly plausible to argue that, for a country with limited food supplies, this was a rational policy, which maximized the chances of survival of the largest number of workers, if not necessarily the survival of those who did not work or found themselves working in nonessential areas of the economy.

Given what we know about collectivization, the famine of 1932–1933, and the Terror of the mid-1930s, it would be far from unreasonable to assume that the Stalinist leadership was basically indifferent to the welfare of the general population, and that food policy was driven solely by the instrumental need to win the war. This is a tempting hypothesis for anti-Stalinists on both the left and right of the political spectrum, but the fact is that without research into the deliberations that went on at the top of the GKO, there is no way to affirm or disprove it. Our argument in this chapter is somewhat different—that such speculations are largely irrelevant. A different political regime, even one rooted firmly in workers' democracy, might have tried to handle the question of food distribution differently, but it would have confronted the same agonizing dilemmas.

There is still one other conclusion that we can draw from this chapter. People on the Soviet home front labored and lived for nearly four years under impossible deprivation, enduring cold, filth, exhaustion, ill health, and malnutrition so acute that it cost many of them their lives. Yet somehow this workforce, as weak and ill as it manifestly was, managed to produce the weapons, the vehicles, the airplanes, and the ammunition needed to crush the Nazis and drive them out of Soviet territory. The motivations that drove people to endure such sacrifices are still largely unknown, and not everyone was willing to make them.[89] For the mil-

---

89. Between January 1943 and November 1944, nearly 1.3 million workers illegally fled their jobs in defense factories, despite the threat of a lengthy spell in the Gulag if

Starvation Mortality in Soviet Industrial Regions 333

lions who did, their persistence and endurance were themselves acts of enormous heroism.

APPENDIX A: CALCULATING THE CONTRIBUTION
OF LEND-LEASE FOOD AID

Table 5.3 summarizes the contribution of Lend-Lease food aid during different periods of the war. How did we do these calculations? The quantity of food despatched to the USSR appears in a number of different sources. In order to calculate the importance of this aid, we need to know two things: (1) a detailed breakdown of the different foods that the USSR received, which allows us to estimate the total calorie content of Lend-Lease aid; and (2) a breakdown of how much arrived in each year of the war, which allows us to assess the differential impact of this food at different stages of the war. William Moskoff gives a detailed breakdown of the different food categories, but he does not divide deliveries by periods. Roger Munting gives a useful breakdown by periods, but his list of food categories is not sufficiently detailed. Neither Moskoff nor Munting provides information on food received from Canada or Great Britain.[90] For tonnage of food aid delivered, we have therefore used M. N. Suprun's figures, which he took from the Soviet archives. These have three advantages. First, they record the amount of food aid unloaded at Soviet ports, as opposed to the amount despatched from Allied ports. Second, they include food from Canada and Great Britain. Third, they offer the most detailed breakdown of food categories, making it easier to calculate total calories. Because the vast bulk of this food was grown in the United States,

---

they were caught. This was equivalent to an annual rate of illegal turnover within the defense sector of 12.5 percent. Most of these so-called "labor deserters" were young people mobilized from the countryside. They did not necessarily drop out of the war effort, however. Many took jobs at other factories; many more (probably the majority) fled back to their native villages and spent the rest of the war working in agriculture. For a detailed discussion see, Donald Filtzer, "Reluctant Fighters on the Labour Front: Labour Mobilization and Labour Turnover in Soviet Industry During World War II," unpublished conference paper, American Association for Slavic, East European, and Eurasian Studies annual conference, 2013, copy available on request from the author.

90. Moskoff, *The Bread of Affliction*, p. 121; Roger Munting, "Soviet Food Supply and Allied Aid in the War, 1941–45," *Soviet Studies* 36, no. 4 (October 1984): 588, table 4.

334   *Donald Filtzer*

it makes sense to use not Soviet nutritional tables, as did Suprun, but nutritional tables published by the United States Department of Agriculture just prior to the Lend-Lease program.[91] For the small number of foods not listed in these tables we have used either the Soviet values or, where these, too, were absent, values from modern sources. From these values we can calculate the total number of calories provided by Lend-Lease food. As Table 5.3 shows, these totaled 22,874,650,250,000 calories.

In March 1944, there were 11.235 million soldiers in the Red Army.[92] Suprun assumes that each soldier consumed 4,000 calories a day—a figure that more or less coheres with the ration allowances cited by Brandon Schechter in his chapter of this volume. From this we can calculate the total daily calorie needs of the army, which come to 44,940,000,000 calories per day. If we then divide the total number of calories in Lend-Lease deliveries (22,874,650,250,000) by the Red Army's daily requirement (44,940,000,000), we find that this food would have sustained the army for 509 days. We should caution that this figure makes no allowance for spoilage or losses during storage and transport from the ports to their final destination. The Soviet Union was renowned even at the very best of times for its large losses of raw materials due to inadequate storage and negligent handling. Canned food may have had low spoilage rates, but leaving bags of flour or sugar out in the rain would certainly have resulted in some degree of loss, although we have no way to estimate it quantitatively. We do not include theft in the loss category, since stolen food would have been eaten by somebody, even if not by those for whom it was intended or those most in need of it.

The figure of 509 days, therefore, should be taken as an upper limit of what Allied food aid would have provided. We next have to break this food aid down by the year that it arrived. For this we used the delivery periods cited by Suprun and Munting.[93] The majority of British food aid

---

91. Charlotte Chatfield and Georgian Adams, *Proximate Composition of American Food Materials,* United States Department of Agriculture Circular No. 549 (June 1940): 18–90, table 2.

92. Mark Harrison, *Accounting for War: Soviet Production, Employment, and the Defence Burden, 1940–1945* (Cambridge: Cambridge University Press, 1996), p. 270.

93. Metric tons for the United States are from Munting, "Soviet Food Supply and Allied Aid in the War, 1941–45," p. 588; Great Britain and Canada, from Suprun, "Prodovol'stvennye postavki v SSSR po Lend-Lizu v gody vtoroi mirovoi voiny," pp. 50–52.

Starvation Mortality in Soviet Industrial Regions   335

and Canadian aid up to mid-1944 arrived prior to June 1942. In order to simplify the calculations we have attributed all of this aid to the period June 1941–June 1942. In row 7 (USA final delivery period), Munting gives deliveries up to May 12, 1945, Suprun up to July 1, 1945. Since we have used Suprun's weights to determine the total number of available calories, we have also taken July 1, 1945 as the end date of the delivery period, that is, 365 days. The two sets of figures are therefore not fully comparable with one another.

Column 1 shows the different delivery periods for the arrival of Lend-Lease food aid. Column 2 shows the number of metric tons arriving in Soviet ports during each delivery period. Column 3 shows these weights as a percentage of the total tonnage. Since the total number of days that the Red Army could be fed by Lend-Lease food was 509, multiplying 509 by the percentages in column 3 gives us the number of days that Lend-Lease food would have fed the army within each period. For example, between June 22, 1941, and June 30, 1942, U.S. food aid accounted for 6.4 percent of total tonnage, equivalent to 33 days out of the wartime total of 509. In this same period British food aid made up 3.2 percent of wartime total, enough to feed the Red Army for 16 days. Finally, Canadian aid in this period made up 4.4 percent of the wartime total, enough to feed the Red Army for 22 days. Thus, these three sources together would have fed the Red Army for a total of 71 days during the first 53 weeks of the war. As there were 374 days in this period (column 5), dividing 71 by 374 tells us that Lend-Lease food would have fed the Red Army for 19 percent of that time (column 6). This is the same as if Lend-Lease food provided 19 percent of the *daily* calories consumed by the Red Army in this period. Assuming that each soldier consumed 4,000 calories a day, 19 percent of this is 760 calories. So 760 is the number of calories that Lend-Lease food would have given each Red Army soldier during the period in question.

Repeating these same calculations for the subsequent periods tells us that during the second year of the war Lend-Lease gave each soldier 1,162 calories; during the third year, 2,014 calories, and during the war's final year, 1,622.

336   *Donald Filtzer*

APPENDIX B: SOURCES OF THE MORTALITY DATA

All data are from GARF, f. A-374, op. 11:

Cheliabinsk 1940:	d. 26, ll. 65–65ob.
Cheliabinsk 1943:	d. 219, ll. 35–35ob.
Cheliabinsk 1944:	d. 282, ll. 27–28ob.
Gor'kii 1940:	d. 26, ll. 9–9ob.
Gor'kii 1943:	d. 218, ll. 6–6ob.
Gor'kii 1944:	d. 279, ll. 53–54ob.
Iaroslavl' 1940:	d. 28, ll. 13–13ob.
Iaroslavl' 1943:	d. 219, ll. 42–42ob.
Iaroslavl' 1944:	d. 282, ll. 38–39ob.
Iaroslavl' province 1942:	d. 161, ll. 20–20ob.
Ivanovo 1940:	d. 27, ll. 22–22ob.
Ivanovo 1943:	d. 218, ll. 10–10ob.
Ivanovo 1944:	d. 279, ll. 61–62ob.
Ivanovo province 1942:	d. 160, ll. 6–6ob.
Izhevsk 1940:	d. 27, ll. 23–23ob.
Izhevsk 1943:	d. 219, ll. 31–31ob.
Izhevsk 1944:	d. 282, ll. 1–2ob.
Kazan' 1940:	d. 27, ll. 18–18ob.
Kazan' 1943:	d. 219, ll. 28–29ob.
Kazan' 1944:	d. 281, ll. 78–79ob.
Kemerovo 1940:	d. 27, ll. 20–20ob.
Kemerovo 1943:	d. 218, ll. 17–17ob.
Kemerovo 1944:	d. 279, ll. 75–76ob.
Kirov 1940:	d. 26, ll. 17–17ob.
Kirov 1942:	d. 163, ll. 7–7ob.
Kirov 1943:	d. 215, ll. 17–17ob.
Kirov 1944:	d. 279, ll. 81–82ob.
Kirov province 1940:	d. 27, ll. 19–19ob.

Starvation Mortality in Soviet Industrial Regions

Kirov province 1942:   d. 160, ll. 9–90b.
Kirov province 1943:   d. 218, ll. 18–180b.
Kirov province 1944:   d. 280, ll. 13–140b.

Kuibyshev 1940:   d. 26, ll. 25–250b.
Kuibyshev 1942:   d. 163, ll. 8–80b.
Kuibyshev 1943:   d. 218, ll. 21–210b.
Kuibyshev 1944:   d. 280, ll. 17–180b.

Magnitogorsk 1940:   d. 28, ll. 19–190b.
Magnitogorsk 1943:   d. 219, ll. 34–340b.
Magnitogorsk 1944:   d. 282, ll. 17–180b.

Molotov 1940:   d. 26, ll. 35–350b.
Molotov 1942:   d. 163, ll. 10–100b.
Molotov 1943:   d. 219, ll. 6–60b.
Molotov 1944:   d. 280, ll. 50–510b.

Molotov province 1940:   d. 26, ll. 36–360b.
Molotov province 1942:   d. 160, ll. 16–160b.
Molotov province 1943:   d. 216, ll. 6–60b.
Molotov province 1944:   d. 280, ll. 48–490b.

Moscow 1940:   d. 26, ll. 33–330b.
Moscow 1942:   d. 160, ll. 18–180b.
Moscow 1943:   d. 219, ll. 9–100b.
Moscow 1944:   d. 280, ll. 45–460b.

Nizhnii Tagil 1943:   d. 219, ll. 21–210b.
Nizhnii Tagil 1944:   d. 281, ll. 41–420b.

Novosibirsk 1940:   d. 26, ll. 37–370b.
Novosibirsk 1943:   d. 219, ll. 12–120b.
Novosibirsk 1944:   d. 280, ll. 60–600b.

Omsk 1940:   d. 28, ll. 42–420b.
Omsk 1943:   d. 219, ll. 14–140b.
Omsk 1944:   d. 280, ll. 69–700b.

Prokop'evsk 1940:   d. 27, ll. 2–20b.
Prokop'evsk 1943:   d. 218, ll. 15–150b.

Prokop'evsk 1944:	d. 279, ll. 77–78ob.
RSFSR urban 1940:	d. 28, ll. 11–11ob.
RSFSR urban 1943:	d. 222, ll. 2–2ob.
Saratov 1940:	d. 26, ll. 55–55ob.
Saratov 1943:	d. 216, ll. 18–18ob.
Saratov 1944:	d. 281, ll. 17–18ob.
Stalinsk 1940:	d. 28, ll. 30–30ob.
Stalinsk 1943:	d. 218, ll. 16–16ob.
Stalinsk 1944:	d. 279, ll. 79–80ob.
Sverdlovsk 1940:	d. 26, ll. 53–53ob.
Sverdlovsk 1943:	d. 216, ll. 20–20ob.
Sverdlovsk 1944:	d. 281, ll. 21–22ob.
Sverdlovsk province 1940:	d. 26, ll. 54–54ob.
Sverdlovsk province 1943:	d. 216, ll. 15–15ob.
Sverdlovsk province 1944:	d. 281, ll. 19–20ob.
Zlatoust 1940:	d. 27, ll. 24–24ob.
Zlatoust 1943:	d. 218, ll. 9–9ob.
Zlatoust 1944:	d. 282, ll. 15–16ob.

BIBLIOGRAPHY

ARCHIVES

Archive holdings are catalogued under their postwar titles as Ministries. Up until the end of World War II, they were known as People's Commissariats.

GARF (Gosudarstvennyi arkhiv Rossiiskoi Federatsii; State Archive of the Russian Federation), Main Reading Room

f. 5422 Central Committee of Workers in State Trade, Public Catering, and Consumer Cooperatives

f. 5446 Council of Ministers of the USSR (Sovet Ministrov SSSR)

f. 5451 All-Union Council of Trade Unions (VTsSPS—Vsesoiuznyi sovet professional'nykh soiuzov)

f. 5456 Central Committees of Workers in Local Industries and Municipal/ Social Enterprises

f. 6822 Council on Evacuation (Sovet po evakuatsii)

f. 7021 Extraordinary State Commission for the Determination and Investigation of Atrocities Committed by German-Fascist Occupiers and their Accomplices and the Damage They Caused to the Soviet Union's Citizens, Collective Farms, Social Organizations, and State Enterprises and Institutions (Chrezvychainaia gosudarstvennaia komissiia po ustanovleniiu i rassledovaniiu zlodeianii nemetsko-fashistskikh zakhvatchikov i ikh soobshchnikov i prichinennogo imi ushcherba grazhdanam, kollektivnym khoziaist-vam (kolkhozam), obshchestvennym organizatsiiam, gosudarstvennym predpriiatiiam i uchrezhdeniiam SSSR)

f. 7678 Central Committee of the Trade Unions of Workers in the Aviation and Defense Industry

f. 8009 Ministry of Public Health of the USSR (Ministerstvo zdravookhraneniia SSSR)

f. 8131 Procuracy of the USSR (Prokuratura SSSR)

f. 9414 Chief Administration of Places of Confinement, Ministry of Internal Affairs of the USSR (Glavnoe upravlenie mest zakliucheniia Ministerstva vnutrennikh del SSSR)

GARF, Reading Room 2

f. A-374 Statistical Administration of the RSFSR (Statisticheskoe upravlenie RSFSR)

f. A-482 Ministry of Public Health of the RSFSR (Ministerstvo zdravookhraneniia RSFSR)

GMMOBL (Gosudarstvennyi memorial'nyi muzei oborony i blokada Leningrada; State Memorial Museum of the Defense and Blockade of Leningrad)

f. RDF Manuscript and Document Collection (Rukopisno-dokumental'nyi fond)

MNM ("A Muzy ne Molchali") Shkol'nyi-Narodnyi Muzei, Shkola No. 235 im. D. D. Shostakovicha; "The Muses Did Not Keep Silent"—the People's School Museum, the D. D. Shostakovich School No. 235)

k.p. [kniga postuplenii—register of accessions] 6920, f. 1

k.p. 4153. f. 2

NA IRI RAN (Nauchnyi arkhiv Instituta rossiiskoi istorii Akademii nauk Rossiiskoi Federatsii; Scientific Archive of the Institute of Russian History, Academy of Sciences of the Russian Federation)

f. 2 Commission on the History of the Great Fatherland War, Academy of Sciences of the USSR (Komissiia po istorii Velikoi Otechestvennoi voiny AN SSSR)

NART (Natstional'nyi arkhiv Respubliki Tatarstana; National Archive of the Republic of Tatarstan)

F.R. 3610 Presidium of the Supreme Soviet of the Republic of Tatarstan (Prezidium verkhovnogo soveta respubliki Tatarstana)

OR RNB (Otdel' rukopisei, Rossiiskaia natsional'naia biblioteka; Manuscript Division, Russian National Library)

f. 368 Konopleva, Mariia Sergeevna, Personal Papers (Lichnyi fond)

RGAE (Rossiiskii Gosudarstvennyi Arkhiv Ekonomiki; Russian State Archive of the Economy)

f. 1562 Central Statistical Administration of the USSR (Tsentral'noe statisticheskoe upravlenie SSSR)

f. 7971 People's Commissariat of Trade (Narodnyi komissariat torgovli)

f. 8875 Ministry of the Metallurgical Industry of the USSR (Ministerstvo metallurgicheskoi promyshlennosti SSSR)

RGASPI (Rossiiskii gosudarstvennyi arkhiv sotsial'noi i politicheskoi istorii; Russian State Archive of Social and Political History)

f. 17, op. 122 Central Committee of the Communist Party of the Soviet Union (Tsentral'nyi komitet KPSS), Organizational Department (Orginstruktorskii otdel)

f. 17, op. 125 Central Committee of the Communist Party of the Soviet Union (Tsentral'nyi komitet KPSS), Propaganda and Agitation Administration (Upravlenie propagandy i agitatsii TsK VKP(b))

f. 74, op. 2 Voroshilov, Kliment Efremovich, Personal Papers (Lichnyi fond)

f. 84, op. 1 Mikoian, Anastas Ivanovich, Personal Papers (Lichnyi fond)

f. 88, op. 1 Shcherbakov, Aleksandr Sergeevich, Personal Papers (Lichnyi fond)

RGVA (Rossiiskii gosudarstvennyi voennyi arkhiv; Russian State Military Archive)

TsAMO RF (Tsentral'nyi arkhiv Ministerstva oborony Rossiiskoi Federatsii; Central Archive of the Ministry of Defense of the Russian Federation)

Bibliography

TsGAIPD SPb (Tsentral'nyi gosudarstvennyi arkhiv istoriko-politicheskikh dokumentov Sankt-Peterburga; Central State Archive of Historical-Political Documents, St. Petersburg)

f. 25 Leningrad City Party Committee (Gorkom)

f. 4000 Institute of Party History under the Leningrad Oblast' Committee of the Communist Party of the Soviet Union, Smolnyi District of Leningrad (Institut istorii partii pri leningradskom obkom KPSS, Smol'ninskii raion g. Leningrada)

TsGALI SPb (Tsentrali'nyi gosudarstvennyi arkhiv literatury i iskusstva Sankt-Peterburga; Central State Archive of Literature and Art, St. Petersburg)

f. 157 Kostrovitskaia, Vera Sergeevna, Personal Papers (Lichnyi fond)

TsGANTD SPb (Tsentral'nyi gosudarstvennyi arkhiv nauchno-tekhnicheskoi dokumentatsii Sankt-Peterburga; Central State Archive of Scientific-Technical Documention, St. Petersburg)

f. 313 V. M. Bekhterev State Scientific Research Institute of Psychoneurology (Gosudarstvennyi nauchno-issledovatel'skii psikhonevrologicheskii institut im. V. M. Bekhtereva)

TsGA SPb (Tsentral'nyi gosudarstvennyi arkhiv Sankt-Peterburga; Central State Archive of St. Petersburg)

f. 7384 St. Petersburg City Soviet (Sankt-Peterburgskii gorodskoi sovet narodnykh deputatov)

f. 9156 Central Administration of Public Health, Leningrad City Executive Committee (Glavnoe upravlenie zdravookhraneniia Lengorispolkoma)

PUBLISHED SOURCES

1941: Poslednie pis'ma s fronta. Moscow: Voenizdat', 1991.

Abdulin, M. G. *160 stranits iz soldatskogo dnevnika.* Moscow: Molodaia gvardiia, 1985.

Abramovich, G. B., and S. S. Mnukhin. "Klinika alimentarnoi distrofii: Izmeneniia psikhiki." In E. M. Gel'shtein, ed., *Narushenie obshchego pitaniia (osobennosti ikh vozniknoveniia i lecheniia vo vremia voiny),* vol. 28 of *Opyt sovetskoi meditsiny v Velikoi Otechestvennoi voine 1941–1945 gg.* Moscow: Medgiz, 1951, pp. 117–119.

Adamets, Serguei. "Famine in Nineteenth- and Twentieth-Century Russia: Mortality by Age, Cause, and Gender." In Tim Dyson and Comac Ó Gráda, eds., *Famine Demography: Perspectives from the Past and Present.* New York: Oxford University Press, 2002, pp. 158–180.

Adamovich, Ales', and Daniil Aleksandrovich Granin. *Blokadnaia kniga.* St. Petersburg: Pechatnyi dvor, 1994.

Agamben, Giorgio. *Remnants of Auschwitz: The Witness and the Archive.* New York: Zone Books, 1999.

Aizenshtat, Yakob. *Zapiski sekretaria voennogo tribunala.* London: Overseas Publication Interchange, 1991.

Antipenko, N. A. *Na glavnom upravlenii.* Moscow: Nauka, 1967.

Apfelbaum-Kowalski, Emil, Ryszard Pakszwer, Jeanne Zarchi, Ari Heller, and Zdzislaw Askanas. "Pathophysiology of the Circulatory System in Hunger Disease." In Myron Winick, ed., *Hunger Disease: Studies by Jewish*

Physicians in the Warsaw Ghetto, translated from the Polish by Martha Osnos. New York: John Wiley & Sons, 1979, pp. 125–152.

Applewhite, Harriet, and Darline Levy, eds. *Women and Politics in the Age of Democratic Revolution.* Ann Arbor: University of Michigan Press, 1993.

Aralovets, N. A. "Smertnost' gorodskogo naseleniia tylovykh raionov Rossii, 1941–1945 gg." In N. A. Aralovets, O. M. Verbitskaia, V. B. Zhiromskaia, Iu. A. Poliakov, and A. I. Repinetskii, eds., *Liudskie poteri SSSR v period vtoroi mirovoi voiny. Sbornik statei.* St. Petersburg: Russko-Baltiiskii Informatsionnyi Tsentr, 1995, pp. 154–159.

Aralovets, N. A., and O. M. Verbitskaia. "Osobennosti smertnosti gorodskogo i sel'skogo naseleniia v tylu v 1941–1945 gg." In Iu. A. Polikaov, ed., *Naselenie Rossii v XX veke: istoricheskie ocherki,* vol. 2, 1940–1959 Moscow: Rosspen, 2001, pp. 106–127.

Aralovets, N. A., O. M. Verbitskaia, V. B. Zhiromskaia, Iu. A. Poliakov, and A. I. Repinetskii, eds., *Liudskie poteri SSSR v period vtoroi mirovoi voiny. Sbornik statei.* St. Petersburg: Russko-Baltiiskii Informatsionnyi Tsentr, 1995.

Astaf'ev, Viktor. *Prokliati i ubity.* Moscow: Terra, 1999.

Baklanov, Grigorii. "Naveki deviatnadtsatletnii." in Grigorii Baklanov, *Voennye povesti.* Moscow: Sovetskii pisatel', 1981.

———. *Zhizn', podarennaia dvazhdy.* Moscow: Vagrius, 1999.

Barber, John. "The Moscow Crisis of October 1941." In Julian Cooper, Maureen Perrie, and E. A. Rees, eds. *Soviet History, 1917–1953: Essays in Honour of R. W. Davies.* Basingstoke: Macmillan, 1995, pp. 201–218.

———. "War, Public Opinion, and the Struggle for Survival, 1941–1945:

The Case of Leningrad." In Silvio Pons and Andrea Romano, eds., *Russia in the Age of Wars, 1914–1945.* Milan: Feltrinelli Editore, 2000, pp. 265–276.

Barber, John, and Mark Harrison. *The Soviet Home Front, 1941–1945: A Social and Economic History of the USSR in World War II.* London: Longman, 1991.

———."Patriotic War, 1941 to 1945." In *The Cambridge History of Russia,* vol. 3, ed. Ronald Grigor Suny, *The Twentieth Century.* Cambridge: Cambridge University Press, 2006, pp. 217–242.

Barber, John, and Andrei Dzeniskevich, eds. *Life and Death in Besieged Leningrad, 1941–44.* New York: Palgrave Macmillan, 2005.

Barkawi, Tarak. "Peoples, Homelands, and Wars? Ethnicity, the Military, and Battle among British Imperial Forces in the War against Japan." *Comparative Studies in Society and History* 46, no. 1 (January 2004): 134–163.

Barnes, Steven A. "All for the Front, All for Victory! The Mobilization of Forced Labor in the Soviet Union during World War Two." *International Labor and Working-Class History,* no. 58 (Fall 2000): 239–260.

Barskova, Polina. "The Corpse, the Corpulent, and the Other: A Study in the Tropology of Siege Body Representation." *Ab Imperio,* no. 1 (2009): 361–386.

Barsukov, A. I., ed. *Prikazy narodnogo komissara oborony SSSR 22 iiunia 1941 g.–1942 g.,* vol. 13 (2–2). Moscow: Terra, 1997.

Bater, James H. *The Soviet City: Ideal and Reality.* Beverly Hills, Calif.: Sage Publications, 1980.

Bazanova, V. "Vchera bylo deviat' trevog." *Neva,* no. 1 (1999): 123–147.

Beevor, Antony. *Stalingrad: The Fateful Siege, 1942–1943* New York: Viking Penguin, 1998.

Bibliography

Belousov, V., *Zapiski dokhodiagi.* Ashkhabad: Turkmenistan, 1992.

Berggol'ts, Ol'ga, *Dnevnye zvezdy; Govorit Leningrad.* Moscow: Pravda, 1990.

———. *Ol'ga. Zapretnyi dnevnik*, edited by N. Sokolovskaia and A. Rubashkin. St. Petersburg: Azbuka, 2011.

Berkhoff, Karel C. *Harvest of Despair: Life and Death in Ukraine under Nazi Rule.* Cambridge, Mass.: Belknap Press of Harvard University Press, 2004.

———. *Motherland in Danger: Soviet Propaganda during World War II.* Cambridge, Mass.: Harvard University Press, 2012.

Bernev, S., and S. V. Chernov, eds. *Blokadnye dnevniki i dokumenty*, Arkhiv Bol'shogo Doma St. Petersburg: Evropeiskii Dom, 2004.

Bidlack, Richard. "Workers at War: Factory Workers and Labor Policy in the Siege of Leningrad." *The Carl Beck Papers in Russian and East European Studies*, no. 902. Pittsburgh, Pa.: University of Pittsburgh Press, 1991.

———. "The Political Mood in Leningrad during the First Year of the Soviet-German War." *Russian Review* 59, no. 1 (January 2000): 96–113.

———. "Survival Strategies in Leningrad." In Robert W. Thurston and Bernd Bonwetsch, eds., *The People's War: Responses to World War II in the Soviet Union.* Urbana: University of Illinois Press, 2000, pp. 84–107.

Bidlack, Richard, and Nikita Lomagin. *The Leningrad Blockade, 1941–1944: A New Documentary History from the Soviet Archives.* New Haven, Conn.: Yale University Press, 2012.

Biess, Frank. *Homecomings: Returning POWs and the Legacies of Defeat in Postwar Germany.* Princeton, N.J.: Princeton University Press, 2006.

Boldyrev, A. N. *Osadnaia zapis': blokadnyi dnevnik*, edited by V. S. Garbuzova and I. M. Steblin-Kamenskii. St. Petersburg: Evropeiskii Dom, 1998.

Borodulin, V. I. *G. F. Lang.* Moscow: Meditsina, 1976.

Brandenberger, David. *National Bolshevism: Stalinist Mass Culture and the Formation of Modern Russian National Identity, 1931–1956.* Cambridge, Mass.: Harvard University Press, 2002.

Braude-Heller, Anna, Israel Rotbalsam, and Regina Elbinger. "Clinical Aspects of Hunger Disease in Children." In Myron Winick, ed., *Hunger Disease: Studies by Jewish Physicians in the Warsaw Ghetto*, translated from the Polish by Martha Osnos. New York: John Wiley & Sons, 1979, pp. 45–57.

Browning, Christopher R. *The Origins of the Final Solution: The Evolution of Nazi Jewish Policy, September 1939–March 1942.* Lincoln: University of Nebraska Press, 2004.

Brožek, Josef, Samuel Wells, and Ancel Keys. "Medical Aspects of Semistarvation in Leningrad (Siege 1941–1942)," *American Review of Soviet Medicine* 4, no. 1 (October 1946): 70–86.

Bulatov, T. *Budni frontovykh let.* Kazan': Tatknigizdat, 1984.

Cegielski, J. P., and D. N. McMurray. "The Relationship between Malnutrition and Tuberculosis: Evidence from Studies in Humans and Experimental Animals." *International Journal of Tuberculosis and Lung Disease* 8, no. 3 (2004): 286–298.

Chatfield, Charlotte, and Georgian Adams. *Proximate Composition of American Food Materials.* United States Department of Agriculture Circular No. 549, June 1940.

Chekhovich, Nikolai. *Dnevnik ofitsera.* Moscow: Molodaia gvardiia, 1945.

Cherepenina, Nadezhda."Assessing the Scale of Famine and Death in the Besieged City." In John Barber and Andrei Dzeniskevich, eds., *Life and Death in Besieged Leningrad, 1941–44.* Basingstoke: Palgrave, 2005, pp. 28–70.

Cherniavskii, U. G. *Voina i prodovol'stvie: snabzhenie gorodskogo naseleniia v Velikuiu Otechestvennuiu voinu (1941–1945 gg.).* Moscow: Nauka, 1964.

Chernorutskii, M. V. "Problema alimentarnoi distrofii." *Raboty leningradskikh vrachei za god Otechestvennoi voiny,* no. 3 (1943): 3–13.

———. "Alimentarnaia distrofiia u vzroslykh." In M. V. Chernorutskii, ed., *Alimentarnaia distrofiia v blokirovannom Leningrade.* Leningrad: Medgiz, 1947, pp. 36–51.

———. "Khod razvitiia alimentarnoi distrofii, ee klinicheskaia kartina i techenie." In M. V. Chernorutskii, ed., *Alimentarnaia distrofiia v blokirovannom Leningrade.* Leningrad: Medgiz, 1947, pp. 193–203.

———, ed. *Alimentarnaia distrofiia v blokirovannom Leningrade.* Leningrad: Medgiz, 1947.

Chernykh, P. Ia. *Istoriko-etimologicheskii slovar' sovremennogo russkogo iazyka,* vol. 1. Moscow: Russkii iazyk, 1993.

Chickering, Roger. *Imperial Germany and the Great War, 1914–1918.* Cambridge: Cambridge University Press, 2003.

Cohen, Jerome B. *Japan's Economy in War and Reconstruction.* Minneapolis: University of Minnesota Press, 1949.

Collingham, Lizzie. *The Taste of War: World War Two and the Battle for Food.* New York: Penguin Press, 2011.

Cronjé, Gillian."Tuberculosis and Mortality Decline in England and Wales, 1851–1910." In Robert Woods and John Woodward, eds., *Urban Disease and Mortality in Nineteenth-Century England.* London: Batsford Academic and Educational, Ltd., 1984, pp. 79–101.

Crowley, David, and Susan E. Reid, eds. *Socialist Spaces: Sites of Everyday Life in the Eastern Bloc.* Oxford: Berg, 2002.

Dale, Robert. "Rats and Resentment: The Demobilization of the Red Army in Postwar Leningrad, 1945–1950." *Journal of Contemporary History* 45, no. 1 (2010): 132–133.

Dallin, Alexander. *German Rule in Russia, 1941–1945: A Study of Occupation Policies.* Boulder, Colo.: Westview Press, 1981.

Davies, R. W., and Stephen G. Wheatcroft. *The Years of Hunger: Soviet Agriculture, 1931–1933.* New York: Palgrave MacMillan, 2004.

Davis, Belinda. *Home Fires Burning. Food, Politics, and Everyday Life in World War I Berlin.* Chapel Hill: University of North Carolina Press, 2000.

Dean, Martin. *Collaboration in the Holocaust: Crimes of the Local Police in Belorussia and Ukraine, 1941–1944.* New York: St. Martin's Press, 2000.

de Certeau, Michel. *The Practices of Everyday Life.* Berkeley: University of California Press, 1988.

Depretto, Jean-Paul. "Stratification without Class," *Kritika* 8, no. 2 (Spring 2007): 375–388.

Direktivy KPSS i sovetskogo pravitel'stva po khoziaistvennym voprosam, 1929–1945 gody, vol. 2. Moscow: Gosudarstvennoe Izdatel'stvo Politicheskoi Literatury, 1957.

Duffett, Rachel. *The Stomach for Fighting: Food and Soldiers of the Great War.* Manchester: Manchester University Press, 2012.

Dunaevskaia, Irina. *Ot Leningrada do Kënigsberga: Dnevnik voennoi perevodchitsy (1942–1945).* Moscow: ROSSPEN, 2010.

Bibliography

Dunham, Vera S. *In Stalin's Time: Middle-Class Values in Soviet Fiction.* Durham, N.C.: Duke University Press, 1990.

Dzeniskevich, Andrei. "The Social and Political Situation in Leningrad." In Robert W. Thurston and Bernd Bonwetsch, eds., *The People's War: Responses to World War II in the Soviet Union.* Urbana: University of Illinois Press, 2000, pp. 71–83.

Ehrenburg, Ilya, and Vasily Grossman. *The Complete Black Book of Soviet Jewry.* New Brunswick, N.J.: Transaction Publishers, 2001.

Elias, Norbert. *The Civilizing Process: Sociogenetic and Psychogenetic Investigations.* Oxford: Blackwell, 2000.

Ellman, Michael. "The 1947 Soviet Famine and the Entitlement Approach to Famines." *Cambridge Journal of Economics* 24 (2000): 603–630.

Erickson, John. *The Road to Stalingrad: Stalin's War with Germany,* vol. 1. New Haven, Conn.: Yale University Press, 1999.

Erisman, F. F. "Pitanie golodaiushchikh." *Russkaia mysl',* no. 4 (1892): 128–155.

Fadeev, Aleksandr. "Leningrad v dni blokady." In Aleksandr Fadeev, *Sobranie sochinenii v semi tomakh.* Moscow: Izdatel'stvo Khudozhestvennaia Literatura, 1969, vol. 4, pp. 109–204.

Fest, Joachim. *Hitler.* Orlando, Fla., Harcourt, 1974.

Festinger, Leon. "A Theory of Social Comparison Processes." *Human Relations* 7 (1954): 117–140.

Field, Catherine J., Ian R. Johnson, and Patricia D. Schley. "Nutrients and Their Role in Host Resistance to Infection." *Journal of Leukocyte Biology* 71 (January 2002): 16–32.

Filtzer, Donald. *Soviet Workers and Late Stalinism: Labour and the Restoration of the Stalinist System after World War II.* Cambridge: Cambridge University Press, 2002.

———. *The Hazards of Urban Life in Late Stalinist Russia: Health, Hygiene, and Living Standards, 1943–1953.* Cambridge: Cambridge University Press, 2010.

Fitzpatrick, Shelia. "Ascribing Class: The Construction of Social Identity in Soviet Russia." *Journal of Modern History* 65, no. 4 (December 1993): 745–770.

———. *Everyday Stalinism. Ordinary Life in Extraordinary Time: Soviet Russia in the 1930s.* New York: Oxford University Press, 1995.

———. *Tear Off Masks! Identity and Imposture in Twentieth-Century Russia.* Princeton, N.J.: Princeton University Press, 2005.

Fomin, V. I., ed. *Kino na voine: dokumenty i svidetel'stva.* Moscow: Materik, 2005.

French, R. A., and E. F. Hamilton, eds. *The Socialist City: Spatial Structure and Urban Policy.* Chichester: John Wiley and Sons, 1979.

Frenkel, Z. G., ed. *Zapiski i vospominaniia o proidennom zhiznennom puti.* St. Petersburg: Nestor-Istoriia, 2009.

Frolov, N. S., ed. *Vse oni khoteli zhit': Frontovye pis'ma pogibshikh soldat, vospominaniia veteranov voiny.* Kazan': Tarikh, 2003.

Frontovaia pechat' o voinakh iz Yakutii. Yakutsk: Knizhnoe Izdatel'stvo, 1982.

Galaninskaia, V. I. *Budni medsanbata.* Saratov: Privolzhskoe knizhnoe izdatel'stvo, 1980.

Ganson, Nicholas. *The Soviet Famine of 1946–47 in Global and Historical Perspective.* New York: Palgrave Macmillan, 2009.

346   *Bibliography*

———. "Food Supply, Rationing and
Living Standards." In David R. Stone,
ed., *The Soviet Union at War, 1941–1945.*
Barnsley, South Yorkshire: Pen &
Sword, 2010, pp. 69–92.

Gardiner, Juliet. *Wartime: Britain,
1939–1945.* London: Headline Book
Publishing, 2004.

Garshin, V. G. "Tam gde smert' pomogaet
zhizni." *Arkhiv patologii* 46, no. 5
(1984): 83–88.

Gaukhman, S. L. "Massovye narusheniia
obshchego pitaniia ('otechnaia
bolezn'): istoriko-literaturnyi ocherk.
Obzor literatury 1915–1935 gg." In M. V.
Chernorutskii, ed., *Alimentarnaia
distrofiia v blokirovannom Leningrade.*
Leningrad: Medgiz, 1947, pp. 9–35.

Gel'shtein, E. M. *Metodicheskie ukazaniia
po raspoznavaniiu i lecheniiu alimentarnogo istoshcheniia.* Leningrad, 1942.

———. *Alimentarnaia distrofiia.* Moscow:
Medgiz, 1947.

———, ed. *Narushenie obshchego pitaniia
(osobennosti ikh vozniknoveniia i
lecheniia vo vremia voiny),* vol. 28 of *Opyt
sovetskoi meditsiny v Velikoi Otechestvennoi voine 1941–1945 gg.* Moscow:
Medgiz, 1951

Genatulin, Anatolii. *Vot konchitsia voina.*
Moscow: Pravda, 1988.

———. *Strakh.* Moscow: Sovetskii voin,
1990.

Gerlach, Christian. *Kalkulierte Morde: Die
deutsche Wirtschafts und Vernichtungspolitik in Weissrussland 1941 bis 1944.*
Hamburg: Hamburger Edition, 1999.

Gertsenberg, E. Ia. "Patologicheskaia
anatomiia i patogenez alimentarnogo
istoshcheniia." In M. V. Kostylev, ed.,
*Trudy Molotovskogo gosudarstvennogo
stomatologicheskogo instituta.* Molotov,
1943, pp. 146–151.

Getty, J. Arch, and Oleg V. Naumov. *The
Road to Terror: Stalin and the Self-*

Destruction of the Bolsheviks, 1932–1939.
New Haven, Conn.: Yale University
Press, 1999.

Ginzburg, Lidiya [Lidiia]. *Blockade Diary,*
translated by Alan Myers. London:
Harvill Press, 1996.

———. *Zapisnye knizhki. Vospominaniia.
Esse,* edited by A. S. Kushner and E. A.
Polikashin. St. Petersburg: Iskusstvo,
2002.

———. *Prokhodiashchie kharaktery: proza
voennykh let; Zapiski blokadnogo
cheloveka,* edited by E. Van Buskirk
and A. Zorin. Moscow: Novoe
izdatel'stvo, 2011.

Gladkikh, P. F. *Zdravookhranenie i
voennaia meditsina v bitve za Leningrad
glazami istorika i ochevidtsev, 1941–1944
gg.* St. Petersburg: Dmitrii Bulanin,
2006.

Glantz, David M. *The Siege of Leningrad,
1941–1945: 900 Days of Terror.* London:
Cassell Military Paperbacks, 2001.

———. *Colossus Reborn: The Red Army at
War, 1941–1945.* Lawrence: University
of Kansas Press, 2005.

Glantz, David, with Jonathan House. *The
Stalingrad Trilogy,* 3 vols. Lawrence:
University of Kansas Press, 2009, 2014.

Goffman, Erving. *Relations in Public:
Microstudies of the Public Order.* New
York: Basic Books, 1971.

Golant, R. Ia. "O nekotorykh psikhicheskikh narusheniiakh v usloviiakh
voennogo vremeni na osnovanii
Leningradskogo opyta dvukh voin."
In R. Ia. Golant and V. N. Miasishchev,
eds., *Nervnye i psikhicheskie zabolevaniia v usloviiakh voennogo vremeni.*
Leningrad: 9aia tipografiia Upravleniia
Voennogo Izdatel'stva MVS SSSR, 1948,
pp. 5–17.

———. "Psikhozy pri alimentarnom
istoshchenii i avitaminozakh." In R. Ia.
Golant and V. N. Miasishchev, eds.,

Bibliography

Nervnye i psikhicheskie zabolevaniia voennogo vremeni. Moscow: Medgiz, 1948, pp. 217–227.

Goncharov, G. A. "Trudovaia Armiia" na Urale v gody Velikoi Otechestvennoi voiny. Cheliabinsk: Cheliabinsk State University, 2006.

Gor'kov, Iurii A. Gosudarstvennyi komitet postanovliaet, 1941–45. Tsifry i dokumenty. Moscow: Olma Press, 2002.

Goukassian. "Hungerdystrophie." In Max Michel, ed., Gesundheitsschäden durch Verfolgung und Gefangenschaft und ihre Spätfolgen. Zusammenstellung der Referate und Ergebnisse der Internationalen Sozialmedizinischen Konferenz über die Pathologie der Ehemaligen Deportierten und Internierten, 5.–7. Juni 1954 in Kopenhagen, und ergänzender Referate und Ergebnisse. Frankfurt am Main: Röderberg-Verlag, 1955, pp. 127–134.

Granin, Daniil, and Ales' Adamovich. Blokadnaia kniga. St. Petersburg: Pechatnyi Dvor, 1994.

———. Leningrad under Siege: First-Hand Accounts of the Ordeal, translated by Clare Burstall and Vladimir Kisselnikov. Barnsely: Pen and Sword, 2007.

Gronow, Jukka. Caviar with Champagne: Common Luxury and the Ideals of the Good Life in Stalin's Russia. New York: Berg, 2003.

Grossman, Vasily [Vasilii]. Gody voiny. Moscow: Pravda, 1989.

———. A Writer at War: A Soviet Journalist with the Red Army, 1941–1945, edited and translated by Antony Beevor and Luba Vinogradova. New York: Pantheon Books, 2005.

———. Life and Fate, translated by Robert Chandler. New York: New York Review of Books, 2006.

Gubergrits, M. M. "Ob alimentarnoi toksicheskoi distrofii," Vrachebnoe delo, nos. 11–12 (1945): 547–553.

Gurov, S. Pokhod i otdykh pekhoty. Moscow: Voenizdat, 1940.

———. Boets i otdelenie na pokhode. Moscow: Voenzidat, 1941.

Hagemann, Karen, and Stephanie Schuler-Springorum, eds. Home / Front. The Military, War and Gender in Twentieth Century Germany. Oxford: Berg, 2002.

Halfin, Igal. Terror in My Soul: Communist Autobiographies on Trial. Cambridge, Mass.: Harvard University Press, 2003.

Harrison, Mark. Accounting for War: Soviet Production, Employment, and the Defence Burden, 1940–1945. Cambridge: Cambridge University Press, 1996.

Harvey, David. The Condition of Postmodernity: An Enquiry into the Origins of Cultural Change. Oxford: Blackwell Publishing, 1989.

———. "Space as a Key Word." In Noel Castree and Derek Gregory, eds., David Harvey: A Critical Reader. Oxford: Blackwell Publishing, 2006.

Hawley, Edith. "Dietary Scales and Standards for Measuring a Family's Nutritive Needs." United States Department of Agriculture, Technical Bulletin No. 8, 1927.

Hellbeck, Jochen. Revolution on My Mind: Writing a Diary under Stalin. Cambridge, Mass.: Harvard University Press, 2006.

———. " 'The Diaries of Fritzes and the Letters of Gretchens': Personal Writings from the German-Soviet War and Their Readers." Kritika: Explorations in Russian & Eurasian History 10, no. 3 (2009): 571–606.

Henze, Charlotte E. Disease, Health Care and Government in Late Imperial Russia: Life and Death on the Volga, 1823–1914. New York: Routledge, 2011.

Hessler, Julie. A Social History of Soviet Trade: Trade Policy, Retail Practices, and

Consumption, 1917–1953. Princeton, N.J.: Princeton University Press, 2004.

Iarov, S. V. *Blokadnaia etika: Predstavleniia o morali v Leningrade v 1941–1942 gg.* St. Petersburg: Nestor-Istoriia, 2011.

Inber, Vera. "Pulkovskii meridian." In A. Notkina, ed, *Sobranie sochinenii v chetyrekh tomakh.* Moscow: Khudozhestvennaia literatura, 1965, vol. 1, pp. 472–502.

———. *Pochti tri goda.* Moscow: Sovetskaia Rossiia, 1968.

———. *Leningrad Diary.* Translated by Serge M. Wolff and Rachel Grieve. London: Hutchinson, 1971.

Inozemtsev, N. N. *Frontovoi dnevnik.* Moscow: Nauka, 2005.

Instruktsiia po ukladke pokhodnykh kukhon. Moscow: Voenizdat, 1942.

Irincheev, Bair, and Artem Drabkin. *"A zori zdes' gromkie": Zhenskoe litso voiny.* Moscow: Eksmo, 2012.

Isserson, O. D. "K voprosu o letal'nosti ot alimentarnoi distrofii v Leningrade s noiabria 1941 g. do noiabria 1942 g.." In Il'ia Davidovich Strashun and E. L. Venderovich, eds., *Alimentarnaia distrofiia i avitaminozy.* Leningrad: Narkomzdrav SSSR, Gosudarstvennoe Izdatel'stvo Meditsinskoi literatury, Leningradskoe otdelenie, 1944, pp. 96–100.

Johnston , B. F., with Mosaburo Hosoda and Yoshio Kusumi. *Japanese Food Management in World War II.* Stanford: Stanford University Press, 1953.

Jones, Jeffrey W. "A People without a Definite Occupation: The Illegal Economy and 'Speculators' in Rostov-on-the-Don, 1943–1948." In Donald J. Raleigh, ed., *Provincial Landscapes: Local Dimensions of Soviet Power, 1917–1953.* Pittsburgh, Pa.: University of Pittsburgh Press, 2001, pp. 236–254.

———. *Everyday Life and the "Reconstruction" of Soviet Russia during and after the Great Patriotic War, 1943–1948.* Bloomington: Slavica Publishers, 2008.

Kamalov, Khisam. *U kazhdoi zhizn'-odna.* Kazan': Tatknigizdat, 1983.

Kay, Alex J. *Exploitation, Resettlement, Mass Murder: Political and Economic Planning for German Occupation Policy in the Soviet Union, 1940–1941.* New York: Berghahn Books, 2006.

———. "Germany's Staatssekretäre, Mass Starvation and the Meeting of 2 May 1941." *Journal of Contemporary History* 41, no. 4 (2006): 685–700.

———. "The Purpose of the Russian Campaign Is the Decimation of the Slavic Population by Thirty Million: The Radicalization of German Food Policy in Early 1941." In Alex Kay, Jeff Rutherford, and David Stahel, eds., *Nazi Policy on the Eastern Front, 1941: Total War, Genocide, and Radicalization.* Rochester, N.Y.: University of Rochester Press, 2012, pp. 101–129.

Kay, Alex J., Jeff Rutherford, and David Stahel eds. *Nazi Policy on the Eastern Front, 1941. Total War, Genocide, and Radicalization.* Rochester, N.Y.: University of Rochester Press, 2012.

Kerner, V. M., ed. *Problema belkovykh distrofii v patologii i klinike tuberkuleza.* Moscow: Biomedgiz, 1935.

Kessler, G., and G. E. Kornilov. *Kolkhoznaia zhizn' na Urale, 1935–1953.* Moscow: ROSSPEN, 2006.

Keys, Ancel, Josef Brožek, Josef, Austin Henschel, Olaf Mickelsen, Henry Longstreet Taylor, et. al. *The Biology of Human Starvation.* Minneapolis: University of Minnesota Press, 1950.

Khlevnyuk, Oleg, and R. W. Davies. "The End of Rationing in the Soviet Union, 1934–1935." *Europe-Asia Studies* 5, no. 4 (1999): 557–609.

Bibliography

Khvilitskaia, M. I. "Simptomatologiia." In M. V. Chernorutskii, ed., *Alimentarnaia distrofiia v blokirovannom Leningrade*. Leningrad: Medgiz, 1947, pp. 128–165.

———. "Diagnoz." In M. V. Chernorutskii, ed., *Alimentarnaia distrofiia v blokirovannom Leningrade*. Leningrad: Medgiz, 1947, pp. 186–203.

———, "Lechenie." In M. V. Chernorutskii, ed. *Alimentarnaia distrofiia v blokirovannom Leningrade*. Leningrad: Medgiz, 1947, pp. 215–227.

Kirillov, V. M., P. M. Kuz'mina, N. M. Paegde, A. A. Permiakov, and S. L. Raznikov. *Gedenkbuch: Kniga pamiati nemtsev-trudarmeitsev Bogoslovlaga 1941–1946*. Moscow and Nizhnii Tagil: BIZ, 2008.

Kirschenbaum, Lisa A. "'The Alienated Body': Gender Identity and the Memory of the Siege of Leningrad." In Nancy M. Wingfield and Maria Bucur, eds., *Gender and War in Twentieth-Century Eastern Europe*. Bloomington: Indiana University Press, 2006, pp. 220–234.

———. *The Legacy of the Siege of Leningrad: Myth, Memories, and Monuments*. Cambridge: Cambridge University Press, 2006.

Klein, Richard. *Cigarettes Are Sublime* Durham, N.C.: Duke University Press, 1993.

Kochina, Elena. "Blokadnyi dnevnik." *Pamiat': Istoricheskii sbornik*, vol. 4. Moscow-Paris: YMCA Press, 1979–1981.

———. *Blockade Diary*. Edited and with an introduction by Samuel C. Ramer. Ann Arbor, Mich.: Ardis Publishers, 1990.

Komskii, Boris. "Dnevnik 1943–1945 gg.," *Arkhiv evreiskoi istorii*, vol. 6. Moscow: ROSSPEN, 2011.

Koshkarbaev, Rakhimzan. *Shturm: Den' 1410*. Alma-Ata: Zhalyn, 1983.

Kotkin, Stephen. *Magnetic Mountain: Stalinism as Civilization*. Berkeley: University of California Press, 1995.

Kozhina, Elena. *Through the Burning Steppe: A Memoir of Wartime Russia, 1924–1943*. New York: Riverhead, 2001.

Kozlova, Natal'ia, ed. *Sovetskie liudi: Stseni iz istorii*. Moscow: Evropa, 2005.

Kravchenko, Victor. *I Chose Freedom: A Personal and Political Life of a Soviet Official*. London: Robert Hale, 1947.

Krotkov, F. G., ed. *Gigiena. Opyt sovetskoi meditsiny v Velikoi Otechestvennoi voine, 1941–1945 gg.*, vol. 33. Moscow: Medgiz, 1955.

———. "Problemy pitaniia voisk v gody Velikoi Otechestvennoi voini." *Voprosy pitaniia*, no. 3 (1975): 6.

Kulagin, G. A. *Dnevnik i pamiat'* Leningrad: Lenizdat', 1978.

Kurkotkin, S. K. *Tyl sovetskikh vooruzhennykh sil v Velikoi Otechestvennoi voine, 1941–1945 gg.* Moscow: Voenizdat, 1977.

Kuznetsov, Anatoly. *Babi Yar: A Document in the Form of a Novel*. New York: Farrar Straus and Giroux, 1970.

Lang, G. F., ed. *Uchebnik vnutrennikh boleznei: Bolezni pochek, apparata neiro-endokrinnoi regulatsii i obmena veshchestv, avitaminozy, ostryi revmatizm, bolezni sustavov i otravleniia promyshlennymi iadami*, vol. 2, no. 2. Leningrad: Medgiz, 1941.

———. "Klinika alimentarnoi distrofii." In I. M. Rybakov, ed., *Trudy pervoi terapevticheskoi konferentsii*. Gor'kii, 1943, pp. 406–424.

Larson, Richard C. "Perspectives on Queues: Social Justice and the Psychology of Queuing." *Operations Research* 35, no. 6 (November–December 1987): 895–905.

Lavrov, B. A. "Ocherk razvitiia vitaminologii v sovetskom soiuze." *Voprosy pitaniia* 7, no. 1 (1938): 30–47.

Lefebvre, Henri. *The Production of Space.* Oxford: Blackwell, 2005.

Lesin, Aleksandr. *Byla voina: Kniga-dnevnik.* Simferopol': Tavriia, 1990.

Levels and Trends in Child Mortality: Report 2010. New York: United Nations Children's Fund, 2010.

Levi, Primo. *The Truce: A Survivor's Journey Home from Auschwitz.* London: Bodley Head, 1965.

———. *Survival in Auschwitz.* New York: Collier Books, 1986.

———. *The Drowned and the Saved.* New York: Vintage International, 1989.

Levi, Primo, and Leonardo de Benedetti. *Auschwitz Report.* Translated by Judith Woolf, edited by Robert S. C. Gordon. New York: Verso, 2006.

Levtov, V. E. and V. M. David. *Budni podviga: blokadnaia zhizn' leningradtsev v dnevnikakh.* St. Petersburg: LIK, 2006.

Lih, Lars T. *Bread and Authority in Russia, 1914–1921.* Berkeley: University of California Press, 1990.

Likhachev, Dmitrii Sergeevich. *Vospominaniia.* St. Petersburg: Izd-vo "Logos," 1995.

Lipskii, A. A. *Golod i vyzyvaemye im bolezni: publichnaia lektsiia.* St. Petersburg: Tipografiia Doma Prizreniia Maloletnikh Bednykh, 1892.

Liublinskii, V. S. "Blokadnye dnevniki. Vospominaniia. Stikhi. Pis'ma." In Ts I. Grin, G. V. Mikheeva, and L. A. Shilov, eds. *V pamiat' ushedshikh i vo slavu zhivushchikh: Pisma chitatelei s fronta, dnevniki i vospominaniia sotrudnikov Publichnoi biblioteki, 1941–1945.* St. Petersburg: Rossiiskaia Natstional'naia Biblioteka, 1995, pp. 147–200.

Livshin, A. I., and I. B. Orlov. *Sovetskaia povsednevnost' i massovoe soznanie 1939–1945.* Moscow: ROSSPEN, 2003.

Loginov, Mikhail. *Eto bylo na fronte.* Kazan': Tatknigizdat', 1984.

Lomagin, Nikita. *Neizvestnaia blokada,* vol. 1. St. Petersburg: Neva, 2002.

———. *Neizvestnaya blokada. Dokumenty, prilozheniia,* vol.2. St. Petersburg: Neva, 2004.

Lomakina, Inessa. *Nasha biografiia: Ocherki istorii proizvodstvennogo ob'edineniia 'Zavod imeni Kalinina,' 1869–1989.* Leningrad: Lenizdat, 1991.

Loskutovoi, M. V. *Pamiat' o blokade: Svidetel'stva ochevidtsev i istoricheskoe soznanie obshchestva.* Moscow: Novoe izdatel'stvo, 2006.

Luknitskii, P. N. *Leningrad deistvuet . . . Frontovoi dnevnik,* vol. 2. Moscow: Sovetskii pisatel', 1964.

Lukovnikov, A., *Druz'ia-odnopolchane: Rasskazy o pesniakh, rozhdennykh voinoi: Melodii i teksty.* Moscow: Muzyka, 1985.

Macintyre, Kate. "Famine and the Female Mortality Advantage." In Tim Dyson and Cormac Ó Gráda, eds., *Famine Demography: Perspectives from the Past and Present.* Oxford: Oxford University Press, 2002, pp. 240–59.

Malakhova, Vera Ivanovna. "Four Years a Frontline Physician." In Barbara Alpern Engel and Anastasia Posadskaya-Vanderbeck, eds., *A Revolution of Their Own: Voices of Women in Soviet History.* Boulder, Colo.: Westview Press, 1998, 175–218.

Manassein, V. A. *Materialy dlia voprosa o golodanii.* St. Petersburg: Tipografiia Imperatorskoi Akademii Nauk, 1869.

Manley, Rebecca. *To the Tashkent Station. Evacuation and Survival in the Soviet Union at War.* Ithaca, N.Y.: Cornell University Press, 2009.

Mann, Leon. "Queue Culture: The Waiting Line as a Social System." *The American Journal of Sociology* 75, no. 3 (November 1969): 340–354.

Bibliography

Margolin, Iu. B. *Puteshestvie v stranu Ze-ka.* New York: Izd-vo im. Chekhova, 1952.

Markwick, Roger D. "Stalinism at War." *Kritika: Explorations in Russian and Eurasian History* 3, no. 3 (Summer 2002): 509–520.

Martin, Bernd. "Agriculture and Food Supply in Japan during the Second World War." In Bernd Martin and Alan S. Milward, eds. *Agriculture and Food Supply in the Second World War. Landwirtschaft und Versorgung im Zweiten Weltkrieg.* Ostfildern: Scripta Mercaturae Verlag, 1985, pp. 181–205.

Mashkova, M. V. "Iz blokadnykh zapisei." In Ts. I. Grin, G. V. Mikheeva, and L. A. Shilov, eds. *V pamiat' ushedshikh i vo slavu zhivushchikh: Pisma chitatelei s fronta, dnevniki i vospominaniia sotrudnikov Publichnoi biblioteki, 1941–1945.* St. Petersburg: Rossiiskaia natstional'naia biblioteka, 1995, pp. 34–146.

Mateshvili, G. I. *Alimentarnaia distrofiia, ee klinicheskie formy, patogenez i lechenie.* Tbilisi: Gruzmedgiz, 1945.

Merridale, Catherine. *Ivan's War: Life and Death in the Red Army, 1939–1945.* New York: Picador, 2006.

Miasishchev, V. N. "Nervno-psikhicheskie zabolevaniia alimentarno-avitaminoznogo proiskhozhdeniia." In V. N Miasishchev, ed. *Nervno-psikhicheskie zabolevaniia voennogo vremeni (po materialam Leningradskikh konferentsii 1942–1943 gg).* Leningrad: Gosudarstvennoe izdatel'stvo meditsinskoi literatury Leningradskoe otdelenie, 1945, pp. 3–13.

Mikoian, Anastas. *Tak bylo: Razmyshleniia o minuvshem.* Moscow: Vagrius, 1999.

Mintz, Sidney W. *Sweetness and Power: The Place of Sugar in Modern History.* New York: Penguin, 1986.

Mitrofanova, A. V. *Rabochii klass SSSR nakanune i v gody Velikoi Otechestvennoi voiny, 1938–1945,* vol. 3. Moscow: Nauka, 1984.

Moreinis, I. Ia. *Uchebnik pishevoi gigenii dlia sanitarno-fel'dsherskikh shkol.* Moscow-Leningrad: MEDGIZ, 1940.

Moskoff, William. *The Bread of Affliction: The Food Supply in the USSR during World War II.* Cambridge: Cambridge University Press, 1990.

Munting, Roger. "Soviet Food Supply and Allied Aid in the War, 1941–45." *Soviet Studies* 36, no. 4 (October 1984): 582–593.

Naiman, Eric. *Sex in Public: The Incarnation of Early Soviet Ideology.* Princeton, N.J.: Princeton University Press, 1997.

Nastavlenie po polevomu vodosnabzheniiu voisk. Moscow: Voenizdat, 1941.

Nikolaev, V. G. *Sovetskaia ochered' kak sreda obitaniia: Sotsiologicheskii analiz.* Moscow: Institut nauchnoi informatsii po obshchestvennym naukam RAN, 2000.

Nikulin, N. N. *Vospominaniia o voine.* St. Petersburg: Izdatel'stvo Gos. Ermitazha, 2008.

Novye vidy produktov, postupaiushchikh na dovol'stvie Krasnoi Armii. Moscow: Voenizdat, 1944.

Ó Gráda, Cormac. *Famine: A Short History.* Princeton, N.J.: Princeton University Press, 2009.

O'Neill, Bruce. "The Political Agency of Cityscapes: Spatializing Governance in Ceausescu's Bucharest." *Journal of Social Archaeology* 9, no. 92 (2009): 92–109.

Oddy, D. J. "A Nutritional Analysis of Historical Evidence: The Working-Class Diet, 1880–1914." In Derek Oddy and Derek Miller, eds., *The Making of the Modern British Diet*. London: Croom Helm, 1973, pp. 214–231.

Opyt sovetskoi meditsina v Velikoi Otechestvennoi voine, 1941–1945 gg., vol. 28, *Narusheniia obshchego pitaniia (osobennosti ikh vozniknoveniia, techeniia, preduprezhdeniia i lecheniia vo vremia voiny)*. Edited by E. M. Gel'shtein. Moscow: Medgiz, 1951.

Osokina, E. A., *Za fasadom "stalinskogo izobilia": Raspredelenie i rynok v snabzhenii v gody industrializatsii, 1927–1941*. Moscow: ROSSPEN, 1998.

———. *Our Daily Bread: Socialist Distribution and the Art of Survival in Stalin's Russia, 1927–1941*. Armonk, N.Y.: M. E. Sharpe, 2001.

Overy, Richard. *Russia's War: A History of the Soviet Effort, 1941–1945*. New York: Penguin Books, 1998.

Palladin, A. V. "Sovremennoe polozhenie voprosa o 'vitaminakh.'" In K. N. Georgievskii, K. M. Kogan, and A. V. Palladin, eds., *O golode*. Khar'kov: Izdatel'stvo Nauchnaia mysl', 1922, pp. 79–94.

Pamiatka voiskovomu povaru. Moscow: Voenizdat, 1943.

Paperno, Irina. "What Can Be Done with Diaries?" *Russian Review* 63, no. 4 (October 2004): 561–573.

Pashutin, V. V. *Kurs obshchei i eksperimental'noi patologii (patologicheskoi fiziologii)*, vol. 2. St. Petersburg, 1902.

Pauer, Erich. "A New Order for Japanese Society: Planned Economy, Neighbourhood Associations and Food Distribution in Japanese Cities in the Second World War." In Erich Pauer, ed.,

Japan's War Economy. London: Routledge, 1999, pp. 85–105.

Pavlov, D. V. *Leningrad 1941: The Blockade*. Translated by John Clinton Adams. Chicago: University of Chicago Press, 1965.

———. "Revisiting the Past: History and Historical Memory during the Leningrad Blockade." *Soviet and Post-Soviet Review*, no. 38 (2011): 105–129.

Pis'ma s fronta 1941–1945 gg.: Sbornik dokumentov. Kazan': Gasyr, 2010.

Podzdniakova, T. S., ed. *Peterburg Akhmatovoi: Vladimir Georgevich Garshin*. St. Petersburg: Nevskii Dialekt, 1994.

Pogonii, Ia. F., ed. *Stalingradskaia epopeia: Materialy NKVD SSSR i voennoi tsenzury iz Tsentral'nogo arkhiva FSB RF*. Moscow: "Zvonitsa MG," 2000.

Pokhlebkin, Vil'iam. *Moia kukhnia i moe meniu*. Moscow: Tsentrpoligraf, 1999.

———. *Kukhnia veka*. Moscow: Polifakt, 2000.

Polian, P. M. *Zhertvy dvukh diktatur: Ostarbaitery i voennoplennye v Tret'em Reikhe i ikh repatriatsiia*. Moscow: "Vash vybor TSIRZ," 1996.

Polzikova-Rubets, K. V. *Oni uchilis' v Leningrade*. Leningrad: Detgiz,1948.

———. *Dnevnik uchitelia blokadnoi shkoly: 1941–1946*. St. Peterburg: Tema, pri uchastii turisticheskoi kompanii "Mir," 2000.

Preobrazhenskii, Aleksandr Grigor'evich. *Etimologicheskii slovar' russkogo iazyka*, vol. 2 (P–S). Moscow: Gos. izdat. inostrannykh i natsional'nykh slovarei, 1959; repr. of 1910–1914 edition.

Prywes, M., and H. Chertok. *Prisoner of Hope*. Hanover, N.H.: Brandeis University Press, 1996.

Punin, Nikolai. "Blokadnyi dnevnik." *Zvezda*, vol. 1 (1994).

Bibliography

———. *Mir svetel liubov'iu: dnevniki, pis'ma.* Edited by L. A. Zykov. Moscow: Artist. Rezhisser. Teatr, 2000.

Pushkaraev, V. S. "Razvitie 'chernogo rynke' v period Velikoi Otechestvennoi voiny i ego vliianie na sostoianie vnutrennego rynka strany." In V. P. Kozlov, M. V. Larin, N. I. Nikiforov, M. V. Stegantsev, A. O. Chubar'ian, and S. I. Chuvashin, eds., *Edinstvo fronta i tyla v Velikoi Otechestvennoi voine, 1941–1945.* Moscow: Akademiia, 2007, pp. 187–193.

Qualls, Karl D. *From Ruins to Reconstruction: Urban Identity in Soviet Sevastopol after World War II.* Ithaca, N.Y.: Cornell University Press, 2009.

Randall, Amy. *The Soviet Dream World of Retail Trade and Consumption in the 1930s.* Houndmills, Basingstoke, Hampshire: Palgrave Macmillan, 2008.

Ries, Nancy. "Potato Ontology: Surviving Post-Socialism in Russia." *Cultural Anthropology* 24, no. 2 (May 2009):181–212.

Romer, Felix,. "The Wehrmacht in the War of Ideologies: The Army and Hitler's Criminal Orders on the Eastern Front." In Alex Kay, Jeff Rutherford, and David Stahel, eds., *Nazi Policy on the Eastern Front, 1941: Total War, Genocide, and Radicalization* Rochester, N.Y.: University of Rochester Press, 2012.

Rossi, Jacques. *Spravochnik po Gulagu: istoricheskii slovar' sovetskikh penitentsiarnykh institutsii i terminov, sviazannykh s prinuditel'nym trudom.* Moscow: Prosvet, 1991.

Rukhovodstvo dlia boitsa pekhoty. Moscow: Voenizdat, 1940.

Rybakov, I. M., ed., *Trudy pervoi terapevticheskoi konferentsii.* Gor'kii, 1943.

Salisbury, Harrison. *The 900 Days: The Siege of Leningrad.* Cambridge, Mass.: Da Capo Press, 2003.

Samoilov, David. *Podennye zapisi,* vol. 1. Moscow: Vremia, 2002.

Samsonov, A. M., ed. *Oborona Leningrada 1941–1944: Vospominaniia i dnevniki uchastnikov.* Leningrad: Nauka, 1968.

Samuels, John, ed. *Ration Development.* Washington, D.C.: Quartermaster Food & Container Institute for the Armed Forces, 1947.

Sanborn, Joshua. *Drafting the Russian Nation: Military Conscription, Mass Politics and Total War, 1905–1925.* DeKalb: Northern Illinois University Press, 2003.

Sandomirskaia, Irina. "A Politeia in Besiegement: Lydiia Ginzburg on the Siege of Leningrad as Political Paradigm." *Slavic Review* 69, no. 2 (2010): 306–326.

Saushin, F. S., *Khleb i sol'* Iaroslavl': Verkhne-Volzhskoe knizhnoe izdatel'stvo, 1983.

Sbornik ukazov, postanovlenii, reshenii, rasporiazhenii, i prikazov voennogo vremeni,1944. Leningrad: Lenizdat, 1945.

Schaible, Ulrich E., and Stefan H. E. Kaufmann. "Malnutrition and Infection: Complex Mechanisms and Global Impacts." Public Library of Science. *PLoS Medicine* 4, no. 5 (May 2007): 0806–0812, www.plosmedicine .org.

Sedel'nikova, Zinaida. *279 dnei voiny: Blokadnyi dnevnik.* Volgograd: Volgogradskii Komitet Popechati, 1995.

Sen, Amartya. *Poverty and Famine: An Essay on Entitlement and Deprivation.* Oxford: Clarendon Press, 1981.

Shalamov, Varlam. "Veismanist." In I. Sirotinskaia, ed., *Sobranie sochinenii v* *shesti tomakh.*Moscow: Terra, 2004, vol. 1, pp. 538–545.

———. "Perchatka." In I. Sirotinskaia, ed., *Sobranie sochinenii v shesti tomakh.* Moscow: Terra, 2004, vol. 2, pp. 283–311

———. "Shakhmaty doktora Kuz'menko." In I. Sirotinskaia, ed., *Sobranie sochinenii v shesti tomakh.* Moscow: Terra, 2004, vol. 2, pp. 392–397.

Shaporina, L. V. *Dnevnik.* Edited by V. N. Sazhin and V. F. Petrovaia. Moscow: Novoe Literaturnoe Obozrenie, 2012.

Shnitser, I. S. "Alimentarnaia distrofiia." *Fel'dsher i akusherka,* no. 3 (1943): 31–35.

Shumilov, Nikolai. *V dni blokady.* Moscow: Mysl', 1974.

Simmons, Cynthia, and Nina Perlina. *Writing the Siege of Leningrad: Women's Diaries, Memoirs, and Documentary Prose.* Pittsburgh, Pa.: University of Pittsburgh Press, 2002.

Simmons, Dana. "Starvation Science: From Colonies to Metropole." In Alexander Nützendel and Frank Trentmann, eds., *Food and Globalization: Consumption, Markets and Politics in the Modern World.* Oxford: Berg, 2008, pp. 173–191.

Skliarchik, L. I., ed. "Konferentsiia Leningradskogo obshchestva psikhiatrov i nevropatologov sovmestno s Psikhonevrologicheskim institutom im. Bekhtereva, posviashchennaia probleme 'Nervno-psikhicheskie zabolevaniia pri alimentarno-avitaminoznykh narusheniiakh' (16–17 oktiabria 1943 g.)." *Nevropatologiia i psikhiatriia,* no. 5 (1944): 74–80.

Skriabina, Elena. *V blokade: Dnevnik materi.* Iowa City: Herausgeber, 1964.

———. *Siege and Survival: The Odyssey of a Leningrader.* Carbondale: Southern Illinois University Press, 1971.

Slezkine, L. Iu. *Do voini i na voine.* Moscow: Parad, 2009.

Slovar' inostrannykh slov. Edited by F. N. Petrov. Moscow: Ogiz RSFSR, 1937.

Slovar' russkikh narodnykh govorov, vol. 6. Leningrad: Nauka Leningradskoe otd-nie, 1970.

Slovar' russkogo iazyka. Edited by S. I. Ozhegov and S. P. Obnorskii. Moscow: Gos. izd-vo inostrannykh i national'nykh slovarei, 1949.

Slovar' sovremennogo russkogo literaturnogo iazyka, vol. 3. Moscow: Izdatel'stvo Akademii nauk SSSR, 1954.

Slutskii, Boris. *O drugikh i o sebe.* Moscow: Vagrius, 2005.

Sobolev, G. L. *Uchenye Leningrada v gody Velikoi Otechestvennoi voiny, 1941–1945.* edited by V. M. Koval'chuk. Moscow: Nauka, 1966.

Sokolov, A. K., "Sotsial'no-trudovye otnosheniia na sovetskikh predpriiatiiakh v gody voiny." In A. N. Sakharov and A. S. Seniavskii, eds., *Narod i voina, 1941–1945 gg.* Moscow: Institut Rossiiskoi Istorii RAN, 2010.

Solzhenitsyn, Aleksandr. *Arkhipelag GULag,* vol. 3 Paris: YMCA Press, 1975.

Sorokin, P. A. *Hunger as a Factor in Human Affairs.* Gainesville: University Presses of Florida, 1975.

"Soveshchanie nachalnikov otdelov agitatsii i propagandy Politupravlenii frontov i okrugov." *Propagandist i agitator Krasnoi Armii,* no. 5–6 (1943): 21–30.

Ssorin-Chaikov, Nikolai V. *The Social Life of the State in Subarctic Siberia.* Stanford, Calif.: Stanford University Press, 2003.

Staleva, Tamara. "Odin god i odin mesiats: Dnevnik Dimy Afanas'eva (1928–1988)," *Vechnye deti blokady: dokumental'nye ocherki* (Moscow: The Author, 1995).

Bibliography

Stalin, I. V., "O zadachakh khoziaistvennikov." *Sochineniia*, vol. 13 Moscow: Gosudarstvennoe Izdatel'stvo Politicheskoi Literatury, 1952.

Stalin, Joseph. *The Great Patriotic War of the Soviet Union*. New York: International Publishers, 1945.

Stephenson, L. S., M. C. Latham, and E. A. Ottesen. "Malnutrition and Parasitic Helminth Infections." *Parasitology* 121, Supplement (2000): S5–S22.

Strashun, I. D. "Vmesto predisloviia: Nauchnaia rabota 1 LMI im. akad. Pavlova za 2 goda." In I. D. Strashun and E. L. Venderovich, eds., *Alimentarnaia distrofiia i avitamonizy*. Leningrad: Gosizdatel'stvo Meditsinskoi Literatury, 1944, pp.3–6.

Strashun, I. D., and E. L. Venderovich, eds. *Alimentarnaia distrofiia i avitaminozy*. Leningrad: Gosizdatel'stvo Meditsinskoi Literatury, 1944.

Strazhesko, N. D. "K voprosu o patogeneze otekov." *Vrachebnoe delo*, no. 6–7 (1933): 321–326.

Suprun, M. N. "Prodovol'stvennye postavki v SSSR po Lend-Lizu v gody vtoroi mirovoi voiny." *Otechestvennaia istoriia*, no. 3 (1996): 46–54.

Suris, Boris. *Frontovoi dnevnik: dnevnik, rasskazy*. Moscow: ZAO Izdatel'stvo Tsentpoligraf, 2010.

Taeuber, Irene B. *The Population of Japan*. Princeton, N.J.: Princeton University Press, 1965.

Tarkhov, N. S., ed."Zimniaia voina": *Rabota nad oshibkami (aprel'–mai 1940 g.): Materialy komissii Glavnogo voennogo soveta Krasnoi Armii po obobshcheniu opyta finskoi kompanii*. Moscow-St. Petersburg: Letnii sad, 2004.

Tartakovskii, Boris. *Iz dnevnikov voennykh let*. Moscow: AIRO-XX, 2005.

Temkin, Gabriel. *My Just War: The Memoir of a Jewish Red Army Soldier in World War II*. Novato, Calif.: Presidio, 1998.

Thurston, Robert W., and Bernd Bonwetsch. *The People's War: Responses to World War II in the Soviet Union*. Urbana: University of Illinois Press, 2000.

Timasheff, Nicholas S. *The Great Retreat: The Growth and Decline of Communism in Russia*. New York: E. P. Dutton and Co., 1946.

Tokarev, Genadii. *Vesti dnevnik na fronte zapreshchalos'*. Novosibirsk: Svin'in i synov'ia, 2005.

Tooze, Adam. *The Wages of Destruction: The Making and Breaking of the Nazi Economy*. New York: Penguin, 2006.

Trentmann, Frank, and Just Flemming, eds., *Food and Conflict in Europe in the Age of the Two World Wars*. New York: Palgrave Macmillan, 2006.

Tumarkin, Nina. *The Living and the Dead: The Rise and the Fall of the Cult of World War II in Russia*. New York: Basic Books, 1994.

Tvardovskii, A. T. *Vasilii Terkin: Kniga pro boitsa*. Moscow: Literatura, 1977.

Ukazaniia po raspoznavaniiu, lecheniiu i profilaktike alimentarnoi distrofii i avitaminozov. Tashkent, 1944.

Ukazaniia po raspoznavaniiu i lecheniiu rasstroistv obshchego pitaniia i avitaminozov. Moscow: Medgiz, 1942.

United States Strategic Bombing Survey, Medical Division. *The Effects of Bombing on Health and Medical Services in Japan*. N.p., June 1947.

United States Strategic Bombing Survey, Morale Division. *The Effect of Bombing on Health and Medical Care in Germany*, 2nd ed. N.p., 1947.

Ustinov, Aleksandr. " 'Zavtra uedem v armiiu': Iz frontovogo dnevnika fotozhurnalista." *Rodina*,no. 6 (2011): 21–26.

Vail', S. S. "O nekotorykh izmeneniiakh kishek, pecheni i podzheludochnoi zhelezy pri alimentarnoi distrofii." In *Trudy pervoi terapevticheskoi konferentsii Gor'kii*, 1943, pp. 429–435.

Valiev, Gamilzhan. *Soldat khatlar.* Yar Chally: 2000.

Van Buskirk, Emily S. "Varieties of Failure: Lydia Ginzburg's Character Analyses from the 1930s and 1940s." In Emily S. Van Buskirk and A. L. Zorin, eds., *Lydia Ginzburg's Alternative Literary Identities: A Collection of Articles and New Translations.* Oxford: Peter Lang, 2012, pp. 125–161.

Varga-Harris, Christine. "Forging Citizenship on the Home Front: Reviving the Socialist Contract and Constructing Soviet Identity during the Thaw." In Polly Jones, ed., *The Dilemmas of De-Stalinization: Negotiating Cultural and Social Change in the Khrushchev Era.* London: Routledge, 2006, pp. 101–116.

Varshavskii, V. S. *Sem' let: Povest'.* Paris: self-published, 1950.

Vasilyev, Pavel. "Alimentary and Pellagra Psychoses in Besieged Leningrad." In Ina Zweiniger-Bargielowska, Rachel Duffett, and Alain Drouard, eds., *Food and War in Twentieth-Century Europe.* Farnham: Ashgate, 2011, pp. 111–124.

Veshchikov, P. I. "Rol' tyla v bespereboinom obespechenii deistvuiushchego fronta prodovol'stviem." In V. P. Kozlov, M. V. Larin, N. I. Nikiforov, M. V. Stegantsev, A. O. Chubar'ian, and S. I. Chuvashin, eds., *Edinstvo fronta i tyla v Velikoi Otechestvennoi voine 1941–1945.* Moscow: Akademiia, 2007, pp. 81–87.

———. ed., *Tyl Krasnoi Armii v Velikoi Otechestvennoi voine 1941–1945 gg.: Dokumenty i materialy. Russkii arkhiv: Velikaia Otechestvennaia*, vol. 25 (14), Moscow: Terra, 1998.

Vikhnovich, V. L. *Dve sud'by v Velikoi Otechestvennoi voiny.* Moscow: Gumanitarnaia Akademiia, 2006.

Vögele, Jörg. *Urban Mortality Change in England and Germany, 1870–1913.* Liverpool: Liverpool University Press, 1998.

Volkov, Igor. *Solntse vskhodit na vostoke*, vol. 2. Kharbin: Izd. Monarkhicheskago ob'edineniia, 1940.

Volkov, Vladimir. *It Happens in Russia: Seven Years Forced Labour in the Siberian Goldfields.* London: Eyre and Spottiswoode, 1951.

Vorontsov, D. P., *Prodovol'stvennoe snabzhenie strelkovogo batal'ona i polka v deistvuiushchei armii.* Moscow: Voennaia akademiia tyla i snabzheniia Krasnoi armii imeni Molotova V. M., 1943.

Vospominaniia frontovikov. Sbornik No.1. Moscow: Voennaia akademiia tyla i snabzhenia Krasnoi armii imena Molotova V. M., 1943.

Voznesensky, N. A. *Soviet Economy during the Second World War.* New York: International Publishers, 1949.

Weiner, Amir. *Making Sense of War: The Second World War and the Fate of the Bolshevik Revolution.* Princeton, N.J.: Princeton University Press, 2000.

Werth, Alexander. *Russia at War, 1941–1945.* New York: Carroll and Graf, 1984.

Wheatcroft, Stephen G. "Soviet Statistics of Nutrition and Mortality during Times of Famine, 1917–1922 and 1931–1933." In *Cahiers du Monde russe* 38, no. 4 (October–December 1997): 525–558.

White, Elizabeth. "After the War Was Over: The Civilian Return to Leningrad." *Europe-Asia Studies* 59, no. 7 (2007): 1145–1161.

Winick, Myron, ed. *Hunger Disease: Studies by Jewish Physicians in the Warsaw Ghetto.* Translated from the Polish by Martha Osnos. New York: John Wiley & Sons, 1979.

Wirtschafter, Elise. *From Peasant to Russian Soldier.* Princeton, N.J.: Princeton University Press, 1990.

Wood, J. V., et al., "Social Comparison in Adjustment to Breast Cancer." *Journal of Personality and Social Psychology* 49 (1985): 1169–1183.

Yakupov, Kharis. *Frontovye zarisovki: Zapiski khudozhnika.* Kazan': Tatkigizdat, 1981.

Zakharchenko, V., and I. Kassirskii, I. *Ukazaniia po raspoznavaniiu i lecheniiu obshchikh rasstroistv pitaniia i avitaminozov.* Moscow: Transzheldorizdat', 1947.

Zemskov, V. N. "Smertnost' zakliuchennykh v 1941–1945 gg." In *Liudskie poteri SSSR v period vtoroi mirovoi voiny. Sbornik statei.* St. Petersburg: BLITs, 1995, pp. 174–177.

Zhou, Rongrong, and Dilip Soman. "Looking Back: Exploring the Psychology of Queuing and the Effect of the Number of People Behind." *Journal of Consumer Research* 24, no. 4 (March 2003): 517–530.

Zima, V. F. *Golod v SSSR 1946–1947 godov: Proiskhozhdenie i posledstviia.* Moscow: Institut Rossiiskoi Istorii RAN, 1996.

———. "Medical Expertise and the 1946–47 Famine: The Identification and Treatment of a State-Induced Illness." In Frances L. Bernstein, Christopher Burton, and Dan Healey, eds., *Soviet Medicine: Culture, Practice, and Science.* Dekalb: Northern Illinois University Press, 2011, pp. 174–194.

Zimnitskaia, G. K. "Blokadnye budni (dnevnik leningradskoi devochki)." In S. E. Glezerov, ed., *Blokada glazami ochevidtsev: dnevniki i vospominaniia.* St. Petersburg: Ostrov, 2012.

Zotov, V. P. *Pishchevaia promyshlennost'.* Moscow: Pishchevaia promyshlennost', 1967.

Zubkova, Elena Iu. *Obshchestvo i reformy, 1945–1964.* Moscow: Rossiia Molodaia, 1993.

———. *Russia after the War: Hopes, Illusions, and Disappointments, 1945–1957.* Armonk, N.Y.: M. E. Sharpe, 1998.

Zweiniger-Bargielowska, Ina, Rachel Duffett, and Alain Drouard, eds. *Food and War in Twentieth-Century Europe.* Farnham: Ashgate, 2011.

UNPUBLISHED TEXTS AND ELECTRONIC SOURCES

Abramovich, D. G. "Serdechnososudistaia sistema i ee otrazhenie v elektrokardiogramme pri alimentarnoi distrofii." Candidate of Medical Sciences dissertation. Saratov, 1944.

Adamskii, Izo Davidovich. Interview by Grigory Koifman. Ia pomniu, http://iremember.ru/minometchiki/adamskiy-izo-davidovich.html

Afanas'ev, Dmitri Vladimirovich. "Dnevnik. Text courtesy of Natal'ia Aleksandrovna Afanas'eva. Excerpts from this diary have been published in: Tamara Staleva, "Odin god i odin mesiats: Dnevnik Dimy Afanas'eva (1928–1988)," *Vechnye deti blokady: dokumental'nye ocherki* (Moscow: The Author, 1995).

"Al'bom diagramm o rozhdaemosti i smertnosti naseleniia RSFSR za gody otechestvennoi voiny," prepared by the Scientific-Methodological Bureau of

Sanitary Statistics, Narkomzdrav RSFSR in 1945, in GARF, f. A-482, op. 52s, d. 188.

Barskova, P. "Avgust, kotorogo ne bylo, i mekhanizm kalendarnoi travmy: razmyshleniia o blokadnykh khronologiiakh." *Nezavisimyi filologicheskii zhurnal* 116 (2012). http://magazines .russ.ru/nlo/2012/116/b10.html.

Bazhenov, Pyotr Fyodorovich. Interview by Iu. Trifonov. Ia pomniu, http:// iremember.ru/pekhotintsi/bazhenov -petr-fedorovich.html.

Bogomolova, Maria Zinov'ievna. Memoirs. Ia pomniu, http://iremem ber.ru/svyazisti/bogomolova-mariya -zinovevna-2.html.

Borisov, Mikhail Fyodorovich, Hero of the Soviet Union. Interview by Artem Drabkin. Ia pomniu, http://iremember .ru/artilleristi/borisov-mikhail -fedorovich-geroy-sovetskogo-soiuza -artillerist.html#comment-963.

Deriabina (Ryzhkova), Klavdiia Andreevna. Interview by Artem Drabkin. Ia pomniu, http://iremember.ru/letchiki -bombardirov/deryabina-rizhkova-klav diya-andreevna-letchitsa-po-2.html.

Golubkova, Iudif' Vladimirovna. Interview by Artem Drabkin. Ia pomniu, http://www.iremember.ru /content/view/385/85/1/3/lang ,en/ (14 March 2010).

Gontsova, Marina Vasil'evna. "Povsednevnaia zhizn' naseleniia industrial'nogo tsentra v gody Velikoi Otechestvennoi voiny (na materialakh goroda Nizhnii Tagil)." Candidate of Historical Sciences dissertation. Nizhnii Tagil, 2011.

———. *Povsednevnaia zhizn' naseleniia industrial'nogo tsentra v gody Velikoi Otechestvennoi voiny (na materialakh goroda Nizhnii Tagil).* Author's abstract of candidate of Historical Sciences dissertation. Nizhnii Tagil, 2011.

Healey, Dan. "Medical Investigations in Stalin's Gulag: A Research Culture behind Barbed Wire, 1930–1956." Paper presented at the Munk Centre for Global Affairs, University of Toronto, February 3, 2011.

———. "Combatting 'Enforced Idleness' in Gulag Hospitals: Labour as 'Therapy' in Stalin's Forced Labor Camps, 1943–1953." Paper presented at the Russian and Soviet Cultural and Social History Seminar, University of Oxford, January 23, 2013.

Kats, Genrikh Zinov'ievich. Interview by Grigorii Koifman. Ia pomniu, http:// iremember.ru/razvedchiki/kats -genrikh-zinovevich.html.

Khodzhaev, Ashraf. "Funktsiia zheludka pri alimentarnoi distrofii." Candidate of Medical Sciences dissertation. Tashkent, 1946.

Kunitsina, Nina Ivanovna. Interview by Artem Drabkin. Ia pomniu, http:// iremember.ru/letno-tekh-sostav /kunitsina-nina-ivanovna.html.

Lesniak, Boris. "Moi Shalamov." *Oktiabr',* no. 4 (1999). http://magazines.russ .ru:81/october/1999/4/lesn.html.

Liubovskaia, Aleksandra Pavlovna. "Leningrad, 1941–1942: Zapiski zhitelia blokadnogo goroda." Text courtesy of Igor' Liubovskii.

"Mobilizatsionnoe predpisanie (oborot)." Soldat.ru, http://www.soldat.ru/doc /original/original.html?img =mobpredpis&id=2

Muzhikov, Anatoly Nikolaevich. Interview by Bair Irincheev. Ia pomniu, http://iremember.ru/minometchiki /muzhikov-anatoliy-nikolaevich .html.

Nash, Douglas. "Tinned Meat in the German Army Iron Ration" and "German 'Iron' Rations (eiserne Portionen)." www.dererstezug.com

Bibliography

/ Tinned_Meat_in_the_German _Army_Iron_Ration.htm.

Peri, Alexis. "Minds under Siege: Rethinking the Soviet Experience inside the Leningrad Blockade, 1941–1945." PhD dissertation. University of California Berkeley, 2011.

Quartermaster School for the Quartermaster General. "Rations Conference Notes," January 1949. U.S. Army Quartermaster Foundation, Fort Lee, Va., http://www.qmfound.com /history_of_rations.htm.

"Risunki: I. A. Liubovskogo." Text courtesy of Igor' Liubovskii.

Shoikhet, Abram Efimovich. Interview by Grigory Koifman. Ia pomniu, http:// iremember.ru/pulemetchiki /shoykhet-abram-efimovich.html.

Sokolova (Moskvina), Vera Vasil'ievna. Interview by Ilya Vershinin. Ia pomniu, http://www.iremember.ru/content /view/302/88/1/4/lang,en/ (23 March 2010).

Steiner, Stephanie P. "The Food Distribution System." M.A. thesis. San Jose State University, 1993.

Tobey, Eric. "The German Army K-Ration." www.dererstezug.com /germanration.htm.

Toker, Meir Faivelevich. Interview by Grigory Koifman. Ia pomniu, http:// iremember.ru/svyazisti/toker-meir-fayvelevich.html.

"Velikaia Otechestvennaia voina i promyshlennoe razvitie zapadnogo Urala." *Entsiklopediia Permskoi Oblasti,* http://ru.wikipedia.org/wiki/Пермь

Weinreb, Alice Autumn. "Matters of Taste: The Politics of Food and Hunger in Divided Germany, 1945–1971." PhD dissertation. University of Michigan, 2009.

Zajicek, Benjamin. "Scientific Psychiatry in Stalin's Soviet Union: The Politics of Modern Medicine and the Struggle To Define 'Pavlovian' Psychiatry, 1939–1953." PhD dissertation. University of Chicago, 2009.

Zamikhovskii, Grigory Efimovich. Interview by Grigory Koifman. Ia pomniu, http://iremember.ru /krasnoflottsi/zamikhovskiy -grigoriy-efimovich/stranitsa-3.html.

CONTRIBUTORS

DONALD FILTZER is Professor of Russian History at the University of East London, United Kingdom. He has authored a number of studies of Soviet workers during the Stalin, Khrushchev, and Gorbachev periods. His most recent book is *The Hazards of Urban Life in Late Stalinist Russia: Health, Hygiene, and Living Standards, 1943–1953* (2010). He is currently writing (with Wendy Goldman) a history of the Soviet home front during World War II.

WENDY Z. GOLDMAN is Professor of History at Carnegie Mellon University. She is a political and social historian of Russia and the former Soviet Union. She has written numerous books and articles about Soviet family policy, industrialization, and Stalinist repression. Her most recent books include *Terror and Democracy in the Age of Stalin: The Social Dynamics of Repression* (2007) and *Inventing the Enemy: Denunciation and Terror in Stalin's Russia* (2011). She is currently writing (with Donald Filtzer) a history of the Soviet home front during World War II.

REBECCA MANLEY is Associate Professor of History at Queen's University in Kingston, Ontario. She is author of *To the Tashkent Station: Evacuation and Survival in the Soviet Union at War, 1941–1946* (2009), and is currently working on a project entitled *Tsar Hunger: Conceiving Hunger in Modern Russian History.*

ALEXIS PERI is Assistant Professor of History at Boston University. She previously held the same position at Middlebury College. She currently is working on a monograph based on more than 120 unpublished diaries from the Leningrad Blockade, which is provisionally entitled *The War Within: How Diarists Endured and Interpreted the Leningrad Blockade.*

BRANDON SCHECHTER is a graduate student in the History Program at the University of California-Berkeley. His PhD dissertation, "Government Issue: The Material Culture of the Red Army, 1941–1945," examines the transformative effect of the Great Patriotic War on Soviet society through everyday objects.

INDEX

Afanas'ev, Dima, 172

agriculture and agricultural production
  decline of during war, 61–62
  losses of following German invasion, 6, 12, 27, 28, 45, 48, 49–50, 52–53, 103, 165, 329

alimentarnaia distrofiia. See nutritional dystrophy

All-Union Central Council of Trade Unions (VTsSPS), 19 (table I.2), 59, 69, 73, 74, 76, 77, 85, 87, 90, 92, 92, 95, 314n64, 316n66

Alma-Ata, 89

amenorrhea, 225, 305

Atwater, W. O., 24

Auschwitz, 241, 255, 256, 263

avitaminosis, 268

Backe, Herbert (author of Hunger Plan). *See* Hunger Plan

Barber, John, 176n50

Bashkiriia, 50, 79

bathhouses, 14

Benedetti, Leonardo de, 256

Beria, L. P. (Commissar of Internal Affairs), 83, 316

beriberi, 31

Berggol'ts, Ol'ga, 236, 242, 258

Berkhoff, Karel, 35

Bidlack, Richard, 168–169, 170, 176n50, 184, 198

Boldyrev, Aleksandr, 206n2, 237, 240

Bordiugov, Gennadii, 39, 40, 41

Bormann, Martin, 5

bread, 4, 11, 27, 32, 42, 45, 47, 55, 60, 61, 64, 68, 69, 70, 79, 86, 93
  rationing of, 12, 15 (table I.1), 22n22, 48, 50, 51, 52, 54, 56, 57, 58 (table 1.2), 65 (table 1.5), 66, 67 (table 1.6), 80, 84
  in Red Army, 109, 112, 115, 116, 117, 118, 128n120, 131, 133n145, 140, 147–148, 149

Brezhnev, Leonid, 39

Central Asian workers, 60, 288, 308, 308n54, 309

Certeau, Michel de, 162n8

Cheliabinsk and Cheliabinsk province, 26, 227, 276n18, 277, 331n88
  infant and child mortality in, 289
  introduction of rationing in, 50
  potato consumption in, 19 (table I.2), 20
  starvation and general mortality in, 259, 274, 275, 292 (fig. 5.2b), 295, 296, 321
  tuberculosis in, 280 (table 5.1)

Cherepenina, Nadezhda, 198, 213

Cherniavskii, U. G., 15 (table I.1), 19 (table I.2), 20n18, 21n21, 21n22, 46

Chernorutskii, Mikhail Vasil'evich, 209, 210, 217, 218, 219, 220, 221, 229, 230, 233, 261

children. *See* food provisioning and consumption; infant and child mortality

cholera, 221

363

collective farm markets. *See* food
   provisioning and consumption
collective farms, 48
collectivization, 47, 102
Collingham, Lizzie, 9
Commissariat of Internal Affairs (NKVD),
   5n2, 13n15, 60, 168, 177, 185n75, 191, 198,
   244, 252, 288, 307, 309, 310, 316
Commissariat of Public Health, 213,
   224n64, 244n151, 245, 248, 250, 315n66
   Institute of Nutrition of, 15 (table I.1),
      246, 248
   Scientific Medical Soviet of, 234, 246,
      247, 248
Commissariat of Trade, 50, 51–52, 53, 68,
   69, 72, 74, 75, 77, 79, 81, 82, 84, 85, 86,
   87, 88, 91, 95, 96, 97
consumption. *See* diet and nutrition; food
   provisioning and consumption
Council for Evacuation, 48
Council of People's Commissars
   (Sovnarkom), 52n21, 54, 59, 60, 75,
   76n71, 77, 85, 87, 88, 90, 91, 93, 94

Darré, R. Walther, 9
Departments of Workers' Provisioning
   (ORSy), 26n27, 74–75, 77, 85, 97
diet and nutrition
   in Germany, 28–31
   in Japan, 31–34
   and malnutrition in modern Third
      World, 278n20
   in Soviet Union: changes in and
      adequacy of, 13–14, 15 (table I.1), 16
      (fig. I.1), 17–18, 20, 21–24, 62–64, 65
      (table 1.5), 327; and dietary
      supplements, 73–74; importance of
      potatoes for, 18, 19 (table I.2), 20, 26,
      272, 315, 316, 327; improvement in
      during 1944, 323, 324, 327–329;
      inequalities and differences in, 24–27,
      63n37; and scurvy, 62, 73, 78
   in Victorian and Edwardian Britain, 31
   See also food provisioning and
      consumption; nutritional dystrophy;

rationing; starvation; starvation
   mortality
distrofik and *distrofiki. See* Leningrad;
   nutritional dystrophy
Dzeniskevich, Andrei, 35

Einsatzgruppen, 5, 10
"energy fraction" (energy balance), 13, 14,
   17, 61, 270, 271
evacuation
   and access of evacuees to food and
      rations, 12, 26, 45, 57, 60–61, 65, 66,
      68, 72, 73, 79, 87, 90, 91, 307, 312
   of doctors, 248, 283
   of food and livestock, 48–49, 104
   impact of on urban populations, 287,
      288
   of industrial plant, 44, 49
   and mortality among evacuees, 244,
      269, 296, 299n43, 329
   sanitary conditions during, 296
   of workers, 44, 87, 96, 287
   See also Leningrad
evacuees. *See* evacuation
Extraordinary Commission on Nazi
   Crimes, 255

Fadeev, Aleksandr, 258
famines
   in Bengal (1943), 163n9
   in Japan during World War II, 34n42
   in occupied Europe during World War
      II, 222
   in Leningrad. *See* Leningrad
   in Russia and USSR: 1891, 214;
      1921–1922, 188n82, 201n33, 221, 284;
      1932–1933, 102, 215–216, 222n55, 260,
      284, 332; 1946–1947, 22n22, 258–259,
      260, 272
food consumption. *See* diet and nutrition;
   food provisioning and consumption;
   rationing
food processing industry
   losses in following German invasion,
      49–50, 102–103

Index

365

food provisioning and consumption

in Red Army: as act of mourning dead comrades, 135–136; and bread consumption, 109, 112, 115, 116, 117, 118, 128n120, 131, 133n145, 140, 147–148, 149; discontents over, 149–150; endangered by theft and corruption, 122–124, 133–134; equitable distribution of by soldiers, 134, 138; and feeding of civilians by army, 156; improvements in, 126–129, 153–154; and Lend-Lease food aid, 104, 118n74, 127, 128, 324–329; logistics of, 129–130; as pact between soldiers and the state, 99, 100, 107–108, 112, 119, 120, 126, 128, 129, 149, 155, 157; and problems faced by Muslim soldiers, 151–153, 155; and reliance on horsemeat, 132–133, 155; and reliance on local resources, 105–107, 324; and spoilage due to neglect, 125–126; and subsidiary agriculture, 105; and tea consumption, 141, 147, 152; and water provision, 145–147 (*see also* tobacco; vodka)

on Soviet home front: and centralized provisioning, 52, 53, 64, 65; of children, 12, 14, 15 (table I.1), 17, 24, 26, 30, 32, 33, 34, 56, 57, 58, 59 (table 1.3), 66, 67 (table 1.6), 69, 72, 73, 77, 86, 88, 97, 119, 156, 166, 167, 175, 185, 192, 306, 311, 330n85; and collective farm markets, 18, 26, 53, 54, 65, 78–83, 92, 316; and contraction of retail trade network following German invasion, 50; corruption and theft in, 84, 85; in crèches and nurseries, 72–73; and decentralized procurement, 12, 46, 53, 54, 55 (table 1.1), 63 (table 1.4), 71, 74, 77, 78, 85, 86, 88, 90, 92, 318; in factory canteens, 14, 21n21, 26, 44, 48, 52, 53, 56, 57, 59, 60, 64, 65, 66, 68–72, 87; and gardens and garden plots (collective and personal), 18, 26–27,

53, 76, 78; impact of German invasion on (*see* agriculture and agricultural production); improvement in during 1944, 323, 324; intra-state conflicts over, 85–92; and Lend-Lease food aid, 324–329; percentage of from different sources, 54–55; prewar inequalities in, 164; in public catering, 71, 74, 97; role of state in, 95–97; role of unions in, 47, 53, 55, 70, 72, 74, 76, 77, 84, 85, 91, 92, 95, 251; and self-provisioning by workers, 92–95, 96; and street trading and unofficial markets, 83, 84, 165; and subsidiary agriculture, 18, 46, 53, 75–76, 77–78, 85, 92

in U.S. and British Armies, 104, 105, 110n42

in Wehrmacht, 104, 105, 106

See also agriculture and agricultural production; diet and nutrition; Leningrad; rationing

Frankfurt, Lilia, 35–36

French Revolution of 1789, 45

Frenkel', Zakharii Grigor'evich, 237

Frunze, 89

fuel shortages, 14, 61, 65, 66, 69, 73, 81, 86, 92, 93, 94, 96, 158

Garshin, Vladimir, 212, 219, 220, 223, 230, 233, 234, 261

Gel'shtein, Eliazor Markovich, 225, 227, 230, 259

Germany

hunger mortality in during World War I, 8, 214, 280

diet and nutrition in during World War II, 28–31, 192n98

revolution of 1918, 45

See also Operation Barbarossa

Ginzburg, Lidiia [Lydia], 164, 172, 173, 180, 220, 221, 238, 239, 241n142, 261, 262, 263

Goering, Hermann, 10

Golant, Raisa Iakovlevna, 228

Index

Gor'kii and Gor'kii province, 14n16, 248, 260, 277, 331
food shortages in, 66, 83
introduction of rationing in, 50
starvation and general mortality in, 291 (fig. 5.2a), 294, 295
tuberculosis in, 280 (table 5.1)
Great Britain
rationing in, 27, 203n139
working hours in, 13n15
See also diet and nutrition
Grossman, Vasily, 129, 154
Gubergritz, M. M., 227, 259
Gulag, 307, 308n53

Halder, Franz (German general), 5
Harvey, David, 162n8
Healey, Dan, 253n178
Himmler, Heinrich, 5
Hitler, Adolf, 5, 7, 8, 9
hatred of Bolshevism, 7
housing conditions, 13, 14, 65, 305
Hunger Plan, 9–11, 209–210, 256

Iaroslavl' and Iaroslavl' province
introduction of rationing in, 50
mortality in, 291 (fig. 5.2a), 294, 295, 296, 299n43
potato consumption in, 19 (table I.2), 20
tuberculosis in, 280 (table 5.1)
Inber, Vera, 206–207, 209, 212, 235n115, 258
infant and child mortality, 269, 288, 289, 329
Ivanovo and Ivanovo province, 80, 81, 82, 276n18, 277
infant and child mortality in, 269
introduction of bread rationing in, 50, 65
starvation and general mortality in, 286, 291 (fig. 5.2a), 294, 295, 296, 299n43
tuberculosis in, 280 (table 5.1)
Izhevsk, 277, 280 (table 5.1), 292 (fig. 5.2b), 294, 295

Japan
diet and nutrition in, 31–34

Jews
genocide of, 2, 3, 5, 6, 7, 10, 28, 38, 40, 219

Kassirskii, Iosif Abramovich, 252, 253, 258, 259
Kazan', 69, 80, 81, 86, 87, 277, 283n32, 296
infant and child mortality in, 269
starvation and general mortality in, 291 (fig. 5.2a), 294, 295
tuberculosis in, 280 (table 5.1)
Kemerovo and Kemerovo province (Kuzbass), 21n21, 276n18, 277
potato consumption in, 19 (table I.2), 20
starvation and general mortality in, 273, 293 (fig. 5.2c), 294, 295, 322
tuberculosis in, 280 (table 5.1)
Khrushchev, Nikita, 38
Khvilitskaia, M. I., 228, 229, 231, 243
Kiev Medical Institute, 227, 283
Kirillov, M., 310
Kirov, 26, 59, 65, 66, 71, 93, 277
infant and child mortality in, 269
starvation and general mortality in, 292 (fig. 5.2b), 295, 296, 300
tuberculosis in, 280 (table 5.1)
Kirov factory, Cheliabinsk, 26, 265, 331n88
Kirschenbaum, Lisa, 177, 262
Klishevich, Nina, 158, 159
Kniazev, Georgii, 172
Kochina, Elena, 174, 176, 186, 187
Konopleva, Mariia, 170, 175
Kostrovitskaia, Vera, 36, 166, 169, 174
Kravchenko, Victor, 267
Kuibyshev and Kuibyshev province, 69, 83
starvation and general mortality in, 267, 273, 291 (fig. 5.2a), 294, 295
tuberculosis in, 280 (table 5.1)
Kuzbass, 21n21, 26, 93, 94, 276n18, 277, 286, 314, 322, 323. See also Kemerovo and Kemerovo province

Labor Army, 307, 308–310, 330, 331
"labor desertion," 322–323n89
Lang, Georgii Fedorovich, 216, 220, 226, 227, 248

Index

Lefebvre, Henri, 162n8, 205

Lend-Lease food aid, 27, 104, 118n74, 127, 128, 266, 272, 321, 324–329, 333–335

Leningrad
absence of protest in, 177–178
attitudes of workers in, 190–191
blockade of, 2, 4, 12, 28, 42, 158, 265n2
blockade diarists, 35; attitudes of toward *distrofiki*, 180–181, 182, 189, 202, 238–241; attitudes of toward workers, 194–195, 196–197; blame food workers for shortages, 183–187, 189–190, 202, 204; blame internal factors for shortages, 168; and perceptions of wartime famine, 159–164; and psychology of queuing, 169–178, 202; significance of, 159–164, 202–205
cannibalism in, 40
and "elite" status of food workers, 42, 183–184, 185–186, 187–189
evacuation from, 69, 80–81, 87, 244, 269n6, 299n43
German plans to starve, 11, 158
and myths and heroic narratives of blockade, 177, 243, 263
people's militias in, 35
position of workers in, 42, 191–194, 195, 196, 197
privileges of party officials in, 198–202
rationing in, 12, 50, 61, 119, 158n2, 165–168, 191–192, 193, 194, 195, 198, 201, 203, 205
starvation in, 21, 47, 64, 179–180, 203, 210, 266, 270 (*see also* nutritional dystrophy)
starvation mortality in, 11, 28, 47n5, 158, 158–159n2, 167–168, 184, 198, 210n15, 266 (*see also* nutritional dystrophy)
theft and corruption in, 168–169, 171, 183–187, 189–190, 204
tuberculosis in, 280–281
worker protests in, 191
See also nutritional dystrophy

Leningrad Blockade. *See* Leningrad

Levi, Primo, 254, 256

Levina, Esfir', 172, 173, 174, 175, 176, 179, 180, 181, 182, 185, 195, 200

Likhachev, Dmitrii, 209

Likhacheva, Anna, 159

Liubimov, A. V. (Commissar of Trade), 84, 87, 96

Liublinskii, V. S., 239–240, 241, 243

Liubovskaia, Aleksandra Pavlovna, 180, 182, 193, 194

Loidin, D. M., 252

Lomagin, Nikita, 168–169, 170, 176n50, 184, 198

Magnitogorsk, 77, 277, 283n33, 305n48
infant and child morality in, 289
starvation and general mortality in, 271n9, 292 (fig. 5.2b), 295, 317, 321, 322n77
tuberculosis in, 280 (table 5.1)

malnutrition. *See* diet and nutrition; nutritional dystrophy; starvation; starvation mortality

Markwick, Roger, 41

Mashanskii, F. I., 222n58, 235, 262

Matus, Kseniia, 174, 175, 183, 184, 198

measles epidemic (1941–1942), 269

Mikoian, A. I., 87, 90

mobilized workers, 4, 12, 4, 45, 60, 61, 65, 66, 67 (table 1.6), 69, 92, 287, 288, 305, 307, 308, 309, 310, 311, 312, 323n79, 330, 333n89

Molotov and Molotov province, 50, 72, 77, 88, 89, 91, 277, 283
introduction of bread rationing in, 50
starvation, starvation mortality, and general mortality in, 211n17, 244, 292 (fig.5.2b), 294, 295, 296, 300n44, 309n54, 317
tuberculosis in, 280 (table 5.1)

Moscow and Moscow province, 3, 5, 11, 74, 77, 83, 84, 89, 90, 92, 120, 125, 140, 231, 234, 236, 245, 248, 258, 273, 276n18, 277, 286, 287, 316n66, 331n88
food protests in, 177

Moscow and Moscow province (*cont.*)
infant and child mortality in, 289, 290 (fig. 5.1)
introduction of bread rationing in, 50
potato consumption in, 19 (table I.2), 20
starvation, starvation mortality, and general mortality in, 249, 267, 270, 273, 285n36, 291 (fig. 5.2a), 294, 295, 296, 297 (fig. 5.3), 299, 300, 301 (fig. 5.4), 302, 303 (fig. 5.5), 306
tuberculosis in, 280 (table 5.1)
Moskoff, William, 46, 95, 267, 324, 333
Munting, Roger, 333, 334, 335

Nesterov, Aleksandr (Sasha), 237
New Economic Policy (NEP), 46
Nikitin, Fyodor, 170, 179, 180, 185, 200
Nizhnii Tagil, 26, 277, 300n44, 311, 315, 330n85, 331n88
labor camps in, 308n53
starvation, starvation mortality, and general mortality in, 273, 308n53, 316, 318, 319 (table 5.2)
tuberculosis in, 280 (table 5.1)
NKVD. *See* Commissariat of Internal Affairs
Nosenko, I. (Commissar of Shipbuilding), 87
Novosibirsk and Novosibirsk province, 93, 276n18, 277
potato consumption in, 19 (table (I.2)
starvation and general mortality in, 273, 286, 293 (fig. 5.2c), 294, 295
tuberculosis in, 280 (table 5.1), 284
nutrition. *See* diet and nutrition
nutritional dystrophy, 21, 42, 59, 73, 88
behavioral and psychological impact of, 179–181, 227–229, 238–241, 262–263
and conflicting narratives of war, 262–263
diagnosis and treatment of, 230–233, 245–247, 249–251, 252, 255–256, 281–283, 284–285, 320–321
differential impact of on men and women, 225–227, 302–305

and evolution and application of the term, 206–208, 244, 245, 251, 252, 256n186, 257–258
evolution of medical understanding of, 212–223, 260–261, 263–264, 284
and famine of 1946–1947, 258–260
in Gulag, 251–254, 263
on home front outside Leningrad, 248–251
in liberated territories, 255–256
importance of research into, 233–235, 246–247
and "moral distrofiks," 241–243
pathogenesis of, 223–227
and popular appropriation of terminology, 235–244
among returning German prisoners of war, 256, 257
and unease discussing its presence outside of Leningrad, 210–212, 247
See also Leningrad; starvation; starvation mortality

Omsk and Omsk province, 71, 89, 90, 93, 276n18, 277
potato consumption in, 19 (table I.2)
starvation and general mortality in, 273, 286, 293 (fig. 5.2c), 294
tuberculosis in, 280 (table 5.1)
Operation Barbarossa (German invasion of the Soviet Union), 4, 5–7
and Hunger Plan, 9–11, 209–210
impact of on Soviet food supplies, 6, 12, 27, 28, 45, 48, 49–50, 52–53, 103, 165, 329
and plans to colonize Soviet Union, 7, 8–11

paëk (ration). *See* rationing: in Red Army
Pavlov, Dmitrii Vasil'evich, 222
Pokhlebkin, Vil'iam, 101n11, 115, 118, 126, 127, 151
Poland
destruction of Jewish population in, 28
partition of by Germany and Soviet Union, 9

Polzikova-Rubets, Kseniia, 241–242
potatoes. *See* diet and nutrition
prison labor, 13n15, 60, 288, 307, 310, 330, 331n88
Prokop'evsk, 273, 277, 280 (table 5.1), 293 (fig. 5.2c), 294, 295, 322. *See also* Kemerovo and Kemerovo province; Kuzbass
protein-energy malnutrition (PEM), 277, 278n20, 281n26
Prywes, Moshe, 253–254
Punin, Nikolai, 170, 237

rationing
  in Germany, 28–31
  in Japan, 28, 31–34
  in Red Army: early failures of, 98–100, 120–121; historiography of, 101n11; ideological significance of, 100; and meanings of *paëk* and *prodovol'stvennye normy*, 100, 107–108, 111, 112–113, 155; organizational principles behind, 109–114; and varieties of foods, 114–119; and women soldiers, 113
  on Soviet home front, 2, 15 (table I.1), 16 (fig. I.1), 17–18, 30, 46, 64, 266; abuse of by factory directors, 59–60, 63n37; differentiations in, 25–26, 57–59, 61; disruptions to, 66, 68; during 1930s, 47, 48; during Civil War, 47, 48; and inability to redeem ration cards, 72, 330; introduction of following German invasion, 50–51; in Leningrad (*see* Leningrad); numbers receiving, 66, 67 (table 1.6), 328; principles behind organization of, 51–52, 56–57, 266, 329–332; and reduction of rations (November 1943), 15 (table I.1), 16 (fig. I.1), 80, 271, 315, 327
  See also bread; diet and nutrition; food provisioning and consumption
Red Army, 3, 5, 6, 8, 27, 39, 43, 44, 45, 47, 48, 49, 66, 68, 70, 96

Sanitary Division of, 246, 248, 255n183
See also food provisioning and consumption; rationing
Red corners, 196
Riabinkin, Iura, 175
Ribovskii, Nikolai, 198, 199
Rosenberg, Alfred, 7–8
Rossi, Jacques, 251, 255n182
Russian Revolutions of 1917, 2, 45

Sandomirskaia, Irina, 221
Saratov and Saratov province, 68, 90, 93, 276n18, 277
  starvation, starvation mortality, and general mortality in, 270, 291 (fig. 5.2a), 295
  tuberculosis in, 280 (table 5.1)
Savinkov, Ivan, 184, 185, 187, 188, 189, 195, 199, 200
scorched earth policy, 103n17
scurvy, 62, 73, 88, 285n36
self-provisioning by workers, 92–95, 96
Sen, Amartya, 163
Shalamov, Varlam, 251, 252
Shaporina, Liubov', 236, 240, 243
Shumilov, Nikolai, 200–201
Shvernik, N. M. (Chair of VTsSPS), 73, 87, 88
sickness absence, 313, 314, 317–320
Simmons, Dana, 215, 219
Six, Franz (*Einzatsgruppe* leader), 10–11
skin infections, 83, 314n64
Skriabina, Elena, 170, 194, 237
Slutskii, Boris, 119, 147, 149, 154
soap shortage, 83, 314n64
Sokolova, Elizaveta Aleksandrovna, 161n6
Solzhenitsyn, Aleksandr, 254, 255n182
Soviet Union. *See* World War II; *individual topics*
Sovnarkom. *See* Council of People's Commissars
SS (*Schützstaffel*), 5, 9
Stalin, J. V., 36, 37, 38, 39, 98–99, 103, 120, 122–123, 126, 129, 204, 316, 332
Stalingrad (Battle of), 6, 131

Stalinsk, 21n21, 277
  starvation and general mortality in, 273,
    293 (fig. 5.2c), 294, 295, 322
  tuberculosis in, 280 (table 5.1)
  See also Kemerovo and Kemerovo
    province; Kuzbass
starvation
  in Germany during World War I (*see*
    Germany)
  in Japan, 33–34
  in Leningrad (*see* Leningrad)
  on Soviet home front, 47, 62, 88, 97, 327;
    among defense workers, 249–250,
    266–267, 271n9, 314–323, 327, 331–332;
    delayed manifestation of, 270–272;
    improvements in clinical diagnosis
    of, 230–233, 320–321; and interaction
    with other diseases and conditions,
    281–282; not discussed outside
    medical literature, 208–209; and
    re-feeding sufferers, 266n2, 270, 313,
    317, 321, 321n77, 323, 327, 328, 332 (*see
    also* nutritional dystrophy: diagnosis
    and treatment); and relationship with
    tuberculosis, 266, 270, 278–279,
    280–281, 282; terminological usage
    of, 265n2
  among Soviet prisoners of war, 257
  See also nutritional dystrophy;
    starvation mortality
starvation disease. *See* nutritional
  dystrophy
starvation mortality, 4, 11, 13, 20, 23n23, 24,
    25, 27, 28, 47, 73, 245, 265, 267, 316, 325,
    327, 329
  age and gender distribution of, 270,
    286–296, 302–305, 329
  among Soviet prisoners of war, 210,
    219, 255
  decline of during 1944, 312, 322–323,
    327
  during famine of 1946–1947, 272
  how recorded in cause of death
    statistics, 244n151 (*see also* starvation
    mortality: methods for estimating)

in Germany during World War I (*see*
  Germany)
in Leningrad (*see* Leningrad)
methods for estimating, 268–269,
  272–277, 322n78
in occupied territories, 28, 276
problems diagnosing as cause of death,
  281–285, 320
and social profile of victims, 306–312
and starvation-tuberculosis complex,
  277, 285, 296–301, 317n69, 321, 329 (*see
  also* tuberculosis)
See also nutritional dystrophy;
  starvation
starvation-tuberculosis complex. *See*
  starvation; starvation mortality
State Committee for Defense (GKO), 77,
  84, 85, 90, 95, 121, 288, 332
State Sanitary Inspectorate (GSI), 274
Strashun, Il'ia Davidovich, 207, 219
Strazhesko, N. D., 216, 248, 260
subsidiary agriculture. *See* food
  provisioning and consumption
Suprun, M. N., 325, 333, 334, 335
Sverdlovsk and Sverdlovsk province, 277,
  282n28, 283, 283n33
  introduction of bread rationing in, 50
  potato consumption in, 19 (note to
    table I.2), 272, 311n60, 315, 316, 327
  starvation, starvation mortality, and
    general mortality in, 249, 273, 274,
    275, 276, 292 (fig. 5.2b), 295, 309, 310,
    310n59, 316, 317, 320n74, 330n87
  tuberculosis in, 280 (table 5.1)
Sysin, A. N., 234–235, 247

Tagillag, 307n52, 308n53, 310n59, 330n87
Tashkent, 89, 211, 249, 270
Tatariia, 50
tobacco
  importance of in Red Army, 113, 129,
    140–141, 149, 151
Tooze, Adam, 7
Trudarmeitsy. See Labor Army
tuberculosis, 25

Index

tuberculosis (*cont.*)
  in Austria and Germany during World
    War I, 280
  in Japan, 31
  in Soviet Union, 266, 270, 277, 278–279,
    280 (table 5.1), 281, 282, 284, 285, 286,
    299, 300, 302n45, 313, 314n64, 317n69,
    318, 322, 329
  in Warsaw Ghetto, 280, 281, 282
  See also starvation; starvation mortality
Tula, 50
Tur, A. F., 231–232
Tvardovskii, Aleksandr, 131, 145
typhus, 221, 269

unions
  ammunition workers, 317, 318
  cement workers, 68
  communication workers, 316n66
  nitrogen and special chemical
    workers, 91
  public catering workers, 74
  ship-building workers, 69, 80, 87
  See also food provisioning and
    consumption
United States. *See* Lend-Lease food aid
Urals
  loss of potato crop in, 19 (note to
    table I.2), 315–316, 327
  poor agricultural productivity in, 26
  See also Cheliabinsk and Cheliabinsk
    province; Molotov and Molotov
    province; Nizhnii Tagil; starvation;
    starvation mortality; Sverdlovsk and
    Sverdlovsk province
Uskova, Natal'ia, 194

Victory Day, 1, 38
Vigdorchik, N. A., 249, 250

vodka
  consumption of in Red Army, 141–145,
    150, 156
Vologda, 19 (note to table I.2), 244, 269n6,
  280 (table 5.1)
Vovsi, Miron Semenovich, 246, 247, 248,
  259
Voznesensky, N. A., 37
VTsSPS. *See* All-Union Central Council of
  Trade Unions

War Communism, 46
Warsaw Ghetto, 4, 217n38, 219, 222, 223,
  270, 280, 281, 282
Wehrmacht, 3, 8, 10, 11, 30, 102, 103n17, 105,
  106, 158
working conditions, 13
World War I
  hunger mortality in Germany during, 8,
    214, 280
  impact of on Hitler's war plans, 8
World War II
  commemoration of in the Soviet Union
    and post-Soviet Russia, 1
  competing narratives of in Soviet Union
    and post-Soviet Russia, 36–41, 42–43
  myth of in Soviet Union, 3, 36, 38, 39, 41,
    42, 177, 243, 263
  population losses, 1–2, 3, 11
  responses of Soviet citizens to, 35, 36

ZAGS, 272, 308n53
Zelenskaia, Irina, 169, 172, 180, 181, 183, 184,
  187, 188, 193, 195, 196, 197, 199, 200
Zemskov, V. N., 307
Zhdanov, Andrei, 198, 204
Zlatoust, 277, 280 (table 5.1), 283n33, 292
  (fig. 5.2b), 295, 317, 321–322
Zubkova, Elena Iu., 40n56, 41